DISNEY
HIGH

DISNEY HIGH

The UNTOLD STORY *of the*
RISE AND FALL *of* DISNEY CHANNEL'S
TWEEN EMPIRE

ASHLEY SPENCER

ST. MARTIN'S PRESS
NEW YORK

First published in the United States by St. Martin's Press, an imprint of St. Martin's Publishing Group

DISNEY HIGH. Copyright © 2024 by Ashley Spencer. All rights reserved. Printed in the United States of America. For information, address St. Martin's Publishing Group, 120 Broadway, New York, NY 10271.

www.stmartins.com

The Library of Congress Cataloging-in-Publication Data is available upon request.

ISBN 978-1-250-28345-0 (hardcover)
ISBN 978-1-250-28346-7 (ebook)

Our books may be purchased in bulk for promotional, educational, or business use. Please contact your local bookseller or the Macmillan Corporate and Premium Sales Department at 1-800-221-7945, extension 5442, or by email at MacmillanSpecialMarkets@macmillan.com.

First Edition: 2024

10 9 8 7 6 5 4 3 2 1

For all the dreamers who once held imaginary wands

CONTENTS

INTRODUCTION

Lizzie McGuire. Zenon: Girl of the 21st Century. The Famous Jett Jackson. So Weird. These were the Y2K-era Disney Channel hits that kept me glued to the living room TV as a kid. I crimped random chunks of my hair like Lizzie and imagined I was performing "Supernova Girl" with Proto Zoa or investigating supernatural mysteries with Fi. It wasn't just passive entertainment. I wanted to be part of those fantasy worlds.

Geographically, I was raised Disney-adjacent in Orlando, Florida. The theme parks were a short drive from my house, and school field trips often involved "educational" scavenger hunts at Epcot and Animal Kingdom. When Aaron Carter and Samantha Mumba headlined a *Disney Channel in Concert* special at what was then Disney-MGM Studios, I was among the throngs, screaming the lyrics to "That's How I Beat Shaq." What a bop. What a time.

I often daydreamed about what it would be like to get plucked out of obscurity and cast in my own star-making Disney Channel vehicle. I was not, however, preternaturally gifted with acting, singing, or dancing abilities of any kind. I attended but one class at the hallowed local acting school that helped launch two of Central Florida's finest: Mandy Moore and Zenon herself, Kirsten Storms. While I don't remember any acting exercises that we learned that day, I do remember how the middle-aged instructor slowly made her way around the room lined with twelve- and thirteen-year-old kids and how she crouched to our level to assess our facial compositions. "Your eyes are a little bit close together," she said, squinting at my hopeful baby face. "That could be a problem."

That was all it took. My self-conscious heart broke as I choked back tears and never went to another session.

Whether or not my pupillary distance would have killed my shot at landing a Disney Channel Original Movie of my own, it was clear my brittle adolescent bones were ill-equipped for the superficial scrutiny that auditioning required, let alone able to withstand what could happen once they were put under the microscope of fame.

But is anyone up to it, really?

It's a rare person, let alone kid, who can weather the rigors of celebrity, and it's a miracle anyone comes out less than completely and utterly ravaged on the other side. The ethical quandaries surrounding children in the entertainment business—one of the only industries in the United States in which it's legal for minors under the age of fourteen to have a professional job—and the regulations that exist to protect them abound.

Many former child actors have spoken about the detrimental side effects of joining the industry at a young age. *Cheaper by the Dozen* and *Camp Rock* actor Alyson Stoner coined the phrase "toddler-to-trainwreck pipeline," and they expound on the industry's inherent issues in an eloquent podcast series called *Dear Hollywood*. Former Nickelodeon star Jennette McCurdy's bestselling memoir, *I'm Glad My Mom Died*, shined a light on the toxic combination of stage parents and showrunners working in tandem within a capitalist machine, and the heartbreaking effects on the child at the center of it all.

Still other performers have spoken about how their experiences on a welcoming TV or movie set saved them from a troubled home life and a darker fate, and there are hundreds who have gone on to lead drama-free adult lives and are often overlooked. The pressures of being a Disney Channel star in the 2000s were especially rigorous. And whenever someone reflects on their early industry experiences, it undoubtedly makes headlines, but each story is only a sliver of the whole.

* * *

As CONSUMERS, THE entertainment we ingest in our youth maintains an intangible hold over our entire lives. If you are reading this book, it is likely that at least one bygone Disney Channel show, movie, or performer wormed its way into your heart and took root. Over the course of the aughts, Disney Channel managed to ascend to extraordinary heights, delivering a sweeping empire of tween-centric content that also made roughly a bazillion dollars. Disney Channel franchises topped music charts, box offices, and TV ratings, in addition to selling a staggering amount of merchandise.

In 2006, Disney Channel was the second-most-watched cable channel in prime time across all demographics (behind only USA and its intoxicating blend of WWE and the dramas *Psych* and *Monk*). And in 2007, Disney Channel claimed the crown. Titles like *High School Musical* and *Hannah Montana* became so ubiquitous that even adults who'd never flipped to the channel or had no children in their lives couldn't escape them. Zac Efron graced the cover of *Rolling Stone*. Miley Cyrus (infamously) posed for *Vanity Fair*. And *Saturday Night Live* and *South Park* made a habit of spoofing the kids' cable channel and its teenage stars.

While I've since graduated to writing for *The New York Times* and the *Washington Post*, I began my career at *J-14* magazine in the early 2010s. There, barely past my own teen years, I dutifully chronicled the goings-on of young talent, including a slate of Disney Channel and Nickelodeon stars, for the pull-out poster crowd. By then, it was clear that Disney Channel was in a league of their own. They operated as a slick machine, both in the way the network's publicity team promoted and guarded its stars (while Nickelodeon was happy to send the entire *Victorious* cast to spend an afternoon go-karting for a *J-14* feature, Disney publicists hawkishly monitored each brief interview they'd occasionally grant), and in the way Disney Channel talent had been coached to navigate the media with carefully honed answers and unwavering charm.

This book explores a variety of experiences that took place at Disney Channel on its journey to becoming that manicured operation. It's an attempt to pull back the curtain on a period of extraordinary change and growth in the 2000s, when a once-overlooked channel morphed into a pop-culture juggernaut, and what that kind of success meant for those who graduated from "Disney High," and for the industry as a whole.

Most of what you might assume about the Disney machine of the 2000s is wrong. As the network's influence grew, it wasn't part of a cohesive establishment, with its many divisions seamlessly falling in line and operating in tandem to achieve a common goal. When the commercial promise of Disney Channel and its stars became evident, the disparate Disney parties were each grappling for a piece of the pie with their own agenda. And there were precarious cracks through which projects and people could slip.

More than one hundred and fifty people who were involved with Disney Channel during the 1990s and 2000s—all instrumental in various ways—spoke to me on the record for this book. Actors. Singers. Showrunners. Writers. Producers. Prop masters. Directors. Acting coaches. Assistants. Teachers. Composers. Stage managers. Editors. Publicists. Makeup artists. Music supervisors. Choreographers. Set designers. Wigmakers. Songwriters. Photographers. Cinematographers. Animators. Mouseketeers. Studio executives. Record label executives. Network executives.

Some sources chose to speak on background or off the record, with the agreement that they would not be identified. And other potential sources and their publicists ignored or politely declined my interview requests. Some were interested but sought approval from Disney, who, according to at least one of those sources, did not grant it. Without the sign-off from the Mouse House, it's understandable that they might not want to risk their relationship with Disney, and by extension, that with Hulu, Marvel, Lucasfilm, 20th Century, or any of the vast properties the greater Disney corporation now owns, by participating in a project that came together outside of Disney's notoriously tight control.

It would be impossible to cover every single Disney Channel show and movie and still stay within an acceptable word count, so I've chosen to focus on those projects that most directly contributed to the commercial rise of Disney Channel and the creation of what the greater public now considers the "Disney Channel brand." Because of this, preschool programming, animated series, and some beloved but less broadly transformative live-action projects are not discussed at length.

Finally, the internet is full of impassioned posts that wander down rabbit holes of theories and speculation about Disney Channel lore. They're often presented with great confidence and full of mis- or disinformation. This book is the first reported exploration of Disney Channel of this magnitude, featuring interviews with a wide-ranging group of people who actually experienced the highs and lows of what it was like to be a part of that system. That said, there are still many more stories to be told beyond these pages. But, for now:

I'm Ashley Spencer, and you're reading *Disney High*.

My tale is done,
there runs a mouse,
whosoever catches it,
may make himself a big fur cap out of it.

—The Brothers Grimm

KEY 2000s DISNEY CHANNEL SERIES AND PREMIERE DATES

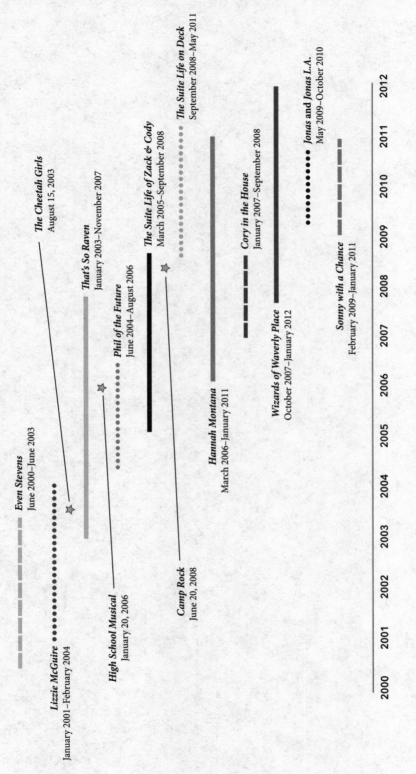

DISNEY
HIGH

Prologue

An inconspicuous van pulled up outside of The Vinings apartment complex in Orlando, Florida, so early that the moon still hung in the dawn sky. It idled in the parking lot, waiting for the arrival of precious cargo to transport to Disney-MGM Studios, nine miles south. Once all were present and accounted for, the vehicle continued on its journey, bouncing down the dusty, still-to-be-paved back roads leading to the new theme park.

The goods in question were a rabble of teenage Mouseketeers. And their final destination every Tuesday through Saturday in the early 1990s was a brightly lit soundstage housed within the 135-acre attraction. In 1989, Disney-MGM Studios (today rebranded as Disney's Hollywood Studios) had been the third Disney theme park to open in Florida. It was partly modeled around the working movie studios of Los Angeles and featured movie-themed rides, as well as a backstage studio tour. But in order to have an authentic backstage tour, Disney needed to give parkgoers a taste of a real production. Enter: a revamped Disney classic that would air on the company's fledgling cable venture, The Disney Channel. A few months before the Berlin Wall fell, *The All New Mickey Mouse Club* rose.

Disney's original Annette Funicello–era *The Mickey Mouse Club* variety show ran on ABC and shot on a closed soundstage at Disney's Burbank, California, studios in the 1950s. Now, this reboot would serve to not only draw viewers to The Disney Channel but also entertain tourists at the Florida theme park, where the cast would delight live audiences with scripted comedy skits and musical performances of contemporary radio hits. Gone were the cutesy mouse ears of yore, replaced by hip letterman's jackets bearing each Mouseketeer's name. It was a new club for a new era.

Looking back, it's easy to brand the cast a veritable who's who of Hollywood icons—stars like Emmy nominee Keri Russell and velvet-voiced boy band king JC Chasez joined the cast early in the show's seven-season run. But at the time, they were just a collection of unknown preteens and teens cherry-picked from around the country (and occasionally Canada) on widespread casting calls. The show avoided casting out of New York and Los Angeles, opting instead to recruit kids from the heartland, the South, and non-showbiz towns from coast to coast in an effort to capitalize on their relatability and authenticity.

In February 1993, a sweeping search was underway to replenish the supply of younger talent for the show's sixth season. The top twenty-three contenders were flown to Florida to undergo multiple days of tryouts on the *Star Search* stage at MGM. Casting director Matt Casella, the producers, music supervisors, and acting coach Gary Spatz were all given printouts to fill in, grading the contenders on a scale of 1–10 in key categories: acting, dance, vocals, camera persona, personality, and appearance. Each performer then received an overall letter grade and commentary.

From Spatz's penciled-in assessment of the seven kids who made the cut: twelve-year-old Ryan Gosling, "*A* (Very good kid)"; twelve-year-old Christina Aguilera, "*A* (Special)"; eleven-year-old Marque Lynche, "*A* (I like this young man)"; twelve-year-old Justin Timberlake, "*B*+ (Raw but good!)"; thirteen-year-old Nikki DeLoach, "*A* (Really like this kid!)"; twelve-year-old TJ Fantini, "*A* (A winner!)"; and eleven-year-old Britney Spears, "*B*+ (Very good! Nice girl)." (Jessica Simpson had also been in the mix, but she bombed her audition and received an inscrutable rating of "??" by Spatz.)

Those newcomers' families were then uprooted to Central Florida, where the young performers were thrust into a well-oiled, star-making venture. The cast filled their production days with on-site acting, singing, and dance lessons between shooting. "It was really like a Juilliard or something," music producer Sarah Elgart said. "They brought in high-level professionals to improve the kids' abilities to be triple threats." Long before Google and Apple popularized the idea of a campus workplace, Disney made the blueprint: Cast members who were still in school did their mandatory three hours of schoolwork a day in the studio class-room. They ate their meals in the park's commissary. There was a fitness room to stay active and a therapist on call to help with mental stress that might arise.

"They were brand-new talent that needed to be developed, and the way they had it set up reminded me of the old MGM studio days," Spatz said. "I hadn't seen anything like that done since the 1930s and '40s. It's obvious if you look at where they are now that this really was an incredi-ble foundation, but you couldn't do that now in any way, shape, or form. The laws wouldn't allow it."

That ample time together created plenty of opportunities for tight bonds and romance to blossom among the cast. Britney Spears and Christina Aguilera harbored crushes on their older co-star Tony Lucca, who dated Keri Russell. "Britney wanted whatever Keri had," Tony said. "If Keri had me, then Britney wanted me." The younger girls idolized Keri, imitating her mannerisms and tying their shirts into knots at the waist because that's how Keri wore hers. When not needed on set, resident rap-scallions Ryan Gosling and Justin Timberlake would steal unattended golf carts and ride them through the theme park. On weekends, the cast would band together for supervised barbecues and beach trips, or some of the older teens would congregate for house parties, where they occa-sionally drank and smoked pot. And nearly everyone loved to, chastely, party at the teen-friendly clubs at Disney's Pleasure Island entertainment quarter (now incorporated into today's much blander Disney Springs).

"My grandmother would drop me, Ryan, Justin, and Britney off at Pleasure Island, and we'd dance," Nikki DeLoach said. "I mean, Britney was eleven. It was insane that we were allowed to do this. But we did. And we were totally fine. We were safe. We were responsible. And then we would make our way back to the pickup spot by eleven P.M. We were allowed to just be kids."

While *The All New Mickey Mouse Club*'s superfans worshipped the cast, the performers' popularity was happening largely in a vacuum. At the time, The Disney Channel was exclusively a premium network for paid subscribers. ("I think my parents *had* to get The Disney Channel because their kid was on it," Mouseketeer Deedee Magno Hall said.) There was no YouTube or social media for Disney to disseminate clips to the masses—or for its stars to use to engage with a wider audience. And when the Mouseketeers returned to their regular schools on season hiatuses, their classmates could be cruel. "M-I-C-K-E-Y B-I-T-C-H," a bully once sang to Lindsey Alley when she walked into the cafeteria at her Lakeland, Florida, middle school. The other kids erupted in laughter. "I went into the bathroom and just lost it," she said. "I remember thinking, *Does everybody hate me?*"

By its seventh season, *The All New Mickey Mouse Club* had gotten wildly expensive to produce. The oldest cast members' contracts were ending soon, and they'd once again need to be replaced with a fresh crop of young stars, meaning a whole new casting search. Plus, a corporate overhaul was brewing at the network. It was easiest for The Disney Channel to just pull the plug entirely when that season ended production in 1994.

It wasn't until a few years later, when Britney and Christina became solo pop stars, and JC and Justin found success with *NSYNC—all on non-Disney record labels—that the media began to marvel at the connective thread of the superstars' early days at The Disney Channel and the show that launched them all. The performers left Disney in their dust as they sold platinum albums, world tour tickets, and endless merchandise. And the Disney executives began to bemoan their losses. "The fact that they became stars *after* they left, that was Disney's mistake," *The All New Mickey Mouse Club* showrunner Dennis Steinmetz said. "They should have held on to them for a while, just to see what happened."

From a business perspective, Disney should have launched those promising young stars' solo careers on Disney record labels. They should have facilitated their cross-platform exposure across the greater Disney corporation's numerous divisions. They should have secured spin-off series, movies, albums, concerts, radio, and promotional opportunities that transcended a cable audience and touched consumers around the world, launching the network's talent to massive fame and bringing in obscene amounts of corporate money along the way.

But no one at Disney was thinking like that. Yet.

1

Changing of the Guard

Michael Eisner was furious. Throughout the eighties and nineties, Nickelodeon had continued to reign supreme in kids' cable programming. Disney's entire brand was built on family entertainment. This was a space in which his company should, theoretically, be thriving.

"I don't understand why this Nickelodeon is so popular!" the Disney chairman would lament in the mid-90s.

In reality, The Disney Channel's programming strategy had been a hodgepodge of chaos since its inception. When James P. Jimirro, who had run Disney's non-theatrical media division, first proposed the idea of a Disney cable channel in 1977, he'd dreamed of a place where the studio's past theatrical material could air on TV and, in turn, promote home entertainment consumption. But back then, Disney was more focused on the growth of its theme parks. Around that time, 70 percent of The Walt Disney Company's revenue came from the parks, and Epcot was about to open in Florida. Meanwhile, the movie studio had hit a rough patch in the years since Walt's death in 1966. Animation was prohibitively slow and expensive. And at the end of the 1970s, home entertainment was only just starting to take off with the advent of VHS tapes.

But cable television was on the rise. As the medium spread throughout the country in the 1980s, compartmentalized channels catering to specific audiences proliferated. MTV for music-loving teenagers. Nickelodeon for kids. A&E for arts lovers. Financial News Network for business junkies. When The Disney Channel launched in April 1983 as a premium cable network, it served as something of a G-rated HBO. If viewers wanted to add "America's family network" to their cable package, they had to pay an extra monthly subscription fee, ranging from $7.95 to $12.95 depending on the area.

In its first decade, The Disney Channel became home to programming like *Welcome to Pooh Corner* and *Mousercise*, which featured classic Disney characters exercising with kids; variety musical shows like *The All New Mickey Mouse Club* and *Kids Incorporated*; and made-for-TV Disney Channel Premiere Films like *The Parent Trap II* and *III*. Plus, it included plenty of airtime for theme park promotions to appease the Disney brass.

They lured new subscribers with "sneak-a-peek" weekends, which gave regular cable users free access to the channel for a brief window before snatching it away again. But while the network was hitting its subscriber targets and attracting critical acclaim, it was clear Disney didn't really know what to do with The Disney Channel as a brand. By the early '90s, in addition to its Disney character–based programming, the lineup featured a scattered mix of Boyz II Men and Willie Nelson concerts and nature programming. They even annually broadcast *The American Teacher Awards* in prime time. By the time *The All New Mickey Mouse Club* aired its last new episode in 1995, the network had no definitive identity, and few consumers talked excitedly about the channel.

Finally, Eisner had had enough. At roughly the same time that The Walt Disney Company snapped up the ABC broadcast network in 1995, Eisner and then–Disney president Michael Ovitz began poaching former Nickelodeon executives to join Disney and push the cable group in a competitive new direction. After ten years as the president of Nickelodeon, Geraldine Laybourne left to become president of Disney/ABC Cable Networks, reporting to then–TV chairman Bob Iger. And Laybourne anointed as the new president of The Disney Channel a woman who'd spent more than a decade with her at Nickelodeon: thirty-eight-year-old Anne Sweeney.

* * *

ANNE SWEENEY'S PARENTS hadn't allowed her to camp out in front of the living room television while she was growing up in Kingston, New York. When *All in the Family* premiered in 1971, the Sweeneys, who were both teachers, would put their three children to bed and invite the next-door neighbors over to watch the groundbreaking sitcom together. But thirteen-year-old Anne, the eldest, routinely snuck out of bed to crouch at the top of the staircase and listen, stifling her laughter so as not to blow her cover. "I remember my jaw dropping at the way these characters spoke to each other and the things that they were discussing," she said. "That was the first moment of clarity for me about what television could be."

While getting her master's in education at Harvard, Sweeney set her sights on forging a career that combined both entertainment and education. Soon after graduating in 1980, she fudged her way into an entry-level job assisting Nickelodeon's then–head of acquisitions, Geraldine Laybourne, by claiming she could type eighty words a minute. In reality, Sweeney said, "It was more like eight." The post was a flop, but Laybourne liked Sweeney's gumption and found another position for her at the channel. Over the next twelve years, Sweeney worked her way up the Nickelodeon ladder to become executive vice president under Laybourne.

It was no small feat to have two women at the top. Corporate entertainment was (and still is) very much a boys' club. Sweeney had watched Paramount head Sherry Lansing's rise from afar in awe, ever since she'd read a 1980 profile in *The New York Times Magazine*, for which Lansing appeared on the cover in a jaunty pantsuit. "I read this article about this woman who made movies, and I will never forget it," Sweeney said. "I stopped and thought, *You can do that?* Because it had never crossed my mind."

After brokering the international launch of Nickelodeon in the UK, in partnership with Rupert Murdoch's Sky Multichannels, Sweeney was asked by Murdoch to oversee the launch of News Corp's new cable channel, FX. She left Nickelodeon in 1993 to help build that interactive network from scratch as chairman and CEO. "Remember, this is all pre–Fox News," Sweeney emphasized.

It was an exciting time of growth and development across the cable industry, but when Sweeney left FX and arrived at her new Disney Channel post in 1996, she found a dismal, uninspired landscape. The legacy staffers on her team had a muted view of their own network's promise. And six weeks into Sweeney's presidency, a Disney animation executive, still riding high from the monstrous success of *The Lion King* and his team's place of prominence within the greater Disney corporation, came to her Burbank office to welcome her to the company. "The first thing he said was, 'I waste more money in a day than you make in a year,'" Sweeney recalled. "I thought, *Okay. I get it.*"

Initial network research showed that when people thought of Disney animated movies, they practically burst with love for the tradition of taking their family to the movie theater to see each new release. When polled about Disney theme parks, there was a similar effusive adoration—even among those who'd never been to Anaheim or Orlando. But when asked about The Disney Channel, the answers became stiflingly polite variations of "It's safe" and "I don't worry about my kids watching it."

"I left that research session saying, 'I want to be a park,'" Sweeney said. "'I want to be the one they talk about.' Even if they've never watched Disney Channel, they can't stop talking about it."

To give The Disney Channel relevance in the broader TV landscape (and within Disney itself), Sweeney and her team would have to completely throw out the old playbook and rebuild the network from the ground up. "At the time that we joined, Disney Channel was not being strategized, targeted, or produced as a kids' channel," said Eleo Hensleigh, who had worked under Sweeney at Nickelodeon and FX and also oversaw marketing and brand strategy at Disney Channel from 1996 to 2007. "The philosophy was that it was for the bill payers because it was a paid channel: you target the parent with the kind of programming that they think kids should watch, and they will feel good about paying the extra monthly charge."

But that programming wasn't igniting loyalty among young viewers. During one focus group session in Chicago, Laybourne and her team asked children to compare Nickelodeon and The Disney Channel to foods. The results: Nickelodeon was pizza. The Disney Channel was broccoli.

It was decided. They'd need to scrap all of the existing programming and develop an entirely new strategy, all the way down to the name of the network. After all, there was no such thing as "The Nickelodeon." Having "The" in The Disney Channel placed it alongside stodgy fare like The History Channel and The Travel Channel. So, in 1997, they became simply Disney Channel.

They also needed to make sure they had a passionate team in place to ignite their robust changes. Six months into her role, Sweeney convinced FX programming head Rich Ross to leave and join her in the mammoth task. "Rich had all the energy. He understood basic cable, the pace, what you needed to do in programming, how to go the distance," Sweeney said. "This was a new take on what we looked like on air. A reset."

MANY KIDS DREAM of becoming an actor or a singer when they grow up. Rich Ross dreamed of becoming a Hollywood businessman. When his childhood friends had been reading *Sports Illustrated*, twelve-year-old Ross had begged for a *Variety* subscription. He learned early on he had no talent for performing, and he didn't attempt any creative roles beyond directing his second-grade class's Thanksgiving play in his Westchester County hometown. "I'm woefully inadequate at things I can be very supportive of in other people," he said.

During his time at the University of Pennsylvania and Fordham Law School, Ross spent his summers interning at the glittery William Morris talent agency, and when it was time to get a real job, he joined Nickelodeon as a freelance talent coordinator. On his first day, he arrived early at the network's New York corporate headquarters to find the floor completely empty. A single light shone down the hallway. There, under its glow, sat a woman eating a very large muffin in a very small office.

"I'm Anne," she said, between bites. "Do you want to join me for breakfast?"

Ross pulled up a chair next to Sweeney and tucked into the mini cereal box he'd brought from home. A friendship quickly formed, and Sweeney began bringing him on to her projects. Ross's original gig had been to book talent for Nickelodeon's inaugural 1987 awards program, *The Big Ballot*, which later evolved into the *Kids' Choice Awards*. That year, he managed to book thirty-five of the thirty-six nominees to appear at the taped event, including Michael Jordan and Madonna. "Every team, every star agreed," Ross recalled. "The only person who wouldn't say yes was Bill Cosby."

From there, Ross ran the Nickelodeon talent department and negotiated programming deals and contracts before moving over to FX in Los Angeles, alongside Sweeney, and then starting at Disney Channel as a senior vice president of programming and production in 1996. "He was just phenomenal at spotting talent," Sweeney said. "He could see beyond the experience or lack of experience and see the potential."

Within the Disney Channel corporate echelons, Ross became "the golden boy," according to *So Weird* executive producer (and national treasure) Henry Winkler. Around the office, Ross often dressed in jeans and loafers, but he carried himself with a dignified presence. At the weekly all-hands meetings each Thursday, he would take center stage in the conference room and go on long-winded soliloquies about the industry and the perceived impact Disney Channel was having.

But with the creatives on various show and movie sets, a different name often took precedence over the years: Gary Marsh.

"Even though it was a big deal when Rich came to town, nobody ever said to me, 'Oh, Rich wants it to be like this,' or, 'Just so you know, Rich took a look at the casting and we're going to go with this kid,'" frequent Disney Channel Original Movie producer Kevin Lafferty said. "It was never that. It was always, 'Gary, Gary, Gary.'"

Marsh was a Los Angeles native who began his career as an assistant to the prolific TV director John Rich. Marsh had also dabbled in political campaigns—including Walter Mondale's failed 1984 presidential bid—and served as the director of movies and miniseries at Columbia Pictures Television before joining the emergent Disney Channel in 1988 as an original programming executive. His previous Disney bosses had been fired in the midnineties Sweeney/Ross transition, leaving him as the sole carryover programming head, focused on original movie content.

"I remember Gary coming into my office, and he was clearly very nervous. Like, *Oh, my god, am I next?*" Sweeney recalled. "I said, 'Tell me what you're working on.' He started telling me stories [about each film], and it occurred to me: I'd found the storyteller. There was no doubt in my mind that he would stay."

But accepting new Disney Channel overlords—brought in from outside the Disney family, at that!—was a tense ask. When Ross initially arrived at his new corner office at Disney Channel's headquarters, he was greeted by an outdated TV encased in wood paneling. Clearly, it had been rarely, if ever, used. But when he walked into Marsh's office, he saw a sparkling modern set.

"Nice television!" Ross exclaimed.

Marsh glanced up from his desk. "Order one," he said flatly.

Oh, boy, Ross thought. *Maybe this is not going to go great.*

But Marsh quickly warmed to the sweeping ideas that Sweeney and Ross were proposing. A month after the TV incident, Marsh knocked on Ross's office door. "I'm not sure how we're going to do it, and I don't know if it's going to work," Ross remembered Marsh saying. "But I believe in your passion."

As Ross's role expanded to general manager of the network in 1999, the team set about leaning into Marsh's strengths—forming relationships with the creatives and identifying relatable narratives. "It was really the beginning of a storied relationship," Ross said. "There was no screaming. There was no drama. Gary had very big energy. Gary had ambition. And Gary had this incredible way of working with writers and directors, which was not my strength. So, we divided and conquered."

While the network heads at ABC, CBS, or NBC would have little to no direct interaction with the production teams of each show, the network executives at Disney Channel were intimately involved. Marsh, whose role encompassed overseeing all original programming and production by 2001, would often help dictate the set designs, sit in on casting sessions, and offer feedback on story arcs. "If it didn't go through Gary, it didn't matter," *Lizzie McGuire* showrunner Stan Rogow said. "*Everything* went through Gary. And anybody who knew anything realized that if you didn't have Gary on board, you didn't have anybody."

ACROSS TOWN, THE Nickelodeon offices at MTV Networks's Santa Monica headquarters featured a whimsical Airstream trailer in the lobby, quirky Astroturf flooring, a one-hundred-foot surfboard suspended from the ceiling, and dozens of TV screens playing their channel's hit series.

By contrast, Disney Channel's high-rise home at 3800 West Alameda Avenue in Burbank was a bland twenty-one-story tower, about a mile from the main Disney Studios lot, which they'd inhabited since 1986. The cookie-cutter, cubicle-filled box was outfitted with fluorescent lights and little evidence of the magical brand identity they were intent on preserving. "When I walked in the door and it was all gray and white, I thought, *Wait, am I in the wrong building?*" Sweeney said. "I was expecting Mickey and Minnie and all this joy."

Sweeney attempted to add softening flourishes, like hanging kids' artwork in the hallways and stationing a six-foot-tall plush Mickey Mouse outside her office. But that innate office rigidity, many say, was the outward manifestation of the long-held, risk-averse tenets of the Disney brand. "When you work there, you have to buy into the ethos that is Disney, and it permeates everything in terms of the way they looked at casting, the way they looked at music, the way they looked at pacing and storytelling," *Bug Juice* creator Douglas Ross said. "I thought, *God, they're so old-fashioned and so scared of their own shadow.*"

And then there was the standards and practices team, colloquially known as S&P. Most TV networks have an S&P division, but because of the brand legacy and the young age of Disney Channel's audience, this particular group was notoriously heavy-handed. They touched every single piece of content that aired on Disney Channel, constantly challenging jokes, looking for potential legal issues, questioning imitable behavior, and pointing out lines and gestures that might be considered offensive in overseas markets.

Over the years, S&P would pick apart everything from which brand of designer flip-flops *High School Musical*'s Sharpay could sing about in "Fabulous" to how much sass Zack could dish out on *The Suite Life of Zack & Cody*. Phrases like "shut up" and "you suck" were automatic no-gos. Adult characters couldn't be seen drinking alcohol or even a Shirley Temple mocktail. A line about an actual hairless cat might be interpreted as innuendo about a vagina, so that was out. The word "war" was banned, and even a pillow fight could be deemed too violent.

So broad was S&P's purview that, at one point, "We had to put a moratorium on farts," said a former S&P manager at the network. (One controversial tidbit that slipped through: naming a *Suite Life* antagonist Ilsa Schicklgrubermeiger—an oversight that rankled the European markets for its intentional inclusion of Adolf Hitler's family name, Schicklgruber. "We were just trying to give her a villainous sounding last name," writer Jeny Quine said. "It didn't get caught until it went overseas.")

The creatives who thrived and had the most longevity at Disney Channel, both before and after the Sweeney/Ross rebrand, tended to be the ones who learned to work within the established system: dutifully incorporating the network executives' exacting input on the desired color of a set rug or slashing a seemingly harmless joke that S&P deemed problematic. Individuals who balked at the oversight and "Disney way" had a rockier road. "Those who tried to run rogue," Hensleigh said, "were usually run out of town."

PART OF THE complete '90s reset was an overhaul of how the network reached its viewers in the first place. Growth was essential. Premium cable was "expensive and exclusive," Sweeney said. "And Disney should never be exclusive." The Disney Channel had initiated a transition from premium to basic cable under former network president John Cooke, allowing cable providers to choose whether they wanted to offer the network as a premium or basic option in their packages.

"They had the brilliant idea that Disney in more homes was more valuable than a profitable, small pay service," Sweeney said. "I thought it was the most genius thing I had seen in business. So, I focused on accelerating the strategy."

In 1996, The Disney Channel was in fifteen million homes. Under Sweeney—who took over Laybourne's job overseeing most of the Disney-owned cable channels, in addition to her Disney Channel presidency, in 1998—they added roughly a million homes a month. Every month. For the next five years.

"We had to quickly matter and figure out a way cable operators would want us badly enough to pay," Ross said. "In the beginning, it was hand-to-hand combat."

The Disney licensing deal, which often lumped Disney Channel into popular packages with ESPN, was among the most expensive for providers. Yet, just five years after the regime change, Sweeney's team had more than quintupled Disney Channel's circulation to seventy-seven million by 2001.

The last major cable company holdout had been Time Warner. The operator's domain included New York City—not only the single largest market in America, but also home to most of the Nickelodeon executives. Because Disney Channel didn't run ads, their growth didn't show up in any advertising reports. And without access to Disney Channel on basic cable in their own homes, the Nickelodeon executives had remained largely unconcerned by Disney Channel's monumental growth—until a deal was brokered with Time Warner, who was in the midst of merging with AOL, in 2000. If the provider wanted to keep offering ABC, Disney demanded, they'd have to include Disney Channel in their basic cable package, too.

"People couldn't believe we had become what we had become—because any competitor would have tried to destroy us. But the people who worked in New York for Nickelodeon really didn't see us coming," Ross said. "And then one day, we were just the most important thing to kids."

* * *

IN THE HIERARCHY of the Walt Disney Company, cable television had been near the bottom of the ladder when Sweeney and Ross arrived in the mid-1990s. "In terms of having an opinion of how to build a business, we were considered to be complete yokels," marketing executive Eleo Hensleigh said. "There was a lot of resistance to the idea that there could be business off of original properties and original characters on the channel."

The studio, theme parks, home video, and consumer products all took precedence. And in the beginning, the other divisions' aspirations for a revamped Disney Channel were that it could become something of a barker channel—a network that existed solely for the purpose of advertising and promoting the other, more lucrative Disney branches.

"I remember getting a call when they were launching one of the first Disney cruise ships. They asked if I could send a crew to film it getting painted in a dock in Italy and make an interstitial about that," Hensleigh said. "I was like, *you honestly think I should make an interstitial about literal paint drying?* It was not relevant to them whether a kid would find that in any way interesting. Every division had an opinion of what Disney Channel should be that would be most valuable to them."

To appease the studio and home video divisions, they developed *Movie Surfers*, an informative series hosted by photogenic teens (including a young Christina "Tina" Milian) who would discuss the latest Disney theatrical and DVD releases and give a behind-the-scenes look at the making of the movies. The Surfers would interview *Mighty Joe Young* actors, hang out with the shaggy dog from *The Shaggy Dog*, or learn how *A Bug's Life* made its computer-animated bloopers. "The big company started to see that our instincts were not to be anti-Disney," Hensleigh said. "We said, 'Let us try to figure out the best way that will work for this audience, and we'll all win.'"

Even after the move from premium to basic cable, Disney Channel steered clear of paid advertising. Instead of the commercials for Nerf guns and Barbies that populated ad breaks on other kids' channels, Disney filled the gaps with their own house-made, short-form content (i.e., interstitials), like *Movie Surfers*. The lack of in-your-face commercials gave parents the peace of mind that their kids weren't being bombarded with ads pushing the latest hair bedazzler or Hot Wheels. But mainly, it was more valuable for the interstitial breaks to serve as a billboard for the greater Disney corporation than to pocket revenue from outside advertisers.

"We were able to calculate the impact that running those spots on Disney Channel had on the rest of the company," Sweeney said. "Advertising would have diminished the amount of time that the company had to talk about itself and promote its visions."

The Children's Television Act of 1990 had mandated that children's programming contain no more than twelve minutes of commercials per hour on weekdays and ten and a half minutes on weekends. And the FCC dictated that advertising for children's products associated with the program was also prohibited. For Disney Channel, that extended to any hint of broader Disney propaganda, including referencing its theme parks, cruise line, or animated films, in its series and movies. (While ABC was able to get away with the *Boy Meets World* characters visiting Disney World in an episode, the fictional families on Disney Channel could never even mention the parks.) But the rule didn't extend to the interstitial breaks. There, Disney Channel could hawk Disney's various assets with abandon—as long as they didn't exceed the time restrictions.

ON THE PROGRAMMING side, Rich Ross had been given six weeks from his initial 1996 start date to come up with the new content strategy. From the twenty-first floor of 3800 West Alameda Avenue, the team mapped out a plan and set about breaking up the network's schedule into audience-specific programming blocks, similar to their strategy at Nickelodeon. There was what became Playhouse Disney for toddlers and preschoolers in the mornings and early afternoons; original movies and series for the older kids in the later afternoons and prime time; and Vault Disney, a space for classic Disney content tucked deep into the night.

The prime-time block aimed at the underserved market of kids aged nine to fourteen and their families was the most crucial. While Nickelodeon dominated in kids' animation with series like *Rugrats* and *Hey Arnold!* and had started venturing into live-action sketch shows with

All That and *The Amanda Show*, there was a distinct gap in prime-time scripted programming for those who had aged out of Nick but were still too young (or, at least, whose parents felt they were too young) for MTV: the tweens.

J.R.R. Tolkien had used the term "tweens" to describe the years that reckless hobbits spent caught be*tween* teenage-dom and adulthood in his 1954 novel *The Fellowship of the Ring*. But, starting in the late 1980s, "tween" began to be used in marketing circles to refer to the precarious time between childhood and adolescence, encompassing a pliable range of years going as low as age eight and up to age fifteen. It's a time when youths face a host of unique physical and emotional challenges—and also begin to wield increased buying power in their homes.

Tweens weren't a natural fit for Disney Channel. In the '90s, the Disney brand name implied babyish fare. Disney's calling cards were kids' animated movies and theme parks. The phrase "Disney adults" did not yet exist. Mickey Mouse was decidedly uncool. The new guard needed tweens to see Disney Channel as fresh and trendy, while dealing with the preconceived notions that came with the name. "People, for the most part, were like, this is not going to work," Ross said. "Anne understood the power of kids. Bob Iger understood the power of television, and they were both very supportive. But a lot of people just didn't believe in it."

As part of the revamp, Sweeney and Ross began using the Disney Channel money that had previously been spent on content acquisitions to make their own original content instead. The network's main priorities would be split across two divisions: original series and original movies. "We had limited dollars to tell a multitude of stories," Ross said. "We needed both to work, and we needed both to be funded."

Key to the early series programming direction was Lee Gaither. Unlike the majority of the other executives, who were white and had migrated to California from the Northeast with degrees from elite private institutions like Harvard, Vassar, Penn, and NYU, Gaither was a Black man from Mobile, Alabama, who had graduated from Auburn, a public university where football is king. He was a veteran of kids' programming at ABC and the USA network, and he was eager to make his mark on the revamped Disney Channel. "No one in the programming room, no one at the networks at the senior level ever looked like me," Gaither said. "I always felt like an alien. But Geri [Laybourne] embraced that part of me in a huge way and forced me to really speak up early on in my tenure at Disney in terms of what was missing in the marketplace."

What was missing, they concluded, was a family-viewing experience. Disney Channel's research showed that '90s millennial kids wanted to be more connected to their parents. It was a notion previously rejected by MTV and Nickelodeon. While Nick shows screamed "for kids only!" with gross-out humor, clueless parents, and copious amounts of slime, Disney Channel now hoped to bring the entire family to the couch with "co-viewing" shows that bridged the generational divide. One early Disney Channel viewer survey asked kids who their heroes were. The executives expected the answers to range from superheroes to historical figures. Instead, almost universally, the answers came back as "Mom," "Dad," "my brother," and "my sister."

"That was a moment when the light bulb went off and we said, 'Oh, we're not paying attention to what makes Disney, Disney,'" Sweeney said. "We needed to recalibrate."

After a few false starts with original game shows like *Mad Libs* and *Off the Wall*, and easy-to-produce nature series like *Omba Mokomba* and *Going Wild with Jeff Corwin*, they shifted their focus to dramas, both in movie and series form, because that was what felt the most true to the Disney brand. If Nickelodeon was burps and pratfalls, Disney Channel was going to be emotion and heart.

At Nickelodeon, the audience inherently skewed toward boys, and they'd had to work to bring in girls with programs like *Clarissa Explains It All* and *The Secret World of Alex Mack*. Disney was the opposite. The brand's princess legacy meant that girls felt more welcome, and they'd now need to work to recruit boys into the mix. "Princesses are one of the biggest franchises for the company, but we were very, very steadfast about not developing princess programming," Hensleigh said. "At the time, a princess program was going to send fifty percent of your audience out of the room." Many of their early Disney Channel movies and series were thus action-packed and male-centric, like *Brink!*, *Johnny Tsunami*, and *The Famous Jett Jackson*.

Other parameters included Disney Channel's much-discussed "sixty-five-episode rule," a policy in which they would cancel most original series once they hit the sixty-five-episode mark. The benchmark was a holdover from the classic programming idea that you'd need sixty-five episodes to have enough content to air repeats five days a week for thirteen weeks, which could then be repeated quarterly to provide a full slate of content year-round.

With sixty-five episodes in the bank, Disney Channel would be able to air consecutive reruns in the same timeslot every weekday (i.e., *The Famous Jett Jackson* at 4:00 P.M., *In a Heartbeat* at 4:30 P.M., and *So Weird* at 5:00 P.M.). After they reached that threshold, the cost to the network to continue making new episodes of the same show was greater than if they ended the series and started fresh with a new show to add to the mix.

Plus, as the young casts got older, the storylines had to remain rooted in material that was appropriate for younger audiences. Unlike *Grease*, where thirty-year-old actors tried to pass as high schoolers, or *Beverly Hills, 90210*, where the cast was mostly in their twenties during filming, Disney Channel followed the Nickelodeon model, casting actual tweens and teens to play their on-screen counterparts. "To me, the most relatable thing was casting someone who was around thirteen to play thirteen," Ross said. "They were all young, and there's a sensitivity to that, and we were very cognizant of it, but we were interested in the audience looking at them and saying, 'They look like somebody I go to school with.'"

Most of the young actors also wanted to evolve and grow, and ending at sixty-five episodes just seemed like the right timeline to allow that to happen. "It was healthy for everybody that they grow up," Ross said. "It was better for us to meet new tweens and teens than to have twenty-five-year-olds playing eighteen-year-olds and the stories they would be involved in. It wasn't that the kids had to stay young. It was that the stories needed to stay young."

2

The Experimental Era

"If you could make any show you wanted, what would it be?"

Rich Ross posed this pie-in-the-sky question to producer Douglas Ross (no relation) during a 1996 *Movie Surfers* development meeting. Douglas thought for a moment. He had long been intrigued by documentaries and had ample experience doing interview segments with kids at PBS and elsewhere. His producing partner, J. Rupert Thompson, had worked on the second season of *The Real World*, a reality show staple at MTV since 1992, and that was top of mind. "All of these data points combined in my brain to make me think I knew exactly what show I wanted to do," he said. "A documentary about kids at summer camp, but cut it like a soap opera."

In the mid- to late 1990s, without a predetermined look and feel for new Disney Channel original series, then–senior vice president of progamming and production Rich Ross and the other network executives were open to throwing ideas against a wall and seeing what stuck—like Douglas's reality show pitch, which eventually became the three-season, summer camp–set series *Bug Juice*. As long as the content was family-friendly and aimed at tweens, the executives entertained creatives who came with passionate ideas, even if they were outside the box.

Another enthusiastic pitch came from Fracaswell Hyman, a writer for the PBS series *Ghostwriter*. Eight years before *Hannah Montana*,

Hyman's Disney Channel show featured a superstar juggling a public and private life. And this superstar was Black.

WHEN HYMAN SOLD *The Famous Jett Jackson* to Disney Channel, he was adamant that the show cast an African American teen in the role of Jett, a mega-famous TV action star trying to live a normal life in his North Carolina hometown. The landscape of Black-led television at the time was overwhelmingly in the comedy space. Nickelodeon had *Kenan & Kel* and would soon develop *Cousin Skeeter*. On network prime time, *The Fresh Prince of Bel-Air* and *Family Matters* had been huge sitcom hits. But to greenlight a family drama from a Black creator that portrayed a Black male lead as a suave teen heartthrob? That was new.

Disney Channel had been making an effort toward diverse casting in their movies and shows, "not because someone told us to," Ross said, "but because we had a diverse audience, and it mattered greatly." (Still, some early Disney Channel Original Movies, like *Halloweentown* and *The Thirteenth Year*, had scarcely any lines of dialogue spoken by people of color.) They auditioned hundreds of Black actors for the lead role of Jett, but it wasn't until Hyman turned on his TV at home and happened to see a Robitussin commercial featuring a kid named Lee Thompson Young that he felt he'd found his star.

"He was just so self-possessed and friendly and talented," Hyman said. "I can't say enough wonderful things about him. He was just what we needed." (Lee later tragically died by suicide at age twenty-nine, after struggling with bipolar disorder and depression.)

But the initiative to tell Black stories and center a Black action hero didn't necessarily equate to equity among the rest of the cast. When the role of Jett's mom came down to two actors, Hyman said some of the Disney suits expressed concern that audiences wouldn't believe the character could be a renowned TV star if she was played by Melanie Nicholls-King, a darker-skinned Black woman with dreadlocks. Their other top candidate was lighter skinned and had a weave. "When you looked at the audition tapes, Melanie was much warmer, much funnier, much more relatable," Hyman recalled. "But I remember having a meeting and them saying the other actress *looked* the part."

Nicholls-King eventually won the role, but over time, Hyman felt he was being undervalued on his own project. After being wooed by Nickelodeon to run *Little Bill*, he left *Jett Jackson* at the end of the first season. New white executives (including Shawn Levy, at the dawn of his career) were steadily brought on board and a blond co-lead was added to the cast. "All the creatives were white, and they brought in a character to be the opposite of Jett," Hyman said. "I just had to divorce myself from the entire thing and say, 'I wish you the best.'"

By 2003, just two years after its final episode, reruns of *Jett Jackson* had been relegated to a 3:00 A.M. time slot. The idea of fostering inclusivity and diversity on the network was something Disney Channel was clearly putting a premium on, but how it played out in practice was a different story. "Disney, from the outside, it's all Tinker Bell and sparkles," Hyman said. "But inside, it's not fantasy land."

WHILE *THE FAMOUS JETT JACKSON* planted the seeds for fame-centric original series, *So Weird* explored the role that music could play in Disney Channel's scripted content—wrapped up in a completely unexpected package.

Long before he became The Fonz on *Happy Days*, Henry Winkler became fascinated with the occult. As a boy, he had once lost and then miraculously found his treasured ID bracelet in Central Park. "I choose to believe that a higher power helped me find it," he said, adding, "And I have always believed since I was that age that I will be in the vicinity when aliens land on the earth, and they will be friendly." That unbridled love of the otherworldly led Winkler to executive produce the Disney Channel Original Series *So Weird*.

No scripted Disney Channel show encapsulates the freewheeling late-nineties era of experimentation better than *So Weird*. A young teen girl named Fi (Cara DeLizia) joins her rockstar mom (Mackenzie Phillips) on tour, where she encounters paranormal phenomena at every stop, while also grappling with the death of her father and directly confronting questions around the afterlife and mortality. It's dark, both in subject matter and cinematography. And Winkler fought to make sure the show didn't talk down to young viewers. "Their fingers are little, but their brains are big," he said. "You can't forget that in making entertainment for them."

Husband-and-wife team Jon Cooksey and Ali Marie Matheson had been working on *Rugrats* at Nickelodeon when development executive Lee Gaither poached them to come to *So Weird* as showrunners. "It took probably ten secret meetings to finally get them to leave Nickelodeon and do the show," Gaither said. "It was a huge, huge thing. Because, suddenly, now Disney Channel was stealing people that were the secret sauce for Nickelodeon." As the concept of family viewing had steadily fallen out of fashion at other networks, *Rugrats* had been a rare show at Nickelodeon to find cross-generational appeal. "*Rugrats* was unique in that it worked for two-year-olds and seven-year-olds and stoned college kids and adults," Cooksey said. "It was for family viewing, and that's what they wanted [at Disney] for *So Weird*—a kind of a teen *X-Files* that kids would watch with their parents."

So Weird overflowed with what Winkler described as "the richness of the humanness." The characters were flawed, fragile, and real. When casting the show's matriarch, Molly, it came down to Mackenzie Phillips or Debby Boone. Boone was the bubbly blond daughter of conservative icon Pat Boone and best known for her moony 1977 cover of "You Light Up My Life." Phillips was the daughter of The Mamas & The Papas' singer John Phillips, and undoubtedly the bigger risk. She'd publicly battled drug and alcohol addictions, been fired from *One Day at a Time*, done multiple stints in treatment centers, and suffered a pair of near-fatal overdoses. Outside of brief single-episodic TV appearances, she had been virtually unhirable since the mid-1980s. "The girl lived a *life*," Winkler said of Phillips. "That power of being able to confront your demons and then put them behind you gives you a weight and understanding of living, of relationships, of acceptance, of warmth, of passion." Rich Ross agreed, and they cast her. "People were like, 'Are you insane?'" Ross recalled. "I was like, 'She's perfect.'"

The ensemble cast included several teen boys, including *Brink!*

heartthrob Erik von Detten and Blake Lively's older brother, Eric Lively, in supporting roles, but the show was centered on Cara DeLizia and her character's experiences navigating the paranormal as a teen girl. Fi followed in the footsteps of spunky Nickelodeon heroines Alex Mack and Shelby Woo, but having a female dramatic lead on a kids' show was still a rare occurrence. And when Cara went through puberty in real life, there was outsized concern, based on focus group results, that young girls who hadn't yet developed wouldn't connect with Fi's curves.

"They would try to hide my boobs with sports bras or baggy shirts," Cara said. "It was a big deal to have a young girl as a female star, so I think they really wanted every girl in the United States to feel like they could relate to Fi. But on the other hand, you also have this young girl that's going through puberty herself, and it's like, 'What the hell are these boobs? They're huge.'"

Disney Channel tested *So Weird* extensively throughout its 1999 to 2001 run, and the results about the content of the show were overwhelmingly positive. Audiences liked the idea of a kiddie *X-Files*, they liked the traveling musical family element that was subtly reminiscent of *The Partridge Family*—they just didn't like the idea of watching it on Disney Channel. Disney was associated with perky, happy fare, not introspective spookiness and haunting melodies. In response, the series began shifting into a younger, goofier place, more in line with viewers' expectations of the network.

By the time Winkler appeared in a guest role on a season 2 episode, he said with an air of sadness, the show had already started to take on "a completely different tone." And ahead of season 3, Cara said her mom (whom she described as "not the most easygoing person") asked that she be released from her contract to pursue other projects. The network complied. "I didn't want to leave. I wanted to stay, and Disney wanted me to stay," Cara said. "But I was a kid. It was out of my control, and it was really hard. That cast and crew were like my family." Disney Channel ended up completely revamping *So Weird* for season 3, axing the showrunners and bringing in a bright-eyed, younger lead named Alexz Johnson to star as Fi's cousin and sing on the show and in side projects. "It was a lot of different emotions," Alexz said. "Cara's character represented *So Weird*, and then I'm coming in as the new kid on the block. It was really delicate."

Even before the shift, *So Weird* had relied on original songs to complement its storytelling. The series was perfectly set up for music integration: Fi's mom, Molly, was a rockstar! She sang original tracks throughout the series. The theme song was an absolute banger. Real-life bands SHeDAISY and The Moffatts had guest appearances. But Disney never released an accompanying *So Weird* soundtrack or promoted the show's music in any way, apart from airing performance clips as music video interstitials to promote new episodes. It was obvious that audiences responded well to music, but without a working and willing relationship between the Disney labels and Disney Channel, the path forward remained unclear.

ONE OF THE most striking indicators that pop music needed to play a role in Disney Channel's reimagined landscape was in its live concert series. Because Disney Channel had space to fill in their ad-free breaks, Rich Ross was able to broker a deal with external record labels like Sony, BMG, and Warner Records: Disney Channel would air interstitial music videos from their relevant young pop acts, if the labels would also offer up their talent for Disney Channel concert specials, to be shot on Disney properties. "Right from the beginning, I said, we need to bring relevant things to kids' lives on the channel," Ross explained. "We felt very strongly that we would buy equity until we could create our own equity."

To make this happen, he turned to Tina Treadwell. She was a fellow Ivy Leaguer who'd worked in commercial casting and production on shows like *In Living Color*, and she had grown up around the music business. Her father, George, was a jazz trumpeter and one of the first Black entertainment managers, overseeing acts like Billie Holiday and Sammy Davis Jr., and cofounding The Drifters (famous for hits like "Under the Boardwalk" and "Save the Last Dance for Me"). "If you can figure out a way to do music specials for kids," Ross told Treadwell during the hiring process, "you can start right away."

Treadwell leapt at the challenge and began sketching out the *Disney*

Channel in Concert series. The taped specials would go beyond straight-forward musical performances and would meld Disney's corporate interests with the audience's desire to get to know their favorite stars. Woven alongside clips from the concerts held at Disney properties, like Disney-MGM Studios or the *Disney Magic* cruise ship, were candid segments that showed the artists exploring the Disney parks, shopping at Downtown Disney, and talking about their personal lives. Early acts to jump on board included LeAnn Rimes, Ray J, Brandy, and Jonny Lang. But the promise of the concert series really clicked into place when the Backstreet Boys backed out two weeks before their scheduled taping.

Desperate for a last-minute replacement, Treadwell flew to Orlando to sign a deal with controversial music manager Lou Pearlman, who had offered up his group *NSYNC as an alternative act for the special. *NSYNC, which included former Mouseketeers Justin Timberlake and JC Chasez, had thus far remained in the Backstreet Boys' shadow in the American market. But *NSYNC's July 1998 *Disney Channel in Concert* special helped them explode. Two weeks after the special premiered, *NYSNC's self-titled album cracked the Top 40 for the first time. "Once it started airing, that's when the tides started changing," *NYSNC member Lance Bass told *Billboard* in 2018. "One morning we woke up, and everyone knew our name."

After that, the *Disney Channel in Concert* floodgates opened. Britney Spears. B*Witched and Five. Jessica Simpson. BBMak and M2M. 98 Degrees and Hoku. The Backstreet Boys scrambled to rebook. As Disney Channel president Anne Sweeney recalled, "The labels were pounding on the door saying, 'Can we get a Disney Channel special with you?'"

The specials were a hit, both in terms of media attention on Disney Channel and the accompanying boosts for the featured artists. But because most of the artists weren't signed to a Disney record label, Disney wasn't reaping the album sales profits that came from their promotion in the concert specials and music videos.

At first, they tolerated the loss in the name of making Disney Channel an arbiter of musical taste. But the cool artists and songs of the day weren't always Disney appropriate. Although labels agreed to alter lyrics to be less suggestive in order to get their artists more airtime on the channel, it only delayed the inevitable, as even the most sugarcoated acts eventually grew up. (See: Britney Spears's "Stronger" music video, which drew a wave of parental backlash when it aired on Disney Channel in 2000.) "When they would become less appropriate," Ross said, "that was the end of the line for us."

Those challenges, coupled with the specials' lack of longevity—"You can't play that same Britney Spears concert five years from now because she's moved on to be a different kind of artist," Treadwell said—saw them phase out the concert series and external music videos completely by 2001.

KIDS MIGHT NOT want to watch the same concert special for years, but they do want to rewatch movies.

While on vacation in Aspen in 1999, Michael Eisner and his wife, Jane, called up various friends to gather a group for a Friday night dinner. One by one, the other couples turned them down. After the fourth rejection, an exasperated Eisner asked, "I don't understand. Why can't you go?"

"Michael, I don't even understand why you're asking us to dinner," the woman replied. "You have a movie coming out this weekend that we want to watch with the kids."

"What? No, I don't," Eisner said, mentally running through the Walt Disney Studios theatrical calendar.

"Yes, you do," she insisted. "*Johnny Tsunami* on the Disney Channel."

Eisner relayed this story to the Disney Channel executives at a budget meeting with a huge grin. "That was the moment where they literally gave us the keys to the kingdom and were like, 'This matters,'" Ross said.

When Anne Sweeney started as Disney Channel president in 1996, research consistently showed that most eleven- and twelve-year-olds were scared of MTV. And while they wanted to be cool and talk about going out with their friends on the weekends, they weren't actually ready for that reality. That conundrum begat the idea of the Disney Channel Original Movie, aka DCOM (pronounced "dee-com," for the devout): a ninety-minute feature that premiered on Friday nights and repeated on

Saturdays and Sundays, offering tweens an exciting weekend activity in the comfort and safety of their homes. The network cultivated a culture of DCOM co-viewing that, for its intended audience, was prioritized as much as a family's weekend outing to a movie theater. "We gave kids something to look forward to," Sweeney said. "And something they could watch as a community."

For the original movies' subject matter, the DCOM team rotated through a mix of sports, fantasy, mystery, and holiday topics. In the early days, movies with male leads were prioritized, following the conventional wisdom that girls would watch content with male stars but boys wouldn't watch female-led entertainment. Around the turn of the millennium, things shifted. "I was doing a lot of research and talking to child psychology experts," original movies executive Denise Carlson said. "When girls start going through puberty, suddenly, they get intimidated, and they lose their feeling of strength. They start worrying about, *Am I good enough?*" So, Disney made sure to dot the DCOM lineup with empowering, female-led films like *Halloweentown*, *Rip Girls*, *Gotta Kick It Up!*, and *Motocrossed*.

Sweeney's background in education meant she was eager to see the DCOMs also serve as a hub for imparting valuable lessons under the guise of entertainment. *The Color of Friendship* taught a generation about South Africa's apartheid. *Miracle in Lane 2* showed a kid with a physical disability triumphing in a competition. And *Tru Confessions* highlighted a tween with a developmental disability. "We never said, 'We're going to teach you about apartheid today,'" Sweeney said. "We said, 'We're going to tell you a story.'"

Original movies head Carol Rubin, one of the only senior holdouts from the pre-Sweeney days, looked for adaptation ideas by browsing bookstores to see which covers of kids' books spoke to her. That's where she found Marilyn Sadler's *Zenon: Girl of the 21st Century*. And producer Sheri Singer, who had worked on The Wonderful World of Disney films through the early '90s, would often bring in script ideas based on real-world events—like twins who played in the WNBA or sisters who were race car drivers.

Because each film only carried a budget between $3.5 and $4.5 million, most of the original movies were shot outside of California, in locales that offered desirable production tax break incentives. Canada, Utah, Oregon, Louisiana, Puerto Rico, and New Zealand all entered the mix and presented unique on-location challenges.

While Toronto could believably double as a generic US city, it wasn't always easy to find uniquely American skills on the ground in Canada. They imported double Dutch jump-ropers from Brooklyn for *Jump In!* and ROTC units from New Jersey for *Cadet Kelly*.

Elsewhere, the cast and crew of *Now You See It* had to evacuate New Orleans ahead of Hurricane Ivan in 2004. They eventually chartered a flight along with the cast of the film *Glory Road* back to L.A., where nervous Disney Channel executives were waiting on the tarmac to greet them.

As each new DCOM script was put into production, the network executives would turn to a pre-approved director list, comprised of mostly white men. Names like Paul Hoen, Duwayne Dunham, Stuart Gillard, and Greg Beeman frequently appeared on the proverbial director's chair. Directors of color (LeVar Burton on *Smart House*, Kevin Hooks on *The Color of Friendship*, Oz Scott on *The Cheetah Girls*, Ramón Menéndez on *Gotta Kick It Up!*) and women directors (Joyce Chopra on *Rip Girls*, Maggie Greenwald on *Get a Clue*, Mary Lambert on *Halloweentown II*, Francine McDougall on *Go Figure* and *Cow Belles*, Allison Liddi-Brown on *Princess Protection Program*) popped up more sporadically.

Unlike the network's previous generation of Disney Channel Premiere Films, which varied in style and tone, the Disney Channel Original Movies soon fell into a cohesive identity: Their stories featured an abundance of heartfelt family and friendship moments. Their sets were filled with primary colors. Their actors were clad in bright costumes. "I remember [DCOM executive] Carol Rubin calling me once after she saw some dailies, and she said, 'Let me be clear, I do not want to see tan. I do not want to see brown. I do not want to see taupe. I do not want to see beige,'" said producer Kevin Lafferty, who worked on many of the Toronto-shot original movies. "Whenever possible, it was always: color, color, color."

Often, new DCOM directors would arrive on set their first day and announce to the crew, "This movie is going to be different from the rest. It's not going to feel like a TV Disney movie. It's going to feel like a real feature film, a real drama." A network executive would then gently pull them aside and remind them, "No, no. Here's the codified look of exactly what we want."

"It was almost like an anthology series," Lafferty said. "If every one had the same lighting and look, they would be perfectly happy with that, kind of like how Marvel is now."

And since movies have long shelf lives, the most popular DCOMs were aired repeatedly. "A lot of people have come up to me over the years and been like, 'Oh, I loved your *Johnny Tsunami* TV show. I watched it all the time,'" the film's star, Brandon Baker, said. "I'm like, 'It was a movie; they just played it so often that you thought it was a TV show.'" (The film would have become a bigger franchise if not for the actual devastating tsunami that hit Southeast Asia in 2004, delaying an eventual sequel until 2007 and leading them to retool the title to *Johnny Kapahala: Back on Board*, omitting the word "tsunami.")

But no matter how popular a Disney Channel Original Movie became, it was made clear that its stars were always replaceable. Kimberly J. Brown played the lead role of teen witch Marnie Piper in the first three *Halloweentown* films, but when it came time to sign on for a fourth film in 2005, her contract negotiations stalled. Having starred in the network's most successful film franchise for the better part of a decade, Kimberly and her team came to the table with a slate of what executive producer Sheri Singer termed "unusual perks." "She wanted a rich deal," Singer said. "It wasn't acrimonious, but I think she wanted her mother to get a shot at writing the story or getting a producer credit, [had limits on] what publicity she would or wouldn't do, what she wanted to get paid. There were just some things that, at least at the time, felt overreaching. And she didn't budge." (Brown has maintained that she was "available and ready to do" a fourth film when "Disney decided to go in a different direction.")

Still, Marsh wanted a fourth *Halloweentown* film, with or without Kimberly. "I know fans were really disappointed," Singer said. "But we had one more story to tell." They pursued two different script ideas, one of which would have been a musical, featuring songs written by Jim Wise, who played Coach Tugnut on *Even Stevens*. They decided on the non-musical version, and Sara Paxton, who had auditioned for virtually every DCOM since *Smart House*, was offered the part of the replacement Marnie in *Return to Halloweentown*.

But no matter how delightful and charming Sara was in the role, she wasn't Kimberly, and many fans didn't appreciate or understand the change. "It's kind of sad because every year like clockwork around Halloween time, the hate messages rain down upon my Twitter and Instagram," Sara said. "*Sara Paxton sucks. We miss the old Marnie.* It's like, do you guys think that we had a fistfight in a parking lot or something? I didn't attack her! It is what it is. They asked me, and I said yes."

At their peak output of twelve movies a year, the Disney Channel Original Movies team was shepherding twenty or more projects at a time through various stages of development. But that abundance quickly proved untenable. "We thought it was a dream come true, and then it became, be careful what you wish for," Rich Ross said. "Monthly, it was hard to find the stories that we felt were right, talent to populate them, marketing dollars to support them, and anticipation to get ready to watch them. We quickly came back and said, this is not going to work."

After spending the late 1990s trying a variety of new programming and greenlighting original series that ranged in genre from reality shows to edgy sci-fi capers and action-drama series, Disney Channel settled into its winning formula for a new millennium: a two-prong balance of dramatic original movies and comedic original series that would form the core of the network for decades to come.

3

Even Stevens:
Talent and Turmoil

"I'm Shia LaBeouf, and I'm going to win an Academy Award one day."

That's how a ten-year-old Shia walked into a *Hey Arnold!* voice casting session and introduced himself to the room. It was a semi-ridiculous statement from a ten-year-old, and an extremely ridiculous statement from a ten-year-old who proceeded to completely bomb that Nickelodeon audition. But Shia's hyperbolic introduction made weary casting director Joey Paul Jensen snap to attention. Who was this brazen kid whose bravado far outpaced his craft? "He had no discipline," she recalled. "He was all over the place and had no understanding of recording." And yet, there was a refreshingly weird spark about this unpolished acting hopeful. Shia lost out on the *Arnold* gig without a second glance. But, eager to learn, he signed up for acting classes with Jensen and then joined her standup comedy troupe, which she'd launched to give kids the chance to perform original material at venues around Los Angeles.

When Jensen was beginning her casting career in the early '90s, she had observed how networks like NBC and ABC were finding massive success with sitcoms centered around the skills of a singular standup comic: Roseanne Barr on *Roseanne*, Jerry Seinfeld on *Seinfeld*, Tim Allen on *Home Improvement*. Why couldn't that model work for children's programming? "That was the biggest thing," Jensen said, "how to convince the executives that we can trust these twelve-year-olds to carry a show."

When Disney Channel started working on a new single-camera sit-com called *Spivey's Kid Brother* in 1999, they brought Jensen aboard to oversee casting. After a nationwide search testing more than two thousand boys for the lead role of Louis Spivey, a hapless kid who dreamed of becoming a standup comedian, Jensen narrowed her selections and brought twelve-year-old Shia to the network as her first pick. By that point, he'd booked a few minor TV roles and she felt he was ready for the rigors of a lead role.

While greatly improved from the *Hey Arnold!* session, he was still a loose cannon. In the *Spivey* audition waiting room, he used a blusterous opening line to scare off the competition. "Hi, I'm Shia, and I'm playing Louis," he cheerfully introduced himself to the other contenders. Inside the Disney casting room, however, he now had enough skill to back up his magnetic antics. Unlike some of the other polished kid actors, Shia retained an unpredictable authenticity. He was a walking ball of energy who deliberately flared his nostrils, scratched his face, and picked his nose while delivering his lines with perfect comedic timing. "Seriously, I've never seen a kid like that ever in my life," Disney Channel casting executive Stacey Pianko said. "It felt like he was this old comedian coming through this young boy's body. He was so intense but so funny at the same time. I was like, oh, God, we have to cast this kid."

Not everyone was convinced. As audition after audition went by, Shia advanced up the ranks, reading for the showrunners, midlevel network executives, and eventually, executive vice president Gary Marsh. Marsh was adamant that Shia was too young, but Pianko stressed that by the time production began on the actual series, he'd be thirteen and the perfect age. Marsh hesitantly gave in, Shia got the part, and filming on the pilot, by then dubbed *Ren's Brother*, began. "When I first saw him, Shia was sitting there reading *Variety* like a sixty-year-old vaudevillian," recalled Tom Virtue, who played the show's patriarch. "He turned to me and said, 'If this thing isn't a hit, we suck.'"

But Shia's job security was anything but certain. After filming the pilot, test audiences didn't respond well to Shia, in particular. They felt his character came across as more of a depressed loner than a comical boy next door. The orders came from above that Jensen needed to recast

Shia and start from scratch on a new nationwide search for his replacement. Skeptical, she agreed to look at an additional six hundred boys for the role of Louis. None, she felt, matched Shia's charisma and talent. "After all is said and done, I still think Shia is the best," she reported back to the network executives.

They weren't going to make it easy: If Shia wanted a shot at keeping the part, he'd need to re-audition and do a new screen test in front of the executives, just like the other new finalists. It was a practically unheard-of move and a humiliating ask for a kid who'd already won the role and filmed the pilot. Jensen delicately explained the situation to Shia and his agent, convincing them to comply with Disney's demands.

As Jensen trudged down the hallway on the twenty-first floor of the Disney Channel headquarters with Shia in tow to read for the executives once again, she glanced back, only to find her young charge had disappeared. Confused, she doubled back and spotted him crouching between two filing cabinets, wracked by heavy sobs. "What do I have to do to prove myself to them?" Shia asked between gasps. "I can't do it again! I can't!"

Jensen bent down to his level and looked him in the eye.

"I felt like Cher in *Moonstruck* when she yells at Nicolas Cage to snap out of it," Jensen recalled. "I was shaking him, like, 'Shia, we can't have this drama right now. You've just got to be funny. This is *your* part.'"

The pep talk worked. Shia booked the part—again—and production began in earnest on Disney Channel's first original comedy series, retitled *Even Stevens*.

EVEN STEVENS HAD its origin in a Bourbon Street bar. Creator Matt Dearborn happened to first meet Disney Channel narrative series executive Lee Gaither at a New Orleans watering hole late one evening while attending a National Association of Television Program Executives conference. They struck up a conversation, and Gaither urged Dearborn to send over a script.

Dearborn, who had established his career working on *The Secret World of Alex Mack* and *Beverly Hills, 90210*, subsequently submitted the *Spivey's Kid Brother* pilot to Disney Channel on spec for $10,000. (The show's original title was a nod to the poison ivy–stricken character in Allan Sherman's 1963 novelty song about a kid at camp, "Hello Mud-dah, Hello Faddah!") He set the series in his hometown of Sacramento and focused on the title family's hapless youngest child, Louis (Shia LaBeouf), surrounded by his family of overachievers: a senator mom (Donna Pescow), lawyer dad (Tom Virtue), athletic older brother (Nick Spano), and brainiac sister (Christy Carlson Romano).

After the Shia casting debacle, Dearborn was still wrapping up his work at *90210* when series production got underway on what was now *Even Stevens*. It was off to a tedious start. They'd shot the first six epi-sodes, but as each new script reached Dearborn, who was serving as an off-site creative consultant, the problems jumped off the page. His origi-nal pilot script had leaned into emotion and family comedy, but the new material was swinging into over-the-top slapstick. People were starting to panic. "It was too broad. It wasn't story driven. It wasn't emotionally driven," he said. "You have to be kind of smart to write dumb humor. And it just missed."

The network's new original series head, Adam Bonnett, put in a fran-tic call for help to Marc Warren and Dennis Rinsler, a pair of former New York City public school teachers who had served as writers and eventual showrunners on ABC's mega-hit *Full House*. They'd recently wrapped production on The WB's *The Parent 'Hood* and agreed to a meeting. The pay at Disney Channel would be less than a third of what they'd been making as showrunners on network shows, but family sit-com work was growing scarce, and the chance to oversee a single-camera show was intriguing. While the pilot Bonnett sent them wasn't very good, they thought, the kid actors were *great*.

"Disney gave us carte blanche," Warren said. "They said, hire who-ever you want. Fire whoever you want. We'll give you a new staff. We'll give you eight weeks to read through the scripts. They couldn't have been more open to us, creatively, coming in and taking over the show."

So, the pair cleaned house. Dearborn was the only one from the original team who was asked to stay on as a writer and producer, and Warren and Rinsler countered the show's zany sound effects and food gags with a more grounded, familial heart. They made the Stevens family half Jewish in a nod to Shia's own family history and were the first Disney Channel original series to have a Hanukkah episode. Alongside the screwball scenarios of Louis creating wacky inventions and Ren moonlighting as a lounge singer, there were dramatic storylines, like a season 3 opening kiss between Louis and his friend Tawny—a development that was written primarily to let Shia kiss actor Margo Harshman, on whom he harbored a real-life crush and later dated.

While many network TV shows were shot at Disney's Burbank studios, no Disney Channel show had merited the cost of renting a soundstage on the home lot. "We couldn't afford it," the network's then–general manager Rich Ross said. In fact, previous Disney Channel series had been mostly shot in Canada to avoid L.A. production costs altogether. *Even Stevens* became one of the first projects to stay closer to home, but it still shot on the far west side of town in Playa Vista, at a former chainsaw factory that had been converted into a studio for *Baywatch* in the early '90s. It was near executive producers Sean McNamara's and David Brookwell's offices—and essentially out of sight and mind from the Disney Channel overlords at 3800 West Alameda in Burbank. "We might as well have been shooting in Tajikistan," Dearborn said.

The most the cast saw of network executives like Marsh and Bonnett was when the kids showed up unannounced at Disney's Burbank headquarters and made themselves at home. "Shia and I would go to the twenty-first floor at the Disney Channel building and just pop into Gary's office or pop into Adam's office and hang out and chat," said A.J. Trauth, who played Louis's friend Twitty. "They didn't even lock their doors. Sometimes they'd have a meeting going on, and we would just walk in."

So hands-off were the Disney Channel executives during *Even Stevens*'s run that no one batted an eye at the show's decision to name the school's gym teacher Coach Tugnut and christen another supporting character Tom Grabowski (which could be pronounced "grab-balls-ski"). "We were just making ourselves laugh," Rinsler said. "If it made us laugh, we put it in. It was fun to trick them. We would say, 'This is totally innocent! It's your dirty mind.'"

In the middle of the second season, they introduced a new character: Beans Aranguren, the middling, bacon-loving kid next door played by Steven Anthony Lawrence. The character's last name was a playful nod to Steve Aranguren, a midlevel network executive tasked with running notes between the suits in Burbank and the creatives on set. Aranguren had won the creatives' hearts early on with his minimal feedback. "We couldn't believe the first table read. He came from Burbank with his briefcase. And he sat there afterward and went, 'It's going to be a good show.' We were like, 'What? That's the notes?'" Warren said. "They just trusted us. For creatives, it was heaven."

THAT TRUST EXTENDED to the network green-lighting an experimental episode that would cement *Even Stevens*'s place in Disney Channel history: "Influenza: The Musical." As part of the initiative to integrate popular music on the channel, Disney Channel had established a pattern of inserting pop star cameos and performances in their shows—Britney Spears and Destiny's Child on *The Famous Jett Jackson*, The Moffatts on *So Weird*, and, in the season 2 premiere of *Even Stevens*, the Hollywood Records boy band BBMak. But there was no precedent for an outright Disney Channel original musical in any form. Greater Disney wisdom held that young audiences loved watching animated musicals or maybe even the occasional Muppet-led musical. But a live-action original musical with kids belting plot-advancing showtunes? No dice. Walt Disney Pictures's most recent prominent attempt had been *Newsies* a decade earlier, and it had disastrously flopped in theaters, bringing in under $3 million at the box office against its $15 million budget. No one was eager to suffer a repeat failure on TV.

Still, *Even Stevens* had long had musical elements percolating behind the scenes: Christy Carlson Romano had a Broadway background; Lauren Frost, who played Ren's friend Ruby, had toured with Barbra Streisand; Ty Hodges, who played Ren's nemesis Larry Beale, was a professional dancer. And on the *Even Stevens* set, Shia, Margo, and A.J. had formed an amateur band that jammed in the studio's conference room during lunch breaks. The show clearly had the talent to put together a full-on musical episode—if they could convince the network executives. "In the beginning, they were saying, 'Nobody likes that, and nobody does that,'" Rinsler said. "And we said, 'Don't worry! It's going to be funny. It's going to be smart.'"

They'd also need to come up with a stellar reason for *why* these characters were all suddenly singing and dancing around the halls of their junior high. They landed on a fever dream: Ren wakes up sick with the flu but doesn't want to ruin her perfect attendance record, so she soldiers on and arrives at school, where everyone is inexplicably singing their thoughts and feelings in Broadway-worthy numbers throughout the day. At the end of the episode, it's revealed that it was all a dream and Ren actually stayed home in bed to recover.

The pitch worked, and they were granted a slightly larger budget for the episode and extra time to record the tracks and rehearse. Warren penned the script, McNamara directed, and Jim Wise—who played Coach Tugnut and had also been a member of the live comedy troupe The Groundlings, alongside Jennifer Coolidge and Will Ferrell—sketched out the lyrics and sound for six musical tracks.

"I tried to make every song sound like a different style," Wise explained. The principal sings the morning announcements like a swinging Motown bop. "Masters of the Gym" utilizes a devil's interval to become a menacing pirate-y anthem as Louis and Twitty endure PE torture. "What's the Matter with Ren" adopts a *Sound of Music* vibe. And for what became the episode's pièce de résistance, Wise looked to The Beatles's "Penny Lane" to inspire "We Went to the Moon," a catchy ditty Ren makes up when she forgets to prepare her report on the space program and can only remember the fact that the astronauts went to the moon in 1969.

When the season 2 episode aired on January 25, 2002, it amounted to twenty-three minutes of what is essentially perfect television. Christy got the chance to shine front and center. The ensemble actors flexed their musical prowess, and those who weren't sonically gifted still gave it their all. Wise even added a special nod to Donna Pescow's career-making role in *Saturday Night Fever* by giving the Stevens parents a disco interlude. Every moment of "Influenza" was utilized to create a campy mini-masterpiece full of lingering earworms.

A testament to its longevity: In 2018, Cardi B posted an Instagram video asking, "Who remembers this song?" before belting "We Went to the Moon" from memory.

THROUGHOUT *EVEN STEVENS*'s production, the relationship between Christy and Shia could best be described as fraught. They harbored the same sibling-like antagonism for one another that their characters did, and the writers used that to fuel their storylines. "In real life, they drove each other crazy," Rinsler said. "When we heard that, we said, 'Oh this will be fun.'"

Christy had been acting professionally since she was six years old, commuting from her family's home in Milford, Connecticut, to New York City for auditions and, eventually, a Broadway stint in *Parade*. She'd performed in national tours of *Annie* and *The Sound of Music*, and had played a singing Chiquita banana in the 1996 Woody Allen film *Everyone Says I Love You* before she and her mom headed to L.A.

For her *Even Stevens* audition, fourteen-year-old Christy wore a crisp blazer, made impeccable eye contact, and owned the room with charisma and humor as she nailed every line. "In the thousands of casting sessions I've sat through, to this day, hers is still the best audition I've ever seen," Dearborn said. Echoed casting director Joey Paul Jensen, "Nothing was out of place. Not her hair. Not a button. Nothing. She was the total opposite of Shia. They both could walk in a room and command the room. They have that ability in common—but it would be like if Robin Williams and Anne Hathaway both came through the door, one after another." (In fact, Christy has said she missed her audition for the lead in *The Princess Diaries* because she was working late one evening on *Even Stevens*.)

The *Even Stevens* writers increasingly leaned into Christy and Shia's tension and pushed the Louis versus Ren storylines to the max, making what was originally a series centered on just Louis into a series centered on sibling rivalry. A season 1 scene in which Ren gets pelted with tomatoes cemented Christy and Shia's animosity offscreen. "She said that Shia was throwing the tomatoes at her face, like really trying to hurt her, and she never forgave him for that," Rinsler said. "He was always giving her a hard time and complaining about her off camera, which she put up with because she felt it made the on-camera rivalry more realistic."

It didn't help that playing the uptight foil to Shia's zaniness was essentially a thankless job. "It's hard to be a really good straight man, and she had a good funny bone," Warren said. "But they were just so different. They didn't really have the patience for each other or that much affection for each other. I don't think Shia was threatened by her as much as maybe she might have been by the attention that he was getting."

While Shia would be literally bouncing off the walls and skateboarding down the halls of the soundstage, Christy would be diligently studying her lines. And as Shia parlayed his *Even Stevens* role into the lead of Walt Disney Studio's theatrical adaptation of Louis Sachar's *Holes* and flexed his acting muscles in the soapy DCOM drama *Tru Confessions*, Christy got pigeon-holed.

It became clear that the network didn't really know what to do with her. Despite her Broadway pedigree and proven chops, she was too mature and poised to be relatable to the average girl, they thought. Her role in the 2002 *Private Benjamin*–like DCOM *Cadet Kelly* amounted to playing yet another high-strung party pooper, this time in the shadow of Hilary Duff's accessible charm. (It may not have been Christy's most impactful role at the time, but in the years since, fans have noted the close-talking chemistry between Christy and Hilary's *Cadet Kelly* characters contributed to their sexual awakening and have dubbed it "the queer girl DCOM Disney never actually gave us.")

Then, in June 2002, Christy made her debut as the titular voice of the animated series *Kim Possible*. According to the creators, the original *Kim Possible* pilot featured the voices of Alyson Hannigan as Kim and David Arquette as her sidekick Ron Stoppable, but the actors' delivery wasn't quite over-the-top enough for Disney Channel animation. Gary Marsh suggested trying Christy as the voice of Kim, and Will Friedle, who appeared on *Boy Meets World* in syndication on the channel, as Ron. "Christy was the first breakthrough of like, wow, this is bringing the show to life," *Kim Possible* co-creator Mark McCorkle said. "There was a genuine spark there." After Christy had been denied additional live-action roles at the network, Kim Possible, whom she voiced for eighty-seven episodes and two DCOMs, was the perfect fit.

When *Even Stevens* ended production, Rinsler and Warren also pitched ABC the idea of having Christy star in an *Even Stevens* spinoff, in which Ren would be working as an intern on Capitol Hill. But ABC wasn't interested. Disney Channel didn't yet have a reputation as a star-maker or hitmaker, and their ideas were deemed of little value to the other Disney TV divisions. "We said, 'You have a talent here. She can dance. She can act. She can sing. She's likable. She has a built-in audience. Why don't you grow that audience with her?'" Warren said. "At that time, ABC did not want to hear anything from Disney Channel. It was almost like, 'Get away from us with this stuff.'"

THOUSANDS OF MILES from Christy's Connecticut upbringing, Shia Saide LaBeouf grew up poor in east Los Angeles with his hippie parents. His father, Jeff, was a brash former rodeo clown and Vietnam War veteran who battled an alcohol addiction and had spent time in prison for attempted rape in the 1980s. His mother, Shayna, was a soft-spoken former ballet dancer and visual artist who once ran a head shop in New York's East Village. Before Shia's parents divorced, they'd all dress up as clowns and sell hot dogs from a pushcart in Echo Park.

Shia's path to Hollywood began when he coveted another kid's Fila sneakers at a Fourth of July picnic in Malibu. The kid told Shia that he'd bought the shoes with money he earned from acting on *Dr. Quinn, Medicine Woman*, and that his job meant he only had to do schoolwork for three hours a day. Shia was intrigued. "It wasn't about acting," Shia told *Vanity Fair* in 2007. "It was about: I hated school, and I wanted Filas."

He procured the name of the sneaker kid's talent agent, Teresa Dahlquist, whom he then looked up in the yellow pages and cold-called, pretending to be a European manager seeking an agent for a promising young actor named Shia LaBeouf. Dahlquist saw right through his act, but was charmed by the chutzpah and signed him.

Still, some say the stories of Shia's upbringing should be taken with a spoonful of salt. "Let me tell you about Shia," Dahlquist said in 2007. "I absolutely adore him, [but he] never let the truth get in the way of a good story."

On set, the *Even Stevens* cast and creatives felt certain that Shia would be the next Jim Carrey or Will Ferrell: a comedic genius with blockbuster box office appeal. "It was as if the rest of us took music lessons, and we were all really good and knew all of our scales, but then Shia just walked in, flipped a guitar around, and knew how to play like Hendrix," said Brandon Baker, who had a recurring role on the series as Louis's rival, Zack. "You just couldn't help but be drawn to him."

But it was also clear that Shia was struggling. During the week, he lived with Jeff in a motel not far from the Playa Vista set, a much closer commute than Shayna's home in the Valley. On weekends, Shia often stayed with co-star A.J. Trauth at his family's apartment in Burbank, where they'd skateboard or hang out at Universal CityWalk. Other times, he'd go surfing at Donna Pescow's family home in Malibu or go snowboarding with Nick Spano at Mammoth Mountain. On Sunday nights, Shayna would collect Shia from wherever he'd been, then drive him to set Monday morning where Jeff would be waiting to take over the weekday guardianship, an on-set requirement for all child performers under age sixteen.

"It's so sad, but kids who have grown up with trauma and not had the most stable home life are the ones that can really dig deep. They can really act," casting director Stacey Pianko said. "They have that range of emotion. They know what real sadness is."

Casting directors in kids' programming are often expected to act as welfare gatekeepers, doing check-ins with a potential hire's family to gauge whether it's a healthy dynamic and if the kid actually wants to do this for themselves. But if a kid is exceptionally talented, they might be willing to overlook certain red flags.

When Shayna would visit the set, she was a quiet presence, frequently hugging and doting on the other kid actors. But Jeff was domineering and chaotic, flirting with female extras and begging to be put on camera himself. (The showrunners eventually let him have a non-speaking cameo in an episode.) "There were obvious things going on," Pescow said. "I didn't know the extent of it. I didn't know the weight of it. But I knew something was a little bit off."

At times, Shia lacked the ability to focus long enough to carry his scenes and memorize his lines, so the showrunners tried coming up with tactics to help. They'd chop up his dialogue so Shia never had large chunks to recite at once. Or they'd instruct him to cross his arms and tuck his hands under his armpits while filming, a trick to center him on the task at hand. Still, some days, it seemed like he didn't want to be there at all. "I was looking to make money," Shia told *The Hollywood Reporter* in 2019. "In a very simple way, to me, having money meant having a family."

The *Even Stevens* producers contacted a child psychologist to discuss how to help Shia, and on a conference call the expert suggested he needed an additional mentor on set. Using funds that were already in the budget for a dialogue coach, they hired a coach named Richard Lyons, who also functioned as a big brother figure, to keep an eye on Shia and provide him companionship and care. That move, Rinsler said, "changed everything" for the show.

Lyons encouraged Shia to make short films during his downtime, and the young actor became more engaged in the creative process, sitting in on meetings in the writers' room and handing out self-written comedy scenes for the producers to perform for his camcorder. "Suddenly, Shia became collaborative and was having a good time," Rinsler said. "Whenever I see Richard Lyons, I say, 'The man who saved *Even Stevens*!' We were floundering."

Overall, most people who worked on *Even Stevens* described the show as a sanctuary from what they were facing in the real world. "Our set really was such a solitude and a home for so many people," Steven Anthony Lawrence, who played Beans, said during a COVID-era cast reunion. "We all took a great refuge in coming to work, because it wasn't work; it was coming to see our family."

As SHIA'S MOVIE career skyrocketed in the years after *Even Stevens*, he faced abuse allegations, multiple arrests, and detailed his treatment for addiction, psychological issues, and PTSD. He drifted away from most of the *Even Stevens* cast as soon as the final episode wrapped in 2002, but as part of his therapy, Shia began journaling about his childhood and relationship with his father, Jeff. Those journal entries became the basis for the 2019 film *Honey Boy*, which told a fictionalized version of Shia's upbringing and time on kids' TV through a character named Otis and his recovering addict father, James. Shia wrote the screenplay and played James, and there are direct references to *Even Stevens*'s dialogue, storylines, and costumes throughout.

Shia had previously sold a never-produced Disney series based on that time in his life called *Rent A Dad*, but *Honey Boy* took on a much darker tone. "It looked so grim in the movie," said Tom Virtue, who played *Even Stevens*'s patriarch. "The way they portrayed the show, even the lighting, in *Honey Boy*—ours was the opposite: It was bright. It was a lot of energy. And a lot of laughs." In the movie, Shia portrayed his dad as physically, verbally, and emotionally abusive. Director Alma Har'el has said it was difficult for Shia's mom to visit the *Honey Boy* set and "watch things happen that she wasn't aware of."

"Everything in the film happened," Shia said at the time. "There's things that happened that aren't in the film, but everything that wound up in the film is what was going on." Those who'd worked on *Even Stevens* were shocked by the painful revelations, both in the film and via interviews Shia gave on the promotional tour. They'd known Jeff was offensive and unpleasant—more than one person described him as an "asshole"—but they hadn't realized the level of alleged abuse Shia had endured while they'd worked together.

Pescow, in particular, was shaken. When she went to an awards-season screening of *Honey Boy* that Shia also attended, she cried throughout the movie. And when the end credits featured photos of a young Shia during the *Even Stevens* years, she said, "That about killed me." As the lights came back on in the theater, she saw Shia standing behind her. "I just grabbed him and he grabbed me," she said. "We stood there and hugged for the longest time, and I said to him, 'Had I known what it was like at that point, I would have made you live with me.' And he said, 'Yeah, I know, but everything's okay.' I was angry and sad and upset and so proud of him."

But then, in 2022, Shia said he made up most of the narrative of *Honey Boy* because the reality "didn't position me as this wounded, fractured child that you could root for."

"I wrote this narrative, which was just fucking nonsense," he told Jon Bernthal on his *Real Ones* podcast. "My dad was so loving to me my whole life. Fractured, sure. Crooked, sure. Wonky, for sure. But never was not loving . . . I turned the knob up on certain shit that wasn't real."

Ultimately, it's impossible to know the whole truth of what went on behind closed doors during that time. "Shia was a great kid. He always knew what he was doing. He always knew how to push buttons and pull levers to his advantage," co-star Nick Spano said. "And I don't expect that's ever going to change."

DURING *EVEN STEVENS*'s original three-season run, it was difficult for the creative team to gauge the show's success. There was no *Even Stevens* merchandise. Shia and Christy weren't making the covers of magazines or doing whirlwind press tours. And the network executives didn't share ratings information with the producers. "We really didn't know how popular it was, other than they renewed us," Warren said. "And when kids heard I worked on that show, they would be excited."

It was popular enough to merit a 2003 DCOM, making it the second series to get such a treatment after *The Famous Jett Jackson*. (*The Even Stevens Movie* controversially cut out series creator Matt Dearborn, who said he had previously talked to Gary Marsh about making the feature. "I called Gary and said, 'Gary, what the fuck?'" Dearborn said. "He goes, 'Yeah, I fucked up. Listen, you can write any movie you want.' And that's when I sold them [the 2006 DCOM] *Cow Belles.*")

Even Stevens won a BAFTA in 2002 (beating *Lizzie McGuire*), and received repeat Daytime Emmy nominations for Pescow's work and the show as a whole. But it wasn't until their final season that they managed to secure a coveted Emmy win.

On May 16, 2003, the cast and crew waited with bated breath inside Radio City Music Hall for presenter Kirsten Storms to announce the winner of the Outstanding Performer in a Children's Series category at the Daytime Emmys. Both Pescow and Shia were nominated, alongside *Reading Rainbow*'s LeVar Burton, and the puppeteers behind *Sesame Street*'s Elmo and Bear from Disney's *Bear in the Big Blue House*. Storms sliced open the envelope and delivered a chipper, "Gotta love the Disney Channel! Shia LaBeouf!" (She pronounced LaBeouf, "LaBoof.")

A seemingly shocked Shia shook his head and pulled his hair in disbelief as he made his way to the stage. "Oh my God, sixteen and got an Emmy. What the hell? Wow, wow, wow," he sputtered into the mic, award in hand. "I don't know how to breathe. Oh my God, oh my God, this is absolutely crazy."

But despite the critical accolades, there was always the feeling that *Even Stevens* was in the shadow of *Lizzie McGuire*, Disney Channel's other single-camera comedy series, which had premiered seven months after them and had merchandise, a soundtrack, a theatrical film, and Hilary Duff's fledgling singing career to send attention its way. Still, "Adam Bonnett called *Even Stevens* their *Seinfeld*," producer Tom Burkhard said. "It wasn't their biggest show or their most successful show, but I think they felt like it was their smartest show."

4

Lizzie McGuire:
The TV Girl Next Door

Night fell on Aaron Carter's thirteenth birthday party at the Bergamot Station Arts Center in Santa Monica. The buzzy gallery space was more fit for wine snobs and art lovers than a newly minted teen pop star. But on that brisk December evening, Mary-Kate and Ashley Olsen and members of the boy band No Authority mingled among suited agents and assistants, ready to toast the pint-sized singer whose second album, aptly titled *Aaron's Party (Come Get It)*, had recently gone platinum.

In a corner, a much less conspicuous thirteen-year-old's wide eyes darted anxiously. She'd been sent to the December 2000 fête with some of the *Lizzie McGuire* writers on a mission: Get Aaron Carter's attention. Their series would debut the following month and they needed a musical guest star to stunt cast for a future episode. "We were told, 'Go find Aaron. We want him to be in an episode,'" series writer Nina Bargiel recalled.

This was how the twenty-seven-year-old writer found herself trailing a nervous tween girl at a tween event where they hoped to get Aaron's team interested enough that they'd acquiesce. It was going terribly. As the evening wore on, the young blond girl grew increasingly smitten with the birthday boy, while the turtleneck-and-leather-pants-clad singer continued to politely ignore her. Despite his aloofness, the *Lizzie* team's persistence and a few key discussions between a Disney casting executive and Aaron's choreographer paid off. And by the end of the night, Aaron had agreed to appear and perform on the show. But when he arrived on the *Lizzie McGuire* set to film the "Aaron Carter's Coming to Town" episode weeks later, he got a shock. As Aaron sat in the makeup chair, the nervous blond girl from the party walked down the hall and into her dressing room. It was Hilary Duff.

He hadn't realized it was *her* show.

A GERMAN EXPERIMENTAL thriller isn't the obvious muse for a Disney Channel hit. But then again, *Lizzie McGuire* was never an obvious tween show. Centered on thirteen-year-old Lizzie, her quirky family, and her supportive best friends Gordo and Miranda, the series drew unlikely inspiration from the R-rated arthouse flick *Run Lola Run* to interweave animated effects and experimental camerawork alongside everyday storylines about school picture day and first bras.

Executive producer Stan Rogow had first stumbled upon the pilot in a pile of scripts that cluttered his office. Hoping to make something his young son could enjoy, he selected two scripts from the stack to pitch to Disney Channel: one, a complex cyber adventure series from *Back to the Future* co-writer Bob Gale; the other, TV writer Terri Minsky's *None of the Above*, about an incredibly ordinary girl named Lizzie McGuire trying to navigate high school as her thoughts are communicated to the audience through voiceover narration. "Bob Gale's was always the no-brainer. It was a classic high-concept Disney show from a legend," Rogow said. "*None of the Above* literally was no concept. It was: here's a girl who has esteem issues and isn't the prettiest or the smartest, and we're going to see what happens to her every week."

The network bought both scripts, but the Gale project quickly fizzled in pre-production. That left *None of the Above*. Gary Marsh, the network's EVP of originals at the time, wasn't thrilled with the show's complete lack of gimmick. So, to elevate it, he and Rogow tweaked the script's voiceover component to become a pop-up animated character, similar to the visualized narration on MTV's *Daria*. They also re-set the pilot in middle school to age it down for the Disney audience.

Now they just needed their perfect star.

FOR HOPEFUL YOUNG actors, auditioning for Disney Channel could be an exhausting effort that might involve seven or eight auditions to the finish-line offer of a starring role. Casting directors often embarked on cross-country tours, meeting kids from the top agencies in all the major markets, sitting in on community theater productions, and overseeing additional open casting sessions. Actors who couldn't audition for Disney in person would send in VHS tapes or, in later years, DVDs and digital clips. "The kids are kids, but they're also commodities," *Even Stevens* and *That's So Raven* showrunner Marc Warren said. "So, the casting sessions are like shopping for a new car or something. 'That one's got dents in it. This one's that.' Nothing was ever said directly at the kid, but there were certain things I'm not that proud of."

Until he left the network in 2009, executive vice president turned eventual network president Rich Ross technically had the final say on all casting. But in the casting sessions at Disney Channel's Burbank headquarters, it was usually Gary Marsh who sat in on the finalists' reads and made judgment calls in the room alongside the producers. Marsh was known to wear a stony poker face—"I never saw him laugh, except when someone was getting fired," one executive producer joked—and often maintained an intimidating façade while young actors performed comedy lines in the room. It served as a test for how well the kids might keep their cool in the face of future critics.

In addition to the standard line-reading, the Disney Channel auditions included an interview component, in which the kids answered softball questions about their own lives. *What are your hobbies? Who are your favorite singers?* "We knew that the writing would stem from their real personalities as much as from the characters that they were playing," Ross said. "If they weren't really comfortable talking about themselves in a very 'this is who I am' way, it was going to be a challenge. I don't think we ever cast someone who flunked the interview."

For *None of the Above*, which later became *What's Lizzie Thinking?* and then just *Lizzie McGuire*, casting director Robin Lippin was tasked with finding a charming tween girl who could master comedy but who also felt relatable and a little bit quirky. She tested a couple hundred girls for the lead role of Lizzie via self-tape and in-person auditions at Rogow's office at Lantana Studios in Santa Monica, including finalists Sara Paxton, Hallee Hirsh, and Hilary Duff. "Everybody wanted that part," Sara said. "I gave it my all."

In the end, it came down to Hallee and Hilary. Hallee had done dozens of episodes of the soap opera *Loving* and recently charmed audiences in *You've Got Mail*. Hilary had starred in the straight-to-video, critically panned *Casper Meets Wendy*, and had recently had her role in the Michael Chiklis–led sitcom, *Daddio*, cut after shooting that pilot. She was ready to quit acting altogether if she didn't get *Lizzie*.

"It wasn't like Hilary was the best actress in the world. I mean, she was twelve," Lippin said. "But I remember the personality. I remember the likability. I remember the adorableness. All of that just came together when she read. I knew that she had charisma. I knew that boys and girls would like her. She wouldn't be threatening."

Hilary Erhard Duff was a Texas transplant who had been raised in Houston and San Antonio. She and her older sister Haylie first began shuttling back and forth to L.A. for auditions in the midnineties with their mom, Susan, while their dad, Bob, stayed behind to run his successful business overseeing a chain of Texas convenience stores. "That's the difference between Hilary and all my other clients: none of my clients had the wealth that Hilary's family had," said Troy Rowland, who became Hilary's acting coach during *Lizzie* and later worked on her management team. "The Duffs didn't *have* to do it. So, if Hilary ever got out of line, they had a very strong hand and could say, 'Hey, do you think we want to be here, away from our nice house in Texas?'" Hilary echoed that sentiment to *Cosmopolitan UK* in 2020: "My mom didn't let me get away with shit. She was like, 'You're not supporting this family, we're not using your money, so you're not calling the shots.'"

Aided by her stuttering squeaks and tendency to nervously bite her lip, Hilary had a casual warmth that carried over into her acting, and a friendly "cool" factor that made her someone kids could hope to emulate. With Hilary as Lizzie, suddenly, the show—and Disney Channel's entire MO moving forward—clicked into place. She was relatable, but also an icon. "That was the magic trick of the show: you had this deathdefyingly cute girl playing the not-cute girl," Rogow said. "And everybody bought it."

They assembled the rest of the cast around Hilary. As Lizzie's best friend, David "Gordo" Gordon, they cast Adam Lamberg, a fifteen-year-old intellectual New Yorker who was small for his age. And as Lizzie's other best friend, Miranda Sanchez, they cast twelve-year-old Lalaine Vergara-Paras. Lalaine came from the musical theater world, where she'd acted in *Les Misérables* on Broadway and played an orphan in The Wonderful World of Disney's 1999 version of *Annie*.

Professionally, she'd gone by just "Lalaine" ever since a talent agent encouraged her to drop her Filipina surname to broaden her casting possibilities. And rather than make her *Lizzie* character Filipina to mirror Lalaine's own background, Miranda was written as Mexican. "I don't know why they just didn't make her character Filipina," writer Nina Bargiel said. "I don't think it would have changed things drastically. It was tough because we couldn't go to Lalaine and be like, 'Hey, tell me about some of your Mexican traditions'—because she wasn't Mexican."

AFTER DELIVERING THE script for the pilot and having some input in casting, Terri Minsky exited *Lizzie* to run *The Geena Davis Show*, which she created at ABC. Susan Estelle Jansen, who'd been a producer on *Boy Meets World*, joined *Lizzie* as an executive producer alongside Rogow as regular series production began in the summer of 2000 at Hollywood's Ren-Mar Studios (the site of Lucille Ball and Desi Arnaz's former Desilu Studios). Rogow was simultaneously serving as EP on the Fox Family series *State of Grace*, starring Mae Whitman and Alia Shawkat, on an adjacent soundstage. He picked *Lizzie*'s spot next door to make it easy for him to shuffle back and forth between the productions throughout the week. "I was Desi for a while," Rogow joked. "Only once did I walk onto the wrong stage."

While filming the live-action, single-camera *Lizzie McGuire* episodes, they relied on animator Debra Solomon to draw each episode's cartoon Lizzie segments on paper by hand. The images were then scanned and colored on a computer before being overlaid on static photographs from the sets, and Hilary recorded her accompanying voice-over lines in a small recording booth on site.

For the kid actors, working on *Lizzie* was a dream gig. "Every week was, what fun thing do I get to do now?" said Jake Thomas, who played Lizzie's little brother, Matt, when I spoke to him for a 2021 *Vice* article. "It really was the best job in the world for a nine- to eleven-year-old. I can't say that there's anything looking back on it that was unpleasant or even difficult. It was just fun." In their down time, the actors would go to Disneyland or socialize at teen clubs in L.A. Once, Clayton Snyder, who played *Lizzie* hunk Ethan Craft, even took Hilary to a dance at his public middle school. "My mom thought it'd be a great idea to invite her," he said. "It ended up being all my fellow classmates just forming a giant circle around her and staring at her the whole night."

Just like on *Even Stevens*, the network executives in Burbank provided notes on each episode. But unlike that other show, here, the suits had Rogow to contend with. "Stan Rogow was a classic firewall producer," writer Tim Maile said. "It was almost reflexive. They would give a note and his impulse would be to say, 'No, we can't do that.'" To Rogow, the network feedback amounted to little more than "make it funnier," and in his mind, *Lizzie* was already as funny as it needed to be.

Rogow made sure every script had what he dubbed "the Gary Marsh three-quarter page" (on a generous day it would stretch to "the Gary Marsh page-and-a-half")—an extended moment that catered to the sentimentality of the Disney legacy. Heartwarming and poignant, just the way Walt would have wanted. To keep the humor that the network now so desired, he'd find creative ways to deliver the schmaltz on screen, like having Mr. McGuire share a heart-to-heart with Matt while hanging upside down from a booby trap.

Rather than break down the series into the then-standard eighteen- to twenty-four-episode seasons, Disney structured *Lizzie* into two thirty-something-episode megaseasons that they shot over two years. The reason seemed to be monetary: with every new season of a show, various union rules dictate that pay scales, and often job titles, receive a bump. To avoid that increase, Disney tacked on season "extensions," adding episodes to the current season that didn't require the accompanying pay-outs. "They kind of did a bait and switch," *Lizzie* writer Melissa Gould said. "So, while I was thrilled to continue working on the show, I felt completely screwed over."

ON *LIZZIE McGUIRE*, the episodic stakes were never too high. But the series quietly pushed the envelope by showing some of the realities kids actually deal with, like the humiliation of shopping for a first bra, Miranda's single-episode battle with an eating disorder, and Gordo be-latedly celebrating his bar mitzvah. "I'm Jewish, and I had dealt with a lot of prejudice growing up. So, to me, it was a little bit personal," said the bar mitzvah episode's director Anson Williams, who is perhaps best known for playing Potsie on *Happy Days*. "It was a kinder, gentler way of maybe stopping a little bit of prejudice."

Several episodes featured a pair of male characters and their pet chimpanzee in a bit that fans have since equated to coded representation of a gay couple raising an adopted child. "We had never intentionally been like, 'This will be a gay couple,'" writer Nina Bargiel said. "There was one draft where the guys were going to Fire Island, and they needed somebody to watch the chimp. That was clearly coded, and I think Dis-ney made us change that."

Other elements of the show were less progressive. Davida Williams, who played Claire Miller, the sidekick of mean girl Kate Sanders, was the most prominent Black actress on the show, but her character was largely one-dimensional. "It was definitely obvious to me that on the network, and on TV in general, there just weren't a lot of people of color," Davida said.

One of the only other Black characters on *Lizzie* was Matt's friend Lanny Onasis (played by Christian Copelin), who was scripted to be completely mute and never spoke a line. According to show writers Doug Tuber and Tim Maile, the series didn't have the money to pay for a new recurring speaking role, so Lanny was created to be mute to fit in the budget. But the network's late-stage effort to diversify the show's casting by finding a Black actor to play him backfired.

"When we originally wrote Lanny, we had in mind kind of a weird-looking Eastern European kid. But Disney Channel said, 'We'd love it if you would cast an African American actor to get some better visual representation,'" Maile said. "Toward the end of the run, a woman approached me and said, 'I've got a bone to pick with the show: Lanny is one of the only Black characters on the show and he never says a word. What's that about?' I couldn't very well say, 'Well, the character was never intended to speak. There was never any money for the character to speak.' But I could see how somebody simply watching the show would go, *what's up with this?* The one Black kid never gets to say a word."

THE NETWORK'S GOALS for *Lizzie McGuire* hadn't initially been anything different or bigger than past Disney Channel series. The benchmark for viewership success, based on the number of households with Disney Channel, had been set at what seemed like a lofty one million before its launch in January 2001. That quickly went out the window.

By its second season, *Lizzie* was averaging around 2.3 million viewers per episode and became the most-watched show on Disney Channel, charging past *Even Stevens*. "Shortly after the show had begun airing, a gaggle of tween girls began serenading me to the *Lizzie McGuire* theme song as I walked home from Hermosa Beach with a surfboard under my arm," said Kyle Downes, who played the geeky oddball Larry Tudgeman. "I remember thinking how surreal a moment in life this was for me. And one not repeated since."

By September 2001, *Lizzie* was being syndicated on ABC's One Saturday Morning, widening its reach, and in September 2002, Disney Channel started airing *Lizzie* seven days a week, rather than just on weekends. In addition to its prime-time slot—by then it was the number one show on cable at 7:30 P.M.—it occasionally aired again at 11:00 P.M. to unexpected success. "I said, 'Who the fuck is watching at eleven at night on the Disney Channel?'" Rogow said. "Well, it was college girls." The situations Lizzie faced on the show spoke to older girls and women who had lived through those awkward adolescent days themselves, and the series served as sweet nostalgia for their own bygone girlhoods. Plus, Lizzie and Miranda's hair and fashion choices were trendily maximalist and chaotic (hairstyles topped with feathers, dice, and pom poms! Outfits pairing paisley with tie-dye!), and the scripts were just plain funny.

Lizzie's wide-reaching popularity even stretched into the homes of stars like Aerosmith front man Steven Tyler, whose children loved the show so much that he agreed to play Santa Claus in a season 2 episode, as long as his kids could appear as well. What was supposed to be a four-hour shoot for his cameo turned into an all-day experience that included Tyler making an impromptu visit to the *Lizzie* recording booth and laying down a rendition of "Santa Claus Is Coming To Town" to sing in the episode.

While *Lizzie* received prime-time Emmy nominations for Outstanding Children's Program in 2003 and 2004, it lost to an HBO documentary special that dealt with 9/11 and another on diversity. "It was like putting the Real Housewives up against *Inside the Actors Studio*," writer Nina Bargiel said. But there were more important metrics of *Lizzie*'s success, like when the cover of an April 2003 *TV Guide* proclaimed, MOVE OVER, MARY-KATE AND ASHLEY . . . LIZZIE McGUIRE IS AMERICA'S NEW SWEETHEART!

Suddenly, as outside media attention rolled in, the greater Disney corporation began considering that Disney Channel's original content might have value of its own. Rogow pushed for the consumer products division to merchandise the show. Until then, Disney's strategy had been almost entirely reliant on merchandising characters from its animated films. The consumer products team understood how to market Simba and Ariel. They didn't quite get the appeal of centering products around a live-action series and its star. At first, "Nobody thought Disney Channel stuff was going to make a lot of money," Rogow said. "They didn't know if it was going to make *any* money."

But the demand was undeniable, and *Lizzie* books, pencils, sleeping bags, jewelry organizers, sewing patterns, diaries, stationery, party supplies, and apparel lines at Kohl's and Limited Too exploded onto shelves. Because Hilary's deal wasn't structured to include a substantial cut of the merchandise, Rogow said, the Duffs weren't interested in Disney profiting from Hilary's face on their assorted products. "Her deal gave her bupkis if she did merchandise. So, rather than have Hilary on merchandise, we had the animated character, which Disney owned," Rogow said. "But it just never really broke through the way it would have had she been willing to do more—or if Disney would have compensated her more."

IN 2001, DISNEY CHANNEL introduced an Express Yourself interstitial campaign with network talent, giving them a platform to voice their own (brand-approved) opinions, discuss their favorite hobbies and music, and share their views of the world. Overseen by the marketing team, each performer would sit down for a thirty- to forty-five-minute interview that would then be chopped up and edited together around various themes to air during programming breaks. "It was really the crescendo of it all," Rich Ross said. "It was transcendental for us because it just underscored our purpose and the [talent's] purpose, which is not always the same."

While the stars of Disney Channel series received media training whenever they did occasional outside press interviews, on the network itself, they had previously only appeared as their scripted characters in their specific projects. Would it be confusing for kids to suddenly see Hilary as Hilary Duff and not as Lizzie McGuire? Or Shia as Shia LaBeouf instead of Louis Stevens? Maybe. But it would also increase the relatability of the talent and forge a connection between them and the audience.

Plus, it would please the actors, who would get the chance to talk about themselves on air before their careers reached a level that merited talk-show appearances. In the Express Yourself spots, Hilary had the space to talk about her "fantasy mall day" and her family's Fourth of July traditions. And when 9/11 happened, the network used the interstitial series to have their stars directly connect with unsettled viewers.

In the immediate aftermath of the 2001 attacks, network president Anne Sweeney dictated Disney Channel's official position: "We are a safe haven." She instructed the programming team to comb through Disney Channel's content library, making sure there was no imagery of buildings collapsing in any episodes or movies. And within weeks of 9/11, the network sent a film crew to the White House to film an Express Yourself interview with First Lady Laura Bush in the Map Room. "That was a very surreal experience. I remember President [George W.] Bush came into the room where we were filming and said hello," Express Yourself director Glen Owen said. "What ran through my mind was, 'Dude, you shouldn't be in here. You should be in a war room somewhere. The world's on fire.'"

Back at a studio in Los Angeles, Disney Channel gathered various talent to film companion Express Yourself interviews with the goal of comforting scared viewers and opening a dialogue with their parents. Without speaking directly about the events that occurred on September 11, the way *Nick News* with Linda Ellerbee might have, they instead had stars like Hilary talk in abstract terms about their love of firefighters and the American flag. Shia even read an original poem. Sample line: "I think through this pain I've learned a powerful lesson, that it's awesome to be an American citizen."

Global affairs routinely impacted Disney Channel's programming decisions. While the animated action series *Kim Possible* frequently showed Kim battling bad guys, none of those showdowns could take place at her high school. In the wake of the Columbine school shooting, the network mandate was that schools on Disney Channel needed to be seen as safe places where nothing too scary occurred. And after the high-profile beheading of journalist Daniel Pearl and other tragedies in the Iraq War, Disney decided it would be too disturbing for the mom on *Phil of the Future* to have a detachable head, as was originally planned, so they scrapped that idea and reshot all of her early scenes with the character as a regular, fully human mom.

In hindsight, the 9/11 Express Yourself clips come across more as nationalistic propaganda than the generic comfort vehicles they were intended to be. Off camera, the actors were more candid with their opinions. "I was very vocal about my disgust for the Bush administration," Nick Spano of *Even Stevens* said. "I remember being dumbfounded and being on set, having those conversations about, wow, this is the dumbest administration we've ever had."

*   *   *

IF THE EXPRESS YOURSELF interstitials allowed the actors to (semi) be themselves on camera, the legendary wand IDs allowed the actors to be themselves on camera while also explicitly promoting the Disney Channel, their respective projects, and drawing attention to the Disney Channel logo, all in a matter of seconds. It was a branding masterclass.

Disney Channel had hired the Razorfish creative agency to come up with graphics and interstitials that would market the brand as "cooler" and older. From the agency's office in New York, creative director Carlos Ferreyros and the team had first revamped the network's logo in 1997 by making new show characters appear inside a Mickey Mouse–shaped TV logo, and again in 2000, to craft a more abstract, transparent corner logo dubbed "peeking Mickey."

For the latter redesign, the goal was that the minimal, mostly transparent Mickey would keep the Disney brand front of mind as it watched the show along with the audience, rather than acting as a barrier between the viewer and the content. The designers debated every detail, focusing on the texture of the ears and how elastic and "jelly-ish" the logo should be as it moved into place.

The Mickey logo serves as a reminder of the magic of Disney, but why not take it a step further, Ferreyros thought. What if the stars of Disney Channel shows appeared in transitional segments drawing the simple new logo with a magic wand? It could invoke the mythology of Sorcerer Mickey and Tinker Bell's pixie dust, while still being a uniquely Disney Channel entity. The agency presented the idea to the Disney Channel marketing team.

"The biggest conversation was, how dorky is this going to be?" marketing and brand strategy head Eleo Hensleigh said. "But there's something about the waving of a wand. It's sort of a wish fulfillment of its own."

In 2003, a dozen or so actors from original series, syndicated series, and DCOMs assembled for the first time at Hollywood's Raleigh Studios to shoot a new round of Express Yourself videos, and then each shuffled over to a white backdrop to shoot quick to-camera introductions that all ended the same way:

"Hey, I'm Hilary Duff from *Lizzie McGuire*, and you're watching Disney Channel."

"Hi, I'm Tahj Mowry from *Smart Guy*, and you're watching Disney Channel."

"Hey, what's up? It's Christy Carlson Romano. You're watching Disney Channel."

After reciting their lines, they'd use a stick wrapped in green screen to draw the outline of the mouse ears—a task more challenging than it appeared. "You're just painting in thin air," *Even Stevens*'s A.J. Trauth said. "You know those Picasso photographs where he paints an entire matador using a light wand in pitch black, and it's incredible? That was not us." (In more recent years, the wand tech has improved. Now, the kids watch themselves on an on-set video monitor that overlays an outline of the ears for them to trace with precision.)

The by-product of the wand IDs and Express Yourself interstitials was the messaging to viewers that these actors were bigger than any single project or character they were known for playing. Suddenly, Gordo wasn't just Lizzie's best friend on *Lizzie McGuire*. He was Adam Lamberg, a well-spoken kid who loved Bob Dylan and Jimi Hendrix. He had authority and purpose. He was a budding celebrity in his own right.

"It was a leap bringing the talent out of their world and into the Disney world," Ferreyros said. "But [Disney Channel] realized, oh, there's a lot of value in connecting with the actual actors and actresses behind the characters."

As *LIZZIE McGUIRE* became the network's biggest hit, Hilary and Lalaine became good friends while playing BFFs on the show. They were always rehearsing and shooting their scenes together at work. And off set, they lived near each other and shared milestones like shaving their legs together for the first time. But as the show was shooting the final few episodes of its run, the unthinkable happened: they had a falling-out beyond repair. "The two girls were literally best friends for three-quarters of the series, maybe more," showrunner Stan Rogow said. "And then they had a blow up that never got healed."

The issues were multifold. Part of the tension was rooted in the season 1 episode "Random Acts of Miranda." Because the writers knew that Lalaine had a singing background and wanted to pursue it further, they wrote a storyline where Miranda bombs as the lead in the school play but wows the crowd with her rendition of the *Mulan* power ballad "Reflection." "Hilary and her mom were very upset by that because their long-term plan was for Hilary to sing," the episode's co-writer, Tim Maile, said. "And, in the overall scheme of *Lizzie*, Lalaine was the one who got to sing first." While Hilary's music career would soon ascend, and she eventually sang a song on the show's soundtrack, she never actually got to perform on the series like Lalaine did.

There was also some insecurity on Hilary's part over where she stood among the cast and crew. Because her character was so central to the show, Hilary had to be in more scenes than everyone else. While the other kids all did their schoolwork together in a classroom, Hilary had a private tutor. While Lalaine played basketball with crew members on the lot or bonded with the other young actors in their downtime, Hilary was busy filming or recording cartoon Lizzie's voiceover.

One day, Susan Duff approached writer Nina Bargiel and told her that Hilary had noticed everyone seemed to spend more time with Lalaine and have a stronger connection to her. Bargiel said she immediately wrote Hilary a letter telling her that wasn't the case, that everyone adored her, and that she understood how it felt to feel left out. "I was like, if you're feeling weird or whatever, you are always free to find me. You're always free to call me. If you need someone to talk to who is not a parent, I am here,'" Bargiel said. "And she came up to me and hugged me. We were crying. I feel like it was a swamp of things. It was this cauldron that just eventually bubbled over."

The tension between Hilary and Lalaine was partly typical teen-girl drama, but it also involved their careers and their managers. "There were a lot of emotional politics that were just unfortunate," Rogow said. "It was a mess." And while most friends who have a falling-out can distance themselves from each other, Hilary and Lalaine's on-screen friendship was a cornerstone of every *Lizzie* episode, and they'd need to continue to spend full days together shooting the series. "It fractured all the way up to the parents," Rogow said. "There were two camps: 'We don't want to work with her,' and 'We don't want to work with *her*.' It was like, oh my God, this is a nightmare. We couldn't solve it."

Production screeched to a halt. The issue eventually escalated to the senior network executives, and they made the call. They'd release Lalaine from her contract six episodes early. The writers could add throwaway lines explaining her character's absence: "Miranda's out sick," "Miranda's still visiting her family in Mexico," etc. "We could never and would never force someone to do [a show they didn't want to do]," Rich Ross said. "For Lalaine, she was ready to go."

Rogow and Jansen gathered the team to break the news. "We were just told, 'Lalaine has left to do something else,'" Nina Bargiel said. "And it was like, what?! It was always phrased in a way where it sounded like it was her choice." Losing Lalaine meant losing a cornerstone of what made the series so special. "Lalaine is very talented," Rogow said. "She made the show funny because she could make a joke work."

There was an attempt to bring her back for the Christmas episode with Steven Tyler. (While it aired as the twentieth episode of season 2, it was actually shot later in the production schedule.) But things quickly soured again. "At the table read, you could tell there was something going on between the two of them. Lalaine was kind of strutting like, 'I'm baaack,' and Hilary didn't like that," writer Doug Tuber said. "After the table read, Stan told us, 'Well, she's not going to be in this one either.' So, we wrote her out."

In 2005, Rogow and *Lizzie* creator Terri Minsky re-teamed on a pilot for a Disney Channel spinoff series centered on Miranda's previously unseen and unmentioned little sister, *Stevie Sanchez*, which would star a young Selena Gomez in the title role. Hilary wasn't involved, and Lalaine reprised her supporting role to film the pilot. The only problem? It was a real downer. "*Lizzie McGuire* was fun and wacky. The tune that I put about fifteen minutes into the *Stevie* pilot was 'Everybody Hurts' by R.E.M. And it fit perfectly," Rogow said. "That's not a show for Disney Channel." And when it went up against the much perkier *Hannah Montana*, it ultimately lost.

Despite the Hilary and Lalaine drama, there had initially been hope that *Lizzie* would be the first Disney Channel original series to extend beyond sixty-five episodes. Some of the creatives remembered Gary Marsh summoning them to Burbank at the start of season 2 and telling them, "The standard business model up till now has been sixty-five episodes, but if you guys take this season and make it even more popular, that can go away in a heartbeat."

But as Hilary's fame escalated and the outside movie offers began to trickle in, negotiating an extended contract with the funds they had available soon became impossible. "We had only so much money," Ross said. "Hilary started getting other things. We had already been piloting Raven's show, and we were just developing more and more." *Lizzie* would have to end at sixty-five, just like all the others.

On June 14, 2002, the *Lizzie McGuire* cast and crew gathered one last time at a bowling alley at Universal CityWalk—"for the one and only, not to be duplicated, utterly stupendous, wondertastic wrap party!" read the invite—and that was that.

Until music and movies entered the picture.

5

Hilary Duff:
Pop Star and Movie Star

Throughout the 1990s, the scope of Walt Disney Records had mostly been confined to animated film soundtracks and Mickey-themed compilations. But a week into Jay Landers's new role as the label's senior vice president of artists & records in early 2000, Disney CEO Michael Eisner announced that, in a cost-saving measure, Disney would be pulling back on new animated musicals for the foreseeable future. Fewer musicals meant fewer musical soundtracks, leaving Walt Disney Records with mostly educational kids CDs "like Mickey Mouse singing the ABCs," Landers recalled. For the man who'd served as a creative advisor to Barbra Streisand and overseen projects with Neil Diamond and James Taylor, it was an unappetizing prospect.

Looking for ways he could make his job worthwhile, Landers quietly signed a thirteen-year-old Mexican American singer named Myra to the label in the spring of 2000. "No one was paying attention" at Disney, he said, "so I didn't ask anyone." At the suggestion of her personal management team, Myra had professionally dropped her last name, Ambriz, and changed the spelling of her first name from "Mayra" to "Myra" to make it easier for non-Spanish speakers to pronounce. "At first, I was really butthurt over it," she said. "There were moments where I truly felt like, *what's my identity?*"

Landers gave Myra a cover of "Magic Carpet Ride" to sing on a *La Vida Mickey* compilation album and, with the help of Disney music executive Mitchell Leib, placed her extremely catchy song "Miracles Happen (When You Believe)" on *The Princess Diaries* soundtrack. In 2001, Myra also released a solo album on Disney's catch-all label, Buena Vista Records, and a Spanish-language album on their artist-focused Hollywood Records.

For the young singer who had grown up with her parents and four siblings in a studio apartment in Northern California, the experience was life-changing and, she said, "a non-stop roller coaster." She barely saw her mom as she toured around the world, but the money from her Disney record advance was enough to buy her family a house. Each week she and her dad, who traveled with her as her guardian, sent half of their per diem money back home to help pay the mortgage and cover other family expenses.

But within two years, it was all over. Myra's family severed ties with her management team, and her time at Disney came to an end. Although Myra's talent and music were exactly in line with young consumers' tastes at the time, Landers's attempts to secure opportunities for her across The Walt Disney Company faced perpetual hostility, and her career didn't take off the way he'd hoped.

"I made these big assumptions that I would be able to use the resources of the company—the theme parks, the channels, the international side," Landers said. "I was delusional, thinking that if I signed her people would get behind her. It was only after the fact that I came to learn how much resistance had been built up between the various Disney divisions."

As Myra put it, "It felt like I was the guinea pig."

ON THE HEELS of the successes and frustrations that came with Myra, Landers happened to turn on an awards show on TV one night in 2002, just as the cameras panned to Hilary Duff. As she waved, the crowd went wild. "You would have thought The Beatles had walked in," Landers said.

He grabbed the remote and flipped to Disney Channel, where he found an episode of *Lizzie McGuire*. Not only was Hilary clearly a star, but she already had the network's support. And, handily, her ratings-busting show incorporated pop music.

Unlike *Even Stevens*, which had relied on DIY sound effects and in-house songs, *Lizzie McGuire* used contemporary hits to score its major moments. It was an expensive touch that *Lizzie* showrunner Stan Rogow had fought for when he hired his old friend Elliot Lurie—the former front man of the "Brandy (You're a Fine Girl)" band Looking Glass, and the composer of the show's theme song—as *Lizzie*'s music supervisor and licensed a variety of tracks under a cost-saving five-year deal.

Landers's mind started racing. What if they created a soundtrack album of pop songs featured on the show, plus a few others that fans could imagine Lizzie *might* listen to if she were real, to create a sort of "Lizzie's playlist" in CD form? *Lizzie* had already wrapped shooting, but new episodes would continue to air for the next year or more. And, if Hilary was interested, the centerpiece of the soundtrack could be a new song recorded by her. Hilary had never sung professionally, but it didn't really matter whether or not she was a skilled singer. They could work around that by picking an easy track and adding copious auto-tune, if required.

Having been burned by seeking cross-Disney support only after he'd signed Myra, Landers changed course and set about discussing the idea of signing Hilary with various parties. Hilary and her mom were thrilled for Hilary's singing dreams to finally come true. And Landers's enthusiasm was music to Rogow's ears. He'd been eager to cross the show into the music space and had been pushing the Disney Channel executives to make it happen.

Next, Landers raced to find support from Bob Cavallo, the chairman of the Disney Music Group (which included Walt Disney Records, Hollywood Records, and other labels), but Cavallo was reluctant to greenlight the project. Landers wanted to tear his hair out. Walt Disney Records was sitting on a pile of gold, and they couldn't see it! He made a plea to Hollywood Records executive Mitchell Leib, who yielded influence with Cavallo, given his decades-long history with Disney and his recent hit soundtracks for teen films like *10 Things I Hate About You* and

Save the Last Dance. "This soundtrack is happening," Leib told Cavallo. "I'll back it. If you don't like it, just look the other way." It wasn't worth the fight. Cavallo stepped aside and let them proceed.

Over the next few weeks, Landers, Rogow, and Lurie worked together to package a cohesive album of twelve tracks, ranging from Smash Mouth's cover of "Why Can't We Be Friends?" to "ABC" by The Jackson 5, "Walk Me Home" by Mandy Moore and, of course, the *Lizzie McGuire* theme song, sung by Angie Jaree. This was pre–iTunes store, which would start offering individual song downloads when it launched in 2003, and it was much easier for fans to buy a soundtrack CD than hunt down each individual track across separate artists' albums.

For the pièce de résistance, Landers selected a cover of Australian singer Brooke McClymont's "I Can't Wait" to give to Hilary. It was an easily performed pop track that was virtually unknown to American audiences. They updated the lyrics to be more tween friendly, and Hilary sang her heart out at her recording session. Unlike other, more trained pop stars, Hilary's singing voice sounded a lot like her speaking voice, which gave it added relatability and instant fan recognition.

"I think she'd be the first to admit that, technically, she's not a terrific singer. But she was good enough," Lurie said. "And with the help of a good producer and modern technology, we got a good performance."

The album came out in August 2002 and went gold (selling at least 500,000 copies) that December and platinum (selling at least one million) the following year. For Walt Disney Records, the *Lizzie McGuire* TV soundtrack was the first record in nearly fifty years not tied to a specific movie that clicked with consumers.

Once again, Landers could barely contain his excitement at their future prospects: What if Hilary Duff became the new Annette Funicello? The former Mouseketeer had given the label Top 10 hits in the mid-twentieth century when Disney had capitalized on her TV popularity and transitioned her to pop songs. Annette hadn't been the best singer or actor on *The Mickey Mouse Club*, but, like Hilary, she had endless charisma and commercial appeal. Hilary could do what Annette had done, and so much more.

Imagine: a performance in one of the theme parks could be filmed as a concert special for Disney Channel, which could be used as a driver for an album to boost her popularity to star in theatrical Disney releases, which could then have accompanying soundtracks—and the cycle continues. This could be the start of shifting Walt Disney Records into a tween-focused brand, saving it from the death knell of Mickey Mouse singing the ABCs.

At the same time, Landers began to use the chokehold that contemporary pop stars had on 2000s tweens to revitalize classic Disney intellectual property. To help make the brand's classic songs hip again, he greenlit a *Disneymania* compilation CD (which would eventually lead to eight more in the series) featuring new recordings of old favorites: *NSYNC singing "When You Wish Upon a Star," Jessica Simpson belting "Part of Your World," and Baha Men jamming to "Hakuna Matata," among others. He gave Hilary "The Tiki, Tiki, Tiki Room," using it to serve as a testing ground to see how audiences would react to her performing completely divorced from her TV character. Even when she was assigned to arguably the worst song of the bunch, the support from Hilary's fans was overwhelming.

And ahead of *Disneymania 2*, Landers created a version of "We Are the World" for the Disney Channel crowd called Disney Channel Circle of Stars, which assembled talent from various shows to record a new version of *The Lion King*'s "Circle of Life" and shoot a collaborative music video that would air on Disney Channel. Alongside confident, eager singers like Hilary and Raven-Symoné, they peppered in those with little desire to fit the pop star mold to even out the gender and series representation. "If you watch, you'll see me in the background, doing some little moves that are very much me being like, *What the fuck am I doing here? How did I get myself into this?*" *Even Stevens*'s A.J. Trauth said. "Looking back, I'm so glad that it exists. But in the moment, I was like, this is not me. This is definitely not me."

Between takes, other defining moments took place at the "Circle of Life" shoot; Christy Carlson Romano pulled Raven and Anneliese van der Pol aside to show them her new breast implants. "I wanted to make an impression," Christy told Anneliese, as they reminisced during a 2023 episode of Christy's *Vulnerable* podcast.

"And you did, girl," Anneliese replied. "I'll never forget those boobs. Best boobs I've ever seen."

A YEAR BEFORE that eventful *Lion King* track recording, Landers rushed Hilary back into the studio for another one-off deal, recording a Christmas album called *Santa Claus Lane* on Buena Vista Records, Disney's catch-all label for projects that didn't quite fit at the more prominent labels. (The album's title track was originally called "Candy Cane Lane," with lyrics entirely themed around sugary treats, but there was concern that might send a bad message to the cavity-prone kids of America, and the song was reworked.) The Christmas ditty appeared in the end credits for Walt Disney Pictures's *The Santa Clause 2*, and Hilary's first performance in front of a crowd was singing it on a *Movie Surfers* interstitial on Disney Channel.

But this was bigger than just Hilary, Landers thought. He reflected on the titanic successes of Britney, Justin, and the other former Mouseketeers who'd struck it big. He even called *The All New Mickey Mouse Club*'s casting director Matt Casella to see if he would come work for Walt Disney Records and help spot talent. (He would not.) And he begged Marsh to do a new iteration of *The Mickey Mouse Club* so that he could sign the new kids to Walt Disney Records. (Marsh declined.)

Signing Disney Channel talent to a Disney-owned label might seem like a no-brainer in hindsight—a version of Walt Disney Records had been around since 1956, and Hollywood Records since 1989. The tools were all there, but the separation and hostility between the various branches of Disney made communication and willingness to forge new paths between them virtually nonexistent. Crucially, the Disney music division fell under the Disney film division, meaning the profits from the music side factored into the studio executives' bonuses—not those of the network executives. "Those siloed businesses are what prevented the great alignments between the record business and Disney Channel coming together prematurely," Mitchell Leib said. "It came together when it just became so fucking obvious."

According to Landers, Disney Music Group chairman Bob Cavallo initially told him not to pursue anything further with Hilary beyond the

Christmas album. Gary Marsh at Disney Channel was also skeptical. "If you fail with Hilary, then she's just a failed singer," Marsh cautioned Landers. "It hurts the show." But Landers had a different perspective. "Do you know how many records Frank Sinatra put out?" Landers asked him. "No! We only remember the hits. If Hilary puts out a song and it doesn't connect, nobody will even know it came out. But if she puts out a song and it's a hit, everyone will know. There's no downside. Nothing ventured, nothing gained."

Landers pushed ahead and set up a meeting with the Duffs. He couldn't offer them an overall record deal, but they could at least discuss the possibility of making a one-off pop album. The Duffs were eager but hesitant to commit, given Hilary's already intense schedule working on films like *Agent Cody Banks* and *The Lizzie McGuire Movie*. They didn't have time to come up with creative ideas or have copious input. They needed a plan that would take care of all the specifics so that Hilary could just pop in and out of the studio between her other obligations.

A follow-up meeting was set with Bob Cavallo—who was slowly coming around to the idea of backing Hilary as the sales data came in from the *Lizzie* TV soundtrack and Hilary's Christmas album—and his son, Hollywood Records's senior vice president of A&R, Rob Cavallo. Patriarch Bob was a legendary producer and music manager whose clients had included Earth, Wind & Fire, Prince, Alanis Morissette, and Green Day. He approached the meeting with the Duffs like he would one with those artists, stressing the creative license that Hilary would be given and how she could be the main idea generator for the project.

It was overwhelming and exactly the kind of album the Duffs *didn't* have time to undertake. They left the meeting with a curt, "We'll think about it."

The Duffs had also been in contact with other labels, as Hilary was under no obligation to stay in house with Disney. But Hilary's music manager, Andre Recke, cautioned them against leaving the fold. "We wouldn't get the attention and the care that we would probably get from Disney or Hollywood Records, who have an invested interest in the brand already," he told the Duffs. They ultimately struck a deal with Hollywood, since Walt Disney Records didn't oversee single-artist albums or marketing. But because Landers had shepherded Hilary's music at Walt Disney Records, he was loathe to let Hollywood snatch away his artist. "It was incredibly uncomfortable," former Hollywood Records general manager Abbey Konowitch said of the tension between the two labels at the time.

The music executives managed to work out a cross-label deal, allowing Landers to have continued involvement on what would become Hilary's debut solo album, *Metamorphosis*. "The only thing I was against was the title because I couldn't spell it," Landers said. They brought on renowned producers and songwriters, including The Matrix, Kara Dio-Guardi, and Charlie Midnight, to craft an album full of pop and rock bops like "Come Clean," "So Yesterday," and "Sweet Sixteen."

"Hilary had so much personality that she was able to convey on a recording," Midnight said in a 2013 MySpace interview. "I'd never worked with anybody that young, so I was very pleasantly surprised that we didn't have to coax a personality out of her. That idea of 'metamorphosis,' that really came from her, that she was going through a metamorphosis."

Metamorphosis was released on August 26, 2003, shot to the top of the charts, and went triple platinum within five months. Hilary embarked on a thirty-plus-date concert tour and took the stage at Z100's annual Jingle Ball at Madison Square Garden that December. As she finished her performance in the iconic New York arena, her team applauded her efforts and congratulated her on a job well done. Hilary didn't seem as enthused.

"I wasn't feeling it. I felt a little hoarse," she told them.

Oh honey, the only time your mic is on is when you say "Woo!" or "Hello, New York," Landers thought. But nobody told her that.

"Hilary uniquely created a business for us because of her magic," Konowitch said. "Hilary had that magic that comes along every ten to twenty years. People *loved* Hilary Duff." With the groundwork laid, Hilary and subsequent teen solo artists' albums moved completely over to Hollywood Records. And a frustrated Landers eventually left Walt Disney Records to go to Nickelodeon, where he oversaw music for the stars of *Big Time Rush*, *iCarly*, and *Victorious*.

"This is the thing that I have to impress upon you," Landers told me.

"There was nobody at Disney who liked the idea of being in the tween business at the labels. It wasn't hip enough. It was too much work. There were one hundred excuses—until it became successful."

THE OTHER KEY component to the entire Disney Channel musical venture in the 2000s was Radio Disney, an AM station for kids and tweens sandwiched between the likes of Rush Limbaugh and NPR.

First founded in Dallas, Texas, in 1996, with a national rollout the following year, the station was an anomaly. It populated its musical lineup with pop hits from artists like Britney, Christina, A*Teens, Baha Men, S Club 7, and the songs that kids just loved, like jock jams, Weird Al parodies, and vintage rock anthems such as "We Will Rock You." The process for vetting the tracks was intense. In addition to the radio staff listening to a potential song multiple times to parse for any inappropriate content, the artist's record label was required to send over the official lyrics for the Disney standards and practices team to comb through, making sure nothing contained innuendos or hidden double entendres.

As Disney's stable of young artists expanded, Radio Disney provided a pathway to amplify their music. But extensive airplay wasn't a given (much to the Disney record labels' frustration). The Radio Disney DJs and producers meticulously kept spreadsheets recording every request from callers to democratically decide which tracks made it to air: Avril Lavigne, "I'm With You," 4,646 requests. Hilary Duff, "I Can't Wait," 7,503 requests. "We wanted kids to have a voice because we felt that they were an underserved audience," said Radio Disney DJ Ernie Martinez, who was known as DJ Ernie D on air. "So, we would literally sit at the computer and write their request down and enter it into a database. Some songs got five thousand to ten thousand requests in a weekend. Some got one."

HILARY DUFF'S POPULARITY quickly exploded far beyond the confines of Radio Disney. And as a Disney Channel star being noticed by the industry at large for the first time, Hilary seemed to effortlessly take on the unscripted role required of her. She was eternally chipper, smiling at red carpet events while being peppered with hard-hitting interview questions like, "What's your favorite food at the Thanksgiving table?" ("I'd have to say my mom's desserts!") and "What's the most boring thing in the world to you?" ("Riding on planes—unless I can watch a movie!").

Even when she and Lindsay Lohan publicly feuded over their on-again, off-again relationships with Aaron Carter, Hilary tried her best to remain positive in interviews. "I'm not here to talk bad about her like she talks bad about me," she quipped to *Access Hollywood* in 2004.

"She was just darling," said Hallie Todd, who played Hilary's mom on *Lizzie*. "She really had this beautiful spirit. It was a lot for a little girl to deal with people wanting a piece of her all the time."

The Hollywood careers of other Disney Channel talent like the Mouseketeers, Kirsten Storms, or Christy Carlson Romano hadn't blown up while they were still attached to their Disney projects. As long as they weren't caught doing anything illegal, there was little outside attention given to how well those performers took up the mantle of role model or brand ambassador, because the cameras weren't on them 24/7.

Now, as Hilary transmitted a sunshiny disposition at every media appearance and public event, the framework was inadvertently being laid for what it meant to be a Disney Channel star. Bubbly and wholesome was just part of who Hilary was. She had little desire to rebel against the system because she could largely be herself within its confines. Plus, by the time she turned sixteen, she'd already finished her obligations to the channel and the *Lizzie* franchise. But later, when future Disney Channel stars' personalities and desires didn't align with those established parameters, that chasm could be catastrophic.

And although Hilary was certifiably sweet, she was also savvy. When *Lizzie McGuire* director Savage Steve Holland grew impatient with how long it took the show's hair and makeup team to work on the kids who, in his mind, were already camera ready just as they were, Hilary reminded him how much was at stake for her as the lead of the show. "This is forever!" she told him. "When I'm on TV, it's like this is my one shot. I'm seen like this for the rest of my life."

It was a prescient observation. In her late teens, as Hilary grew up and moved beyond her *Lizzie* days, she developed an eating disorder over the pressure she felt to be thin on camera, and she struggled with "trying to navigate becoming a person that I wanted to be outside of who everybody wanted me to be," she said on the *Good Guys* podcast in 2023.

While Disney Channel represented a bubble of G-rated content and talent, Hilary was also experiencing fame as a teenage girl at a time when Hollywood and the media were still the Wild West in terms of sexualizing underage stars. When Hilary was fifteen, a male *Rolling Stone* reporter made a point to mention her pink thong, which he had caught a peek of when she crouched down to sign an autograph for a fan in a wheelchair at the 2003 Teen Choice Awards. At that same event, host David Spade addressed Hilary in the audience during his monologue, "You're almost sixteen? Sweet. As my good buddy R. Kelly says, 'If only she was two years younger.'" It was a pre-#MeToo world and the dawn of exploitative internet gossip blogs. But if anyone could handle it, Disney insisted, their stars could.

"The kids who make it through to here are the Navy SEALs of the kid talent," Gary Marsh once said of the network's roster in the early 2000s. "They are thoroughly trained, ferociously talented, and tenacious. It's not by accident they rise to the top."

BACK IN 2002, as *Lizzie McGuire* was wrapping up production on the series, showrunner Stan Rogow had begun journeying to the Disney lot to meet with Dick Cook, the head of Walt Disney Studios, about the possibility of making a *Lizzie McGuire* feature film. Until then, the studio had mostly been pulling from children's and YA literature (*Holes*, *The Princess Diaries*) or vintage Disney fare (*The Parent Trap*, *Freaky Friday*) for their live-action family films. But Cook was interested in synergizing the disparate film and TV businesses, and, with Rogow's urging, saw *Lizzie* as a solid entry point to horizontally integrate the brand.

Rich Ross, then the network's president of entertainment, was delighted. From the earliest days, he and Disney Channel president Anne Sweeney had been pushing to utilize their content across the parochial

Disney divisions. At first, because they needed other divisions' help in launching the revitalized Disney Channel, and more recent, when it started to become evident that cross-promotional opportunities could be mutually beneficial to everyone involved.

Disney Channel had traditionally used its Disney Channel Original Movies as a way for their most prominent talent to flex their acting wings and remain satisfied with their opportunities in house. But Hilary's star had risen so fast that another DCOM wasn't a big enough incentive to dangle. A theatrical film would have a more robust budget and, in turn, a much bigger star salary. "It wasn't about them doing the feature-length version of *Lizzie McGuire*. It was about Hilary getting to do a movie," Ross said. "For the first time, the network and the studio were kindred spirits."

Cook approached Walt Disney Studios development executives Doug Short and Karen Glass, who had previously shepherded *The Princess Diaries*, to oversee the feature. Cook wanted the *Lizzie* film to be similar in tone to the Anne Hathaway–Julia Andrews charmer—but they'd need to do it for roughly half that film's budget, at just $17 million. "We were pretty much at the lowest-level budget because this was a huge risk," Short said. "*Will people pay to see something that they have on their TVs already?* This was something that hadn't really been done, and we weren't sure if people would follow the show to the theater. We just didn't know."

Disney needed to get the *Lizzie* movie done quickly to capitalize on the popularity of the show. But they'd need to make sure potential movie-goers didn't just envision the film as a ninety-minute episode of a series they could watch at home. One of the most blatant ways to achieve that differentiation would be to change the setting. They'd uproot Lizzie from her comfortable suburban existence and send her abroad.

Forty years after *Gidget Goes to Rome*, the American-girl-finds-love-and-adventure-in-Europe genre was having a major moment. Mary-Kate and Ashley Olsen had perfected the formula in their straight-to-DVD romps *Winning London*, *Passport to Paris*, and *When in Rome*, and former Nickelodeon star Amanda Bynes was attached to her own trans-Atlantic theatrical film, *What a Girl Wants*.

Ensconced in the midcentury glory of the Polo Lounge at The Beverly Hills Hotel, Short, Glass, Rogow, and *Lizzie* executive producer Susan

Estelle Jansen had a series of meetings to flesh out the plot and feel of what was originally titled *Ciao, Lizzie!* and later became simply *The Lizzie McGuire Movie*. The film would follow Lizzie's eighth-grade class's graduation trip to Rome. The scenery would be stunning. The new love interest (and, plot twist: eventual villain), Paolo, would be dreamy. And it would feature a musical finale bigger than anything they could have imagined on the series.

The studio executives selected an unlikely candidate to direct: Jim Fall, an indie filmmaker whose biggest hit had been the low-budget gay rom-com *Trick*, which had premiered at the 1999 Sundance Film Festival. "I didn't know what the hell *Lizzie McGuire* was," Fall said. "I had never seen the TV show, but I read the script, and I realized, oh, this is actually a romantic comedy with a $17 million budget set in Rome."

After his initial meeting with Short and Glass, Fall left them with five pages of single-spaced notes detailing what was wrong with the original script and how he'd fix it. (Step 1: Nix a roller-skating scene in the Pantheon.) He was the most enthusiastic option they had. "I think the studio ultimately very much wanted somebody outside of the *Lizzie McGuire* TV show world, probably so they could feel like they were controlling me," Fall said. "But they never did. I never got pushback on anything. I just made the movie."

ALL OF THE main cast returned for *The Lizzie McGuire Movie*—except for Lalaine. There were initial discussions with her about coming back to play Miranda, but it was an immediate no on her end. Plus, "I don't believe that Hilary wanted her to be part of the movie," said Robin Lippin, who oversaw casting for both the series and film. "It probably would have been uncomfortable for both of them." So, it was made clear that Miranda would not appear in the script, other than an offhand mention to once again explain her absence.

New cast members included comedian Alex Borstein of *MadTV* fame, who signed on to play the domineering chaperone Miss Ungermeyer. (Fall recalled that Ellen DeGeneres also wanted the part, though others had no such memory.) Brendan Kelly, who was concurrently playing a homophobic white supremacist on HBO's *Oz*, joined as Paolo's stoic bodyguard. And Canadian actor Yani Gellman won the part of Paolo—the Italian pop star who woos Lizzie by showing her the sights of Rome, before it's revealed that he's just using her to embarrass his ex-girlfriend, an Italian singer named Isabella who happens to look exactly like Lizzie with brown hair. "I always imagined myself to have, if nothing else, a great love and appreciation for Italian culture," said Yani, who previously had a small part on *The Famous Jett Jackson* and a larger part in the DCOM *Tru Confessions*. "I think that fed into the role."

When Hilary and her mom initially met with Fall to discuss the film at a Starbucks on Santa Monica Boulevard, Hilary's first question was, "I don't have to kiss Gordo, do I?" It wasn't a dig at her co-star Adam Lamberg, but at the thought of having to kiss someone she'd worked alongside for years. And in the 2000s, there were no such things as intimacy coordinators to make on-screen kisses less uncomfortable or traumatic. (Some Disney Channel shows occasionally found creative ways to have their scripted kisses not involve an actual lip-lock, like when a luggage cart blocked Lilly and Oliver's *Hannah Montana* finale kiss.)

But the *Lizzie McGuire* series had ended with the romantic tension building between Lizzie and Gordo, and the last scene of the film features them sharing a blink-and-you'll-miss-it peck on the lips. "I think that's the first take and only take," Fall said of what made it to camera. "Maybe I would have wished the kiss lasted a little longer, but in retrospect, I think she did it right."

WHILE THE EXECUTIVE producer is king on a TV set, in movies, it's the director who holds the most creative power. After writing an early draft of the script, Susan Estelle Jansen was no longer involved in *The Lizzie McGuire Movie*. That left Stan Rogow, now serving as an executive producer on the film, as the sole ambassador from the *Lizzie* TV team, watching as an outsider took over his former domain. "Stan was pissed that nobody was hired from the TV show," Fall said. "So, I think he didn't like me from the get-go. I didn't find him particularly personable or enjoyable—and he was trying to fire me the whole time."

Rogow remembered it less dramatically. "At the end of the day, I got to do what I wanted," he said, "because I just would go in and recut it where necessary."

Meanwhile, the cast and their families had spent two years growing close with the TV team, and they were now starting fresh with complete strangers in all departments. Tensions, at times, ran high. One day, Fall said he went to check on Hilary and found her with her mom in her trailer, crying over one of Lizzie's costumes that she didn't like. "That was shocking because I'd never seen Hilary upset," Fall said. "But the dress was bad, so I get it."

While costume designer Monique Prudhomme's looks for the other movie characters worked, it seemed there were issues with some of the costumes she was creating for Lizzie. Rogow, eager to contribute, sprang into action. He secured costume designer David Robinson, who had crafted the outlandish wardrobe for *Zoolander*, to join the team and reconceive Lizzie's outfits in a more fashion-forward direction.

For a whimsical runway fashion montage, Robinson created outré pieces from unlikely sources: Lizzie's igloo dress was made from four inflatable children's igloos he found at a Canadian Tire store in Vancouver. Her dangling Styrofoam hat look was inspired by a drag queen walking the streets of New York as Tippi Hedrin in *The Birds*, complete with avian mobile. And, for the big musical number, Robinson plated lambskin leather in metallic green and purple for Lizzie and Isabella's complementary looks as they sang to an audience inside a computer-generated Colosseum.

"The green-screen people were like, well, the costume can't be blue or green, and it can't have any sparkly, shiny stuff on it," Robinson said. "I went, 'Hello! We're doing a movie about a teenage girl as a pop star! What you're describing is absolutely everything that's going to be on this costume. You'll have to figure it out!'"

And they did.

PRODUCTION ON *The Lizzie McGuire Movie* in the fall of 2002 was tight. After a few weeks of prep in Vancouver, they spent a month shooting

exterior scenes in Rome, then another few weeks back in Canada shooting interior scenes, including the megawatt musical finale. That climactic Colosseum performance, during which Lizzie realizes she's being
used by Paolo and sings a triumphant duet with Isabella (also played
by Hilary) to a packed crowd, actually took place on a soundstage in
Vancouver.

From its conception, *The Lizzie McGuire Movie* hinged on the music.
Like the TV soundtrack, which had come out a couple of months before
the movie shoot began, the film would be populated with a variety of
pop songs, along with a new track or two for Hilary to record and promote across Disney platforms. And this time, in addition to providing
the pop single "Why Not" for the film's soundtrack, Hilary would get to
sing on screen, too.

To create the centerpiece single that Lizzie would belt on stage in the
Colosseum scene, Fall reached out to composer Dean Pitchford. Pitchford was already a legend in the movie musical world for his work on
Fame and *Footloose* in the 1980s. And with *Lizzie*, the composer began
by thinking about a song that could put a conclusive crescendo on the
film, something that spoke to both the beauty of the scene's Italian setting and the magic of Lizzie realizing her full potential and growing up.
"What we *don't* need here is a pop tune," Pitchford concluded as he
thumbed through the script. "What we need here is a showtune."

He solicited Matthew Wilder, who had written the music for Disney's *Mulan* and produced No Doubt's smash album *Tragic Kingdom*,
to collaborate on the track. And the combination of their unique skills
blended to create the soaring "What Dreams Are Made Of," a Europop-
tinged, starry-eyed anthem for the ages. "This song is not being sung at
an Anaheim stadium. It's being sung at the Colosseum," Pitchford said.
"What better excuse could we possibly have for writing a Eurovision
Song Contest song?"

Fall and the rest of the studio team loved it. But Pitchford recalled
concerns that "What Dreams Are Made Of" wasn't edgy enough for
the direction the Duffs hoped Hilary's music career would go. "Hilary's
camp was not as wowed by it. They wanted something more along the
lines of Alanis Morissette," Pitchford said. "They wanted a song to be-

gin her pop career, whereas our first objective was to serve the motion picture. And that was exactly the crisis. Matthew and I wrote a song for Lizzie McGuire. Hilary Duff and her camp wanted a song for Hilary Duff." Eventually, Hilary's team conceded. She could work an edgier sound into her debut solo album *Metamorphosis* that would be released the next fall.

While Hilary was busy shooting *The Lizzie McGuire Movie*, her older sister Haylie did the pre-records on her vocals at a studio in L.A. The ballad version of "What Dreams Are Made Of," however, was recorded in Nashville, with local singer Amy Owsley and track producer Mark Hammond providing the singing voices for Isabella and Paolo. "I did the piano version and sent it in just as a demo," Hammond said. "I had no idea that it was going to go into the movie at all. In fact, I didn't find out about that until the night of the premiere."

THE LIZZIE MCGUIRE MOVIE wasn't by any means a critical darling when it opened in theaters on May 2, 2003. *The Washington Post* called it "a smug, cutesy music video/fashion show for Duff," while Roger Ebert observed that the film and its implausible storyline seemed only to serve as "a showcase" for Hilary to launch her "show-biz career."

But it didn't matter. No one expected *The Lizzie McGuire Movie* to be an Oscar darling. This was a movie for the fans, and they came out in droves to see Lizzie's Roman holiday unfold. It opened at number two, behind *X2: X-Men United*, with a $17.3 million haul, earning out its small budget instantly. In the weeks before the movie arrived in theaters, Disney president Bob Iger had initiated discussions for a sequel and potential *Lizzie McGuire* high school–set series on ABC, and studio chief Dick Cook offered Hilary a multipicture deal for future theatrical films at Disney that would be produced by Debra Martin Chase, who had overseen *The Princess Diaries* and The Wonderful World of Disney's *Cinderella.*

On the *Lizzie* TV series, Hilary's original $8,000-per-episode base salary had been raised to $15,000 by the show's end (a substantial bump, thanks to the shrewd negotiating skills of Susan Duff and Hilary's management team). And Rogow had helped the Duffs negotiate a $1 million salary for Hilary for the *Lizzie* feature film. For the sequel, the studio initially offered Hilary $2 million, twice her haul on the first film. But Susan wanted them to double it again.

"I'm serious," a source recalled her telling the Disney executives, which included Iger. "Hilary helped you build your music business *and* the Disney Channel, and you're not giving her what she's worth."

It was a valid assertion, and Hilary was a valuable enough asset that Disney was willing to negotiate—to a point. The amount on the table for Hilary (who wasn't present or involved in the business meetings) escalated to $4 million for the sequel. And while the studio wasn't willing to shell out the $5 million that Susan ultimately wanted—a sum that was equal to what Hilary's former co-star Frankie Muniz had reportedly made for their MGM movie *Agent Cody Banks*—they agreed on $4 million, plus a $500,000 bonus if the first *Lizzie* movie grossed $50 million, and a percentage of the sequel profits.

But during this same time, Susan had acquired the script for *A Cinderella Story* and was shopping it around as a Hilary-led project to the major studios—excluding Disney. "Dick Cook was so pissed off that her reps had gone out with this other script and not even shown it to Disney while they were in the middle of this [*Lizzie*] deal," producer Debra Martin Chase said, "that he called off the [multipicture] deal."

With that friction still hanging in the air, the *Lizzie* sequel negotiations continued. Until Susan made a fatal miscalculation.

"Give us the $500,000 bonus now, or we walk," she told them. The first film hadn't yet reached the box-office threshold to trigger that bonus, and Disney refused. Instead, they reiterated their offer and gave the Duffs a Saturday deadline to accept. The cutoff, a mere week and a day after *The Lizzie McGuire Movie* hit theaters, came and went without a peep, and that was the end of the Duffs' working relationship with Disney film and TV for the next several years. "Basically, it came down to: She called our bluff, and we called her bluff," studio executive Doug Short said. "And we just walked away."

Susan's decision to take the negotiations public and give interviews discussing her displeasure with the dealings only solidified Disney's decision to stand their ground. "It was a bold move that wasn't going to go anywhere," Rogow said. "When I'm getting calls from Bob Iger, you know that the buck has stopped someplace. Iger told me a line I'll never forget. He said, 'Stan, you know I'm known as pretty unflappable. She's flapping me.'"

Still, many of those who worked on *Lizzie* perceived Susan Duff's actions to be in the service of protecting Hilary and her interests rather than exploiting her. "She always struck me as a mom looking out for her kid versus a mom looking out for her kid's career," *Lizzie* writer Nina Bargiel said. Susan insulated Hilary from the business side of the business, but behind the scenes, she made sure to multiply whatever obligatory money was put into Hilary's Coogan Account, a locked bank account mandated by California law where fifteen percent of a child performer's earnings must be set aside by the employer and are only touchable by the performer once they turn eighteen (or are legally emancipated).

And the Duffs invested a significant portion of the rest of Hilary's paychecks in stocks, Texas oil, and real estate to set her up for success, no matter what direction her career might take in the future. "Susan was often not appreciated for how hard she would fight to get what she considered to be a fair deal for her daughter," Rogow said. "A line she often used was, 'Disney is always marking down my kid,' like a discount at a department store. Susan had her own ways of expressing it that often chaffed people at Disney. That was unfortunate because what she was basically saying was: Be fair to her."

With Disney in the rearview, Rogow negotiated an offer from NBC boss Jeff Zucker for a thirteen-episode order of a new high school–set series starring Hilary on that network. They couldn't make it a *Lizzie McGuire* spinoff series, since Disney owned *Lizzie*. But it would essentially be the same low-concept scripted series with Hilary now navigating the highs and lows of high school. Disney's offer for the *Lizzie* ABC series had been $35,000 per episode. Now, NBC was offering Hilary a whopping six figures per episode. "It was a breathtaking amount," Rogow said.

Still, Susan passed on both.

"All I was able to say [to the Duffs] at that point is, it's going to be a long time before you get an offer like you just got from Disney on the movie. It's going to be a long time before you get an offer like you just got from Jeff Zucker at NBC," Rogow said. "I know enough about the business to know that."

Instead, the Duffs took Hilary to Warner Brothers, Universal, and MGM, where she starred in *A Cinderella Story*, *The Perfect Man*, and *Material Girls* in quick succession, earning a rumored $2 million for each film. Susan served as a producer on all.

And when *Lizzie McGuire* ended its run, the lesson that Disney Channel took from the show's unprecedented success wasn't that the network needed more single-camera, low-stakes comedies—it was that it needed more stars. A marketable, beloved star like Hilary was the key that could unlock movie franchises, record deals, and merchandising opportunities across the Disney landscape and bolster the Disney Channel brand on a whole new level.

They were starting to see the future.

6

That's So Raven-Symoné

There is no Disney Channel as we know it today without *Who Wants to Be a Millionaire?*. The gameshow never aired on the network, yet the ongoing rise of Disney Channel was dependent on the ABC series's instant success—because it essentially killed network sitcoms.

When *Who Wants to Be a Millionaire?* premiered in August 1999, it quickly became a prime-time smash, drawing up to thirty million viewers three nights a week. Viewers tuned in en masse to experience the anxiety-inducing thrill of watching Regis Philbin psych out players with exaggerated pauses and wry quips. They relished the schadenfreude of seeing contestants miss easy answers and the emotional pull of cheering for an underdog with a tear-jerking backstory.

It took less than three years for *Millionaire* to flame out as a prime-time phenomenon due to overexposure, but in that time its meteoric rise showed network executives what they believed to be the way of the future: unscripted TV. Game shows and reality shows are cheap to produce and quick to manufacture. Rather than pay expensive salaries to a cast of demanding actors and navigate an opinionated writers' room, unscripted series often mean executives only have to deal with one potentially demanding host and a stable of cheap, non-union "real" people.

With drama and comedy ratings dwindling and the threat of a potential writers' strike looming in 2001, ABC, NBC, CBS, Fox, UPN, and The WB all rushed unscripted series into production that could keep them afloat during any potential dispute. Over just a few seasons, the slate of those networks' scripted comedies shrunk by nearly half. Even ABC's TGIF programming block, a staple for the network since 1989, was scrapped. Sitcoms' enormous writers' rooms—which could sometimes house twenty or more writers on a team—all but vanished. The strike never materialized, but the damage was done. And the creatives who had been working on those series had to look for work elsewhere.

"I'm sure the Disney executives just thought they became geniuses, but what really happened is they suddenly had access to network writers, directors, actors, crew, wardrobe," said *Phil of the Future*, *The Suite Life of Zack & Cody*, and *Jessie* producer Adam Lapidus, who had previously written on *Full House* and *Smart Guy*. "All these people who were doing network shows, we're all unemployed. So, we all went to Disney Channel."

It was an arena many had previously snubbed their noses at. Cable, and especially *kids'* cable, was perceived as second-rate, and its accompanying paychecks were meager. Many of the unions' scale minimums for basic cable were a fraction of network salaries. In the 2000s, the young Disney Channel lead actors' base salaries almost always started at $8,000 to $10,000 per episode, plus prepaid residuals and 5 percent salary bumps each subsequent season. (To compare: Frankie Muniz's 1999 deal for *Malcolm in the Middle* on FOX started at $20,000 per episode.) And veteran actors and producers who had been able to negotiate making $30,000–$50,000 per episode for a network TV show could find themselves stuck in the $15,000-and-under range at the notoriously tight-fisted Disney Channel. "We didn't have the precedent of prime time that we'd had before," said *The Suite Life of Zack & Cody* showrunner Danny Kallis, who counted *Who's the Boss?* among his past credits. "And they were crying poverty."

"It was terrible money," echoed David DeLuise, who signed on to play the *Wizards of Waverly Place* patriarch in 2006 after previously acting on network sitcoms, including NBC's *3rd Rock from the Sun*. "They were like, 'We don't negotiate. You either want the job or you don't.' It was an awful contract."

For the creatives, it was an adjustment, not only in terms of salary, budget, and expectations, but also in the type of content they were producing for a young audience. "How do you shift gears to write for tweens?" *That's So Raven* writer Michael Carrington said. "You can't do sex. You can't do drugs. You can't even do anything too risqué. On Mondays, we would go around the room, and I would say to my writers, 'What did you do this weekend? Anything we can use?' And of course, someone would tell some dirty story about hookers and coke, a debauched weekend, and we would all laugh and go, 'Hold on. What if we change coke to candy and hookers to a massage? I think we have a story.'"

He added, "The reason for the success of these shows, in my opinion, is because we were all veteran sitcom writers. We weren't children's writers. Because all the networks gave up on us, it was Disney Channel's game. They got lucky."

AT THE TURN of the century, Disney Channel had been eager to break into the multi-camera comedy space with the influx of network creatives available. *Lizzie McGuire* and *Even Stevens* had soft launched the idea of adding original comedies to their lineup, but those were single-camera shows that followed the same production process and achieved a similar visual result as the network's earlier dramas. Disney Channel's vice president of original programming Adam Bonnett worshipped at the altar of classic multi-camera sitcoms like *Laverne & Shirley* and *I Love Lucy* and wanted to bring something like that to Disney Channel.

Bonnett had begun his career as Rich Ross's assistant in the talent relations and casting department at Nickelodeon, before Ross brought him over to manage current series at Disney Channel in 1997 and to later also oversee the development of new series. If Gary Marsh (who became the executive vice president of original programming and production in 2001) was the keeper of the Disney legacy, harping on sentimentality and preserving the emotional heart of the brand, the more exuberant Bonnett was the keeper of the comedy. "We used to call Adam and Gary the sieve, and if it made it through both of them we knew it was good," *Hannah Montana* producer Douglas Lieblein said. "If it was funny enough for Adam and serious enough for Gary, we knew we had something."

AIRING SYNDICATED EPISODES of network multi-cams like *Boy Meets World*; *Sister, Sister*; and *Smart Guy* had shown Disney Channel that the audience appetite was there. Plus, shows like those were quicker to produce, and the energy that came with filming in front of a live audience was something kid viewers around the world responded to well. "The nature of a multi-camera show is you're sharing the laughter," Bonnett said. "There's a simplicity to a multi-camera show that I think appeals to a broader audience. It can be so visual, even if you don't speak the language, you know what's going on."

Meanwhile, a man named Michael Poryes needed a job. He had been a writer for *The Facts of Life*, *Saved by the Bell*, *Small Wonder*, and a bevy of other shows, but the work had dried up. When he heard that Disney Channel was interested in launching an original multi-cam sitcom, he approached Bonnett with a few pitches. None of them resonated, but Bonnett decided to pair Poryes with another writer named Susan Sherman to hone a script she'd previously pitched. Together, Poryes and Sherman crafted the *Absolutely Psychic* pilot, centered on a teen girl who could see the future and her non-psychic best friend. "It had a touch of *Absolutely Fabulous*," Bonnett said. "It was a female buddy comedy, and they were these bigger-than-life, outrageous characters."

In the lead role of Rose, they cast Shanelle Workman (the older sister of *Modern Family* actor Ariel Winter). For Rose's zany best friend, they chose fifteen-year-old Raven-Symoné, who blew the producers away at her audition. Unlike most of the other candidates, Raven completely memorized the five pages of *Absolutely Psychic* dialogue required. While the other hopefuls were glancing down at their scripts, Raven's hands were free to help fully throw herself into the physicality of the scene. She wasn't just good. She was incredible.

It shouldn't have come as a shock. Raven-Symoné Christina Pearman had been working since she was sixteen months old. After doing print modeling in her hometown of Atlanta, she signed with Ford Models, and her family moved to New York when she was a toddler. While one parent worked, the other would take her to auditions, until she landed the plum role of Lisa Bonet's stepdaughter, Olivia, on *The Cosby Show* at age three and shot three seasons of the hit NBC series in Queens. Next came music and movies. Raven would stay at the recording studio until one in the morning perfecting the tracks on her first hip-hop album at five years old, "knowing that this is the next step in your career, so suck it up and let's do it," she later recalled. She had gone on to co-star in *Hangin' with Mr. Cooper* and the Eddie Murphy–led *Dr. Dolittle* films. And for Disney Channel, she had previously co-starred in two of the *Zenon* movies as Zenon's friend Nebula. By her midteens, she was a seasoned professional.

According to Gary Marsh, after Raven auditioned for the sidekick on *Absolutely Psychic*, they asked her to read again for the lead role, then gave her the choice between the two parts. Sensing the sidekick would have more comedic material to work with, he's said, Raven initially opted for that part.

Poryes doesn't remember Raven having the power to choose. "She was asked to read both and she did wonderfully in both," he said. "But in what world do you look at an actress [and say], 'Would you like to be the star of the show? Or the co-star of the show?'" Poryes added, "If I wanted her for the central character, I would have really pushed for that."

But while shooting the pilot, it was undeniable that Raven, whose boundless energy radiated from her every pore, inherently made the friend character the focal point of each scene.

Everyone was in agreement: Raven wasn't an Ethel. She was a Lucy.

Casting director Joey Paul Jensen was brought on board to re-cast the rest of the series around her. Shanelle re-auditioned to play the friend, but the flipped dynamic felt too forced, and they let her go. With Raven in the lead, they needed someone goofier and more animated to play off of Raven's antics. Lauren Frost from *Even Stevens* was considered, but she withdrew to star in her own doomed Disney Channel pilot, *Virtually Casey*. In the end, they cast musical theater actor Anneliese van der Pol as Raven's BFF Chelsea, and added Orlando Brown, who had co-starred with the Olsens on *Two of a Kind*, as the girls' other friend Eddie. Rondell Sheridan and T'Keyah Crystal Keymáh joined as Raven's parents, and Kyle Massey, who had lost out on the role of *Even Stevens*'s Beans, landed the part of Raven's younger brother, Cory.

Now that the show was a star vehicle for Raven, it needed a new name. Lucille Ball got *I Love Lucy* to center herself and her comedy right from each episode's opening credits. Raven would now have *That's So Raven* to follow suit, making her one of the first Black female stars to ever have her name in a comedy series title.

To MAKE A kids' multi-cam sitcom is an incredibly difficult task, one many network heavyweights who look down on the genre would struggle to pull off. It's a regular sitcom pushed to an exaggerated extreme—and with the added restrictions of kid hours, a heavy-handed standards and practices division, and a paltry budget. In *Raven*'s case, that meant about $500,000 per episode, to start. (To compare: even when you subtract the six main *Friends* actors' $1-million-each per-episode salary, the final season of that series still cost around $4 million per episode to produce.)

Plus, under California law, child performers have to do at least three hours of schoolwork a day, and the network must provide an on-set teacher. It's the studio teacher's job to keep track of the minors' limited work hours and make sure the kids are staying within the requirements. Once they hit the work-hour limit, the kids will "pumpkin"—industry verbiage alluding to the stroke-of-midnight transition of Cinderella's carriage back into a garden gourd—and quickly be ushered off the set. "It's miraculous how good the shows are because you're never saying, 'Is this the best version of the scene?'" *The Suite Life* writer Tim Pollock said. "You're saying, 'Do we have this good enough to go to the next thing because we have to go, go, go!' Every episode is a race."

For kids younger than sixteen, the teachers also serve as the de facto welfare monitors on set and are responsible not only for kids' education but also their well-being. "If parents had a problem, they'd call us," Rich Ross said. "If kids had a problem, we found out about it from the teachers."

While the kids' hour limits were strictly enforced down to the minute on Disney Channel sets in the 2000s, there were occasional sneaky exceptions when the creatives needed extensions to wrap up a scene. If a director called "action" before the kid's time limit ran out, they could finish shooting the scene at hand. So, occasionally, a director would call "action" just before the limit, then let the cameras roll while they captured additional takes without calling "cut" in between.

Actors' parents often urged the teachers to look the other way and let their kids work just a little bit longer, said *Hannah Montana* studio teacher Linda Stone, who also worked as a teacher on everything from *Family Matters* to *Hook*. "I'll be the 'heavy,'" she said of having to constantly put her foot down. "Part of my job is to protect the production company, and if there's a violation, it can get to be really difficult for them. If it's a second or third offense, they can lose their permit to employ minors for a time."

But, sometimes, there was "a little bit of collusion," *Even Stevens* and *That's So Raven* showrunner Marc Warren admitted. "The parent might take the social worker out for a smoke or a coffee for ten minutes while we got that last shot that we needed. We tried not to abuse that, and we never kept the kid for, like, six extra hours. It was usually a matter of minutes."

There were also sanctioned ways to ditch the restrictions entirely. If a minor is a high school graduate, they can work as an adult performer and are exempt from child labor laws. Many teen performers take the California High School Proficiency Exam to test out of school early and increase their day-to-day workload. Raven, Demi Lovato, and others chose this route.

THE EXCITEMENT AROUND Disney Channel's first multi-cam sitcom was high as *That's So Raven* began production in the fall of 2001. They'd staffed *Raven* with pedigreed creatives from top-rated, Emmy-winning network series, and unlike the single-camera shows of the past, which were shot out of order and not easily observed by the higher-ups, *Raven* and other multi-cams shot in a rigid schedule that the network executives could track like hawks.

Most multi-cam Disney Channel series followed a one-episode-a-week formula of a table read on Mondays, blocking on Tuesdays (where the actors would physically be on the stage reading lines from their scripts), and run-throughs on Wednesdays to see it all come together. Then, because the studio audience was mostly kids who couldn't sit captive for an extended time, the cast and crew would shoot half the episode sans audience on Thursdays, then play back those scenes on monitors for the crowd who attended the live Friday tapings, where they shot the remaining scenes.

Raven marked Poryes's first time running a show, and the pressure was mounting. As filming got underway, the *Raven* set became a place of tense chaos. *Even Stevens*'s early production problems had concerned the on-screen comedy missing the mark. *Raven*'s issues were the backstage culture. "Michael is a driver," director of photography Alan K. Walker said. "He drives everybody to the brink." While *Lizzie* and *Even Stevens* had kept generally sane hours, with days wrapping up by 6:00 or 7:00 P.M., the *Raven* crew would often find themselves working exhaustive network hours, staying until two or three in the morning to rewrite lines and overhaul scenes. "There wasn't a show that I worked in prime time where the hours weren't absolutely crappy [to start]," Poryes said. "So, I brought that same sensibility to *Raven*."

Writer Dava Savel, who had won an Emmy for the landmark "The Puppy Episode" of ABC's *Ellen* that featured Ellen DeGeneres's character coming out, had been recruited to work on *Raven* as a writer and co–executive producer. One day, Savel was taking a walk on the Sunset Gower lot with *Six Feet Under* showrunner Alan Ball, whose series shot on a nearby soundstage.

"What time are you here till?" Savel asked.

"Oh, we're out of here by 6:00 P.M.," Ball replied.

Savel lost it.

"Come. On. You're doing *Six Feet Under* for HBO! I'm doing fucking *That's So Raven* for Disney Channel, and I'm going home at two in the morning," she groaned. "What is the problem here?"

The problem, some concluded, was Poryes. The writers' room, in particular, was in his line of fire. While *Lizzie McGuire* showrunner Stan Rogow had ignored most of the network's suggestions on his show, it seemed to the *Raven* writers that Poryes felt beholden to incorporate all notes, resulting in an endless stream of rewrites and flip-flopping decisions. "It's like you're going to war, and all of a sudden your general is conceding every battle," writer and producer Michael Feldman said. "You begin to lose faith in what you're doing because it's like, what's the point?" On the flip side, Poryes felt some of the staff were undervaluing *Raven* and treating it as a subpar kids' show rather than the distinguished sitcom he wanted it to be.

A whiteboard in the writers' room paid tribute to the canceled good ideas they'd had. They doodled gravestones laying to rest each eliminated zinger or killed scene, alongside other epitaphs that more broadly read "RIP sleep" and "RIP happiness." "People were quitting the show at a time when nobody was quitting shows," said Feldman, who had joined *Raven* after a wave of early staff exits. "It was like, holy shit, what did I get myself into?"

One writer broke out in hives. Another hid in their office all day, sprawled on a couch with their stomach in knots. The performers were exempt from Poryes's demands. "He was great with the kids," Savel said. "Michael never showed anything but adoration for the cast, but he was brutal on the crew."

Reflecting decades later, Poryes shrugged off the discord. "The only real truth in the entertainment industry," he said, "is that you will never, ever know the real truth."

DOWN IN PLAYA VISTA, *Even Stevens* showrunners Marc Warren and Dennis Rinsler were shooting the final episode of that series when they learned of the creative debacle happening at *Raven*. Half of *Raven*'s first season had already been shot, and things were imploding. "They said, 'We're having a crisis on this new show,'" Warren recalled. "'We're firing the showrunners, and what you did on *Even Stevens*, we want you to come over and do it on *Raven*.' We had no downtime at all. We switched jobs, like, that day."

The two men were asked to visit the *Raven* set that evening to watch the run-through and provide feedback. When they arrived, they found a series in shambles. Warren referred to it as "a shit show." Rinsler deemed it "a hell hole." Either way, it was a certified disaster. "When we got there, the writers looked shell-shocked," Rinsler said. "I said, 'Come on, everyone, we're here to have fun!' And they looked at me like I was crazy."

Ahead of the new showrunners' arrival, Poryes had been removed from the set in the middle of production one afternoon, as one source recalled, literally kicking and screaming. "I was railroaded," Poryes said. "Disney did not handle it correctly . . . It was done in a classless, embarrassing way." Poryes said he was blindsided by his firing and had hoped to continue to have a role on the series in at least a consulting capacity, but Rinsler and Warren weren't interested.

"It was right up there with Trump conceding to Biden," Savel said. "There was no peaceful transfer of power."

SENSITIVITY AND INCLUSIVITY, even if underbaked by today's standards, were crucial to Disney Channel's programming of the time. And the *That's So Raven* cast reflected what Rich Ross once called a "thrilling" move to mirror the reality of the network's diverse audience on screen. *The Famous Jett Jackson* paved the way, and Disney Channel had recently debuted the original animated series *The Proud Family* in 2001. That show was about a Black family, voiced by Black actors, and helmed by Black showrunners Bruce W. Smith and Ralph Farquhar. Now, with *Raven*, they had a flagship live-action sitcom with an almost completely Black principal cast.

But although *That's So Raven* had shifted focus to a Black family when Raven was recast as the lead, its showrunners and top-billed creatives remained starkly white. For all the public platitudes about representation on the network, during the first season of *That's So Raven*, there were no Black writers in the writers' room.

"I think that was a mistake on my part," Poryes said, noting that "none" of the potential writers that were suggested to him were Black. "What I should have done was cast the best writers I could find, and then find Black writers that I felt had potential and bring them on and mentor them. I regret that."

An exception to the off-camera whitewashing in the early days was Eric Dean Seaton, a Black, young-and-hungry stage manager (a job that's also known as the first assistant director, or AD) who had worked on the sitcoms *Smart Guy*, *Eve*, and *Girlfriends*. While he really wanted to direct, the best opportunity for Black creatives at the time often meant finding work on a Black-led show as an AD.

"The onus was if you have a Black cast, you get Black ADs because you need someone who can talk to the cast," Seaton said. "You can look back at the history of a lot of shows of color and see very few directors of color, very few crew members of color. *Moesha* was an exception. *The Parkers* was an exception. But women or people of color were not something that was encouraged or hired."

Disney Channel honored Raven's requests to have a Black hair and makeup team for her own needs, but most Black barbers weren't unionized at the time, and union rules prevented those barbers from being employed by the network on unionized sets (which most Disney Channel series were). That meant the Black male cast members were left to figure out their hair on their own, or take their chances with the provided hairdressers. Some opted to have their personal barbers come to their dressing rooms or go off site to a barbershop instead.

"Think of the lead Black actors on the show having to get their hair cut in their dressing rooms. That happened for five years," Seaton said. "Orlando, Rondell, Kyle. It was atrocious. The people that are in the hair room can't do their hair, yet you won't let in people who can."

After the new showrunners Marc Warren and Dennis Rinsler arrived, they set about diversifying the *Raven* writers' room with Black writers for season 2 and beyond. They hired people like Al Sonja Rice, who'd worked on shows including *The Parent 'Hood* and *In Living Color*, Edward C. Evans from *The Jamie Foxx Show* and *Living Single*, and Michael Carrington, who had started as a standup comic before becoming a voice actor on several episodes of *The Simpsons* and a writer on a slew of Black-led network sitcoms including *Martin* and *The Sinbad Show*. By season 2, Carrington said, "*Raven* was the most African American writers I've had in a writers' room, maybe ever."

The legendary Debbie Allen directed multiple episodes, as did Seaton, and Carrington penned a season 3 Black History Month episode called "True Colors" directed by Raven's dad. Inspired by a much-publicized 2003 discrimination lawsuit against Abercrombie & Fitch, "True Colors" went beyond honoring historic African Americans and blatantly called out contemporary systemic racism when Raven Baxter becomes the victim of a racist hiring manager at the mall. As was standard when episodes dealt with culturally sensitive issues, a consultant was brought in to help oversee the material and shape the plot. "Originally, I pictured that Raven [Baxter] would come back in whiteface and get hired that way," Carrington said, "but the consultant said, 'No, no. Come up with a scenario where she can still be a Black person and solve the problem.'"

THAT'S SO RAVEN was originally expected to premiere in early 2002, about a year after Lizzie's debut. But the tumultuous creative changes contributed to delaying its run until after the entire first season had been shot. "When we did that first year and it didn't air, I thought, 'Well, this is never going to see the light of day,'" co-star T'Keyah Crystal Keymáh told MadameNoire years later.

When the show finally premiered in January 2003, it was another instant hit and quickly began drawing around two million viewers an episode. By season 3, it was averaging three million—surpassing Lizzie McGuire—and the 2005 two-part special episode "Country Cousins" (in which makeup, prosthetics, and computer magic helped Raven play an uncle, elderly aunt, and a baby, in addition to her usual role) brought in more than four million viewers.

A new Disney Channel formula had been born, and its loud colors and louder line deliveries would define the network for the next decade. That's So Raven marked a dramatic departure from Lizzie McGuire and Even Stevens in look and feel. Raven leaned in to broad physical comedy, numerous pratfalls, and ample use of a laugh track. (The latter effect was dubbed over the actual kids' laughter from the live audience, which would inevitably dwindle after the second or third take.) And Disney Channel's initial crop of female-driven comedy series—Lizzie, Raven, and the animated Kim Possible—was attracting loyal viewers and fueling Disney Channel to dominate as the number one basic cable channel for kids nine to fourteen in prime time.

Backstage, with the new creative team in place, *That's So Raven* became "the most well-run machine you've ever seen," writer and producer Dava Savel said. The crew went from pulling all-nighters to clocking out when the clock struck 6:00 P.M. But it wasn't without its difficulties. In a post-*Lizzie* world, the network executives had increasingly begun to care about what was happening on their shows, and the notes began to flow. Excessively. A stable of mid- and lower-level network executives shuffled back and forth from Burbank to *Raven's* Hollywood lot, circulating feedback between the two sides.

"It became a game. You didn't really have to address the notes. You just had to acknowledge them somehow," Warren said. "But the stuff we got away with on *Even Stevens*? Forget it."

Micromanaging was rampant. The network executives wanted input on everything from the colors of various props to which actor got cast for a two-line role. The inordinate oversight was a greater Disney tradition going back decades. When *Raven* producer Walter Barnett worked on the early-nineties Disney Channel series *Adventures in Wonderland*, he said they had "monthly meetings with Michael Eisner and Jeffrey Katzenberg on details as small as the Mad Hatter's buttons on his jacket."

Now, on the *That's So Raven* set (which filmed at Hollywood Center Studios in season 2 and beyond), most of the network executives, from Gary Marsh on down, joined the show's Wednesday run-throughs to offer their input. "The Disney Channel feedback was like no other feedback I'd ever seen, and haven't seen since," Seaton said. "When they would give notes, they would give notes line by line, page by page."

For example, in a season 2 episode the writers needed a reason for Victor Baxter to exit a restaurant scene so that chaos could unfold. The script had him leave to go pick up a party clown to bring to the event. Back came a network executive's note: "Wouldn't the clown drive himself?"

"It was a silly note," Warren said. "Like some kid's going to be sitting home going, 'Hey, wait a second, wouldn't the clown drive himself? This episode's terrible! We hate the show!'"

The physical nature of the comedy on *Raven* provided another level of complication. Original series head Adam Bonnett had an obsession with using Raven's physical comedy gifts to channel the legendary Lucille Ball. He left books about the black-and-white series in the writers' room and urged the staff to watch reruns of the classic sitcom. "We have a Lucy here," he'd enthuse. "And that's what you've got to give us, more Lucy!"

The structure of each episode was such that it culminated in a zany block comedy sketch, often involving an elaborate and messy gag. And production designer Jerry Dunn, who had previously worked on *Mad About You* and *The Nanny*, needed to create the magic on a shoestring budget. He was initially given only a single carpenter, a painter, and a couple of thousand dollars a week to build the sets. "The expectations of the Disney Channel were extreme," Dunn said. "They were pretty ridiculous with what they wanted versus what they wanted to spend."

The crew had to get creative. But somehow, they made it work. Like in season 3, when they shot an outlandish scene where Raven goes to a natural history museum and falls into a giant exhibit on the human stomach—rather than build an entirely new museum set, they just shot it on the neighboring lobby set of *The Suite Life of Zack & Cody*.

"Would I have loved to pay people more? Of course, that's a given," former Disney Channel president Anne Sweeney said. "But we made do with what we had. And I really think that, salaries aside, a lot of great creativity came out of doing less and really focusing on what we had in our hand."

By THE TIME she starred on *That's So Raven*, Raven had more experience in movies, TV, and music than many veteran adult performers. "We used to write the craziest shit for her," Savel said. "We wrote the show backwards, starting with the big block comedy scene, and then figured out how she got there. Because nobody did physical comedy like Raven."

On set, Raven would listen as directors explained the scenes, then nod in quiet understanding when they finished. She'd rehearse each scene barefoot on stage, ready to throw herself completely into whatever zany antics the scene called for. "Literally, from her toes on up, every part of her was in it. She would act with her toes," writer and producer Michael Feldman said. "She used her entire body as a tool." And when it was time to perform for the cameras, she sprang to life and surpassed expectations. "Whatever was funny, she would make ten times funnier," Seaton said.

Raven won five NAACP Image Awards and two Kids' Choice Awards for her work on *That's So Raven*. But for her, the performances are all a blur. "I do not remember as soon as the camera starts," she told TV One in 2021. "Something clicks off and I do what I'm trained to do." When she turned eighteen, Raven started going to therapy and learned that she disassociates completely while acting. "I black out," she said. "I turn into who I'm supposed to be when the camera's on, and I come back to when 'normal' life resumes."

When she wasn't in character, Raven took the time to study all the moving parts of the production, shadowing various crew members and learning the art of TV making. "Everybody wants to be a writer or a director. Nobody wants to be a line producer [the person in charge of managing a show's episodic budget]," *Raven* line producer Patty Gary Cox said. "But she was interested in knowing what I did. That amazed me. It all mattered to her. It wasn't just her little world, it was how she fit into the big picture of the world around her."

DURING A TIME when lithe Victoria's Secret models were exalted as the ideal build for thirteen-year-olds in suburbia to strive for, Raven's mere presence as the dazzling, curvy lead on a kids' series was revolutionary. "I want to bring a new beauty to television," she told the *Los Angeles Times* in 2006. "I would love to bring what normal people look like to the screen. I would love to watch people who look like me."

But Raven wasn't immune to critiques. When she was a young kid on *The Cosby Show*, she was shamed for craving bagels and other food on offer at the on-set catering table (known as craft services) and said someone on that set once told her she was "getting fat." By 2003, when she was seventeen and working on *Raven* and *The Cheetah Girls*, she was on the Zone diet. Raven has said her dad suggested she get a breast reduction, and she ended up having two reductions and liposuction before she turned eighteen.

And when she pursued her singing career, she endured negative feedback while touring; comments like how she "was too big to be doing an hour and a half concert," and "I don't know how she can dance being that big." At the time, she publicly laughed off any pressure. "My fans know I love my cheese grits with shrimp, and I'm not giving them up to be a size two," Raven said in 2005. "I don't even worry about that type of stuff that much."

But some inside Disney HQ *were* worried. "There was a lot of shit going on because Raven had a propensity to gain weight," Savel said. "Disney Channel was going crazy about it. And they handled it in really bad ways. But it was never to her face."

While shooting the second season of *That's So Raven*, Raven was eager to do an episode that centered on her character's body insecurities. In "That's So Not Raven," a thinner model is chosen over Raven Baxter to appear in a fashion show, and she embarks on a crash plan to lose weight. But, by the end of the episode, Raven decides her body is perfect just as it is and confidently struts the runway. It was a powerful message of body inclusivity at a time when it wasn't the norm. But according to multiple people involved in the episode, a network executive instructed the show's visual effects team to manipulate the footage to make Raven appear thinner in the episode's final scenes. The rationale seemed to be that it wasn't believable for Raven to look the same weight at the end of the episode, after her character had spent a week doing intense dieting and exercise.

"It was shameful," Feldman said. "I don't know how they could look at themselves and do that. The very thing that she wanted to do a story about was literally done to her. It's still a shocking thing to me that they were that tone-deaf." (Adam Bonnett did not recall any such edits being made on that particular episode and said it's "not something I would have asked for," though he did remember the same postproduction technique being employed in a latter episode where Raven attends a school dance. "There was some stuff done to make Raven['s attire] look more flattering in certain scenes," he said, noting that "flattering" is a subjective term and that they "wanted to protect Raven.")

Disney Channel wasn't unique in monitoring the weight of its stars—"I was on an ABC show once and the star walked in, and there was a StairMaster and boxes and boxes of Atkins bars," Savel said. "They didn't say anything. They just put it in her dressing room"—but the fact that Disney's talent were teens and kids made the physical assessments more appalling. "I was in my own turmoil of weight battles," Raven has said, looking back on the *Raven* years. "I'm like, 'Dang, y'all got it good nowadays. Y'all got it so much better. You guys can embrace your body without judgment of anything.'"

Raven also knew she was "not straight" from age twelve, but it would be another decade before she publicly came out. Until then, Raven was pushed to conform to a specific type of feminine mold at public appearances. "I remember that I wore Abercrombie & Fitch jeans, a stereotypical lesbian vest, a tie," Raven told *Variety* in 2019, "and one of the members of my team went up to my mom and was like, 'She looks too much like a lesbian. Can you tell her to put on a skirt and makeup? Because then they'll accept her and come to her concert.'"

Much had changed by the time Raven reprised her iconic role for the *Raven's Home* reboot on Disney Channel in 2017, when, she said, the network offered to make Raven Baxter a lesbian in a nod to the actual Raven's now-public queerness. She declined, saying it didn't make sense for the character. "Disney understood me," she told the *Los Angeles Times* in 2018. "They knew it's not about my sexual orientation. It's about having fun, it's about family, it's about comedy, it's about good content . . . I love them forever for embracing me."

FOR MOST OF *That's So Raven*'s run, an imposing figure stood just off camera: Raven's father, Christopher B. Pearman. He doubled as Raven's manager and had been an instrumental part of her career since her toddler days on *The Cosby Show*. While Rich Ross, who took over the Disney Channel presidency in 2004, described Raven's mom, Lydia, as "one of my all-star moms" who "allowed her to have a safe place to grow," Chris was more complicated.

Many who worked on *Raven* described Chris as a nice guy who was fun to be around but who also appeared to have a tendency to be controlling and self-serving. "There are certain parents that are there for their kids. And certain parents that are there for themselves," Poryes said. "He walked the line. He was very hard on her."

Chris had co-produced the *Raven* theme song and negotiated a consultant credit for himself on the show, and he also wanted to write and direct. He became a fixture in the writers' room and on the studio floor, and some wondered how much of Raven's earnings were being used to fund his own seemingly extravagant lifestyle.

When Raven turned eighteen, she had the power to remove her dad as her manager. And she did. "I can tell you exactly when it was," stage manager Eric Dean Seaton said. "It was whenever *Spider-Man 2* came out. We went to go see *Spider-Man 2*, and we got there a little early and were sitting outside. She said, 'Eric, I'm going to part ways with my dad.' Just a matter-of-fact sentence. I laughed, and she's like, 'No, I'm serious.' That was a Thursday or Friday. And by that Monday, he was gone."

Chris was rarely on set for the remaining episodes of the series, and Raven "was a lot more jovial after that," director of photography Alan K. Walker said. "We saw a change in her. She was a lot more relaxed, and her self-confidence rose up quite a bit."

Decades later, when asked on a podcast what institutionalized change she would implement for young performers, Raven said, "I truly believe that the parents should not be the managers of the children. They should be removed. The parents should be the parents and also keep a job and not live off the child while the child is working."

WHILE ON HIATUS from filming the first season of *That's So Raven*, Raven signed on to *The Cheetah Girls*, a Disney Channel Original Movie about four friends who become a superstar musical group. The film launched one of the network's most successful DCOM franchises, but it almost didn't happen.

After producing the groundbreaking Brandy- and Whitney Houston–led *Cinderella* for The Wonderful World of Disney, as well as *The Princess Diaries* for Walt Disney Pictures, Debra Martin Chase and her team had originally shopped the idea of a *Cheetah Girls* TV series to Disney Channel as part of Chase's overall deal with Disney. But with the focus increasingly on the expansion of Disney Channel in overseas markets, every potential new series needed to be run past the international team to assess its viability abroad.

"The international people were like, 'We don't believe these girls. We don't think these Black and brown girls would live on Park Avenue and lead this kind of lifestyle. So, we don't think we can sell this,'" Chase recalled. "Needless to say, I was furious."

Fortunately, the network's original movies weren't put through the same rigors—they didn't need to sustain year-round viewership, and the other markets could take or leave a one-off film. "Gary Marsh, to his credit, said, 'Look, I have less control over the TV series. But if you reboot this as a movie, I'd really like the movie,'" Chase said.

With Raven set as the anchor character Galleria, they cast two members of the real-life hip-hop girl group 3LW: Adrienne Bailon as Chanel; and Kiely Williams as Aqua. (Solange Knowles was initially cast to play Aqua, but her dad pulled her before production began so that she could focus on her solo singing career.) "Adrienne had never read a script before. She came in [to audition] and read all of the stage directions with her lines," Chase said. "But she had that sparkle and that energy."

And though the main characters in Deborah Gregory's book series (on which the film was based) are Black, Latina, or mixed race, Chase said she pushed for the fourth lead to be played by a white girl on screen. "I wanted every girl to see themselves in the Cheetah Girls," the producer said. So, she cast blond and bubbly Sabrina Bryan, whose strength was her dance experience, as Dorinda. It wasn't until later that Chase learned Sabrina was partly of Mexican-Spanish descent and her actual last name was Hinojos.

Cheetah Girls was groundbreaking in terms of representation on screen and behind the camera: it featured Black and Latina stars, a Black director (Oz Scott), writer (Alison Taylor), and executive producers, including Chase and her producing partner Whitney Houston. That dynamic proved powerful to viewers. "*The Cheetah Girls* was the first movie I saw that specifically glamorized Black and brown girls' dreams," Zeniya Cooley wrote in a Refinery29 article on the film's twentieth anniversary. "It declared that my goals were worthy of glittery outros, fairy-lit bedrooms, and cityscape backdrops."

When they shot the New York–set film over three weeks in Toronto in the fall of 2002, the biting Canadian air led to some of the movie's most memorable looks, born out of necessity to keep the young cast warm as the temperature dropped. Costume designer Resa McConaghy configured the big finale's velour tracksuits to double as crucial heat incubators. She layered a thin set of thermals underneath and added matching vests, head-warmers, and gloves to protect the talent. And, yes, she's aware that most of the "cheetah" patterns seen on costumes throughout the film are actually leopard print. "If we had only done cheetah, I would have had to paint them by hand," she said of the print's scarcity.

Between takes, Raven was the most reserved of the four stars and preferred to focus on her work. But when they were all together, the girls loved to belt a cappella renditions of Houston's "I Will Always Love You" at every turn. Adrienne would start the refrain and the others would fall into line. "In the makeup chairs, in the transport vans to set," makeup artist Shauna Llewellyn said. "They loved to hold the 'I' in 'I will always love you' for as long as they could."

On set, director Oz Scott pushed the film beyond what was expected and tried to incorporate believable pop star elements throughout. "MTV really affected our style of filming, where it became more handheld, more cinéma vérité," he said. "I said, 'The audience is watching music videos, guys. Let's lean into it.'" The network brought in the songwriting and producing team of brothers Greg and Ray Cham, who had also created a slate of original tracks for the 2002 America Ferrera–led dance DCOM *Gotta Kick It Up!*, to work on the music. But despite investing in song rights and hiring songwriters to create original tracks for the film,

Walt Disney Records didn't originally plan to release a *Cheetah Girls* soundtrack. No DCOM had ever received a standalone soundtrack at that point, and when they invited label executive Jay Landers to screen an early cut of the film and determine its soundtrack potential, Chase remembered him initially dismissing it. "He was like, 'I don't get this movie. I don't really see it,'" she said.

It wasn't until just weeks before the film's release in August 2003 that the label hesitantly decided to release the film's eight tracks on CD and cassette. Requests for the songs poured into Radio Disney, and the album ended up going double platinum. Imitating the concurrent success of Hilary Duff's record releases and concert tours, Disney eventually worked with The Cheetah Girls to record six albums and embark on multiple national tours. They were a tween sensation.

In 2006, Disney filmed *The Cheetah Girls 2* on location in Barcelona, making use of tax credits in Spain and the opportunity to bolster Disney Channel's European market presence. They brought in director Kenny Ortega, fresh off of *High School Musical*, to oversee the sequel, and Raven was made an executive producer. But whatever harmony had occurred between the actors on the Toronto set of the first *Cheetah Girls* evaporated in Barcelona.

A distinct divide had formed between Raven and the other three girls. "Raven was a significant star, and the other three felt like they were the stars," one of the sequel's choreographers Chucky Klapow said. "I just remember constant tension. I remember the girls being mean to Raven. I remember Raven couldn't stand the girls. It was very intense, very serious. It was a constant political battle of trying to calm everybody down and just get through this movie."

It became two cliques: Adrienne, Kiely, and Sabrina versus Raven and Belinda Peregrin, who played the Spanish singer Marisol. By the time filming wrapped, Raven was over the drama. She did not sign on for the third *Cheetah Girls* film—shot in India to forge a stronger alliance with the valuable South Asian market and help the network's expansion there—or travel with the other girls for an eighty-plus-date concert tour in 2006. "I don't think I was surprised, but I was disappointed," Chase said of Raven's departure. But Disney wasn't willing to let a successful franchise go just because Raven walked away. They simply pushed on with The Cheetah Girls as a trio.

In a post-*Lizzie* world, every Disney Channel project was a potential lucrative franchise opportunity. There were *Cheetah Girls* and *That's So Raven* merchandise lines targeted at nine- to fourteen-year-old girls that included fragrance, makeup, dolls, books, Game Boy Advance games, and a Macy's partnership. The *Raven* products alone were estimated to bring in nearly $400 million by 2006.

But while the power of Disney Channel grew and stars like Hilary Duff, and later Miley Cyrus, Selena Gomez, and Demi Lovato, landed on the covers of major magazines, Raven struggled to transcend the Disney Channel bubble. At her nineteenth birthday party, when *That's So Raven* was in the middle of airing its third season, only a solitary paparazzo showed up outside the celebratory venue. "It was so sad," Raven told *Newsweek* writer Allison Samuels in 2005. "I mean, I was dressed up and ready to party and not one flash went off. My mom is always telling me not to leave the house with my sweats and T-shirts that might have jam from breakfast on them. But I know they don't even know who I am."

In that article, titled "Why Not Raven?," Samuels wondered, "Anyone who's stood in line at a supermarket knows who Paris, Jessica, Mary-Kate, Ashley, Hilary and Lindsay are. Too many late nights and too little body fat, a surfeit of fast cash and a bare minimum of clothing have made them tabloid princesses. So why aren't the tabs on a first-name basis with Raven? . . . Could it be—we're just taking a wild guess here—because Symoné is African-American, not even close to a size 2 and prefers sweats and T-shirts to Dolce & Gabbana?"

On Disney Channel, *That's So Raven* didn't receive an accompanying theatrical movie like *Lizzie* or even a Disney Channel Original Movie like *Even Stevens* and *Jett Jackson* did before it. Several of the *Raven* writers worked on a treatment for an announced 2007 *That's So Raven* DCOM that would have seen Raven go to fashion school, but it didn't materialize.

And *Cheetah Girls* was an ensemble project. Walt Disney Studios did develop two star vehicles for Raven in the form of an *Adventures in Babysitting* sequel and an adaptation of Meg Cabot's novel *All-American Girl*, about a teen who saves the US president, but both iterations withered on the vine. (*Adventures in Babysitting* would eventually happen as a 2016 DCOM starring Sabrina Carpenter and Sofia Carson.) Raven was also set to star in Warner Brothers' remake of *Sparkle* but that likewise fell apart, and the role eventually went to Jordin Sparks.

While Raven's music made it onto the *Princess Diaries 2* and *Ice Princess* soundtracks, her two solo albums with Hollywood Records failed to crack the Top 50 of the Billboard 200. (Hilary, Miley, Selena, and Demi's albums at the label all made it to the Top 10, and often to number one.) "Raven had a whole different view of her career than we did," former Hollywood Records general manager Abbey Konowitch said, noting that Raven wanted "to go a lot faster into the R&B world" and "expand quicker than the brand wanted her to expand." He added, "That made it much more difficult for her to be successful."

Selena Gomez would later voice her own frustration at not being allowed to incorporate hip-hop influences on her Hollywood Records albums because she was "too young." And music producer Greg Cham, who worked on the *That's So Raven* and *Cheetah Girls* soundtracks, surmised that, when it came to hip-hop and R&B, Disney "loved the sound; they didn't love the culture."

Outside of Disney, the opportunities for Raven were likewise skewed. When *Vanity Fair* put together their memorable It's TOTALLY RAINING TEENS issue in July 2003, Hilary Duff, Mandy Moore, Amanda Bynes, and the Olsen twins made the front cover, while Raven—the only Black star included in the nine-person cover shoot—was relegated to the fold-out flap. (She and fellow inside-cover star Lindsay Lohan struck up a friendship at the shoot that led them to become roommates for a time.) "She's a Black girl. To me, it just wasn't the same," *Raven* stage manager and director Eric Dean Seaton said. "I don't know that she had the launching pad the same way they did."

*   *   *

WHEN HILARY DUFF'S star power grew, *Lizzie McGuire* had to be cut off at sixty-five episodes. As *That's So Raven* reached that pivotal episodic threshold, Disney Channel had another obvious hit that made sense to extend. "It was the type of show that was built to be able to continue," Rich Ross said. "It re-ran really well. The physical comedy worked for boys and girls. It worked for everyone, and we needed content."

The threat of losing Raven to non-Disney projects wasn't as high as it had been with Hilary, and they were able to retain her for a fourth season with the addition of a producer credit. Most of the ensemble cast returned, except for T'Keyah Crystal Keymáh, who played Raven's mom and left to care for her grandmother who was suffering from Alzheimer's. She had also expressed frustration at the lack of material for her character. "As talented as T'Keyah was, there wasn't much for her to do," Seaton said. Just like that, matriarch Tanya Baxter was written off, leaving her family behind as she moved to London to go to law school.

Immediately after production on that final season of *That's So Raven* wrapped in 2006, many of the creatives went to work on the show's spinoff series. Disney Channel had experimented with a planted spinoff starring Alyson Stoner (see: the season 3 *Raven* episode "Goin' Hollywood"), and there had been talks about another version of the show that would follow Raven Baxter to college, but the former was too similar to *Hannah Montana* and the latter was quickly deemed too mature for the network.

Instead, showrunners Marc Warren and Dennis Rinsler returned to oversee *Cory in the House,* and actors Kyle Massey and Rondell Sheridan reprised their roles as little brother Cory and patriarch Victor Baxter, with the premise that Victor gets a job working as a chef in the White House and Cory joins him in the nation's capital. The series premiered to a massive 7.6 million viewers in January 2007, but beyond those initial numbers, *Cory* largely failed to re-create the *That's So Raven*'s magic without, well, Raven. Still, it was doing well enough and was intended to have a full three-season run. Then, near-catastrophe struck.

A season 2 episode involved a scene where Cory goes overboard on a large boat. On a network show, the budget might have allowed the production to buy a boat, saw off the underbelly and fin, and sit the vessel on the soundstage floor. But a Disney Channel budget could only stretch so far. Their boat was a rental, so they couldn't physically alter it. To get the shot, they needed to keep the boat perched atop its trailer to stay upright.

According to Warren, the plan was for Kyle to say his lines at the edge of the boat, then a stuntperson would step in to leap off the side of the boat and drop onto a stack of thick, padded mats below. Instead, Kyle jumped over the edge of the boat himself. "Kyle thought it would be really funny if he did the fall," Warren said. "So we yell 'cut.' He says, 'I'm doing it!' And he falls off the boat." (Production designer Jerry Dunn and that episode's director, Eric Dean Seaton, recalled that Kyle had permission to do the jump himself.)

Kyle, who was sixteen years old at the time, hit the mats at an angle, rolled off, and smacked his head on the hard floor. He was rushed to the hospital, trailed by concerned members of the crew. "That was the lowest moment of my career," Seaton said. "It was just a freak accident." Once medically cleared, Kyle returned to set to continue filming additional episodes of the series. (The Masseys eventually sued the production company and some of those involved in 2010 and alleged that Kyle suffered ongoing physical and mental pain for years after the fall, but the case was dismissed by the parties before any proceedings.)

With the accident tension simmering, the 2007–2008 writers' strike sealed *Cory in the House*'s fate. Production had to go on hiatus, and it never resumed. "The show kind of just fizzled out on a bad note between the accident, the [threat of the] lawsuit, the writers' strike," Rinsler said. "When it came time to settle the strike and get back to work, [the network] said to us, 'No more, we're done.' And *Cory* was canceled."

DURING ITS RUN, *That's So Raven* received a host of NAACP Image Awards and two prime-time Emmy nominations for Outstanding Children's Program. It lost the Emmy in 2005 to a Linda Ellerbee special for Nickelodeon about the Holocaust, and again in 2007 to an Ellerbee episode of *Nick News* about autistic children. But *Raven*'s impact was bigger than any hardware.

As the show succeeded, it proved *Lizzie McGuire* hadn't been just a random fluke. "Once an ugly stepchild, the Disney Channel has become a prized possession for the larger corporation," *Fortune* declared. Bonnett began sending tapes of *Raven* episodes to potential creatives to lure them to Disney Channel and show them the exact kind of multi-cam comedy he'd like them to re-create in future series. And during production breaks on *Raven*, its crew members worked on pilots for new Disney Channel series, including *The Suite Life of Zack & Cody*, *Hannah Montana*, and *Wizards of Waverly Place*. When production on *Raven* ended in 2006, many of those individuals moved over to the new series, ensuring a cohesive look and feel to Disney Channel's multi-cam ventures.

"People always talk about *Lizzie McGuire*, *Even Stevens*—and those were great shows that got us a lot of attention," Bonnett told the *Los Angeles Times*, "but it wasn't until *That's So Raven* came on that we really exploded."

7

The Suite (and Not-So-Sweet) *Life*

Disney Channel had a boy problem. In the 2000s, Disney Channel's audience was skewing about 60 percent female and 40 percent male. In the binary terms of consumer research, male viewers still preferred Nickelodeon and Cartoon Network, where action series thrived and on-screen burps, farts, and gross-out humor were not only tolerated but encouraged.

"We had the tween business, which was massive. We had the preschool business, which became massive, and then boys became third," former Disney Channel president Rich Ross said. "They were the hardest for us to get."

The data showed that tween boys did not want to buy merchandise that advertised their affinity for Disney Channel shows or its stars. Nor did they buy Disney Channel soundtracks or attend Disney-related concerts at the same rate as their female counterparts. Instead, they pledged their allegiance to video games. "We had a vast viewership, including boys," Ross stressed. "The problem was boys *acknowledging* they watched Disney Channel."

The Disney Channel executives tried to add a variety of goofy, high-energy male characters to pull boys in, even on shows that starred girls. Hence the existence of supporting characters Rico on *Hannah Montana* and Max on *Wizards of Waverly Place* as "ports of entry" for younger male viewers. "There was always a younger brother or friend," former Disney Channel PR head Patti McTeague said, "so that the sibling in the house, whose tween sister was watching and controlling the remote, had something they could relate to."

To further alleviate the boy problem, Disney created a separate programming block on the ABC Family and Toon Disney cable channels called Jetix in 2004, and they eventually rebranded the whole Toon Disney network into Disney XD, a platform aimed at boys aged six to fourteen but carefully billed as "boy-focused, girl-inclusive." Soon after Disney XD's launch, however, that brother channel likewise proved more popular with girls than boys.

But what Disney Channel lacked in an equal spread of viewers across genders, they made up for in inspiring zealous devotion from their female audience. "Every girl possible would be tuning in to what we had. We over indexed in a very big way," original programming executive Adam Bonnett said. "That maybe skewed our Nielsen numbers a little bit, but what it ended up doing was creating such a fever and passion for our content that you just couldn't deny."

Still, any potential Disney Channel show that could draw more boy viewers without isolating existing female viewers was exalted. Thus, hopes were high for *Phil of the Future*, a comedy about a time-traveling family who gets stuck in the present, with a tween boy in the title role. On *Phil*, however, the creatives were instructed to deploy broad sitcom comedy tropes within the series' single-camera framework. It was a confusing ask. "If we could go back and redo things, I would love to take a whack at *Phil of the Future* as a multi-camera show," Bonnett said.

Instead, the single-camera series, starring Raviv Ullman (who went by Ricky professionally at the time) and Aly Michalka, underwent several showrunner changeovers trying to find a formula that worked, until Disney Channel pulled the plug after just forty-three episodes. "If you know what big is, you know when you have something big," Ross said. "So, when shows did just okay, we said, that's life. You can't force it."

MEANWHILE, IN 2004, Irene Dreayer was on the hunt for new talent. The independent producer prided herself on her ability to sniff out potential superstars, who she would then bring to TV networks to develop

projects around. She'd previously found success with Tahj Mowry for
Smart Guy at The WB, and with his older twin sisters Tia and Tam-
era Mowry for *Sister, Sister*, which originally aired on ABC. When both
of those series started airing in syndication to great ratings on Disney
Channel, she called Bonnett to ask what talent the network needed for
their own new shows.

"Find me boy twins," Bonnett instructed.

Dreayer had recently seen the Adam Sandler film *Big Daddy* and
thought the young boy starring opposite Sandler could be worthy of a
show of his own. Given the frequency with which twins were employed
to play the same kid role, Dreayer wondered if that might be the case
here. She scanned the credits. Cole Sprouse *and* Dylan Sprouse. Perfect.

A further dive would reveal that the brothers had gotten their start
as toddlers in a shared role on the ABC sitcom *Grace Under Fire*. Cole
had also appeared as Ross's son on *Friends*. At eleven years old, the
boys were already established sitcom actors. Dreayer set up a meeting.
"Dylan and Cole were hysterically funny," Dreayer said. "We made the
deal right then and there."

Bonnett paired Dreayer and the twins with a hotel-set pilot that
Disney had bought from former *Who's the Boss?* producer Danny
Kallis and *Family Matters* producer Jim Geoghan, and tailored it to
fit the Sprouses. It marked the first and only time a Disney Channel series was specifically developed for new-to-the-network talent.
"What if two Bart Simpsons lived in a fancy hotel?" became the internal logline of the *Eloise*-inspired *The Suite Life of Zack & Cody*, about
twin boys named Zack (Dylan) and Cody (Cole) Martin growing up
in an upscale Boston hotel where their single mom works as a lounge
singer. Kallis and Geoghan had been shopping a version of *Suite Life*
to various networks for years. At one point, they'd even hoped a young
Alfonso Ribeiro would star as the hotel-dwelling kid with a lounge-
singer father.

Rather than bring in an outside production company, like how
Brookwell McNamara Entertainment had worked on *Even Stevens* and
That's So Raven, Disney Channel utilized its recently created inter-
nal division called It's a Laugh Productions, allowing them to further

streamline contracts, costs, and the need to involve outside parties on their series. (They had a similar setup for many of their DCOMS, which operated under various production company banners but were actually run by the same team.)

The *Suite Life* pilot beat out another potential show starring identical siblings: *Triple Play*, executive produced by *That's So Raven*'s Dava Savel and centered on identical triplets played by Alyssa, Kaitlyn, and Lauren Gainer—yet another set of lookalikes found by Dreayer. A young Zac Efron played their older brother. "Oh my God, I remember telling Zac Efron that it was not going ahead, and he was crying," Savel said. "He was so sweet. I swear to God, this is verbatim. I said, 'Zac, you are not meant to do television, sweetie. You are a movie star. And that's what you're going to do.'"

The Suite Life of Zack & Cody, which was set almost entirely within the fictional Tipton Hotel, was essentially Disney Channel's first workplace comedy. "We would talk about *The Suite Life* being our version of *Mary Tyler Moore* in a way," Bonnett said. "We wanted a place where everyone felt like a family even though they all just kind of worked together."

The hotel premise also allowed for an unusually robust cast of adult characters to rotate around the kids. There was Mr. Moseby, the uptight hotel manager played by Phill Lewis (they'd also considered putting Ribeiro in that role); Arwin, the hotel engineer played by Brian Stepanek; and the bellhop, Esteban, played by Adrian R'Mante. And after testing Jane Lynch, Debbie Gibson, and Taylor Dayne to play Zack and Cody's mom, Carey, they decided to cast Shakespearean theater actor Kim Rhodes.

Still, Disney made it clear that the adults were not to draw attention away from their younger co-stars. When Rhodes went to get her hair dyed to believably match the boys' sandy locks, she said the network sent over a color palette of the hotel's colors, with approved hues for her hair that would easily blend into the background.

The kids were the stars.

* * *

CRUCIALLY, *THE SUITE LIFE* also had the potential to be a "gender-neutral" show for viewers, thanks to boisterous boy leads and the substantial supporting roles of two slightly older, slightly aspirational female characters. "They wanted me to beat the pants off of *SpongeBob* and get boys," Kallis said. "Mind you, the day of the first script reading after they picked up the pilot, the executives came up to me and said, 'You realize this is really about Maddie and London, right?' They kept wanting to be reassured they wouldn't lose their girl viewers."

As Maddie, the smart and relatable every-girl working the candy counter in the hotel lobby, they cast Ashley Tisdale. And to play *Suite Life*'s spoiled hotel heiress London Tipton, a character inspired by Paris Hilton, they turned to veteran Disney Channel actor Brenda Song. The girls had originally auditioned for each other's parts but, Kallis said, "I just felt that Ashley would be the better Maddie and Brenda would be the better London—and, in no small measure, I was amused by the idea that the Asian character wasn't the brainiac."

Brenda grew up idolizing Cindy Crawford and dreaming of being on *Star Search*. Her Hmong dad and Thai mom had both immigrated from Thailand to Sacramento, where her mom had Brenda when she was just seventeen. Though the family didn't have much money, Brenda's grandmother emptied her savings account to put Brenda in acting lessons. By the time Brenda was six, her mom was driving her the five-and-a-half hours back and forth from Sacramento to L.A. for auditions. And when Brenda was fifteen, she graduated high school through homeschooling and got accepted to Harvard University just as she booked *The Suite Life of Zack & Cody*.

She turned down Harvard to do the show. As a result, "I didn't go to my first house party until I was twenty," she later told *Glamour*. "I saw marijuana for the first time and thought it was potpourri and threw it away. That's how naïve I was."

On the *Suite Life* set, Brenda was always on time, exceedingly polite, and memorized her lines at lightning speed. On breaks, she'd chat with the crew about literature and practice punch lines with Kim Rhodes. Everyone loved her. "Dylan had an insane crush on Brenda. It was very sweet," producer and writer Jeny Quine said. "There was one episode where London was dating someone, and we were like, let's keep Dylan off the set because he did not want to see his beloved kissing someone else." Brenda could make funny scenes hysterical, like when Moseby taught London to drive and asked her if she knew how to use the shifter. "Oh, you mean the PRNDL?" she replied, innocently sounding out the word as "prindle." It was sitcom comedy gold.

Brenda had first come into the Disney Channel fold with a co-starring role in the 2000 Disney Channel Original Movie *The Ultimate Christmas Present*. That had led to a supporting role behind Lindsay Lohan in the 2002 DCOM *Get a Clue*, another supporting part on *Phil of the Future*, and yet another supporting role in the 2004 DCOM *Stuck in the Suburbs*. But it was only in the 2006 DCOM *Wendy Wu: Homecoming Warrior* that she received top billing. "I don't think they felt they could do a show where an Asian character could carry the title role," casting director Joey Paul Jensen said. "They always saw her as being part of an ensemble. I just don't think it was in the ethos at the time." Still, Brenda has praised the network for "giving this little Asian American girl a chance in Hollywood," she told *W* in 2019. "They were giving me my own TV movies when people weren't doing that."

Throughout the 2000s and beyond, the executives calling the shots on who did or didn't get to be Disney Channel stars were overwhelmingly white. And as much as Disney was lauded at the time for diversifying their on-screen representation, there were still cultural and ethnic stereotypes and skewed opportunities playing out in their shows—like having American-born actors perform with pronounced Spanish and Indian accents on *Suite Life* and *Jessie*, and reducing the already rare roles played by Black actors during *Hannah Montana*'s run (Frances Callier, as Roxy the bodyguard, and Andre Jamal Kinney, as Jackson's best friend Cooper, both disappeared by that show's third season).

While *Suite Life* was still in production, Brenda began branching out from Disney and exploring theatrical movie roles. She auditioned for Clint Eastwood's 2008 film *Gran Torino*—a role that would have let her speak Hmong on screen—but, she said, Disney didn't allow her to move forward because of an implied rape that takes place in the film. Many of the Disney Channel actors' contracts included verbiage that prevented them from pursuing outside projects that were "inconsistent in content, taste, and sensibilities with the traditional and family-oriented values" of the Disney Channel brand, unless they obtained express written permission from the network.

Brenda pushed again in 2009, auditioning for and winning a role in David Fincher's *The Social Network* that included a scene hooking up with Andrew Garfield in a bathroom stall. Again, Disney Channel pushed back. Gary Marsh "did not want her to do that movie," said *Suite Life* creative consultant Billy Riback, recalling a conversation he'd had with Brenda. "She said, 'You don't understand. I'm not asking for permission. I'd like your blessing.' And [Marsh] went, 'Well, you do not have my blessing.' She did it anyway. And she was great."

For Dylan and Cole Sprouse, the *Suite Life* set provided a stability they had yet to know in their young lives. "A lot had happened in our lives that was difficult then," Dylan posted on Instagram in 2020, "and this show, in a way, saved us."

The boys had been born in Italy, where their parents, Melanie Wright and Matthew Sprouse, were teaching art and physical education at an English language school. Several months later, the family moved back to Long Beach, California, and before the twins turned one year old, Melanie and Matthew had split, and Dylan and Cole were acting professionally. "My mother needed an income," Cole said on the *Call Her Daddy* podcast in 2023. "It started really as a means to put bread on the table."

As production on the *Suite Life* pilot began, it was clear that Melanie, who had signed the twins' contracts and was serving as their guardian, was struggling with mental health and addiction issues. "The night of the pilot, I got very concerned about their mom," showrunner Danny Kallis said. "I said, here's what we do. I'll let Disney know. We'll put them up at the hotel right up the block. Tell the boys simply that we don't want to risk them being late. And let's get them out of the house for the next two weeks while the parents figure out what to do." By the time regular production on the series was underway in late 2004, their dad, Matthew, had been assigned sole custody.

Frequent *Suite Life* director Rich Correll had experience working with young twin performers, having already directed Mary-Kate and Ashley Olsen on their various shows since they were nine months old. (The only time the girls were ever late to set, he said, was when they bought a Learjet on their *So Little Time* lunch break and had trouble deciding the color of the interior.) Because he'd also been a child actor, Correll said he was intent on fostering a fun, family atmosphere at work and making sure the young stars felt safe and loved. He and his wife, Beth Correll, who served as an assistant director on *Suite Life*, took Dylan and Cole under their wing during production. "My wife was like their surrogate mother," Rich said. "They still, to this day, send her Mother's Day cards."

Rather than commute back to their dad's house in the Valley each night during shoot weeks, the Sprouses would periodically stay at the Corrells' home, which was a four-minute drive from the studio. Rich was an avid collector of horror and sci-fi memorabilia, so the house was filled with artifacts from Hollywood hits. There was also a movie theater, a ground-level trampoline, a zip line into the pool, and a garage full of go-karts. At Halloween, the Corrells opened up their home to the public to tour the memorabilia, and the boys (as well as Miley Cyrus and other network stars) would often dress up in costumes and scare the unsuspecting visitors. On at least one occasion, the *Suite Life* cast went to the Playboy Mansion to see the elaborate Halloween decorations that Rich orchestrated there every year. "It was during the afternoon," said Adrian R'Mante of an outing he said he went on with the Sprouses, Brenda, Ashley, and the Corrells, stressing that it was a "work environment" as they toured the grounds, including the infamous grotto.

Years later, when producer Adam Lapidus ran into Cole at one of Rich's Halloween parties in the late 2010s, Lapidus recalled Cole telling him "that us and Rich and Beth really gave [him and Dylan] the support and the family that they needed at the time. I was crying, because you hear so many horror stories. The fact that them being on the show was actually something that helped them was so heartwarming."

As was the case with many of those who worked on Disney Channel shows, *The Suite Life* crew said they viewed their role as going beyond that of mere creative contributors. "It's more than just a show, you're creating an environment," said line producer Patty Gary Cox, who had a reputation for being a comforting "mother hen" on her sets. "These kids are going to remember this. The things that we create on stage are things that they'll take with them forever, and you want it to be positive."

But sometimes the kids were the ones having to act like adults. Both Sprouses were known to be protective of those around them and seemed to sharply discern the power they wielded as stars of the show. Rather than use that power to act out and make demands, they took it upon themselves to speak up for their much older crew and co-stars. "I cuss like a sailor, and there was a very brief period of time early on where someone had a problem with that and was really going to make it a big problem for me," Kim Rhodes said. "The boys were like, 'We worked with Adam Sandler. There's not a word we haven't heard. Stop it.'"

Later, Rhodes became pregnant in real life during the show's third season. Rather than write the storyline into the show—an unwed pregnant mom was simply a bridge too far for Disney Channel—the scripts occasionally made jabs acknowledging her character's weight gain. Again, the boys stepped in. "There was this line that Dylan was supposed to say about 'Mom putting on weight,' and he kept skipping it in rehearsals," Rhodes said. "Finally, in front of the studio audience, he got called out. We were like, 'Say your line!' And he said, 'No, I would never disrespect my mother that way. I will not disrespect Kimmy that way.'"

Another quintessential memory for Rhodes was when Ashley Tisdale refused to leave her side at a red-carpet premiere where Rhodes, who has since learned that she is autistic, said her "crippling social anxiety" started flaring up. "Ashley took my hand, and she said, 'I've got you,'" Rhodes recalled. "She didn't tell people why she was doing it, but she didn't step away from me. She held my hand the entire length of that red carpet, and I don't know what would have happened to me if she hadn't been there."

Other times, the twins pulled co-stars into publicity opportunities they wouldn't otherwise have been part of. "At a photo shoot, they'd go, 'Where's Adrian? He's supposed to be here. We want Adrian,'" said

R'Mante, who played Esteban. "There are some iconic marketing photos that were used for years of us on the little bellhop carts. I was in those photos because Cole Sprouse pulled me in and included me."

Outside of Disney, the Sprouses' management team was busy attempting to make them the next Mary-Kate and Ashley Olsen. At age thirteen, they signed with the Olsens' Dualstar Entertainment and launched their own deodorant, hair gel, sportswear, and a magazine. But unlike Raven and Hilary, the Sprouses had zero interest in pursuing a singing career—though they were roped into a Disney Channel Circle of Stars rendition of "A Dream Is a Wish Your Heart Makes." "Dylan and Cole from day one were like, 'We do not sing,'" *Suite Life* producer Adam Lapidus said. "They were adamant about that. They said, 'Don't try. We can't.'"

BY THE TIME *The Suite Life* was underway, the network executives had grown comfortable with constant input and oversight, and they were increasingly relying on testing from focus groups to determine what should be included on their series. Sometimes, they'd show a new episode to a room of eight to ten kids, then spend an hour and a half dissecting every aspect of the show that the tiny sample set liked or didn't like.

Director Rich Correll had been a child actor on *Leave It to Beaver* and *Lassie* before becoming a producer and director as an adult. His dad was radio star Charles Correll (best known for voicing one of the first radio sitcoms, *Amos 'n' Andy*—a serial about two Black men voiced by two white men)—and friends with Walt Disney. As a kid, Rich would go to Walt's house and ride the mogul's famous backyard train. Seeing the contrast between the innovative Disney he recalled from his youth and the by-the-book Disney he was now working for, Correll had little respect for the Disney Channel executives dictating things from the Burbank headquarters, a place he termed "The Black Tower."

"Disney had hired a group of people to run this division that were muscle bound from patting themselves on the back," Correll said. "Not really talented people, but just lucky people who thought they were talented."

For Correll, who'd been a producer on *Happy Days* under the tutelage of the legendary Garry Marshall, the network notes and weekly meetings at Disney were now excruciating. Marshall had taught his team to always have a solution for something they didn't like—"You can't say, 'That isn't funny,' or 'That doesn't work.' You have to say, 'That doesn't work, and here's what *will* work."—but those giving notes at Disney often did not.

To many of the creatives, it seemed to be notes for notes' sake. One network middleman got yelled at for reporting back to his boss that all was good with a script draft. They *needed* notes to show they were doing their jobs. And the exertion of control extended across all creative facets. "Now that I'm out of the business, I'll tell you: Disney is the most micromanaged company. It was horrific," producer Adam Lapidus said. "If we wanted to hire a one-line actor, we had to send the Disney executives three choices and they would choose, not us."

One of the most egregious decisions the network made was hiring a convicted sex offender for a small voice role on *The Suite Life of Zack & Cody*. Brian Peck had previously worked with Nickelodeon as an actor and dialogue coach on shows including *All That* and *The Amanda Show*, but he had also already spent sixteen months in jail at the time he provided the voice of London's talking mirror in three episodes of *Suite Life*.

In 2004, Peck pled no contest to charges of lewd acts and oral copulation with a male minor he'd previously coached. Drake Bell of Nickelodeon's *Drake and Josh* publicly came forward as the victim at the center of that case in 2024, and it was also revealed that Rich and Beth Correll wrote letters defending Peck at his 2004 sentencing. The Corrells have since apologized—"If we had known the truth at the time the letters were written, we never would have written them," they wrote in a statement to *Variety*—and stated they had no involvement in Peck's *Suite Life* hiring.

Peck was never on the *Suite Life* set with the actors, and he recorded his vocals in postproduction. "How that ended up happening, I'm not sure. But I know for a fact that if he was on-camera talent that was going to be on the set, the checks and balances that we had in place at the time would have caught that," former original series head Adam Bonnett said. "The minute that we found out who he was, I was contacted and a change was made to re-voice the mirror."

Another bombshell hit the *Suite Life* set in 2008 when the Sprouses' personal manager, Josh Werkman, whom they had worked with since they were eight years old, was convicted of misdemeanor child molestation. The case did not involve the Sprouses, and their family cut ties with him immediately. "It was shocking," producer Irene Dreayer said. "I never, ever imagined anything like that to happen." Werkman had been a major presence in the Sprouses' lives and had guided their careers, securing the Disney deal and their outside partnerships. "My big concern at that point was, were the boys affected physically. Because I knew they were affected emotionally. He was really important to them," Lapidus said. "That was rough, and just really sad."

As PRODUCTION ON the third season of *The Suite Life of Zack & Cody* came to a close, Disney Channel began working on a spinoff series called *The Suite Life on Deck*. The network had originally been interested in a companion series that centered on London and Maddie on a ship, and showrunner Danny Kallis had hoped he could keep *The Suite Life of Zack & Cody* going, running both shows simultaneously. But, according to Kallis, Disney couldn't reach an agreement with Ashley Tisdale over her share of the merchandise profits on a spinoff. "I get a call a couple of months later, 'They can't make a deal with Ashley. Could we put the boys on the boat instead?'"

The *Suite Life of Zack & Cody*, as well as previous shows like *Lizzie McGuire* and *That's So Raven*, had received periodic season extensions, sometimes stretching their number of episodes into the thirties for a single season. That tactic, many creatives felt, was a monetary decision on Disney's part to delay salary and title bumps for new seasons. But after *The Suite Life of Zack & Cody* spent a year and a half filming its thirty-nine-episode(!) second season, things changed.

"We felt in the moment that this is not fair, and we looked into ways to fight it," said writer and producer Jeny Quine, who got pregnant, had a baby, took maternity leave, and returned to work during the course of that single gargantuan season. "At the end of the day, it ended up being

Dylan and Cole [who changed things] because they didn't want to be working for a year and a half straight."

The Suite Life of Zack & Cody had already reached the sixty-five-episode threshold after just two seasons, and its third season was reduced to twenty-two episodes. Then, by subsequently making *The Suite Life On Deck* a separate series rather than just another season of *Zack & Cody*, Disney was able to avoid renegotiating new season-4 salaries for most of the crew—who were on three-season basic cable contracts in alignment with their collective bargaining agreements—and instead revert them back to the season-1 scale minimums, as if they were starting on a new show.

"I think Disney thinks they are so huge that it doesn't matter what they pay anybody," director of photography Alan K. Walker said. "No matter how good you are, you're still a line item."

Series executive Adam Bonnett insisted that the spin-off decision wasn't part of some "Disney master plan" and that saving money wasn't the reason for the overhaul on this or any other Disney Channel series that followed suit. "We did change the titles of our shows in latter seasons, but it was simply to keep the creative fresh," he said. "Each reason why the name was changed is different from show to show . . . It had nothing to do with contracts and saving money and all that kind of stuff. I mean, it's just ridiculous."

Still, there were measures taken to ensure that *On Deck* classified as a new series and not a continuation of *Zack & Cody*. "It was absolutely financial because there were very specific rules that we had to follow in terms of characters and sets and premise to make sure it was a new show," Lapidus said. "We had to walk a very fine line to figure out, how many characters can we take and still call it a new show?"

As a result, series matriarch Kim Rhodes was not invited back. Another near casualty was Phill Lewis, who played Mr. Moseby, and whom the network pushed to axe from *On Deck* until the creatives won the battle to keep him. And, with a starring role off the table, Ashley Tisdale didn't return, opting instead to pursue singing and the possibility of bigger projects after the success of *High School Musical*.

The initial plan was to replace Ashley's character, Maddie, with a new female character close to London's age, so they almost cast Tiffany Thornton. But Tiffany was simultaneously cast on *Sonny with a Chance* and unavailable. And when the network passed along a tape that fourteen-year-old Debby Ryan had submitted from Texas, they rejiggered the part to suit her, aging the Bailey character down and making her a cohort for the boys rather than London. "Debby had the Disney look," Kallis said, "the chipmunk cheeks, the big eyes, the whole nine yards."

Whatever the actual reasoning for the spin-off approach, *The Suite Life on Deck* premise—the twins now went to boarding school on a cruise ship that sailed around the world—paired well with Disney Channel's international focus and Disney's cruise line business. The showrunners toured one of the Disney ships docked at Long Beach for inspiration, and while Zack and Cody couldn't be on a Disney cruise ship or reference the Disney brand on the show at all due to FCC regulations, the very basis of the series subliminally instilled the idea that cruises are great fun to viewers watching at home.

The Suite Life on Deck premiered to 5.7 million viewers in 2008 and continued to perform well. But it was not entirely smooth sailing on set. While the teenage cast members occasionally got into competitive spats and feuded over who had a crush on whom, the bigger problem was, once again, the adults.

According to multiple sources who worked on the two *Suite Life* series, showrunner Danny Kallis's leadership style grew more intense on the sequel series, and the former *Smart Guy* and *Who's the Boss?* producer often yelled to get his point across. "Danny could be the sweetest human being in the world, but he was a little of the old-school, yell-y, angry showrunner [mentality] at a time when that was not appropriate anymore, especially on a kids' show," said producer Adam Lapidus, who had first worked with Kallis on *Smart Guy* in the '90s. "He would never directly be abusive to the children or things like that, but he was a tense guy who got stressed." Countered director Rich Correll, "A lot of people thought Danny was a pain in the ass. I thought he was very, very loyal to the show. I thought he was a good showrunner."

Things reached a tipping point while filming the second season of

The Suite Life on Deck. Kallis was fired and one of the show's executive producers, Pamela Eells O'Connell, who'd previously produced *Married . . . with Children* and *Ellen*, was promoted to oversee *On Deck* for the remainder of the series. Kallis said he was caught completely off guard by his ousting. "The mouse is cheap, and the mouse is heartless," he said. "No one ever told me why I was let go, other than they were 'protecting their set' in the most vague way possible."

When asked about the firing, Adam Bonnett said, "It was just time. But more importantly, he had a number two in Pamela Eells, who was so good at what she did, that it gave us the confidence that she could pick up the ball and run with it."

To some, Kallis's exit was a relief, as the *Suite Life on Deck* soundstage became a calmer place. "I always felt like [being a showrunner] was such a stressful job that I understood when you lost your shit," said Lapidus, who stepped into the number-two role. "Then, suddenly, when Pam was there, it's like, oh, no, you can actually do this job and not yell at people."

Still, executive producer Irene Dreayer stressed that any negativity from Kallis "didn't really permeate the atmosphere" during his previous years overseeing *Suite Life*. "There was so much love on that set," she said, noting that "eighty-nine percent of the time, Danny was terrific." And, she added, "When it escalated, he was taken off the show."

OVERALL, WHILE MANY creatives described their time working on a Disney Channel show as "one of the best jobs I ever had," others bemoaned the company's "culture of fear," in which everyone, at every level, was replaceable. "Disney did operate from an MO of fear," *That's So Raven* showrunner Dennis Rinsler said. "My personal opinion was that they felt they got better cooperation if everyone was in fear."

That unease may have helped keep some problematic whims in check, as there seemed to be less tolerance for overt, out-of-line behavior, in comparison to what some have alleged was allowed to transpire at other networks. When there were blatant enough issues, above-the-line creatives could be fired in the middle of production, despite their series' success.

"I mean, nothing excuses the behavior of a toxic showrunner or toxic person, but we were kid-driven family [entertainment]. And that is distinctly different from Nickelodeon, which is a place where it's for kids only," former Disney Channel president Anne Sweeney said. "We had a lot of people on staff who really cared deeply about our talent and knew their families and were very, very protective of these kids. It wasn't because Disney told us to. I think when people signed up for Disney Channel, they signed up for a way of thinking about kids and families."

But, as was the case with Michael Poryes, who returned to co-run *Hannah Montana* after being fired from *That's So Raven*, the network could give second chances to certain individuals—provided their behavior hadn't affected the "health and happiness" of the talent, which Bonnett said was always paramount. ("I wouldn't give Disney executives that much credit that they wanted a happy set," Lapidus argued. "I think they wanted a smooth-running set.")

And even talent could be expendable when they crossed a stark enough line. Mitchel Musso, who co-starred on *Hannah Montana* and later had a starring role on the Disney XD series *Pair of Kings*, was released from the latter project after he got a DUI. Driving under the influence of alcohol or drugs was explicitly listed in talents' contracts as an activity that carried an "undue risk of injury or death" and, therefore, could be grounds for termination.

"Whether you're starring on a Disney Channel show or whether you're developing a Disney Channel show, you're working for The Walt Disney Company," Bonnett said. "There's an expectation that you adhere to certain values that were important to us."

AFTER SEVENTY-ONE *The Suite Life on Deck* episodes spanning three seasons, plus a *Suite Life* DCOM, the Sprouses were legally adults by the time *On Deck* finished taping in 2010. Their base salaries had been contracted to go from $8,000 per episode each on the first season of *The Suite Life of Zack & Cody* to $13,781 per episode each in that final *On Deck* season (plus contingent bonuses). And Dylan said they were eager to stay on the network. "I mean, we had a really awesome idea for where the show needed to go. We were eighteen," he told *Vulture*. "If that isn't old enough to know exactly what the show needs, then . . . well, I would beg to disagree."

The twins had both been accepted to New York University, but they initially hoped to defer their enrollment for a year and put together a third *Suite Life* iteration. The network was also keen, and they discussed having the Martins serve as mentors to a new young boy navigating life growing up in a hotel. But the parties couldn't land on how exactly that would play out. Instead, Dylan and Cole continued on to NYU, where they graduated with honors, studying video game design and archeology, respectively.

"Dylan and Cole were very secure. They had an attitude like, 'We don't need this job,'" Lapidus said. "I think they liked it, but they felt like if this all went away tomorrow, [they]'d be fine. I wish more actors had that attitude."

The *Suite Life* franchise was a ratings hit for Disney Channel and a star-making vehicle for the Sprouses. But the combination of the twins' disinterest in engaging with the wider Disney ecosystem and the tween boys of America's disinterest in engaging with Disney Channel–related products meant *Suite Life* never achieved the wider cultural impact that other female-led Disney Channel shows of the era did. And it would take a romantic high school musical that had the trifecta of singing, sports, and a merchandising empire to truly catapult the network to new heights.

8

High School Musical:
The Little Movie That Could

When Lucas Grabeel graduated high school, he ditched his Missouri hometown and headed west to Los Angeles, where he embarked on a glamorous new life working a minimum-wage job at a Blockbuster in a Sherman Oaks strip mall. Between shifts, the self-described "shit-kicker from a small town" trudged to countless failed auditions. His biggest break had been a co-starring role in the third *Halloweentown* film, but he still hadn't made enough money to quit the Blockbuster gig. After filming, he had to go back to work at the store, stocking the shelves with DVDs that occasionally featured his face on the boxes.

Lucas grew up doing musical theater. Getting the chance to act with *Singin' in the Rain* legend Debbie Reynolds in *Halloweentown High* had been a thrill. So, his manager sent him a script for another Disney Channel Original Movie, the still-untitled *High School Musical*, thinking it could be a good fit. But Lucas was twenty years old and had never been a huge Disney fan. He read it, and judged it. Hard.

"Dude, this is the worst script I've ever read," he told his manager. "And I feel like it's going to be the worst thing I ever do if I book this."

"Lucas, what else are you doing?" his manager sighed. "Are you happy at Blockbuster?'"

Lucas was, in fact, miserable at Blockbuster. So he headed to casting directors Jason La Padura and Natalie Hart's office and auditioned for the part of the film's lead boy, Troy: the star athlete torn between basketball and musical theater. The casting team deemed Lucas a better fit for supporting character Ryan Evans, the flamboyant theater kid forced to live in his power-hungry sister Sharpay's shadow. They put him through to the final callbacks, which entailed an all-day session of sudden-death auditions for the six main roles and tested the top fifty or so contenders' singing, dancing, and acting abilities.

When Lucas arrived at Madilyn Clark Studios in North Hollywood for the callbacks, he found himself in a frenetic sea of teen actors and their momagers. "I was probably one of five people who didn't have their parents there," he said, adding dryly, "because I was an adult."

After passing the first round and reading lines with several potential Sharpays, Lucas stepped outside to escape the noise and sulk. As he lit a cigarette, the door suddenly burst open behind him. A frazzled, nineteen-year-old blonde scampered out, centering herself in his gaze.

Ashley Tisdale had been working since she was three years old. She was born and raised on the Jersey Shore, where she did local theater at the Jewish Community Center and booked dozens of commercials. She'd played Cosette in a national tour of *Les Misérables* at age eight, and had done the South Korea tour of *Annie*. After moving to Los Angeles at age twelve, she began appearing in guest roles on a steady string of TV shows including *The Amanda Show*, *Charmed*, *7th Heaven*, and *Beverly Hills, 90210*, before landing the role of Maddie on *The Suite Life of Zack & Cody* and later voicing Candace on *Phineas and Ferb*. Her grandfather was Arnold Morris, the famed Ginsu knife infomercial pitchman, and now, Ashley was pitching herself as the sharpest choice for Sharpay in *High School Musical*.

"We need to run lines together. We need to rehearse the song together," a breathless Ashley told Lucas. "Disney wouldn't give me a part, and my team has been working to get me into this round of auditions for Sharpay, and I only found out about this two days ago, and—"

Lucas stared back, mouth agape. "I'm just like, what are you doing? I don't know who you are. And I don't understand why you're telling me this," he reminisced, eighteen years later.

Against his better judgment, Lucas agreed to practice with her. They'd have to perform together for the casting team, director Kenny

Ortega, and the other executives shortly, so what could it hurt? They ran the scene—and Ashley promptly delivered a flurry of notes, critiquing Lucas's delivery and pacing, and proposed an unscripted bit.

"At the end," she concluded, "I'm going to add this thing, where I'm going to order you to get my bag, and I'm going to leave, and then I'll be like, 'Ryan!' and you grab my bag and run off after me."

The whole thing was extremely Sharpay. By this point, Lucas was enraged. "I was just *flummoxed* that someone had the balls to walk up to another actor and tell them what to do in an audition," he said. Still, he couldn't deny that it was a good idea for a bit.

As the day wore on, Lucas's judgment and indifference toward the film began morphing into a desperate desire to be cast. He'd met the choreographers and seen the musical elements of the story start to come together in ways that weren't evident on the page. Plus, it could be his golden ticket out of Blockbuster. He *needed* this part. He agreed to Ashley's plan, all the while still quietly burning with hatred for his scene partner. "I walked into that audition room seething because of how much I disliked her," Lucas said.

But his animosity and Ashley's competitive hunger fueled the perfect dynamic as they bandied Ryan and Sharpay's lines and sang a duet of "You Can't Stop the Beat" from *Hairspray*.

"They were great together, and what you see in the movie is what they did that day," executive producer Bill Borden said. "She thought she was a star. And he was like, *what the hell's going on here?*"

BORDEN HAD FIRST started kicking around the idea of doing a Disney Channel musical, something like a *Grease* for kids, while working on the 2004 DCOM *Tiger Cruise* with Hayden Panettiere and Bill Pullman. *Tiger Cruise* was a somber film about military families stuck on a navy boat when September 11 happened, but Borden had snuck in a lively galley scene that let the young cast bang on pots and pans in an impromptu jam session. "Watch *Tiger Cruise* and you will see the start of *High School Musical*," he said.

At Disney Channel HQ, president of entertainment Gary Marsh had likewise become enamored with the idea of doing a musical. *The Chee-tah Girls* had been a huge success, but it wasn't an all-out foray into the genre. The Cheetah Girls sang pop songs as staged performances. They didn't erupt into spontaneous outbursts of plot-advancing numbers. What would happen if Disney pushed a musical to the limit? Marsh approached Disney Channel president Rich Ross, asking if he could pursue a full-blown musical DCOM endeavor.

"I was like, 'Sure. Sounds fun,'" Ross recalled. "I never quite understood or appreciated what it could be, but I appreciated that he wanted to give it a whirl." After all, in the nearly thirty years since Olivia Newton-John and John Travolta had crooned on the bleachers of Rydell High, no live-action movie musical about teens had managed to generate the same nation-sweeping fervor.

Post–*Tiger Cruise*, Borden and his producing partner Barry Rosenbush were in the midst of rewrites with screenwriter Peter Barsocchini on another, non-Disney movie. While waiting for their meetings to start, the three men began discussing what a Disney Channel musical could look like. They liked the idea of a *Romeo and Juliet*–esque romance about star-crossed high school lovers, but knowing that the network was still eager to draw in more boy viewers, a sports component also seemed necessary.

Barsocchini had been on the basketball team at his Catholic prep school in the late 1960s. One day, on a sweaty post-game bus ride, the star of the team had leaned over to him and quietly made an offhand comment. "I always wanted to dance ballet," he said. "But if you ever tell anyone, I'll kill you." That star athlete, Barsocchini said, was Lynn Swann, who would later become an NFL superstar and play in the Super Bowl with the Pittsburgh Steelers. And that anecdote became the perfect sports-driven tension to add to their Disney Channel musical idea: a high school sports star who secretly wants to do musical theater. (Ballet, they decided, would have been asking too much of the boy viewers they wanted to hook.) For the music, they could use covers of '70s and '80s tracks that would feel new to their millennial audience, and maybe they could even add an original song or two.

The men pitched an outline for an untitled *High School Musical*

Project to original movies executive Denise Carlson, who recognized the potential in the idea and kicked it up to her boss, Michael Healy. Healy loved it but had some instructions: age it down to middle school to better suit the network's demographic, and ditch the cover songs for all original tracks. Disney doesn't want to pay for songs they don't own.

Barsocchini got to work on the script, weaving together a tale of warring school cliques. At its heart, Troy Bolton, the basketball star who was scared to embrace his theatricality, and Gabriella Montez, the new girl in school who also happened to have perfect pitch. (Barsocchini named her Gabriella after his daughter and dubbed the school's resident brainiac Taylor after his stepdaughter.)

The producers flat-out ignored Healy's mandate to age down the characters, and Barsocchini made sure to print *High School Musical Project* on every treatment of the script to drive home the movie's high school setting. "I kept saying, my daughters want to see what's down the road," he said. But they agreed to adjust the music as requested.

Not having any experience with actual musicals, the men bought a book about Broadway shows to guide them. They learned there were certain song choices that reliably occurred at pivotal moments: the opener, the duets, the eleventh-hour track. Barsocchini mapped out places in the script where those types of songs could be slotted in, then they turned in the script to Healy. He sat on it for a few weeks before kicking it up to Gary Marsh.

Marsh was enchanted. He allowed them to keep the high school setting, but they would obviously need a real title. "We came up with pages and pages and pages of different titles, and none of them quite worked," Carlson said. In the end, Marsh suggested stripping back the placeholder title, in the same way The Disney Channel had simplified its own name.

The film would just be *High School Musical*.

Now, TO FIND a director. Rather than turn to their usual stable of Disney Channel Original Movie directors, they wanted a leader with a very particular set of skills in musicals and choreography. The network sent producers Borden and Rosenbush a list of a dozen names to choose from. One immediately leapt out: Kenny Ortega.

Borden had worked with Ortega on the 1981 Francis Ford Coppola musical *One from the Heart*, and they'd gotten along well. Ortega had gone on to receive early acclaim for his "Try a Little Tenderness" choreography work with Jon Cryer in *Pretty in Pink* and the "Twist and Shout" parade sequence in *Ferris Bueller's Day Off*. But in the years since, Ortega had found himself in movie jail. He had directed two theatrical films for Disney in the early '90s, *Newsies* and *Hocus Pocus*. Both flopped. (It would take years for them to become modern cult classics, and *Hocus Pocus*'s belated rise in popularity was largely thanks to its annual autumnal airings on Disney Channel.) He'd then turned to piecemeal TV work, directing episodes of *Gilmore Girls* and choreographing the 2002 Olympics opening ceremony in Salt Lake City. He was desperate to get back into movies and thought directing a TV film could lead to more theatrical work.

Ortega's agent presented him the *High School Musical* script as an option. "I read it and I said, 'Ya know, this reminds me of growing up, this reminds me of my high school musical theater days,'" Ortega told *The Hollywood Reporter* in 2019. "I thought: It's under the radar, it'll be invisible, and it'll give me a chance to warm up and maybe prove myself again."

WITH ORTEGA ON board, casting was set in motion. The brother-and-sister team of Jason La Padura and Natalie Hart had become a go-to casting unit for Disney Channel Original Movies. They'd already successfully cast the *Halloweentown* films and *Twitches*. Now, with a summer 2005 production deadline looming, they faced the daunting task of assembling an ensemble of triple-threat kids inside a two-month casting window for *High School Musical*.

They filled the supporting adult roles with relative ease. For the eccentric theater teacher, Ms. Darbus, they tested Judy Garland's daughter Lorna Luft, but it was *A Chorus Line* actor Alyson Reed who won the part. For Troy's dad, they selected Bart Johnson, whose mom had been a hairstylist on *Newsies* and counted Ortega as a family friend.

For the six main teen roles, the casting directors tested hundreds of performers in their oversized trailer on the Universal lot. The top three to eight contenders for each of the principal parts were then sent to a day-long group bootcamp at Madilyn Clark Studios in North Hollywood. There, the fifty or so hopefuls were paired and re-paired as they danced, sang, and read scenes for La Padura and Hart, network casting executive Judy Taylor, producers Borden and Rosenbush, and Ortega. Later in the day, as the cuts progressed, Marsh, Healy, and Carlson joined to assess the lucky few who remained.

Corbin Bleu was already part of the Disney Channel family, even if audiences weren't aware of it yet. After acting on the big screen in Fox's *Catch That Kid* and Universal's *Galaxy Quest,* the sixteen-year-old had just landed a guest part in the still-unaired *Hannah Montana* pilot as Miley Stewart's crush. (In reality, it was Miley Cyrus who had a huge crush on Corbin while filming. "She was not shy at all," he said. "She had no problem being like, 'You're *so* cute.'") And Judy Taylor recommended Corbin for the part of Ryan in *High School Musical.* That wasn't a fit, but they called him back to read for Chad, Troy Bolton's best friend and fellow basketball star. Corbin serenaded them with "I Would Die 4 U" by Prince, and went through to the final callbacks.

There was just one issue. Corbin had grown up in a dancing and acting family—his dad is actor David Reivers, who later played Corbin's dad in *Jump In!* and *High School Musical 2*—but Corbin had not grown up in an athletic family. And the actors hoping to be cast as Troy or Chad would need to prove that they could convincingly portray a varsity basketball player. Assistant choreographer Chucky Klapow, who had worked with the WNBA and danced for the L.A. Sparks, had been tasked with coordinating the basketball routines for the tryouts.

Ortega knew he wanted to cast Corbin as Chad; he just needed to make sure Corbin could manage the basketball component. The director set up a meeting for Klapow to assess Corbin's sports skills one-on-one and report back. Ahead of the callback, Corbin's dad took him to Sport Chalet to buy a jersey, shorts, and a basketball so that he would arrive looking the part. "Think of the ball as just another prop in a dance routine," his dad told him. "The steps to the game are your choreography."

Dressed in his full basketball garb, complete with sweatbands and headband, Corbin dribbled, drove, and maneuvered the ball to the beat, convincing Klapow that he was a skilled basketballer. "This kid can dance *and* play!" Klapow reported back to Ortega. "He's perfect."

"It wasn't until the very first day of basketball practice in Utah where they went, 'Oh shit. He can't play,'" Corbin said. But he dedicated himself to improving. And just like his on-screen character, "There was never a moment that I didn't have a basketball with me. I actually slept with it. I would wake up walking and bouncing the ball, just so I could be comfortable enough to make it look like I knew what I was doing."

Pre-auditions, the lead role of Troy Bolton had been offered to singer Jesse McCartney. But the Hollywood Records artist didn't want to be seen as a "Disney star" and turned it down, leaving La Padura and Hart to start from scratch. As they began their search, a possible contender sprang to their minds. They'd first met Zac Efron when they cast him in a guest role on The WB soap *Summerland*, which, coincidentally, also starred Jesse McCartney. Zac had tested so well with that show's audience that he was brought back as a series regular the following season.

Unlike most of the other young actors, Zac and his family had stayed based in their Central California hometown near San Luis Obispo rather than relocate to Los Angeles for his budding career. He had floppy hair and a gap between his front teeth. "He didn't have any of that Hollywood polish at all," Hart said. "It's sort of what endeared him to us, because he was just a good guy and a lovely kid."

The casting directors knew that seventeen-year-old Zac could act, but they needed to find out if he could sing. They called him in, and his mom drove him the three hours down from San Luis Obispo for a five-minute singing session with Hart and La Padura. His voice was good enough, and he could also play basketball. "He was fine," Disney Channel Original Movies executive Denise Carlson said of his sports skills. "Would he have won an all-city championship? Probably not." Still, Corbin said, "Compared to me, Zac was Michael Jordan."

They put Zac through, along with Hunter Parrish, who'd been in *Sleepover* and would soon have a breakout role on Showtime's *Weeds*; Drew Seeley, who'd had small roles on *Dawson's Creek*, *One Tree Hill*, and the DCOM *Stuck in the Suburbs*; and Michael Copon, who had played the Blue Power Ranger on TV and had appeared in one of Raven's music videos.

For the part of Gabriella, the female lead and Troy's love interest, Vanessa Hudgens was an obvious choice. She had booked a string of smaller parts over the years, starting with the edgy indie film *Thirteen* and had recently co-starred in Universal's theatrical family sci-fi flop *The Thunderbirds*. "As soon as I met her, I was like, that's her," La Padura said. "She ticked all the boxes. She's multicultural. She's beautiful. She could sing. She could act. It was like, there's nothing wrong with this girl." They put Vanessa through to the finals, along with Bianca Collins, who had co-starred in *Tiger Cruise*, and Diana DeGarmo, who had been voted the runner-up on season 3 of *American Idol* earlier that year.

When it was time for Zac and Vanessa to be paired up to read at the callbacks, Vanessa started to panic. She ran over to Hart.

"Oh my god, I don't know if I can read against him," Vanessa said.

"What's wrong?" Hart asked.

"He's too cute," she whispered urgently.

"Great." Hart grinned. "Use that."

If Lucas's animosity toward Ashley made them stand out in their callback, Vanessa's puppy dog eyes for Zac pushed their chemistry over the edge. "It was magic," Hart said.

At 7:00 P.M., the dance studio closed and the team decamped back to Disney Channel HQ with the final four contenders for Troy and Gabriella to do one last round of chemistry reads. It had come down to Zac and Vanessa, and Michael Copon and Diana DeGarmo. As they read through the karaoke meet-cute and school rooftop scenes, the room was divided on which pair to cast.

"I looked at Zac Efron, and he reminded me of the actor who played Romeo in Franco Zeffirelli's *Romeo and Juliet*, who I had the biggest crush on when I was a little girl," Carlson said. "I was like, *this* is the guy who our audience is going to be all over. But not everyone felt the same."

They sent the actors home, and the executives spent the next few weeks deliberating. Zac and Vanessa? Or Michael and Diana? Some were on the fence about Zac, in particular. His singing skills were unpolished.

Michael had a stronger voice, better teeth, and a more athletic build. They spread the headshots across a table. Kenny Ortega jabbed his finger at Zac's portrait. "This is our guy," he said, growing annoyed that it even had to be debated. "I can direct him. I can get what we need from him. He's a star. You don't like his teeth? We'll fix his teeth. You don't think he has a great singing voice? We'll address that. But we need him to be Troy Bolton." The naysayers surrendered.

As PRODUCTION NEARED, an additional casting search took place in Utah, where they found supporting actors like Olesya Rulin, who played the musical's composer, Kelsi. Ortega and the choreographers also held a massive audition of more than five hundred Utah-based backup dancers. One of those dancing hopefuls was nineteen-year-old KayCee Stroh, a Salt Lake City dance instructor who had done local theater but mostly given up on her dreams of acting and singing professionally.

KayCee had trained in jazz, hip-hop, and ballet. She could outdance almost anyone. But unlike the cookie-cutter, willowy dancers that populated the stage and screen in the mid-2000s, KayCee had curves. She didn't look like the other girls, and the cultural stigma against plus-sized bodies was rampant. "I remember really only having, like, Kathy Bates or Kathy Najimy to look up to," KayCee said. Given the climate, she approached the *High School Musical* casting session with zero expectations. She brought several of her students to try out with her, hoping the auditions could be a good opportunity for them, even if she didn't make the cut.

When it was KayCee's turn to perform a group number for the panel of choreographers, she handed over her résumé and took her place with the other girls, all a size six or smaller. For ninety seconds, she gave her all. Then, Kenny Ortega stopped the music. Rather than give the group feedback, he stood up from behind the casting table and walked over to KayCee. He grabbed her hands and looked her in the eyes. "I *love* you. You're different," he said. "Please tell me that you sing."

Ortega eventually offered KayCee a small speaking and singing role as Martha Cox, a bookish student who secretly loves to "pop and lock and jam and break." She became a fan favorite, returned for both sequels, and by the third film had her role expanded to make Martha the head cheerleader of East High.

"My entire life, and especially my career as a dancer, I felt like I always had to fight harder to be there and fly higher to prove myself," KayCee said. "And the thing that was always such a struggle for me was the one thing that made me unique and stand out that day."

At the same time that Raven-Symoné was being pressured to lose weight and the rest of the female leads on Disney Channel were categorically thin, KayCee's casting represented a small act of defiance and a step toward size inclusivity.

WHILE THE *High School Musical* cast was being assembled, the producers scrambled to get the movie's music in place. In order to crank out a slate of original tracks in time, they'd need to work with a variety of songwriters and producers rather than hire one cohesive composing unit the way a traditional musical would. Luckily, Steven Vincent, the head of Disney Channel's music ventures, had a seemingly infinite database of songwriters and music producers at his disposal. He had a reputation for knowing exactly who to call for any project's musical needs.

For *High School Musical*'s pop-driven tracks and power ballads, he looked to Matthew Gerrard and Robbie Nevil, who had worked on The Cheetah Girls' and Hilary Duff's early music. For a hip-hop–infused basketball track, he hired fellow Cheetah Girls veterans, brothers Greg and Ray Cham, to compose "Get'cha Head in the Game." And he put in a call to David Lawrence, who was in the midst of working on an ill-fated musical with Blake Edwards about 1920s gangsters, to compose the film's score.

Vincent wondered if Lawrence and his writing partner, Faye Greenberg, might also be interested in tackling a song for a cafeteria scene that was originally written as a non-musical moment but now needed a breakout showtune. Lawrence and Greenberg pounced, crafting a "Bohemian Rhapsody"–tinged ensemble track for the East High cliques to sing as they collide around the lunch tables: "Stick to the Status Quo."

"They cut the leash and just said, 'Go,'" Lawrence said. "I was like a kid in a candy store."

Once the cast was finalized, the performers began recording the tracks at various studios around Los Angeles. They'd need to have the tracks completed to lip-sync to them while filming, so everything had to be in place before they left for the Utah film shoot. But as recording got underway, Vincent grew increasingly concerned about Zac Efron's singing ability and whether or not he had the range to master the tracks. "With Zac, I remember always not liking what was going on, and what people were saying about his range," songwriter and music producer Matthew Gerrard said. "There was a bit of an unfair assumption beforehand."

Vincent asked the Cham brothers, who were working on "Get'cha Head in the Game," to cut a separate demo track with Zac in order to get a sense of his prowess in the studio. That session, during which Greg Cham concluded Zac "wasn't Jesse McCartney, but he could carry a tune," led Vincent to decide that Drew Seeley—who was signed to Ray Cham's production company—would sing for Troy in *High School Musical* instead. "We get a call from Steve, who says, 'Everybody thinks that Zac is cool, but he's not good enough,'" Greg Cham recalled. "So we cut a deal for Drew, and away we went." While Zac recorded parts of the songs, twenty-three-year-old Drew recorded his own full versions of the tracks.

Drew wouldn't be credited, but Disney was used to doing a bait and switch with their Disney Channel Original Movie singing roles. When Taran Killam auditioned for the part of pop-star heartthrob Jordan Cahill in the 2004 DCOM *Stuck in the Suburbs*, the comedian confidently belted a pop version of "Unchained Melody" at his final audition (where he was coincidentally up against Drew Seeley for the part). But while Killam got the role, and he was the one who glued chunky, highlighted extensions to his head to embody the character, he didn't actually record any vocals for the film's soundtrack. "By the time I said yes, the wheels were already in motion," said Killam, who studied musical theater at UCLA. "They'd already recorded something, and they just ended up having me lip-sync." (Music producer Robbie Nevil sang on those final tracks instead.)

There was no question that Drew was a stellar singer. If anything, he was *too* good. During his first *High School Musical* recording session for Troy, he belted "Breaking Free" with perfect pitch and the depth of a tenured pop star. He was asked to tone it down to be more believable as a kid who's never even been on stage before. But no matter how polished Drew may have been, he wasn't Zac.

"What I was advised was, 'Let that happen,' which is kind of contrary to how I generally work," Rich Ross, then–Disney Channel president, said of using Drew's voice in lieu of Zac's and the potential blowback. "Technically, it was my call, but I knew the repercussions would not be great."

Borden said he was in a mixing session where Zac's voice was used "when we could." And, in Borden's opinion, Zac's voice alone would have been good enough without bringing in Drew. "I thought he was fine. It's not a live performance. Lots of big stars autotune to get the pitch right," he said. "We could have done it, but the decision was above my pay grade."

In the end, Zac's vocals were virtually nonexistent on the published tracks. And Zac was, understandably, upset. "In the first movie, after everything was recorded, my voice was not on them," he told the *Orlando Sentinel* in 2007. "I was not really given an explanation. It just kind of happened that way."

They had all been cast as triple threats. Now, Zac was the only one deemed unsuitable to fulfill his singing duties. By summer, rumors were flying about who really sang for Troy Bolton. "To set the record straight, the majority of what is sung in the movie is definitely sung by someone else," Zac told Digital Spy in August 2006. "His name is Drew Seeley. He's a great guy. I sing like the beginnings and ends of all the songs, and hopefully I can fix that in the future. I'm going to sing in *Hairspray* which is the next film I'm doing . . . That will be all me, thank God."

The initial plan had been that the *High School Musical* audience would be none the wiser to the subbed-in singer. Disney would simply list the vocalists by their character names on the soundtrack, and the fictional "Troy" would be the only one getting credit for the vocals. It had worked on *Stuck in the Suburbs*, and they'd done the same thing with Paolo in *The Lizzie McGuire Movie*. But when *High School Musical* became a global sensation, they had to come clean. The kids were doing too much press, and the questions about the recording process had become too difficult to dodge. Zac had been put in an incredibly awkward position.

"Zac was like, 'I will represent this, but I will not in any way allude to it being different than it is,'" Ross recalled. "That, ultimately, was challenging."

WHEN THE ACTORS convened in Utah to shoot the first film in July 2005, Zac was a different person from the boy they'd met at the callbacks that spring. Disney had sent him to cut his hair and close that contentious gap between his front teeth. They shot mostly on location at East High, a real Salt Lake City high school, whose students were on summer break. Since the school didn't have air conditioning, production snaked huge portable AC units through the hallways to cool off the performers, who sweltered under the production lights in the poorly ventilated gymnasium and classrooms.

To keep things simple without needing to change the signage on East High, they gave their fictional school the same name. The actual school team is the East High Leopards, but to give Disney licensing ownership over any potential *High School Musical*–themed merchandise, they switched up the on-screen mascot. Since there was a huge leopard statue cemented in the middle of the school lobby where they'd be filming, and one big cat could pass for another, the Leopards became the Wildcats.

Off set, the main cast stayed at the midrange Little America Hotel in Salt Lake City. Although they were all playing high schoolers, their actual ages spanned from sixteen to twenty-four. Sometimes, they'd all hang out together, playing the lobby piano or hanging out in the hotel pool and hot tub. But usually they peeled off into separate age groups. Lucas, twenty; Monique Coleman (who played Scholastic Decathlon queen Taylor McKessie), twenty-four; and choreographer and dancer Chucky Klapow, twenty-four, would have wine and cheese nights in one of their hotel rooms, while Zac, seventeen, Vanessa, and Corbin, both sixteen, would play *Super Smash Bros. Melee* and make instant mac and cheese in one of theirs. Having just turned twenty, Ashley was caught in the middle and floated between the groups.

One night, during the two weeks of intense dance rehearsals at the start of production, members of the various posses gathered in Klapow's hotel room for a rare wild night of intermingling as the Bacardi Razz and Cherry 7UP on ice flowed. The chemistry that Zac and Vanessa had at their final audition had continued to escalate during rehearsals. Vanessa was, by now, head over heels. But Zac had a girlfriend back home, and he had thus far not entertained his co-star's advances.

"Hey, can I talk to you for a minute?" Zac asked Klapow, as he pulled the choreographer out into the hallway. "I don't know what to do, man. Vanessa is super into me, and I have feelings for her, too. I don't want to do the wrong thing with my girlfriend. But I also don't want to shut Vanessa down and ruin the chemistry in the movie."

Klapow encouraged Zac to explore things with Vanessa. They were so young, and what happened in Utah would probably stay in Utah. If Zac's other relationship wasn't that serious, he should just end things with his girlfriend and test the waters here, Klapow advised.

When the two guys went back into the hotel room, the party vibes had devolved into melodrama. Vanessa was in tears, crying in the locked bathroom with Ashley. It seemed as if the tipping point of her unrequited love had been reached. Corbin tried to console her from the other room until Zac knocked on the bathroom door, and Ashley left the two of them to talk alone.

"I remember the moment that Vanessa and Zac were talking in the bathroom, and then they came out holding hands," Lucas said. "I mean, it was so high school. It was like, 'He broke up with his girlfriend, and we're together now.'"

From that day on, Klapow said, "Zanessa was born."

WHILE LOVE WAS blossoming between the cast, not all of their characters got to follow their hearts in the film. During rehearsals, Lucas approached director Kenny Ortega and asked him if his character, Ryan, was gay.

"Well, that would be one choice," Ortega replied. "I don't think Disney is going to allow us to be overt with this. We obviously can't say anything concrete. You can't have a boyfriend. You're not going to be kissing any guys. When I was in high school, I was still confused and didn't know exactly who I was. So, maybe that's the way we go about this."

America was still two years away from Hilary Duff's "that's so gay" PSA condemning using the word "gay" to mean something bad. And while Ortega has said, "Disney is the most progressive group of people I've ever worked with," having an overtly gay character just wasn't on the table for kids' television, which was hyper-wary of isolating viewers and drawing controversy in 2005. That same year, the creator of *SpongeBob SquarePants* had been pressured to label SpongeBob as "almost asexual," after Christian activist groups accused the Nickelodeon show of promoting a homosexual agenda between the fictional invertebrate and his starfish friend, Patrick. (It would take until 2019 for a Disney Channel character, Cyrus Goodman on *Andi Mack*, to blatantly say "I'm gay" on screen. And it wasn't until 2023 that *High School Musical: The Musical: The Series* would directly confirm Ryan's sexuality by having Lucas cameo and kiss a man.) Still, they had some fun with the idea in *High School Musical*. While the wannabe baker Zeke pined for Sharpay in the film, Lucas and Ortega added the unscripted assumption that Ryan was secretly pining for Zeke, throwing lingering looks his way and wishing he could taste that creme brûlée instead. Most of those nods were cut in the final version.

Off screen, when Rich Ross succeeded Anne Sweeney to become the president of Disney Channel Worldwide in 2004, he also became one of the first openly gay network leaders in TV history. He had been in a long-term relationship since the 1980s with his eventual-husband Adam Sanderson, who joined Disney's marketing team in 1997.

"I was extraordinarily lucky that, from the day I started working, it never was a barrier for me. Everyone was fine with it," Ross said of his sexuality. "In that same manner, when you're the first, you know you're the first."

Of the six *High School Musical* leads, two were Black (Corbin and Monique), three were white (Zac, Ashley, and Lucas), and one was Filipino (Vanessa, although her character, Gabriella Montez, remained Latina, similar to what happened when Lalaine played Miranda Sanchez on *Lizzie McGuire*). "None of that diversity was on paper," La Padura said. "Kenny said to us he wanted to make this generation's *Grease*. And it was just, go ahead and do it."

But for Corbin, the truly special moment in his Disney Channel trajectory was moving from sidekick in *High School Musical* to leading man in the ratings-busting 2007 DCOM *Jump In!* "I went from playing a token best friend to actually playing the lead heartthrob," Corbin said. "*Jump In!* was huge."

And while the fact that Monique was a Black actor playing the smartest girl in school in *High School Musical* was special, the white hairdressers on set didn't know how to properly style her hair. She had to take it upon herself to integrate headbands into her character's wardrobe to cover up their mistakes.

For Monique and Lucas, *High School Musical* served as more than just a fun stepping stone in their careers like it did for the younger cast. It was a lifeline to stability. Before the paychecks began to roll in, Monique returned home after the shoot to an empty bank account and a three-day eviction notice on her apartment door. She couldn't afford cable, so she watched the movie when it aired on Disney Channel with the children she babysat for ten dollars an hour.

"All of the other kids were working actors. Monique and I were not," Lucas said. "Ours was a totally different experience." And there were times when the two of them were treated as lesser than the other main cast members. Like when they were left out of a portion of the third film's promotional tour, overseen by the studio. "Disney really broke my heart," Monique said on the *Vulnerable* podcast in 2022, adding, "They said something about there not being enough room on the plane."

THROUGHOUT FILMING, Kenny Ortega had been determined to make *High School Musical*'s choreographed numbers as crisp as anything he'd done in the past for the stage or screen. But his drive for perfection could also be relentless. At every turn, he expected flawlessness. "Kenny was very particular and very hard-assed," Lucas said. "It was tense at times."

Added Corbin, "Even though we worked kid hours and everything was within those legal confines, we were still treated as adults. We were pushed to our max. I don't think that was anyone's fault back then. Culture changes and evolves. That's just what it was at the time, and everyone was okay with it, and you dealt with it." (Reflecting on his 2022 guest role in the Disney+ reboot *High School Musical: The Musical: The Series,* Corbin marveled at the treatment of that show's young cast and "how much was taken into account of their mental health, of not pushing them too far.")

Toward the end of the *High School Musical* shoot, Rich Ross journeyed to Utah to visit the set while they were shooting the karaoke scene at a ski lodge. He made time for one or two Disney Channel Original Movie set visits per year, and the dailies on this film had been coming back promising. As Zac and Vanessa began singing "The Start of Something New," Ross stood on the side of the set watching with Vanessa's parents. "I literally burst out crying—and I'm not a crier," Ross said. "But there was something about it. It was perfect. They were perfect. It felt perfect. And the explosion of it, it was them finding each other, and us finding our footing."

Back in L.A., he put in a frantic call to Anne Sweeney, who was at that time the Disney Media Networks president, to rave about how incredible the film was shaping up to be. "Let's call Bob," she said. Together with Marsh, they went to Bob Iger's office and showed him rough footage of three scenes. "Watching it, I was thrown back into my love of musical theater," Sweeney said. "Everything I had done in high school just met me on the screen." Iger, who was then Disney's president and chief operating officer, agreed that the movie had outsized potential and, for the first time ever, he authorized an increase to a DCOM's marketing budget to ensure audiences would know how to find it. A few weeks later, Iger officially replaced Michael Eisner as CEO of The Walt Disney Company.

HIGH SCHOOL MUSICAL was made on a $4.2 million budget, a meager yet typical amount for a Disney Channel Original Movie at the time, and given the standard twenty to twenty-five days to shoot. But the final result is a camp masterpiece.

To watch it is to be transported into an alternate candy-coated universe void of cynicism and trendiness. Every single actor is giving 110 percent. No matter how cheesy the line. No matter how ridiculous the circumstance. They are fully committed to the task at hand and selling it with their whole beings. Even the "bad" acting moments are achingly endearing. "Nothing here is better than your average high school production of *The Music Man*," *Entertainment Weekly*'s critic wrote, "but *High School Musical*, with its big throbbing heart, gives out all the right messages without being slow-witted or preachy."

It was wholesome. Sincere. Perfect. The cinematic encapsulation of a production that Zac later referred to as "hands-down, the most honest, carefree, passionate experience of my life."

Sure, like the rest of the Disney Channel Original Movies slate, *High School Musical* was technically geared toward tweens and their families. "We weren't trying to do *Lawrence of Arabia*," Barsocchini said. "We were trying to make a movie that kids could watch and their parents wouldn't gag." But there's a universality to *High School Musical* that nothing before it on Disney Channel had yet achieved. Ms. Darbus, the theater teacher, speaks like a mid-Atlantic broad from a 1940s melodrama. There are quirky background actors and offhand dialogue that feel more at home in a Garry Marshall film than a Disney Channel Original Movie.

"No one ever said, 'Hey, guys, we're making a super cheesy, over-the-top bubblegum movie that is going to make people smile. And that's all that matters,'" Lucas said. "Everyone, from the top down, was so invested and so serious about it. And, ultimately, I feel like that attributed to its success."

The cast was first introduced to Disney Channel viewers in a New Year's Eve special, and the network began running the interstitial music video for "Breaking Free" before the film's release. Walt Disney Records released the soundtrack on iTunes on January 10 to build momentum. Then, on January 20, 2006, *High School Musical* arrived on Disney Channel.

The ratings for the Friday night premiere at 8:00 P.M. Eastern/7:00 P.M. Central were a jaw-dropping 7.7 million viewers in 5 million households, a new network record. (*Cadet Kelly*'s premiere in 2002 had drawn

7.8 million total viewers, but the number of total households was less than half of *High School Musical*'s.) And the real sign that it was going to be huge was in the repeat ratings. One day later, the Saturday night re-run drew another 6.1 million viewers. It rated number one in all of TV for women eighteen to forty-nine. The co-viewing the Disney Channel executives had so long desired was finally happening at historic levels. Rich Ross sent out an email congratulating the team. "By the way," he wrote, "the world just changed."

But even more impressive was what was simultaneously happening on the music side. "The day after it premiered, I think the most requested song was 'Breaking Free,'" former Radio Disney DJ Ernie Martinez said. "And we didn't have it in rotation. We didn't even have the song from Disney Channel yet. There was not any pre-planning."

Even with virtually no radio support outside of Radio Disney, the *High School Musical* soundtrack reached the Top 10 on the Billboard album chart within two weeks of release. "Breaking Free," Troy and Ga-briella's climactic ballad, made the biggest jump for a single in Billboard Hot 100 history at the time, rising from number eighty-six to number four in a single week.

The network executives quickly lauded the success, speaking about *High School Musical*'s unprecedented achievements as if they had been part of a long-sought, targeted agenda. "Surprised? No," Gary Marsh told *The New York Times* three weeks after the film's release. "Thrilled? Absolutely."

In reality, it cannot be stressed enough how little anyone involved thought *High School Musical* was going to move the needle for the net-work before it aired. Sure, they knew it was good by Disney Channel Original Movie standards. Great, even. But beyond that, no one ex-pected much at all. "We thought it would work," Ross said, "not become a cultural phenomenon for the rest of our livelong days."

Cases in point: The cast's contracts were essentially the standard Disney Channel Original Movie contracts, with no sequel options or franchise potential. (Borden, sensing that Zac had star power during casting, asked the network to make Zac's contract a multipicture deal. "The quote I got back was, 'We don't do that,'" he said.) They didn't have a superstar executive producer like *The Cheetah Girls*' Whitney Houston, or a stunt-cast household name like *Halloweentown*'s Debbie Reynolds or *'Twas the Night*'s Bryan Cranston. They hadn't invested in videographers to capture on-set footage to use in promotional materials. While *The Cheetah Girls* and *Tiger Cruise* had red carpet premieres with celebrity guests, photographers, and legions of screaming fans, the "premiere" for the first *High School Musical* was a private screening on the Disney lot for the cast and crew on a Saturday morning, accompanied by cake and ice cream. The biggest guest in attendance was Siegfried Fischbacher, of Siegfried and Roy, who was friends with Ortega.

"The truth was, there was a real feeling that trying to combine music and basketball might not work for the audience," Disney Channel marketing executive Eleo Hensleigh said. "The cast was relative no-ones. It wasn't starring Hilary Duff. Ashley Tisdale had the biggest résumé in that group. The fact that it hit lightning in the bottle to the extent that it did was a surprise."

Each time *High School Musical* shattered a record for Disney, a few weeks would go by and it would break its own milestone again. "A lot of people considered kids' programming sort of a backwater, and then came *High School Musical*," DCOM executive Denise Carlson said. "Suddenly, it's like, oh, wait, kids' programming can make money and can be a phenomenon. And now, suddenly, everybody wants to pay attention to it."

At a business lunch with Sweeney, Bob Iger greeted her with a bigger-than-usual smile. "When I got home last night, my sons insisted on performing 'Get'cha Head in the Game,'" he told her. "They were totally swept up." By March, the *High School Musical* soundtrack was the number one album on the Billboard 200—the first TV soundtrack to reach the top since *Miami Vice* in 1986. By the end of the year, it had sold 3.7 million copies, was the bestselling album of any genre, and had gone platinum or gold in more than a dozen other countries.

On YouTube, fans made sing-along videos to the musical numbers en masse, prompting Disney's notoriously aggressive legal team to spring into action. "I got a call from legal to say, 'We own the music, and people can't use our music.' Legal was very unhappy," Ross said. "I called

Anne and said, 'We have dreamt about this. All over the world, there are thousands of videos karaokeing our songs!' We went to Bob, and Bob said, 'Let it happen. Rich and Anne are right: we have dreamt about this.' It was the beginning of what TikTok became."

In just a few short months, *High School Musical* was generating revenue for The Walt Disney Company across ten separate divisions: from music and home entertainment (the top-selling TV-movie DVD release of all time) to theme parks (an in-park live show), publishing (a series of junior novels whose inaugural tome made it onto the *New York Times* bestseller list for sixteen weeks), theater (a licensable stage production that middle and high schools could perform), merchandise (digital cameras, branded Uno cards, posters, pajamas, board games, video games), and more. There was even an ice show.

By the end of 2006, Disney estimated that almost ninety million people in more than one hundred countries had seen *High School Musical*. And that August, *High School Musical* finally broke Disney Channel's Emmys losing streak when it won the original children's programming category and beat Linda Ellerbee's special about Hurricane Katrina, an HBO documentary about Tourette's, and an animated series for babies set to a compilation of classical music. It also took home an Emmy for choreography—an honor shared between Ortega, Bonnie Story, and Chucky Klapow, because Ortega changed their official titles from "associate" and "assistant" choreographers to the more general and encompassing "choreographers" to ensure they'd be eligible.

Disney Channel was finally a respected contender.

9

Even More *High School Musical*:
Stardom and Sequels

Almost immediately after *High School Musical*'s January 2006 release, the network hastily cobbled together a massive press tour for the cast. There was no time to coach the kids or ease them into it after the film's ratings and chart success. They needed to capitalize on the momentum ASAP.

Disney flew the cast to New York to perform on *Today*. They sat down with *Life*, *Seventeen*, *Teen Vogue*, *Teen People*, *Bop*, *J-14*, and dozens of other outlets. Monique Coleman joined *Dancing with the Stars*. Hollywood Records—which didn't have the capacity to sign all of the main actors as solo singers—chose to forge record deals with Corbin Bleu and Vanessa Hudgens, while Ashley Tisdale signed a separate deal with Warner Brothers. (At the following year's Radio Disney Music Awards, the Hollywood Records executives morosely observed the throngs of fans angling to catch a glimpse of Ashley. "Did we make a mistake?" Bob Cavallo asked Abbey Konowitch. Looking back, "I don't think we made the wrong decision," Konowitch said. "But, it was an awkward time.")

While Ashley had been on a slow-burn rise to fame with *Suite Life*, the rest of the cast were thrown into the deep end without a life raft. Unlike the talent who appeared on Disney Channel Original Series, many of the movie actors didn't receive robust media training—because few journalists had been interested in covering past DCOMs. "We didn't get media training. Our media training was experience," Corbin said. "It's insane how much press we did. I mean, just weeks upon weeks of eight-hour days, ten-hour days, press junkets. It seemed like it never ended."

(Former Disney Channel PR head Patti McTeague said the *High School Musical* cast would have been "briefed" prior to doing any media interviews. "The briefings included message points," she said, "but to encourage authentic interviews, we asked that interviewees provide their own anecdotes and point of view in interviews. It's an acquired skill.")

It was impossible for any of the *High School Musical* stars to leave their homes without being recognized. From the moment they were out in public, they were met with starstruck kids and pushy parents. Beyond just the excitement of meeting a celebrity, it seemed like everyone was eager to assess if they were actually "good kids" whom the children of America should be hoping to emulate. There was constant pressure to be polite, perky, and endlessly accommodating, no matter how rude or uncomfortable an encounter might be.

"I remember developing so much anxiety over it," Corbin said. "We had become these role models, and especially 'Disney role models.' I felt this pressure to have this positive attitude, and I never wanted to create any sort of negativity whatsoever."

Their *High School Musical* contracts, like those for many Disney Channel Original Movies, came with an explicit "morals" section, broadly stipulating that they couldn't behave in a way that would "degrade" themselves in society, bring "public hatred, contempt, scorn, or ridicule," or "shock, insult, or offend the community or ridicule public morals or decency." And the baked-in expectation of what representing the Disney brand entailed was a hazy yet omnipresent force.

"It was definitely something that was just expected and not really ever explained," Lucas Grabeel said. "One of the questions I've been asked the most in interviews is, 'What advice would you give to kids?' Or 'What do you want to say to kids looking up to you right now?' It's like, how are we great role models from just making a movie? You do realize that we're just actors who got a job dancing and singing and being super cheesy in this movie that totally blew up."

From the network's side, as with all Disney Channel projects, "At the end of the day, it's a job," former original programming head Adam Bonnett said. "These kids have a job to do, and part of that job is ensuring that they're consistent with the values of The Walt Disney Company."

The *High School Musical* kids were also making a significant amount of money. Yet there were no Disney financial advisors assigned to educate the talent and their families on how to navigate this influx of wealth, whether it was from the films themselves or the outside deals they were being offered because of their Disney success. There was no guidance on how to save and budget or how to assess what a good deal looked like versus a scam.

"All of a sudden, coming into good money as a sixteen-year-old, my family was definitely not equipped to know what to do with it," Corbin said. "My parents did well, but the kind of money that I started making was not something that we had ever experienced before. So many actors, myself included, went to business managers and handed everything over—and it's not the best thing to hand over that kind of control."

WITH BOTH THE *Cheetah Girls* and *High School Musical* franchises in play, the Disney Music Group began to test the waters of doing concert tours with Disney Channel's made-for-television acts. After the proven success of a 2005 Cheetah Girls Christmas tour, Disney's Buena Vista Concerts and AEG Live plotted an extensive fifty-plus-date *High School Musical*: The Concert tour that would take the film's cast across the United States and South America from the end of 2006 through the spring of 2007. Contracts were drawn up and sent to the six main *High School Musical* cast members to sign. Everyone agreed, with one exception: Zac Efron. "Zac made the decision not to do the concert tour. He was like, 'I didn't sing it, so I'm not doing it,'" Rich Ross said. "That was disappointing."

Drew Seeley took Zac's place to sing Troy's parts on tour, and Kenny Ortega, who had ample experience choreographing and directing tours for Cher, Michael Jackson, and Gloria Estefan, returned to direct the live show. In addition to the songs from the film, Ortega worked to incorporate elements of the cast's numerous side projects in the setlist: Vanessa and Corbin performed tracks from their Hollywood Records releases. Ashley was given permission to sing three songs off her solo album, even though it was a Warner Brothers project. Monique did a bit of ballroom dancing in a nod to her *Dancing with the Stars* run. And Lucas served as emcee.

The tour sold out arenas across the country, packing in audiences of screaming kids and their indulgent, or at least tolerant, parents. "I've driven Lynyrd Skynyrd and Led Zeppelin, and I've never seen fans go crazy like this," one of the tour bus drivers told the cast. "You guys are like the fucking Beatles."

In South America, the shows were bigger, often filling entire stadiums, and the crowds were rowdier. The performers were given military escorts to and from their hotels and the venues. At one airport, an official took their passports and refused to return them unless they took pictures and signed autographs for his children. "That time on the road was the best two months of my life. But it was also some of the darkest moments, as well," Lucas said. "The scale of everything was just unimaginable. They worked us so hard. I mean, we didn't really have days off. And you get to these moments of like, what am I doing? I am a monkey performing on a stage."

They were just getting started.

WITHIN TWO WEEKS of *High School Musical*'s January 2006 premiere, the network had ordered a sequel and approached the cast to sign new single-film contracts, just as they had done with the casts of *Zenon*, *Halloweentown*, and any past Disney Channel Original Movie deemed worthy of a sequel. The previous September, Gary Marsh had been promoted to a newly created position, president of entertainment for Disney Channel worldwide, overseeing the development and production of all original programming across the globe under network president Rich Ross. And Marsh took a heavy hand as the *High School Musical* sequel progressed.

Peter Barsocchini returned to write the script, this time inspired by his youth working as a caddy at a country club. The sequel would follow the gang out of East High as they spent the summer at a country club owned by Ryan and Sharpay's parents and learned a hard lesson in classism. While Ryan and Sharpay vacationed, the rest of the kids would toil away at summer jobs as cooks, lifeguards, and caddies. And since Sharpay had been a breakout character from the first film, she'd be given even more to do this time. The movie's budget increased from $4.2 million to a previously unheard of $6 million, and the pressure manifested tenfold.

After the cast finished the US leg of the concert tour, they only had a week off before going back to the studio to record the soundtrack for *High School Musical 2*. Two weeks later, they were in dance rehearsals and then on location shooting for a month. When they returned to East High to shoot the sequel's opening scenes in April, classes were in session for the school's actual students. The local teens would lean out of their classroom doors and squeal when they caught a glimpse of the actors in the hallway. The cozy sanctuary of a set had become a fishbowl.

But production on *High School Musical 2* primarily took place at the members-only Entrada resort in St. George, Utah, about four hours south near the Arizona and Nevada borders. The venue, with its red rocks, waterfall pool, and eighteen-hole golf course, made an excellent stand-in for a New Mexico country club. And the main cast members could unwind in their adjoining casitas, which they stayed in at the property's The Inn at Entrada. In their downtime, they helped each other with laundry, ordered takeout, or occasionally coerced an obliging cast member to prepare a home-cooked meal for everyone. Once or twice, some made the ninety-minute journey south to Las Vegas to party.

But mostly, they worked. And worked. And worked.

THE SEQUEL DOUBLED down on the musical campiness of the first film. There's Sharpay's glittering, Busby Berkeley–esque poolside ode to consumerism, "Fabulous." And the subliminally flirty "I Don't Dance" duet, where Ryan and Chad have a jazzy, tension-filled showdown on a baseball mound that culminates in them, without explanation, wearing each other's clothes. "Clearly, when you go back and watch it there is so much sexual innuendo in there, and it's amazing," Corbin said. "I personally don't think I was aware of it at the time."

But no number more exemplified the agony and ecstasy of teendom than Troy's literal spiral on a golf course, "Bet On It." The solo song required Zac to run, twirl, and tumble across a setting-sun–dappled golf course, racing headfirst into the throes of an existential crisis. Because the sequence takes place at dusk, Ortega and the team only had a twenty- to thirty-minute window each evening to film it at golden hour, meaning the "Bet On It" shoot actually took place over two weeks. Every evening, Zac and the crew would stop whatever other scene they were shooting to rush to the golf course and capture a segment of the track before the sun set. Much of the choreography was crafted last minute, based on the environment and lighting they had to work with that day. "Okay, jump on these rocks now!" or "Let's strut up this hill!" They'd decide on the spot.

"Zac was so trusting and so committed to any idea that Kenny and I would throw at him," choreographer Chucky Klapow said. "We didn't feel like it was silly or camp at the time. We felt like it was strong and powerful. It wasn't until we saw all the chunks cut together at the end that we realized, oh, this is *a lot*."

ALSO A LOT: the level of attention being paid to the film throughout the shoot. Disney PR had now deployed a round-the-clock team to take on-set photographs and record behind-the-scenes footage for electronic press kits and interstitials. Reporters visited the set to observe the shoots and interview those involved. Whenever a scene wrapped, they'd grab a performer for interviews before releasing them to take a brief break. "Everyone was so famous so quickly," dancer Bayli Baker Thompson said. "The set had gotten a lot tighter, people were a little bit more stressed, because now we had this thing to live up to."

Lucas had torn his meniscus while working on a separate movie project and had pushed through the pain during the *High School Musical* concert tour. Although there'd been a massage therapist, chiropractor, and nutritionist on the road, the grueling schedule—and on-stage cartwheels—had exacerbated the injury. Now, on set for the sequel, he required a back brace and knee braces, and during one on-set interview he mentioned to a reporter that he was feeling better because he'd taken a Vicodin that day. He was swiftly reprimanded by the film's producers. "I was like, what? It's true. I'm in pain. I took a painkiller. I'm not abusing it. My body is fucking falling apart," Lucas said. "They were like, 'Publicity-wise, you can't say that you're taking Vicodin while you're shooting a Disney movie.' I was like, okay, cool, well, no one told me."

Prop master Scott Arneman had worked on most Utah-shot Disney Channel productions since 2001's *The Luck of the Irish*. The stress and chaos of *High School Musical 2* made him stop working with the network for a decade. Because the attention on Disney Channel content now mirrored that of the greater Disney brand, Arneman's job had become less about choosing the best props for a scene and more about jumping through endless red tape on clearances and approvals. (One lesson learned the hard way: The *High School Musical* prop team had made a replica of Ashley Tisdale's actual pink-jewel-encrusted cell phone for Sharpay's device in the first film. When the company that had accessorized Ashley's original phone saw the film, Arneman recalled, they sued Disney for using their design without permission.)

And Ortega's expectations for the film had also reached near-impossible heights. He pushed for perfection from everyone working on the sequel, and his flair for dreaming up creative changes on the fly had gone from requesting those changes to demanding they happen at a moment's notice.

"Kenny was out of control. Now, he had all this authority to just say, 'We need headsets for this dance number!' It's 9:30 at night in St. George, this tiny town, where am I going to get headsets for all these dancers?" Arneman said. "On the first film, he was totally reasonable and fun to work with. But by the second one, it was, 'I want this! I want that! Make it happen.' It went from fun to 'Oh, God, I'm going to cry. I can't wait till this night is over.'"

* * *

THE INTERNAL DYNAMICS of the cast were another roller coaster. Zac and Vanessa had been dating since their early declaration of love during the first film's rehearsals. But there were occasional breakups and on-set fights. "He was the sun and moon to her," Lucas said. "Poor girl." Later, during the third film, Vanessa asked Barsocchini if she could use his office. He obliged. "I hear her dragging Zac into this office," he said, "and then I just hear yelling." He added, "Do you know how long relationships last at that age? That was a real blessing to hold it together for three movies."

Ashley and Vanessa had developed a close friendship that was also fiercely competitive. Some days, they would be as tight as sisters. Other days, they didn't speak. Lucas said he and Monique were "kind of together for a minute," then went back to being just friends. And the tension that he and Ashley had harbored at the callback auditions basically continued throughout their entire *HSM* journey. "We were not close. We were not good friends. Let's be honest, okay?" Ashley has said of her relationship with Lucas. "We hated each other."

But, most crucially, in the year and a half between filming *High School Musical* and *High School Musical 2*, Zac had become a Star with a capital "S." *High School Musical* made America fall in love with him, and the opportunities beyond Disney Channel were aplenty. While everyone else had been traveling on the *High School Musical* concert tour together, Zac had filmed Universal's movie musical *Hairspray* with John Travolta, Michelle Pfeiffer, and Queen Latifah. Universal reportedly paid him a mere $100,000 to play teen idol Link Larkin, but at least they hadn't done him dirty by subbing in someone else's singing voice. Zac felt like he was becoming valued by Hollywood at large—if not by Disney. Now, on the *High School Musical* sequel, he had enough cachet to stand his ground and do all his own singing.

"Personally, I feel no competition with the cast because I'm not going for the same things they are," he told a *New York Times* reporter on the set of *High School Musical 2*. "A lot of them are doing teen music things, and tours, various TV deals and other Disney TV movies and

Disney albums. That's the last thing I want to be doing at the moment." He added, "I'm setting my sights a little bit higher."

A division had formed. Zac, while still kind and polite, returned to Utah with his dream of becoming a full-fledged Hollywood star within reach. He was more aloof with the cast and crew and mainly kept to himself or with Vanessa. The principal actors had all been seen as equals while making the first film. Now, Zac had been singled out as the one with the most promise. And the rest of the cast noticed. "It's hard when you're going through that and people are getting asked different questions and getting different jobs, when you started basically at the same spot," Lucas said. "It was a huge adjustment."

BY THE TIME of *High School Musical 2*'s release in August 2007, Disney Channel knew what they had on their hands. The sequel got a proper red carpet premiere at Disneyland, attended by most of the network's stars, plus celebrity parents eager to score points with their kids. Cindy Crawford and her brood arrived by helicopter, and even company VIPs Mickey and Minnie Mouse made an appearance.

More than 17.2 million viewers tuned in to the US premiere of *High School Musical 2* on August 17, 2007, allowing it to handily beat the series finale of *The Sopranos* that had drawn 11.9 million viewers on HBO two months earlier. *High School Musical 2* was the most-watched basic cable telecast of all time, beating the previous record held by a Monday Night Football game on ESPN in 2006. And with kids eleven and under, who accounted for 6.1 million of its viewers, it was the most-watched TV broadcast of all time.

"Take a bow, Disney Channel entertainment [president] Gary Marsh, Rich Ross and the rest of the exec team that backed the notion of a kid-friendly tuner last year when most of us were going, huh?" *Variety* wrote at the time. "The kids of today—singing and dancing, Mickey and Judy style? Just goes to prove the industry cliche about zigging when others are zagging."

Disney Channel had become a domineering force in cable television. It was now available in more than ninety-two million homes and steadily topping the prime-time ratings for all of basic cable. But unlike most television networks, the value in the ratings bonanza for Disney Channel didn't lie in increased ad revenue. The value was in how those eyeballs on the channel could translate into merchandise and music sales. And because Disney owned the publishing and the masters of all the network's original songs in their entirety, the profits were massive.

"You're talking about a seventeen million audience for *High School Musical 2*," Disney music executive Mitchell Leib said. "What? Is every kid in America watching the Disney Channel? The answer is yes. And then guess what? Is every kid in America buying a *Cheetah Girls* soundtrack and a *Hannah Montana* soundtrack and a *High School Musical* soundtrack? Yes."

BUT NOT ALL *High School Musical* news was good news. In early September 2007, just weeks after *High School Musical 2* premiered on Disney Channel, someone leaked private photos of Vanessa Hudgens posing in her underwear and in the nude. Vanessa was eighteen at the time of the online leak, but the amateur photos had reportedly been taken years earlier when they were sent to a former boyfriend.

Rich Ross was in Australia on a business trip when he awoke to the story splashed on the front page of a local newspaper. "I knew then that, clearly, it was going to be everywhere," he said.

Back in Burbank, Vanessa came to Anne Sweeney's office in tears.

"That was one of the most heartbreaking moments I remember," said Sweeney, who was then the president of the Disney/ABC Television Group. "It was not an interrogation. It was more of an, *Oh, God, how could this happen to this kid? How in the world does someone get access to a child?* And the word to underscore was 'child.' She was just a kid."

The public distribution of the images, which happened without Vanessa's involvement or consent, amounted to child pornography. Disney lawyers swooped in, highlighting that Vanessa was underage when the photos were taken and threatening severe legal action to any outlets that posted the images. "I remember feeling so angry at whoever it was who was out there exploiting her," Sweeney said.

But the novelty of celebrity hacks and the persistent idea that Disney stars should be infallible role models meant that a frenzy of judgment and shaming of Vanessa ensued. "It was at a moment in time where celebrities were starting to realize that what they thought was private wasn't necessarily staying that way," Ross said.

For many pundits and commenters, the blame lay more on Vanessa for taking the photos than on the person who betrayed her and leaked them. "She's damaged," one L.A. mom told *Reuters*. "She's got this teeny-bop audience, young preteens and younger, who are admiring her and thinking she's this wonderful, pure innocent person." And the public messaging from Disney Channel did little to change these victim-blaming perceptions.

"I want to apologize to my fans, whose support and trust means the world to me," Vanessa wrote in a curated statement days after the leak. "I am embarrassed over this situation and regret having ever taken these photos."

Tabloid rumors swirled that Disney was planning to axe Vanessa from the third *High School Musical* film, for which cast negotiations were ongoing. But Disney stressed that they were still in talks with *all* of the main cast. "Vanessa has apologized for what was obviously a lapse in judgment," then–Disney Channel PR head Patti McTeague said in a statement. "We hope she's learned a valuable lesson."

Despite the scolding tone of that statement, those on the ground say that behind the scenes, the matter seemed to be handled with a more compassionate hand by the network brass. "What I heard in the hallways wasn't, 'This is a property. We don't want to fuck it up,'" *High School Musical* writer Peter Barsocchini said. "There was an attitude from people like, 'She's just a kid. Give her a fucking break.'"

Looking back, the network executives reiterated to me that they never considered removing Vanessa from the film or punishing her in any way. "We made the decision that Vanessa was part of the family, and she was going to stay part of the family," Ross said. The stated "lesson" they imparted on Vanessa, Sweeney said, was, "Protect yourself. Protect your privacy. Protect your being."

"From a Disney perspective, it wasn't, 'You're a bad girl. You shouldn't have done this,'" Sweeney reflected sixteen years later. "It was, 'You're a young woman. Be careful out there.' I know the media ran with it like this scolding, but she was surrounded by a lot of women in corporate jobs who didn't want to see anything bad happen to her."

Women, while not as prevalent at the executive level as men, played crucial roles in Disney Channel's ascent. (Exhibit A: executive vice president of production Susette Hsiung, who oversaw the projects' budgets and was described by one male producer as "a tough motherfucker" who was "in many ways, the heart and muscle and brain of keeping the operation going.")

By this point, Sweeney was overseeing all of Disney's television properties, including ESPN and ABC. And she was long familiar with the sexism that permeated the media landscape. When Paramount chief Sherry Lansing had stepped down three years prior, Sweeney took on the mantle of "the most powerful woman in Hollywood."

Yet, when Sweeney joined the other Disney executives to pose for photos with the cast at the *High School Musical 2* premiere, a tabloid identified her as "Zac Efron's mom," assuming she must have been accompanying him to the event. "The sexism was rampant. It was constant. And I didn't take the time to think about it very much, or react to it," she said. "I just kind of parked it."

The Vanessa incident highlighted to Sweeney and the rest of the executives that the nature of celebrity—especially what was expected of young female celebrities—was rapidly changing with the dominance of the internet and the rise of social media. It was clear there was more that needed to be done to protect and train Disney Channel's stars, but it would take until 2009, after the *High School Musical* franchise had ended, for institutionalized action to take place.

WHEN PLANS FOR a third *High School Musical* film were first percolating, the network had pushed for it to be a Halloween-themed Disney Channel Original Movie. Supernatural DCOMs were some of the most successful draws on the network. In the network executives' minds, it made sense. Why not put the East High kids in an otherworldly adventure?

The creative team recoiled. "It was outrageous," executive producer Bill Borden said. "There were magic books and time travel. It was insane." They were saved from that fate by Dick Cook. The Walt Disney Studios chief had been one of several Disney executives invited to watch the *High School Musical* concert tour's stop at the Staples Center back in January 2007. The second film had still been in development then, but Cook sidled up to screenwriter Peter Barsocchini at the show and told him he was interested in making a third film as a theatrical release.

For the studio, the risk of putting *High School Musical* on the big screen was low. *The Lizzie McGuire Movie* had proven that fans would follow their favorite characters from their living rooms to their local movie theaters. And Disney Channel had already done the heavy lifting to build a fan base and develop *High School Musical* into a $200 million franchise that had generated more than $1 billion in operating profits for Disney over two fiscal years. If the studio could make a theatrical movie for $30 million or less, the potential for substantial global margins was huge. Unlike Disney's *Pirates of the Caribbean* or *Chronicles of Narnia* franchises, where a film's budget could stretch beyond $200 million and required aggressive marketing campaigns to turn profits, with *High School Musical,* they could essentially sit back and reap their rewards stress free.

The creatives were thrilled to migrate their TV success to the big screen and not be cornered into making a trippy, fantasy-filled DCOM. Returning director Kenny Ortega floated the idea of shooting it in 3-D and dubbing it *High School Musical 3-D.* Instead, the third film stuck to two dimensions and became *High School Musical 3: Senior Year,* following the gang as they navigated their final days of high school and fretted over college admissions and scholarships.

But as divergent as the network and studio executives had been during the *Lizzie McGuire Movie* days, the tension was even higher now. Moving a massive franchise from the network to the studio meant Disney Channel giving up complete creative control. "It was emotionally hard," Sweeney said. "Because the people at the channel, Rich and Gary, really understood the essence of the property. And it's never easy to hand over your baby and say, 'Oh, but the character wouldn't do that,' or 'They wouldn't say that to each other.' The handoff was tough."

Plus, if *High School Musical 3* was a theatrical property instead of a network release, that chunk of revenue would be sucked out of the network's profits and executives' bonuses. "We did argue for years to try to get a piece of what we had created, but to no avail," Sweeney said. "And it got to a point where I'd rather us be successful in the process of creating great IP than be successful in arguing for a small piece of it."

As A THEATRICAL feature, the *High School Musical 3* budget ballooned sevenfold from that of the original TV film to $30 million. They could now spend $1 million on the set design for a single musical number—a quarter of the entire budget of the first film. The small band of musicians that had been used to create the score on the first two films was expanded to a full-sized orchestra. And Zac Efron had been able to negotiate a $3 million paycheck—a sum worth more than fifty times the average DCOM lead-actor contract.

But by centering *High School Musical 3* on graduation, they were making a definitive farewell film to end a three-part saga. With Zac's movie career ascending and starring roles in big-screen comedies, romances, and artsy indie films on deck, there was little chance he would return for a fourth *High School Musical* film, no matter the offer on the table.

Instead, they left the door open for the franchise to continue without him, introducing a few younger characters in the third film to test if they might be able to carry a fourth vehicle. The role of Sharpay's new minion, Tiara, almost went to Sarah Hyland, but Disney liked the idea of adding a British actor (Jemma McKenzie-Brown) to further cash in on the franchise's popularity in the United Kingdom. And Matt Prokop beat out Taylor Lautner for the role of Troy's hapless basketball protege, Jimmie "The Rocket Man" Zara.

On set in Utah, it felt like the growing pains from the second film had settled. No one expected this shoot to re-create the innocent magic of the first, and the studio wasn't nearly as heavy-handed as the network had been with their day-to-day production oversight. When it was released in more than 3,600 movie theaters on October 24, 2008, *High School Musical 3* exceeded expectations, proving that the franchise could officially shatter records in any medium.

The G-rated film opened at number one at the box office, beating the R-rated horror sequel *Saw V* and pulling in more than $42 million its first weekend. It kept the same pathos of the first two films and didn't attempt to deviate into edgier territory to draw in new crowds. "What Disneyland's Main Street is to suburban planning, this movie is to adolescence," *Time*'s Richard Corliss wrote in his review. The movie also soared in markets abroad, where it opened in dozens of countries, including the UK, Germany, and Spain. Rich Ross's push to amplify Disney Channel's presence overseas had paid off handsomely. And while it was robbed of any Oscar nominations, Zac and Vanessa did perform "Last Chance" as part of a musical movie medley at the 2009 Academy Awards.

In total, *High School Musical 3* made more than $90 million domestically and $252 million at the global box office, putting it on par with the margins of classic films like *Alien* and *Fried Green Tomatoes*. East High didn't have extraterrestrials or murder, but it did have Troy and Gabriella dancing on a school rooftop in the pouring rain.

ALMOST IMMEDIATELY AFTER *High School Musical 3: Senior Year* hit theaters, Dick Cook was prepared to greenlight a fourth film, following a new group of kids and possibly bringing back some of the original cast. The writers and producers discussed ideas with the studio for how it could work. Perhaps the East High arts program could be in trouble, and the Wildcats alumni would need to come back and help put on a fundraiser show.

But Disney Channel had had enough. Walt Disney Pictures had just co-opted a *Hannah Montana* movie, and the network executives were tired of watching the theatrical division continue to benefit from their homegrown franchises. The studio had intruded on their territory for the last time. After the Disney Channel executives made an appeal to Bob Iger, Cook eventually dropped the idea.

There was still talk of bringing the *High School Musical* franchise back to cable and continuing the story on Disney Channel. They toyed with ideas about a DCOM where a new group of kids put on a Halloween or Christmas play, or they might turn the whole of East High into an immersive *Sleep No More*–type experience, where the kids did stationary performances in various parts of the school. The network even publicly announced *High School Musical 4: East Meets West*, with Jeff Hornaday replacing Ortega as director. Barsocchini got as far as writing a treatment of a script that would expand the HSM universe to introduce the Wildcats' rival, West High. The lead would be a female volleyball star from East High who falls in love with a male soccer star from West High. But none of those concepts went ahead.

Instead, Disney made a direct-to-video spin-off, *Sharpay's Fabulous Adventure*, with just Ashley Tisdale (opposite a young Austin Butler). And in 2011, the network announced their "most ambitious series to date," converting the *High School Musical* franchise into a musical series called *Madison High* that would follow a new group of kids at a different school so that they could film locally in L.A. They shot the pilot and recorded songs with the cast, which included Beanie Feldstein, Katherine McNamara, Genevieve Hannelius, Leah Lewis, and Luke Benward. Only Alyson Reed as Ms. Darbus returned from the movie cast. But it wasn't sustainable. Creating an entire musical experience in each episode was deemed too expensive and too complicated for the network. It never made it beyond the pilot.

In 2016, Disney Channel tried again, even holding open casting calls for a new *High School Musical* film. But those plans fizzled, too. It wasn't until the streaming platform Disney+ began to take shape, and creator Tim Federle found the magic formula to capitalize on nostalgia and attract a new generation of fans with the meta *High School Musical: The Musical: The Series*, that the franchise was finally revitalized in 2019.

Still, the legacy of the original *High School Musical* trilogy changed everything. While Ryan Murphy insisted *Glee*, which premiered in 2009, wasn't inspired by the Disney films, the target audience for that Fox show was the same teens who had been the target audience for Disney Channel a few years before. *Glee* had an easier road to success because its teen and twentysomething viewers had now been primed to obsess over singing high schoolers. "When *Glee* showed up, it was all warmed up," Ross said. "The viewers were unapologetic lovers of that genre."

Musical DCOM franchises became the norm on Disney Channel for decades to come, from *Camp Rock* and *Teen Beach Movie* to *Descendants* and *Zombies*. "*High School Musical* became the first of many things that blew the doors off," Sweeney said. "Generations started to sing and dance again." And, perhaps even more important for the network, Disney Channel's stars started to be catapulted to multi-hyphenate celebrity status while still working for the channel. They were becoming teen idols.

10

The Rise of *Hannah Montana*

On Friday afternoons at 4:00 P.M., a line of pulsating energy snaked around Stage 9 at the KTLA Studios on Sunset Boulevard. When the doors pushed open, scores of screaming children, and their amenable parents, climbed the risers to fill the two hundred or so audience seats facing the soundstage. High on adrenaline and free pizza, they cheered for the cast so loudly between takes that the crew struggled to hear stage directions. The cacophony made adult audiences at network sitcoms seem like demure funeral guests. These kids were animalistic.

The hottest ticket in town was an audience seat at a taping of *Hannah Montana*.

"A boom in children's entertainment has created a new blood sport in Hollywood," *The New York Times*'s Brooks Barnes wrote in 2007. "What admission to a private preschool is to some parents in New York, a trip backstage at *Hannah Montana* has become to certain moms and dads in Hollywood."

As the cast got their final hair and makeup done before each Friday shoot, the audience would watch a previously aired episode of *Hannah Montana* to get them hyped for what they were about to see live. "Sometimes I'd look out and watch the kids who were watching the monitor," executive producer Steven Peterman said. "And I'd see kids mouthing the dialogue because they had watched the episodes so many times they had them memorized."

On one particular day in 2007, among the throngs of mostly young girls and their moms, a balding, middle-aged man sat with a blank look on his face as the warm-up guy chattered through a series of asinine jokes. There sat Larry David, at the height of his *Curb Your Enthusiasm* fame, diligently playing the pre-show games with his two daughters, Cazzie and Romy. David had called the producers begging for audience tickets to make his girls happy. "There's Larry David having to pass a balloon without using his hands," Peterman said. "I'm thinking, *This is unbelievable*."

A few weeks later, one of the *Hannah* scripts called for a celebrity cameo to illustrate the exclusivity of a restaurant on the show. The original plan was to have Gary Marsh appear as himself.

"Don't you know who I am? I'm the president of Disney Channel entertainment!" he'd say in the script.

"And I'm the president of the I-don't-care club," the maître'd would retort, before letting Hannah Montana waltz right in.

But Marsh was busy traveling overseas that week. They'd need a last-minute backup. Someone suggested calling David. The comedian was notoriously press shy and shunned the spotlight outside of his own creative work, but it was worth a shot. He'd just been at a taping and seemed willing to do the previously unimaginable to please his kids.

Peterman called him up with the request. If David would be willing to appear as himself, they could also write in small roles for his daughters in the scene, and let them spend the whole day on the *Hannah* set with the cast.

"I never do this. I never do this," David fretted. "When is it?"

"Next week," Peterman replied.

"We're filming *Curb*," David said. "Can you move it?"

"We don't have any other episodes ready. It has to be next week," Peterman said, before adding a final twist of guilt. "Listen, maybe something will come up later in the season. You're a wonderful father to have considered doing it. I thank you for even entertaining the idea."

A long pause from David.

"Don't call anybody yet. Give me fifteen minutes."

David called back a few minutes later, as promised. Good news.

He'd rearranged the *Curb* shooting schedule so that he could film a *Hannah Montana* scene with his daughters instead.

FOLLOWING THE SUCCESS of The Cheetah Girls and Hilary Duff, as well as the wider popularity of *American Idol* and Britney Spears, Disney Channel had been eager to create a series around a singular fictional pop star. "Britney went from being an artist that young kids loved to watch to one where parents were starting to question whether she was the right role model for them," original series head Adam Bonnett said of Britney's *In the Zone* era, during which she made headlines for kissing Madonna at the VMAs and having two quickie weddings in a single year. "So we thought, hey, let's create a pop star, even if it's a fictional pop star, that could fill that void that felt right and appropriate for kids."

Despite the contentious firing of showrunner Michael Poryes during the first season of *That's So Raven* over his clash with the writers, he was subsequently given the opportunity to try his hand at writing a pilot based on the idea of a girl who lives a double life as a pop star.

It was the beginning of *Hannah Montana*.

What Poryes said he didn't know at the time was that Rich Correll, the frequent *Suite Life* director, and his writing partner Barry O'Brien had already pitched a similar pilot to Bonnett. Theirs, Correll said, was called *Where's Xandra?*, about a regular girl named Alexandra who moonlighted as a popstar called Xandra. According to Correll, his and O'Brien's script included key details, like that secret closet full of pop star clothes, and it followed a plot similar to a season 1 *Hannah* episode where Miley's date buys them tickets to a Hannah Montana concert and she spends the evening in a *Mrs. Doubtfire*–esque rapid shuffle between identities.

When Correll found out what was going on, he was shocked. "Adam Bonnett was standing on stage at *The Suite Life of Zack & Cody*, and I remember him saying to me on a break, 'You know, I hope you won't be too unhappy, but we took an idea that's very similar to something you pitched, and we're making a series out of it,'" Correll said. "I was like, 'What do you mean?' You never say to somebody, 'I hope you're not going to be too unhappy, but we just stole your house and your car.'"

The Writers Guild took the matter to arbitration, and Correll and O'Brien were eventually given co-creator credits on *Hannah Montana* and a cut of the show's profits. (Making things even messier, a comedy writer named Buddy Sheffield claimed *he* originally pitched Disney a pilot about a regular kid who secretly lived a pop star life, called *Rock and Roland*, in 2001. Sheffield sued over the alleged similarities and lack of compensation, and he and Disney settled out of court in 2008.)

Meanwhile, as Disney moved forward with Poryes's *Hannah Montana* script, veteran TV producer Steven Peterman, who had overseen the later seasons of *Murphy Brown* and created *Suddenly Susan*, was in need of a new showrunner job. Network comedies still hadn't recovered from the early-2000s reality TV onslaught, and, like so many out-of-work sitcom producers before him, he and his writing partner Gary Dontzig found themselves just desperate enough to consider Disney Channel. Bonnett showed the duo three unrelated pilot scripts to potentially oversee. Of those, Peterman and Dontzig felt Poryes's *Hannah* script had the most potential.

"His script was kind of schlocky, typical silly kid-show stuff," Peterman said. "But what I liked about Michael's *Hannah* script was that being famous didn't solve this girl's problems, it just complicated her life more."

Peterman was more enthusiastic about it than Dontzig, but they worked with Poryes to retool his script to get it into pilot shape. They killed off the mom character to give the teen protagonist more vulnerability. The dad went from being a songwriter to a musician. And popular girls named Amber and Ashley were added as the school bullies.

The network was pleased and made Peterman and Dontzig an offer to run the show. The pair had recently been fired after helming a pilot at a different network, and Peterman—described by one of his colleagues as "the nicest man in showbiz"—wasn't keen on inflicting the same pain upon Poryes. So, he pushed Disney to allow Poryes to stay on as an executive producer. Dontzig couldn't stomach being attached to the project for at least sixty-five episodes, so he bowed out entirely. And Peterman and Poryes forged ahead as a showrunning duo, on the hunt for a star to play a star.

DISNEY CHANNEL ROUTINELY sent casting directors on broad, nation-wide searches for fresh talent, and now that they had the *Hannah Montana* script and showrunners locked down, the search for this specific project kicked into overdrive. Casting directors Lisa London and Catherine Stroud saw more than 1,200 girls, testing their acting, singing, and dance skills in multipart auditions for the lead character, then named Zoe, who moonlighted as the pop star Hannah Montana. Authenticity was key. Marsh wanted someone who could actually sing, both to make the pop star element believable and to carry a potential solo music career, à la Hilary Duff.

The widespread casting call reached the talent agent of an eleven-year-old girl in Tennessee: Miley Cyrus, née Destiny Hope Cyrus, but dubbed "Miley" for her exceptionally smiley nature as a baby by her country music singer father, Billy Ray Cyrus.

Miley's agent was asked to send tapes of all her female clients between the ages of eleven and sixteen to Disney. Miley, just squeaking into the age range, read for the part of Zoe's best friend, Lilly. Almost immediately, London and Stroud called, wanting Miley to make another tape, this time reading for Zoe. Bursting with excitement, Miley hastily recorded a new tape. But the ensuing rejection was swift: Disney felt she was too young and too small to play the lead. "We showed them Miley's tape, and they said no," Stroud said. "Then we showed them Miley's re-tape, and they said no."

Miley continued on with sixth grade in Thompson's Station, on the outskirts of Nashville. She'd missed fifth grade there when the family moved to Canada to be with Billy Ray while he shot his TV show, *Doc*. Her embryonic acting career had included a small part on that series, as well as a bit role in Tim Burton's *Big Fish*. But now, Miley was getting bullied by Tennessee mean girls who made her days miserable, and she dreamed of getting out.

Back in L.A., London and Stroud spent six months trying to find any-one better than Miley for the role. They went to agents and managers. Put up casting notices in performing arts schools. The long list of girls who read for the part included Vanessa Hudgens, Shailene Woodley, Lucy Hale, Sarah Hyland, Sara Paxton, Ashley Benson, Jennette McCurdy, Taylor Momsen, and Daniella Monet. They also considered Brie Larson and the singer JoJo, who both passed on auditioning. (Gary Marsh had initially offered Aly and AJ Michalka the roles of Zoe and Lilly, but they turned it down. According to Bonnett, Aly, in particular, "really wanted her music career and her acting career to be very separate.")

Finally, the Disney Channel executives agreed to give Miley another chance. She was six months older by then. Maybe they could make it work. They asked Miley to come to L.A. and audition in person. Her mom, Tish, wrote a note excusing Miley from cheerleading practice, and they ventured west. The Cyruses had assumed Miley would be one of a select few finalists still up for the lead role, which had now changed names from Zoe to Chloe. Instead, they found fifty other would-be stars preparing to read in the waiting room.

The girls were called in one by one to audition for a panel that in-cluded London and Stroud, Judy Taylor, Peterman, Poryes, and Lee Shallat Chemel, an Emmy-nominated and pioneering female director who would be directing the *Hannah* pilot. When it was Miley's turn, she sang some bars from "Mamma Mia" and read a scene from the pilot script. "She hits some stuff organically, and it's hysterical. She misses other things by a mile," Peterman recalled. "She talks too fast. She doesn't wait, and she doesn't listen to the other lines. But she's just got so much energy, and she's so *alive*."

It was difficult to get a read on the room, and the Cyruses returned home to Tennessee without any news. Then came the call: they wanted Miley back in L.A. to read again. The number of potential Chloes had dwindled down to thirty. Tish and Miley made the cross-country trip and did the whole spiel again. Marsh was still hesitant about Miley. Testing showed southern accents didn't play well to coastal audiences, and Miley's Tennessee twang was thick. He consulted with Walt Dis-ney Records executive Jay Landers and showed him a tape of Miley singing. In Landers's opinion, she had everything they could hope for in an artist. "Think about Shania Twain," Landers told Marsh. "She's made the country thing a universal thing. Who knows?"

After two in-person rounds of "finalist" auditions with dozens of other potential Chloes in the waiting room, Miley was expecting another grueling cattle call when the third audition request came and she flew out to L.A. once again. But now, there were only three girls left: Miley, Daniella Monet—who'd most recently played Jason Alexander's daughter on the CBS sitcom *Listen Up*—and Taylor Momsen, who'd played Cindy Lou Who in *Dr. Seuss' How the Grinch Stole Christmas* and had a part in *Spy Kids 2*.

For her final audition, Miley wore a T-shirt that read *I should have my own TV show* as she delivered her lines and sang an original song she'd written called "Beach Weekend" with a big grin. After the girls left, Marsh went around the room asking everyone's final thoughts.

Taylor Momsen was, according to Poryes, "a very distant third." They ruled her out. Daniella Monet, who would later co-star on Nickelodeon's *Victorious*, was the obvious choice for the part. Her singing voice wasn't as strong as Miley's, but her acting was polished. She nailed every line, and she came with years of sitcom experience already under her belt. She would clearly be a pro on set and would be able to jump into the deep end of all that the series and Disney demanded of her.

"She's definitely better," Peterman told Marsh. "She knows where the jokes are. She knows how to deliver them—and the more I watch her, the more bored I get. I know exactly what she's going to do before she does it."

And then there was Miley.

"I watch Miley, and I don't know what the hell she's going to do next," Peterman said. "But I cannot take my eyes off her. *And* she can sing."

Poryes, Bonnett, and Chemel agreed.

"Okay," Marsh said. "Let's pull the trigger."

MILEY'S CONTRACT, WHICH she had signed when she made it to the final three, had a base salary of $8,000 per episode for the first season, with a standard 5 percent bump each year. (Taylor Momsen and Daniella Monet had also signed contracts as finalists—though, with their more significant past credits, they would have earned $10,000 per episode to start, had either been chosen.)

But the producers still needed to finalize the rest of the cast. Disney had planned for Mitchell Whitfield (best known as Rachel's ex-fiancé, Dr. Barry the orthodontist, on *Friends*) to play Chloe's dad, a busy studio musician who would only occasionally pop in and out of scenes. Poryes had originally envisioned Chloe as a Jewish teen girl in New York, and Whitfield, himself a native Brooklynite, paired well with that setup. But now that the lead was a very southern Gentile, they might need to reconsider his casting.

While Miley did chemistry reads with potential actors to play her character's best friend, Tish Cyrus floated the idea of Billy Ray auditioning to play Miley's dad on screen. He wasn't really doing anything at the moment, and maybe the Cyrus family could all move to California and recenter their lives around this new joint project. London and Stroud were intrigued. They approached the showrunners about meeting with Billy Ray.

"Our first reaction to being told Billy Ray wanted to read was just, 'Shit,'" Poryes said. Miley being Billy Ray's progeny hadn't helped her get the part. Her dad's fame had waned in the decade since his breakout song, "Achy Breaky Heart," and he was completely unknown to Disney Channel audiences. Plus, he didn't have any experience doing comedy. His main acting credits were the PAX TV drama *Doc* (in which he played the doc in question: a rural, God-fearing man who joins a New York City practice), and David Lynch's *Mulholland Drive* (a minor role as the pool guy who beats up Justin Theroux).

But, wanting to keep the mother of their new star happy, the network agreed to humor the Cyruses and allowed Billy Ray to read. When he arrived in Burbank for the meeting, he had his guitar in hand. "It's like Linus with his blanket. He's nervous, and he's holding that guitar," Stroud said. "And he was so over-the-top handsome. We're like, holy crap. And then, all he does is talk about his children. We were dying. It was so endearing."

Charm is always a good thing in TV. And when it was time for Billy Ray to read with Miley, it was a slam dunk. Miley had been stiff and hesitant reading with the other adult actors, but with her actual dad she was completely at ease. "You can't buy that kind of chemistry," Poryes said. "It blew us away." To finish the deal, Billy Ray and Miley did their special real-life handshake, and then he sat down with his guitar and they sang a duet of his song "I Want My Mullet Back." "Everyone in that room could see the magic," Stroud said. "And that, for us, was the moment where the show really came together."

Because the real-life father-daughter casting would now be a selling point of the show, they needed to rewrite Billy Ray's character so that he had a reason to be home all the time. His character name became the playful Robbie Ray, and his storyline would now be that of a musician who had given up his career to support his daughter's dreams.

Art would soon imitate life.

As SHOOTING ON the *Hannah Montana* pilot got underway in 2005, a flurry of adjustments were made throughout. One of the biggest: changing Miley's character name from Chloe Stewart to Miley Stewart, just like they'd turned Rose Baxter into Raven Baxter on *That's So Raven*. "As we were working with Miley, we started to see her as the embodiment of what this character was," Peterman said. "We just thought it was easier for everybody, and it's such a great name." (Billy Ray has also said that his frequent slip-ups calling Miley by her real name during the shoot contributed to the switch.)

The script was rewritten to incorporate more southern slang, though the show's hallmark catchphrase, "Sweet niblets!," was the invention of either the Upper East Side–raised series writer Todd Greenwald or inspired by Peterman's youth in Wisconsin surrounded by corn. (Both men take credit.) Miley's character had originally been written to be shy and withdrawn when not performing as her Hannah Montana alter ego, but that didn't jibe with Miley's spitfire personality. So, her character now became similarly outspoken and goofy.

Likewise, Jackson Stewart, Miley's onscreen older brother, was written to be cripplingly introverted, only speaking through an orangutan pup-pet named Fletcher that he carried everywhere. But when they cast Jason Earles in the role, his comedic chops and gift for physical comedy made them reconsider. "I was dreading the prospect of potentially spending three or four years talking through this hand puppet," Jason said. "I took lessons with a puppeteer and spent so much time with that damn puppet, but you've never seen anybody more thrilled that work went to waste."

When Jason had auditioned for *Hannah Montana*, he told the cast-ing directors, "I'm over eighteen, but I can play younger." The vague phrasing signaled that he wouldn't have to work kid hours or receive on-set schooling (music to casting's ears), but it also belied his actual age at the time—twenty-seven. Legally, casting directors aren't allowed to ask actors their specific age as part of the casting process, and he'd already had small parts playing teens on *That's So Raven* and *Phil of the Future*. "It wasn't until maybe the sixth or seventh episode of the series that they realized how old I actually was," Jason said.

In the end, the decade-plus age gap between Jason and the rest of the actors playing kids on the show was seen as an asset. He took on the role of mentor and served as a crucial bridge between the creatives and the young cast, which also included Emily Osment as Lilly. Miley and Emily trusted Jason's acting expertise and listened to his notes, and he, in turn, was a conduit to the writers' room, letting them know of any grievances among the cast. "He led by example. His work ethic and the way he approached the craft of acting, the kids all looked at him and thought, 'Oh, that's what I should be doing,'" writer and producer Douglas Lieb-lein said. "The show would one hundred percent not be what it was if it wasn't for Jason being an adult in that position and teaching those kids how to do the job that they were completely unprepared for."

But while Miley and Emily looked up to their older co-star, they strug-gled at times to get along with each other. The two girls had gelled when they were first cast as best friends on *Hannah*. Then, they got to know each other. Emily was from an industry family. Her dad, Eugene, was an acting coach, and her older brother, Haley Joel, had been Oscar nomi-nated for his work in *The Sixth Sense*. "Emily was very professional. She was very 'Hollywood,'" said Hiromi Dames, who played socialite Traci Van Horn on the show. "She knew everything she was supposed to do. She was almost like an athlete, and her dad was on the side coaching her."

The Cyruses were . . . not that way.

"Miley flew by the seat of her pants a lot of the time," Lieblein said. "There was a little bit of animosity there because Miley was getting all the attention from doing none of the work. There were about three episodes where they weren't speaking to each other."

During the course of the show there were jealous fights over cute guest stars, and an early tiff in the on-set classroom required parental intervention to broker peace. But, as Peterman put it, the girls "were smart enough to work things out. They figured out that it was more fun when they were not fighting."

BEFORE PRODUCTION ON any Disney Channel series began, Rich Ross hosted a "family dinner" for the cast and their parents, a tradition he'd first begun while working at Nickelodeon. "I wanted to open the door if people needed things, and leave no mystery to the man behind the curtain," he said. "From the beginning, I always knew the talent would be our calling card, and they knew I cared deeply." At the gathering for *Hannah Montana*, he recalled Miley being "very clear" about her intentions in the industry and telling him, "Hilary Duff is my role model. That's what I want to be. That's *who* I want to be. This is an opportunity."

As regular season production got underway on *Hannah*, Miley approached her calling with grit and determination, despite her lack of industry experience. "Miley was just fearless," Jason Earles said. "She was always willing to be the butt of a joke. That was really mature of her, and also really smart—because it made her one thousand times more relatable than some of the other leading teenage girls on other shows."

To capture performance footage for the show, production set up an actual concert for Miley to perform as Hannah at the Glendale Centre Theatre. They gave out free tickets and filled the venue with kids who had no idea who Miley, or Hannah, was. Despite her anonymity, the energy was electric. Miley had a natural stage presence. She'd grown up on tour with her dad and was comfortable with the technical side of performing, unfazed by the hot lights or the feedback from the microphone. "She was incredible at that concert," Peterman said. "That's part of when I knew, 'Oh, my God, what have we got here?'"

But back on set, Miley was less competent. She was still learning the difference between stage left and camera left, and it was clear that she and others in the young cast weren't quite ready for the pressure of filming in front of a live audience. Instead, they filmed the first few episodes without an audience to ease them into the routine.

By the time the fourth episode rolled around, production had to cut the cord and attempt a live show. As the audience took their seats, the cast could hear the buzz of the crowd from backstage. The first scene they were going to shoot was a tricky one. On the Stewart living area set, Emily had to ride in on a skateboard and do an awkward robot dance. Miley had to convincingly have an anguished, one-sided phone call. And Jason had to launch a marshmallow off a spoon and catch it in his mouth. "I remember how white they were, how nervous they were," Peterman said. "We said, 'Just breathe. If you hear laughter, wait. Don't say your next line or they won't hear you.'"

Original programming head Adam Bonnett stood to the side, watching anxiously. The crew held their breaths.

"ACTION!"

Emily whizzed by on the skateboard. Miley slowed down and paused for laughs. And Jason banged his fist on the spoon just right to flip the marshmallow into his mouth. "They were all perfect. Nobody dropped a line," Peterman said. "And the audience went nuts."

Bonnett could barely contain his glee.

"Oh, my God. Oh, my God! We've got a hit," he told the producers afterward.

"Adam, we've been telling you that for weeks," a slightly annoyed Peterman replied.

Bonnett shrugged. "I don't know it's a hit until the audience tells me it's a hit."

*   *   *

To guarantee eyes on *Hannah*'s March 24, 2006, premiere, Disney Channel sandwiched it between the debut of the DCOM *Cow Belles*, starring Aly and AJ Michalka, and an encore showing of *High School Musical*. *Hannah* brought in 5.4 million viewers, the highest ratings of any series premiere in the network's history.

"The first week that the show was out, I was at the gym and this thirty-year-old tatted-up dude came up to me and was like, 'Bro, that new show? You're funny as balls on that thing,'" Jason Earles said. "I was like, 'Oh, do you have kids?' And he's like, 'Nah, man, I just de-stress with Disney Channel.'"

Los Angeles Times TV critic Robert Lloyd described *Hannah* as "not the finest of its kind" but a "solid little sitcom that will help move a lot of units when thirteen-year-old star Miley Cyrus starts fulfilling that re- cording contract she's also been signed to." The network quickly upped the first season order from twenty to twenty-six episodes. While Disney could tout that *Suite Life* was a top-five series for kids on basic cable, *Hannah* was the number one show on basic cable with kids *and* tweens. And in the hearts of tatted-up gym rats.

Miley still needed some handholding to hit the jokes as they con- tinued filming season 1, but her effervescent energy was nearly enough to carry her through. She also perfected the "Lucy sees a spider" face— sitcom shorthand for the classic "Ewww" expression Lucille Ball often made on *I Love Lucy*—and the writers made sure to pepper it into most scripts. "Look, I love Miley. When we first got her at twelve years old, she couldn't act," Lieblein said. "You couldn't give her something and then expect she was going to do the work and come back. But then there was a moment where that changed."

That breakthrough came in season 1, episode 24, "The Idol Side of Me." The script included a scene where the school's flakey-follicled pest, Dandruff Danny, shakes his debris all over Miley. It gave no direction for how Miley should deliver the line that immediately followed the dousing, but Miley made the choice to turn it into a gag, sputtering "pffft" between each word as she spit fake dandruff flakes out of her mouth. Take after take, she nailed it. Finally, the episode's director, Fred Savage of *The Wonder Years* fame, asked Miley to do one more take—this time delivering the line in a straightforward manner, without the theatrics. Miley nodded. But as she walked back to her mark, she mumbled under her breath, "Alright, here's one the unfunny way for Fred."

"When we're behind the monitors, we can hear everything the cast says, even when they're mumbling it and they don't want us to hear them," Lieblein said. "We all went, 'She's absolutely right.' It was the defining moment where we knew: She knows what funny is, and she created that herself. We don't have to keep holding her hand."

WITH MULTIPLE SUCCESSFUL multi-camera sitcoms now simultaneously underway, the network executives decided to bring a fan-favorite sitcom trope to Disney Channel: crossover episodes. *The Suite Life of Zack & Cody* shot in the same building as *That's So Raven* at Hollywood Center Studios (now Sunset Las Palmas Studios), and *Hannah Montana* filmed at KTLA Studios (now Sunset Bronson Studios), about a six-minute drive away. Just as Garry Marshall had once done with *Happy Days* and *Laverne & Shirley*, Disney Channel pulled players from their various sitcoms together for two sets of Frankenstein-ed episodes, *That's So Suite Life of Hannah Montana* in 2006 and *Wizards on Deck with Hannah Montana* (bringing in the later series *Wizards of Waverly Place*, which also shot at Hollywood Center) in 2009.

Most of the actors loved having the chance to do something different and interact with the other casts. But there were challenges. Like when *Wizards on Deck with Hannah Montana* shot in the midst of Miley Cyrus and Selena Gomez's spat over Nick Jonas (whom they both dated at various points). Across that trilogy of episodes, Miley and Selena avoided having any scenes together. While perhaps also the result of scheduling issues, "The way that I remember it is that *The Suite Life* was the no-man's-land between the other two shows," *Suite Life* writer Tim Pollock said. "Selena didn't want to do *Hannah*, and Miley didn't want to do *Wizards*. Dylan and Cole had to do each of those shows to make it work."

A scheduled break between filming part two and three of *Wizards on Deck with Hannah Montana* episodes also caused continuity issues. In the months between shooting that *Suite Life* episode and the companion *Hannah Montana* episode, the Sprouses experienced a growth spurt, their voices changed, and Dylan injured his arm. They had to hide Dylan's cast under assorted props and alter the boys' audio tracks in postproduction to create a semblance of unity across the episodes.

Getting the various shows' creative teams to cooperate was another headache. Each group of writers punched up the lines for their own characters on the other shows, while the producers had to jockey for power on the temporarily shared sets. "There were more egos involved with figuring out how all the showrunners worked together than with bringing the kids together," Bonnett said. Added *Wizards of Waverly Place* creator Todd Greenwald, "It was not fun to write, and we didn't want to do it. But the fans loved it, so it's hard to argue with that."

But even on the day-to-day *Hannah Montana* set, the working relationship between *Hannah*'s two showrunners, Poryes and Peterman, was a delicate balance: Peterman, a laid-back, steady ship; Poryes, an uptight bundle of nerves. "I love Michael like a brother, but we had different styles of working, and there were a lot of times where we battled each other," Peterman said. "He would chase ideas like a dog in the park, but he brought a wonderful whimsy to the show."

Unlike on *Raven*, where Poryes's impulses had gone unchecked, here, Peterman served as a crucial buffer, both between Poryes and the writers, and Poryes and the network executives. "Steve kept Michael focused on what he needed to do, and I think Michael benefited from that," director of photography Alan K. Walker said. "He became a changed guy."

Co-producer Lieblein described the setup a little more bluntly. "Peterman's tragic flaw is he's way too nice of a human being. And Poryes is incredibly brazen and pushy," he said. "My job for five years became stepping in between Mommy and Daddy." On set with the actors, Poryes was once again pleasant and generous. But in the writers' room, he struggled to make decisions and could lose his temper. Still, "He was not Dan Schneider at all," Lieblein said, drawing the comparison to the allegedly volatile Nickelodeon showrunner. "I don't think Poryes has the talent, but he's a very nice person."

By season 2, *Hannah Montana* was Disney Channel's crown jewel. In 2008, Disney merchandise aimed specifically at tweens aged nine to twelve—a sector driven by *High School Musical* and *Hannah Montana*—surged from the previous year's $400 million to an eye-watering $2.7 billion. "This show became something bigger than the channel," Peterman said. *Hannah Montana* had enough clout to attract a deluge of celebrity guest stars, including Ray Liotta, Sheryl Crow, Brooke Shields, Vicki Lawrence, Heather Locklear, The Rock, Lisa Rinna, Donny Osmond, Ray Romano, Jon Cryer, and Dr. Phil, and generated a steady stream of media coverage.

But, as was often the case, the showrunners found that praise and rewards from the Disney Channel brass were hard to come by. "If we were on any other network, you would be asking me where my wife and I want to go on vacation during the hiatus and what kind of car I would like as a gift," Peterman once told Bonnett. Instead, Peterman reflected, "They didn't want anyone to get too uppity."

While the creatives were able to win the occasional network arguments they might have otherwise lost due to *Hannah*'s outsized success, they were also under more scrutiny. "We were the cash cow," Lieblein said. "The executives in charge of steering the train are now afraid that if it goes off the rails on their watch, they'll get fired. So they micromanaged us." And again, the budget for the show was kept tight, no matter how much the series succeeded.

When it was time for the season-3 wrap party, the showrunners wanted to throw a bigger than usual fête to thank everyone for their hard work and celebrate the show's massive achievements. They had leftover money in the budget and submitted a request to the network. It was denied. If the show had leftover money in their budget, they would need to return it to Disney. "The number they offered us to spend on the party would have maybe covered drinks and hotdogs at the Holiday Inn near the Burbank airport," Peterman said. "We were really upset, and maybe I could have handled it better. But I was tired, and I was angry about that nickel-and-diming."

Instead of accepting the offer, Peterman and Poryes composed a letter in reply.

"We understand that there are budget constraints, but we just don't feel we can do a wrap party the way we want to do it with that kind of money," they wrote. "We will pay the difference. But unfortunately, we have a limited amount of money, so we won't be able to invite any of the Disney executives to the party. We're very sorry about that."

The network executives promptly approved the bigger budget.

A SIGNIFICANT PART of *Hannah Montana*'s budget went toward creating a believable pop star look. To construct Hannah's signature blond mane, renowned wigmaker Natascha Ladek sourced untreated human hair from Russia. Once the pale-blond tresses arrived in L.A., she'd take six bundles of hair, each from a different head, and hand weave the strands into a lace cap, then hand dye chunky lowlights throughout. Over the course of the *Hannah Montana* series, tour, and movie, Ladek created about ten custom Hannah wigs of varying lengths and styles. Each wig took eighty to one hundred hours to make and cost roughly $6,000.

"The lighter the hair and the longer the hair, the more expensive it is," said Ladek, whose other work includes Jennifer Lopez's *Selena* wigs and Angela Bassett's *Black Panther* locs. "It's also the quality. Is it straight? Is it shiny? How much natural moisture is in the hair? It's a process. It's almost like buying diamonds."

While the wigs were an instant hit, the network was less enthused by Hannah's pop star wardrobe in season 1. They brought in costume designer Dahlia Foroutan ahead of season 2 to elevate the clothes with a more aspirational slant going forward. Many of the most memorable ensembles from the show—think: Hannah's zebra-striped T-shirts, oversized belts, miniskirts, and combat boots—are her creations. But despite the character being wealthy and famous, Disney didn't want any extravagant couture in Hannah's closet.

Aspirational but still obtainable was the name of the game. So, Foroutan shopped at trendy, youthful boutiques on Melrose Avenue, scoured Nordstrom, and visited the celeb-adored Kitson to create Hannah's fashion-forward style. For Miley Stewart's more down-to-earth looks, she sourced pieces from Forever 21, H&M, Target, and local shops in Malibu. Over time, both sides of the character's style evolved. "We would push her outfits to the limit," Foroutan said. "I always wanted it to look cute. Disney sometimes wanted me to push it past looking cute. It started looking clownish."

In later seasons, Miley began taking a stand. "She would just be like, I'm not coming out of my dressing room, or I'm just not putting it on," Foroutan said. "She had to really start getting strong and standing up. I don't think they had a choice but to respect it."

And as with Raven, there was once again concern over a star's body type on screen. This time, some middling network executives worried that Miley's lanky frame might reinforce the notion that to be a pop star, you needed to be ultra-thin. "Miley was naturally very skinny, and they wanted me to cover up her body as much as possible, especially her arms. They didn't want to create an image of 'This is what beauty is. You have to be super skinny,'" Foroutan said. "They wanted her to be aspirational, but they didn't want it to be harmful to the kids."

WHEN MILEY JOINED *Hannah*, effectively so, too, did the extended Cyrus clan, whom Miley used to describe as "the real Beverly Hillbillies." Tish and Billy Ray first met at a nightclub in 1991 and married a year after Miley was born. They settled on a sprawling farm in Franklin, Tennessee, just south of Nashville. There, they raised their large, blended family, consisting of Miley, her younger siblings, Braison and Noah, and Tish's two children from a previous relationship, Trace and Brandi, whom Billy Ray legally adopted. (Billy Ray also has a son named Christopher, born seven months before Miley, with another woman.)

Because the *Hannah* soundstage was actually two stages that had been combined into one, Billy Ray and Miley occupied a whole suite that included their separate dressing rooms, a sitting area, and a kitchen. Tish's mom, Miley's "Mammie," served as Miley's on-set guardian and ran the MileyWorld fan club out of the shared kitchen, where she sorted through mountains of fan mail and playfully chastised her granddaughter as she ran by with an "Oh, Miley! You're crazy!" Other times, she'd call Miley out if she felt her behavior got too unruly. "If Miley was being a brat, her grandma just wouldn't have it," Jason Earles said. "There was no room for her to be a bad person."

And then there was Miley's godmother, Dolly Parton. Billy Ray had opened for Parton at several concerts in the early '90s and appeared in her "Romeo" music video as Parton's strapping boy toy. They'd developed a close bond, and when Miley was born Parton told him, "She's got to be my fairy goddaughter." While working on season 2, the Cyruses alerted the showrunners that Parton would be open to appearing on the show. Peterman called her up, and they worked out a guest role for her playing Miley Stewart's Aunt Dolly.

"Alright, that all sounds fine," Parton told him. "I'll be there."

"Fantastic!" Peterman replied. "Is there anything you need when you get here?"

"Darlin'," she said, "all I need is a toilet and a place to hang my wig."

THE BOND THAT Billy Ray and Miley had developed during her childhood growing up on the road was more like that of two friends than a parent and child. Tish, who also served as Miley's manager, was the one who had to discipline and put her foot down when either of them crossed a line. When a season 2 episode of *Hannah* involved a Cinderella-inspired fantasy sequence in which Robbie Ray charges down the stairs calling Miley Stewart a "useless freeloader" and yelling at her to clean the house, Billy Ray instead entered with his soft drawl, kindly requesting Miley please do what he asked.

The producers called cut and pulled Billy Ray aside.

"You've got to yell at her," they told him.

"I've never yelled at Miley," he said. "I'm afraid I'm going to scare her."

In the balance of power, "Billy was the child, and Miley was the adult a lot of the time," Lieblein said. "She never, ever showed up late or unprepared. And we're talking about a thirteen- or fourteen- or fifteen-year-old girl. On the other hand, Billy would often just be lost. We'd be like, 'Where's Billy Ray?' He was supposed to be on set, and then we call him and he'd be, like, in Vegas."

Poryes agreed, "I always say Billy was the biggest baby on the set. He was my biggest problem, but he wasn't a *big* problem."

Those who worked on the show described Billy Ray as a gentle, tenderhearted man who generously shared his time and emotions with the other actors. Jason Earles lived an hour-and-a-half commute away from the studio during the first season, so Billy Ray offered for him to stay with the Cyruses whenever he'd like and dubbed him "Jason Ray Cyrus." Other times, Billy Ray would wander around the set, having heart-to-hearts with the other actors when he should have been working.

But it was very clear to everyone involved that Billy Ray didn't enjoy doing *Hannah Montana*. Playing second fiddle on a kids' sitcom wasn't exactly creatively fulfilling. He did it for Miley. "Billy Ray Cyrus didn't need to be there, and he didn't want to be there," said Frances Callier, who played Hannah's bodyguard, Roxy. "You think about that: You don't need the money. You don't have to get up at six o'clock in the morning every day. But you'll do it for your child. I thought that was beautiful."

As time went on, however, Miley's success seemed to weigh on Billy Ray. Her superstardom served as a constant reminder of the ways in which his own star had fallen. "I have always been known as Billy Ray Cyrus' daughter," Miley told *The New York Times* in 2006. "Now, they say my name."

It was a classic Hollywood story of shifting stardoms, just playing out through a father and daughter rather than a couple. "Billy lived *A Star Is Born*," Lieblein said. "He was the biggest star in his country music world for a very long time. His little girl would come on stage with him, and she would be this little treat for the audience. One hundred thousand people were there screaming, 'Billy!' Then, he thinks, *Oh, I'm going to do this little Disney Channel show and help launch her career*. By the end of the first season, she had changed the way tickets were sold to concerts in America, and he couldn't sell out 6,500 seats at Primm, Nevada. When that happened, we went, 'We all know how this ends, right?'"

Between *Hannah* scenes, Billy Ray would retreat to his dressing room, where the crew quipped he was having "a creative moment," as they suspected he imbibed alcohol and weed. "We would always joke about it. Billy Ray would joke about it. Miley made jokes about it," Lieblein said. "But I never saw him visibly drunk. I never saw him visibly high. I will say it would be impossible to tell the difference." Others said Billy Ray's habits were an issue that interfered with his work. "He would come on set, let's say unprepared and not focused, and we all knew what was going on," Poryes said. "We just couldn't do anything about it, as much as we tried. We had a show to do."

By season 4, Billy Ray was miserable. "It got to the point where Billy was like, 'She's the show. You don't need me anymore. You can write me out,'" Peterman said.

Added Poryes, "At his soul, he is a loving guy and a very devoted dad. He got himself into something that turned out to be way more than he thought it was. If it was just Billy making the choice, he probably would have left the show. He was there for Miley, and he stuck it out for 101 episodes for Miley."

In 2010, Billy Ray filed for divorce from Tish. And when *Hannah Montana* wrapped for good, he promptly moved back to Tennessee, while the rest of the family continued on with their lives in L.A. One month after the final *Hannah* episode aired, he gave a melancholy interview to *GQ* magazine, lamenting the ways in which *Hannah* had ruined his life, Satan was attacking his family, and how he'd lost control of his daughter, who was now eighteen and, in his view, surrounded by enabling "handlers."

"I'll tell you right now—the damn show destroyed my family," he said, adding that he wished the series had never happened. "I'd take it back in a second. For my family to be here and just be everybody okay, safe and sound and happy and normal, would have been fantastic. Heck, yeah. I'd erase it all in a second if I could."

On *Hannah*'s fifteenth anniversary in 2021, Miley expressed the opposite sentiment. She sent flower arrangements to many of those involved with the show and penned a letter to her former alter ego, writing in a two-page handwritten memo that "breathing life into you for those six years was an honor." She ended with, "Not a day goes by where I forget where I came from. A building in Burbank, California, with a room full of people with the power to fulfill my destiny. And that they did. They gave me you. The greatest gift a girl could ask for. I love you, Hannah Montana."

11

Miley Cyrus:
Rock Star and Role Model

A decade and a half before the advent of *Hannah Montana* and Miley Cyrus, Hollywood Records was losing upward of $20 million a year. By the early 1990s, they'd earned a reputation within the industry as "the *Titanic* captained by the Three Stooges." While Walt Disney Records was the home of Disney movie soundtracks and Mickey-themed compilations, its sister label Hollywood was attempting to be a "real" music venture with acts like Insane Clown Posse on its roster.

Still, the contemporary argument that Hollywood Records should have signed Justin Timberlake, Christina Aguilera, and Britney Spears when *The All New Mickey Mouse Club* ended in 1995 would have been laughable at the time. The label had begrudgingly taken on The Party, a manufactured group made up of five MMC members, in 1990. They'd hired Debbie Gibson to produce The Party's first album, and The Disney Channel aired a tie-in concert special. But the group never broke out beyond the audience of the TV series itself. And, at the time, that audience was *small*. The Disney Channel was still exclusively a premium cable offering, and Radio Disney didn't exist.

"Horrendous, that's what it was," former Hollywood Records and Walt Disney Studios music executive Mitchell Leib said of the attempt to make The Party happen. "You could not compete in the real music industry—radio, MTV—with The Party."

By the mid-2000s, however, the entire Disney political system and

America's musical landscape had been overhauled. With Disney Channel now on basic cable, the advent of the internet, the creation of Radio Disney, and the corporate divisions working (reluctantly) in tandem, the old system need not apply. "At MTV, if a music video got four or six plays a week, that was good to start," said Abbey Konowitch, who worked in programming at MTV before becoming general manager of Hollywood Records from 2001 to 2011. "At Disney Channel, I was getting things played that many times in a day, totally targeted to the right audience."

After the success of Hilary Duff's music, many incoming Disney Channel stars' contracts included language that gave the Disney labels the first right of refusal to consider them for solo music ventures, in addition to their projects' soundtracks. "We commissioned the songs," Leib said. "We owned one hundred percent of the publishing. We owned one hundred percent of the master." Even with those stipulations, the actors on Disney Channel shows were eager to be signed. "I don't recall too many who said no," Konowitch said. "We had a lot of meetings with virtually everyone who ever thought they could sing or wanted to sing, and there's only so much room in the pipeline for us to do a good job."

One of Hollywood Records's biggest mid-aughts successes was the songwriting sister act Aly & AJ, comprised of Aly and AJ Michalka, who co-starred together in the DCOM *Cow Belles*. Their 2005 debut Hollywood album *Into the Rush* sold a million copies worldwide. Their 2007 follow-up *Insomniatic* doubled the sales. But getting signed to Hollywood wasn't a guarantee for Disney Channel stars, especially for supporting players. *Hannah Montana*'s Mitchel Musso released an album with Hollywood, but his more prominent co-star Emily Osment put out her 2010 album on an independent label. "They needed to be good, and frankly, they needed to be great in our mind," Konowitch said. "Because they were representing the whole company."

After the first *Hannah Montana* soundtrack was released on Walt Disney Records in October 2006, *Entertainment Weekly*'s review sniffed at its lyrical messages "about how totally awesome it is to be famous, yet go unrecognized at will—a nice fantasy for Brangelina, but a weird one to push on little girls." Yet, it became the first TV soundtrack to debut at number one on the Billboard 200 album chart, and beat new releases from My Chemical Romance and John Legend (and Taylor Swift's debut album, which arrived the same day at number nineteen).

To follow that success, Disney Music Group head Bob Cavallo came up with the idea of making a split-personality album to introduce Miley Cyrus as a solo artist, beyond the character she played on TV. While sold as a single unit, the 2007 double album, *Hannah Montana 2: Meet Miley Cyrus* was divided into two parts from two different labels: the *Hannah Montana* album, with Miley performing as Hannah, was produced by Walt Disney Records, and the Miley album, with Miley singing original songs not heard on the series, by Hollywood Records.

The *Hannah* songs served as promo for the series and its merchandise. The Miley songs were pushed to Top 40 radio and introduced her as an artist in a broader market, which in turn introduced those outside of Disney Channel's viewership to Miley's music—and potentially turned them into new *Hannah Montana* viewers. "Miley wanted to express herself as a music artist, and this was a great way for us to grow our two businesses simultaneously," Konowitch said. Miley's personal music manager was Jason Morey, whose father, Jim, had helped shepherd the careers of heavyweights like Michael Jackson, Mariah Carey, and Miley's godmother, Dolly Parton. And, Konowitch added, "Unlike Hilary Duff, which was us finding our way, and management finding their way, Miley Cyrus and Hannah Montana was a group of top-level professionals."

While Nickelodeon's *iCarly*, which had premiered in September 2007, often beat *Hannah Montana* in the Nielsen ratings, that show and its star, Miranda Cosgrove, weren't embedded in the broader cultural zeitgeist on anywhere near the same level as *Hannah* and Miley, thanks to the increasingly multilateral Disney approach and Miley's strong music management team. Yet, Miranda's advance for her first album at Columbia Records was $450,000. Miley's advance for her first album at Hollywood: a mere $65,000.

Hannah Montana 2: Meet Miley Cyrus debuted at number one, just as the first soundtrack had. And following the album's June 2007 release, the labels set up a fifty-plus-date Best of Both Worlds concert tour to run from October 2007 through the following January. Production on *Hannah Montana* season 3 would have to wait—convenient timing, given the industry-wide writers' strike that was taking shape.

Miley had previously performed as Hannah Montana on select dates of The Cheetah Girls' The Party's Just Begun tour in the fall of 2006. Now, she would be performing as both Hannah and herself. Kenny Ortega, who had already shot the first two *High School Musical* films, signed on as the tour's director and choreographer. And the Jonas Brothers, who had recently joined the Hollywood Records fold, would serve as the opening act.

When the concert tickets went on sale, unexpected mayhem ensued. The shows sold out in minutes, in part due to brokers scooping up huge swaths of tickets and reselling them at exorbitant prices. "Hell hath no fury like the parent of a child throwing a tantrum," vice president of Ticketmaster Joe Freeman told the *Los Angeles Times* amid the chaos. "People who have been in this business for a long time are watching what's happening, and they say there hasn't been a demand of this level or intensity since the Beatles or Elvis."

The immediate solution to the uproar over the ticket shortage was to release a batch of forty-five thousand seats that had been withheld, now made available only to members of the MileyWorld fan club. But fifteen years before Taylor Swift's Eras tour Ticketmaster debacle led to Senate hearings, the demand to see fourteen-year-old Miley Cyrus inspired a similar outcry. Politicians got involved. Investigations into scalping laws were launched. Fan club members sued over their lack of access to priority tickets. Parents were desperate.

Radio stations around the country inexplicably decided the best way to do ticket giveaways was to get *Hannah Montana* fans' dads to race each other in high heels. In St. Louis, the winner of a fifty-yard dash was a man competing as a favor for his boss, who had a young daughter. In Connecticut, a participant in a forty-yard dash was later charged with workers' compensation fraud after viral video footage showed him running in drag while simultaneously claiming he was too injured to work. Elsewhere, a Texas mom helped her six-year-old daughter write an essay about her dad dying in Iraq to score four tickets to Miley's Dallas show. The only problem? The child's father was still alive and had never served in Iraq.

When the tour began, Miley performed to the sold-out arena crowds with the power and confidence of an industry veteran twice her age. The audiences, mostly comprised of very young girls, were enthralled, seeing the icon they knew from TV in the flesh—and wig. "Her ability to own the stage was like no one else I've ever worked with," then–Disney Channel president Rich Ross said. "She could just connect with every single person."

Ahead of the tour, Walt Disney Studios head Dick Cook decided the studio should film one of Miley's shows and release a 3D concert movie in theaters. It was an ultra-low-budget, low-risk effort, and the plan was to put the *Hannah Montana & Miley Cyrus: Best of Both Worlds Concert* 3D film in theaters for just one week starting February 1, 2008. But when the film opened, it managed to top the box office and gross $31.1 million on opening weekend: the highest per-screen average wide release in movie history (a feat helped by 3D ticket prices averaging double that of a standard ticket), and the biggest Super Bowl weekend opening ever. They extended its run and continued raking in profits for weeks to come.

After the fury of so many not being able to score live concert tickets, the movie gave fans a chance to have the best seats in the house to watch Miley perform. "This was pure fun and entertainment. I had no delusions of winning any awards," director Bruce Hendricks said. "This was just catering to a rabid fan base that wanted to see their idol."

And following the success of the tour movie and the rush of seeing the impact of her performances and music on so many fans, Miley returned to the *Hannah Montana* set in August 2008 to shoot season 3 with a newfound sense of self. She'd always been confident, but now she recognized just how big her place in the world had become. "She wasn't just a little kid acting on the show anymore," series costume designer Dahlia Foroutan said. "She was a TV star, and she was a rock star. And she knew it."

*   *   *

During *HANNAH MONTANA*'s run, the Cyruses had independently been in talks with a national retailer to launch a line of "Miley" clothing, similar to what the Duffs had done with Stuff by Hilary Duff after her *Lizzie* days. Within a matter of weeks in 2008, Miley's parents filed a petition to legally change her name from "Destiny Hope Cyrus" to "Miley Ray Cyrus," and her Smiley Miley, Inc, corporation filed trademark applications for "Miley" apparel, accessories, furniture, and more.

When the Disney executives caught wind, they weren't pleased. It could be confusing for fans, they argued. Kids might buy a "Miley" shirt thinking they were getting a Miley Stewart shirt, instead of a Miley Cyrus shirt. But, if the Cyruses nixed those merchandising plans, Disney could consider new ways to give Miley an increased share of the company's own profits.

Miley's initial *Hannah Montana* contract included her receiving the standard 5 percent of the show's net merchandising receipts on solo Miley or Hannah products, as well as half of that for products that featured her alongside other talent. One mid-2006 agreement had bumped her cut to 6 percent for the first $4 million made on any *Hannah Montana* products that involved her name or likeness, then 7 percent when net proceeds reached $4 million, then 8 percent on anything over $6 million. Plus, for signing that updated deal, she was given $75,000 up front, as well as a $1 million bonus for every $12 million in additional net merchandising receipts.

Later, in 2009, the Miley Cyrus x Max Azria fashion line at Walmart served as a "cross-category merchandising opportunity involving entertainment and product" that, while wholly separate from *Hannah Montana*, featured tie-ins with Miley's Hollywood Records music and world tour, and was sold alongside Disney's exclusively licensed *Hannah* apparel line.

"Millions went into her pocket because we named the character Miley, essentially," producer Douglas Lieblein said. "Had we not named the character Miley, she would never have had that argument."

The real money to be made on Disney Channel series was often in the ancillary ventures that actors and other creatives were usually cut out of. (Showrunner Michael Poryes sued Disney in 2008 over his contingent compensation, and he and Disney eventually settled for an undisclosed sum. Co-creators Barry O'Brien and Rich Correll filed a similar suit, which also went to arbitration; however, their arbiter sided with Disney.) "Miley sharing in the profit of the show to me, personally, was justice," Lieblein said. "She contributed, and she deserved every penny."

Beyond the feared Miley Stewart vs. Miley Cyrus confusion, Miley herself struggled with the implications of the Clark Kent vs. Superman dichotomy at the heart of *Hannah Montana*. "The concept of the show is that when you're this character, when you have this alter ego, you're valuable. You've got millions of fans, you're the biggest star in the world," Miley said on a podcast in 2021. "Then the concept was that when I looked like myself, when I didn't have the wig on anymore, no one cared about me. I wasn't a star anymore . . . That was drilled into my head: without being Hannah Montana, no one cares about you."

In many ways, the Disney star who would have best understood what Miley was experiencing was Hayley Mills, one of Disney's first teen superstars, who had grappled with growing up in the spotlight while under contract for a series of Disney family films, including *Pollyanna* and *The Parent Trap*, in the 1960s.

"I began to observe a peculiar phenomenon: there were *two of me*," Mills wrote in her memoir. "There was the me who I thought I was—looking at the world, trying to make sense of everything. And then there was this identical twin—'Hayley Mills'—staring back at me: an image projected by my movies, by the Disney publicity juggernaut, by the hundreds of interviews, magazine stories and articles, which combined to create a character I didn't even recognize . . . The other twin was far prettier, wittier, and sexier than I actually was. Who was this Hayley Mills? The real one could only be a huge disappointment."

For Disney, the emphasis on the Hannah Montana character was, ultimately, about money. The horizontal integration across the greater Walt Disney Company was in full swing, and the network now worked closely with the consumer products division from the very inception of their shows, making choices about costume colors and characters' hobbies in line with what might be the most sellable in merchandise form. The goal was to place *Hannah Montana*, which was licensed in

177 countries, at as many touchpoints for kids as possible—from the mall, to the internet, to TV, movies, iPods, Radio Disney, live concerts, and more.

"People were buying into the aspirational rockstar," Rich Ross said. "The cosplay of that show was Hannah, not the everyday high schooler. Not that she wasn't great in both worlds, but merchandise is about aspiration."

THE INEXTRICABLE BY-PRODUCT of the nonstop interest in all things *Hannah Montana* was the nonstop demand placed on Miley Cyrus. By its second season, *Hannah Montana* was the number one basic cable show among tweens and kids over six, and second only to *American Idol* in those demographics across all of TV. Its success was mostly due to Miley. She filmed the show during the week, and on weekends and hiatuses she did mini concert tours and appearances, filmed movies, attended media events, posed for photo shoots, and recorded new music. "I never understood how that worked. I always felt like if you put in your full time on the show, how can you be given more time to do the music stuff?" co-star Jason Earles said. "You don't really get to restart the clock, do you? But it seemed like sometimes it did just restart."

While Rich Ross said Disney maintained a master calendar, showing Miley's commitments each day across *Hannah* and other music, promotional, and film commitments, loopholes abounded regarding whose responsibility it was to track all of those additional hours. Once Miley turned sixteen, neither a teacher nor guardian was legally required to be present at, say, an evening recording session at a studio. And under California law, the impetus is allowed to fall on teenagers who are between sixteen and eighteen to present their work permits at each off-set site and track their own work hours. "I can't imagine any actors I've worked with going up to a production company and saying, 'You have to wrap me by ten o'clock, otherwise, I'm going to turn you in for a violation,'" *Hannah Montana* studio teacher Linda Stone said. "I don't think it's ever happened."

In addition to her workload, Miley devoted ample hours to giving back. Disney had a long-standing partnership with Make-A-Wish, and like many of the Disney Channel stars, Miley recorded video messages for seriously ill fans, met Make-A-Wish recipients after Friday tapings, and visited children's hospitals while on tour. "She spent more time with Make-A-Wish kids than you could possibly imagine. She would play songs for them. She would have them hanging out in the dressing room. She would give them props and little costume pieces," Jason Earles said. "There were times where the ADs would be like, 'Miley, we need you to come to set!' and she's like, 'Piss off. I'm going to spend ten more minutes with this family.'"

While on tour, Stone recalled how she and Miley once visited a local Target and filled several shopping carts with toys to take to young patients at a nearby children's hospital. But when they arrived at the venue for her scheduled visit, Miley was escorted to a room where several board members had convened with their own offspring, who were eager to meet the star. At first, Miley obliged, but as it became clear the leaders had no intention of taking her to visit the actual patients before she had to leave, she snapped.

"You know, I came here to see the kids, and I wanted to give them the toys myself," Miley told the room full of suits, as a publicist yanked at her arm. "All of you here, you can afford VIP tickets to my concert, and I would meet your kids and grandkids personally after the show. But my purpose today was to come here to see the kids who can't do that."

As much as Miley loved being able to brighten kids' days, it added another layer of pressure. Hers was an extreme workload for anyone, and especially for a teenage girl. "Miley never got to rest," costume designer Dahlia Foroutan said. "She was exhausted. She was emotional." In response, executive producers Peterman and Poryes said they began rearranging the *Hannah* production schedule to give Miley more time to recover from her off-set obligations. The young actors would no longer be required at the Monday table reads, giving Miley a day to potentially sleep in after her weekend commitments.

"Nobody knows how much was on her shoulders and how much she had to carry for a long time," Peterman said. "There were times when Miley was being pulled in three directions. One was the necessities of filming the show. One was the Disney appearances and recordings. And once she blew up and had her separate management, they had their own agenda. Everybody's pulling at her. And her family was a little nervous about saying no to people because nobody knew how long this was going to last."

Unlike elite athletes, whose recovery days are prioritized to increase their performance and longevity, Miley was on a hamster wheel with no off ramp. "I didn't get recovery days. That was not important for someone that was making so much capital for such a big corporation," Miley said on Joe Rogan's podcast in 2020. "Off days are days that money's not coming in, and I definitely, probably didn't get the training that I needed to say, 'Hey, I don't want to do this until I'm fifteen; I want to do this until I'm eighty.' That wasn't always considered."

ON SCREEN, *HANNAH MONTANA* presented a sanitized, kid-friendly version of the downside of fame to its viewers as Miley Stewart juggled boys, school, and concerts. Off screen, the option of switching fame on and off with the flip of a wig wasn't afforded to Miley Cyrus. *Hannah*'s storylines would have had to incorporate TV-MA material to accurately reflect what Miley was going through on a daily basis.

Roving packs of paparazzi, sometimes thirty or forty strong, would wait outside the Cyruses' home and follow Miley everywhere. Grown men took upskirt photos of her while she ran errands at age seventeen. Blogger Perez Hilton shared a link to those intrusive photos, and he often dubbed her "Slutty Cyrus" in his viral posts.

Lurking over every young female star in the late aughts was America's preoccupation with the idea that any of them could be about to "pull a Britney." The twenty-six-year-old pop icon had spent 2007 and 2008 in the throes of crisis, shaving her head, being taken from her home in an ambulance, losing custody of her children, and eventually, being placed under what was expected to be a temporary conservatorship. In 2007, Britney's little sister, Jamie Lynn Spears, who had a Nickelodeon series of her own, announced her pregnancy at age sixteen, and Lindsay Lohan was arrested for drunk driving and cocaine possession just weeks after checking out of a treatment center for the second time. All of these headlines added to the fervor that young female stars were all teetering on a perilous tightrope over imminent depravity.

While Vanessa Hudgens's perceived loss of innocence when her nude photos were leaked had been instant tabloid fodder, young male celebrities, like Zac Efron and the Sprouses, were largely excluded from such scrutiny. "The young women on the channel we were on were so heavily sexualized from such an earlier age than my brother and I," Cole Sprouse said when I spoke to him for *The New York Times* in 2022. "There's absolutely no way that we could compare our experiences."

Even in the earliest days of Miley's *Hannah* fame, interviewers were obsessed with her virtue and often fantasized about what a public spiral could look like. A *USA Today* reporter fretted that the current "young hot starlets gone wild" culture would mean that, at fourteen, "pretty Miley will soon start doing nutty Britney Spears–esque things, like not wearing underpants."

By the end of 2007, the public obsession with Miley was in over-drive. And the cruel outside observations became invasive violations of her privacy. That year, someone leaked photos that Miley had posted on her private MySpace page, showing her and a girlfriend sharing a piece of candy mouth-to-mouth and posing in a hotel room. Scandalized parents and nosy teen bloggers questioned her sexuality. "There was nothing wrong with it. It's two girls at a sleepover," Miley said at the time. "If all of a sudden that's bad, then what is the world coming to?"

But Miley's role model status meant that any perceived misstep was spotted and decried. When a scene in the *Best of Both Worlds* 3D concert film showed Miley and Billy Ray riding in the back seat of a Range Rover without seatbelts on, Consumer Reports put out a statement citing data on traffic fatalities and the responsibility that Disney and the Cyruses had to set an example. Billy Ray quickly issued a public apology. "We got caught up in the moment of filming, and we made a mistake," he told *People*. "Seatbelt safety is extremely important."

In early 2008, when Miley was fifteen, another batch of her personal photos leaked. This time, it was a slew of selfies showing her in semi-provocative poses, pulling her shirt up or her pants down to expose her midriff, and posing wet but clothed in a shower with her bra visible. A nineteen-year-old scammer in Tennessee took credit for illegally hacking her MySpace data and using the same password to access her Gmail account, where he said he found the photos and posted them online. (He was never charged.) Blogs and fan sites were quick to spread the images, and on Fox News, Bill O'Reilly dedicated a segment to maligning what he termed the "teasy, peek-a-boo" photos.

Then, a few weeks later, professional photos of Miley taken by lauded photographer Annie Leibovitz for *Vanity Fair*'s June issue began to circulate. In one image, Miley is draped across Billy Ray's lap, holding his hand. In a solo shot, she looks over her shoulder with tousled hair and red lipstick while wrapped only in a satin sheet; her upper back is exposed, giving the appearance that she's topless.

"An editor at a tabloid told me that all the celebrity weeklies have been ratcheting up their focus on her," journalist Bill Handy wrote in the magazine's accompanying profile. "With Lindsay Lohan rehabbed and Britney Spears under psychiatric care, the tabs are looking to Cyrus to flame out, or at least do something mildly outrageous."

Mission accomplished.

As the leaked images from the shoot spread, America collectively lost its mind. On *The View*, Elisabeth Hasselbeck and Joy Behar debated who was to blame for the offensive images, and Howard Stern weighed in on his radio show. "The picture disturbs me," Stern said of the father-daughter photo. "It looks like his daughter is his girlfriend. He's trying to be hot." Jamie Lee Curtis wrote an entire blog for *The Huffington Post* defending Miley and blaming the adults around her at the shoot. "I feel for her," Curtis wrote. "Of course she is embarrassed."

Miley quickly put out a statement, apologizing and saying the shoot was supposed to be "artistic" and that she did, in fact, feel "so embarrassed" by the end results. Meanwhile, a spokesperson for *Vanity Fair* defended Leibovitz, stating, "Miley's parents and/or minders were on the set all day. Since the photo was taken digitally, they saw it on the shoot and everyone thought it was a beautiful and natural portrait of Miley." (Ten years later, Miley would tweet "IM NOT SORRY" on the anniversary of the shoot. "Fuck YOU," she added in her post, along with an image of a *New York Post* cover touting MILEY'S SHAME.)

The shoot caught the Disney Channel executives completely off guard. The Cyruses hadn't alerted them to the *Vanity Fair* coverage, and they only became aware once *Entertainment Tonight* began airing promos about the images and reporters called for comment. "A situation was created to deliberately manipulate a fifteen-year-old in order to sell magazines," Disney Channel PR head Patti McTeague told *The New York Times* at the time.

Looking back, McTeague, who left the network in 2023, said, "It was a different time, but I think that most parents even today would go, 'Hmm, fifteen? That makes me uncomfortable.'" She added, "What I said then is what I believe today, and that is that they manipulated something. If she was eighteen, it would be a very different story because she can make decisions for herself."

The wave of interest in a young Disney Channel star's personal life and off-set decisions was uncharted territory for everyone involved. Hilary Duff had unwittingly established the mold for what it meant to be a "Disney Channel star," but when her outside music and movie career had exploded, *Lizzie McGuire* was already done filming. Hilary wasn't doing triple duty filming a Disney show, recording Disney music, and attending Disney Channel promotional events all at the same time. The *That's So Raven* and *Suite Life* casts, while popular with tween magazine readers, weren't landing high-profile magazine covers or being breathlessly blogged about by tabloids and scared moms.

It wasn't until 2006, when the joint forces of *High School Musical* and *Hannah Montana* invaded every living room in America, that Disney Channel stars suddenly began to receive the prying-eye treatment usually reserved for mainstream pop stars and celebrities who were decades their seniors. The rise of those Disney Channel projects coincided with the rise of social media, blogs, and the rubbernecking over Britney's and Lindsay's public struggles. SHOULD 'HANNAH MONTANA' BE SEXY?, posited an ABC News headline, along with an article that speculated the *Vanity Fair* shoot was a calculated move to transition Miley from a "wholesome" TV star into a "femme fatale." Meanwhile, Eminem—a then-thirty-six-year-old man—rapped about masturbating to an episode of *Hannah Montana* in his song "3 A.M."

Back in Burbank, the corporate office was buzzing in the aftermath of the *Vanity Fair* shoot. "There was this real somber feel coming into the office because people didn't know what to do," one former junior programming staffer recalled. At the weekly all-hands meeting on the twenty-first floor, department heads rattled off updates on their projects, and network president Rich Ross gave his usual soliloquy about the network's latest triumphs and what it meant for the industry at large. Then, in his closing remarks to the fifty or so employees gathered around the conference table, he turned his attention to Miley.

"If we didn't want to deal with any human drama, then we would just make animated shows," he told the room. "But we tell human stories and we use human players. Our actors are people. More importantly, they are children, and they are finding themselves in the world."

To those in the room, it felt like a defining moment. "He just spoke about her with such respect, about the journey that she was on as an adolescent," the junior staffer remembered. "I felt like he turned the wheel, like, this is not something that we are going to be ashamed of. And it set the tone for how we were all supposed to feel about it."

Outside of the office, however, a concerned Ross and the head of the Disney/ABC Television Group, Anne Sweeney, hopped on a plane to Nashville to have a tense meeting with Tish and Billy Ray Cyrus, who had returned to Tennessee ahead of filming Walt Disney Studio's upcoming *Hannah Montana* movie there. "Everyone was pretty upset," Ross said. "Because precocious and rebellious, we get. But we have a pact with our audience, and we're not going to do anything that is going to purposely cross the line. That's not an easy conversation—and the economics were not insignificant, obviously, at that point."

As the *Hannah Montana* retail revenue approached $1 billion, there was a real fear that these scandals could derail the entire franchise. More than three million viewers tuned in to the show on a regular basis. The *Hannah Montana* movie had been granted a $30 million budget. Miley had signed a seven-figure book deal to put out a memoir with Disney's publishing branch, Disney-Hyperion. And her sixteenth birthday was slated to shut down Disneyland that fall with a corporate-sanctioned blowout bash that would serve to cross-promote various Disney initiatives and be attended by more than five thousand fans at $250 a ticket. There was a lot on the line if parents stopped allowing their kids to partake in any of it.

"For Miley Cyrus to be a 'good girl' is now a business decision for her," Marsh told the May 2008 issue of *Portfolio Magazine*. "Parents have invested in her a godliness. If she violates that trust, she won't get it back." The corporate fear wasn't what the young audience might think of the headlines surrounding Miley. It was how offended their parents might be.

But Miley was Miley, and she wasn't going to quietly conform, no matter the stakes. During a performance of her hit single "Party in the USA" at the 2009 Teen Choice Awards, she danced by a pole mounted on top of a prop ice-cream truck. The sequence was relatively tame and lasted approximately two seconds, but controversy ensued over the "stripper pole" and her "questionable dance moves."

Disney Channel's official comment was no comment: "Disney Channel won't be commenting on that performance, although parents can rest assured that all content presented on the Disney Channel is age-appropriate for our audience—kids six to fourteen—and consistent with what our brand values are," read the statement. The network, at least publicly, was drawing the line between the content they put on their channel and what existed outside of it, and making clear that whatever their stars chose to do off set was out of their purview and beyond their control. "I would do that pole dance a thousand times again, because it was right for the song and that performance," Miley told *Parade* in 2010. "But, dude, if you think dancing on top of an ice-cream cart with a pole is bad, then go check what 90 percent of the high schoolers are really up to."

Two months after the Teen Choice Awards incident, Rich Ross left the Disney Channel presidency to become chairman of Walt Disney Studios. The move had been in the works for months, reportedly predating the firing of studio chairman Dick Cook that September. And while many in the industry had speculated that Disney Channel's president of entertainment, Gary Marsh, would be named Ross's successor, the role instead went to Carolina Lightcap, a senior Disney Channel executive whose in-house experience had largely been in the network's preschool venture and in overseeing the Latin America expansion from the Buenos Aires office. "She came from a different side of the business," original programming head Adam Bonnett said laconically. Marsh, meanwhile, took on expanded duties as chief creative officer, but eschewed the top business role. "Gary was always just as passionate about the creative as he was about the business side, and he never wanted to let his passion for the creative suffer in any way," Bonnett said. "The timing just didn't feel right for him."

But when Ross departed in 2009, some say Disney Channel's internal approach to talent relations changed. As Lightcap focused on other priorities and Marsh was pulled in additional directions with his new role, "I felt like we lost something," the former junior programming source said. "From the top down, the culture just shifted a little bit. When Miley would do something controversial, people were saying rude things about it in meetings and rolling their eyes, like, 'When are we going to get her off the air?' It was like, 'Oh, she did something! We're going to pull this episode premiere until things quiet down.' It became more negative. I mean, it's not that Gary was ever in those meetings saying anything bad. But nobody was saying anything *good* either."

PERHAPS AT LEAST part of the outsized public outrage surrounding Miley's behavior can be attributed to many people's assumption that the southern girl they saw on kids' TV would be a chaste beacon for conservative America and its causes. Instead, they were confronted with a wild-child hippie, who just happened to be from Tennessee and raised a Southern Baptist. She espoused her love of *RuPaul's Drag Race* alongside her love of Jesus and supported gay marriage before it was legal. She spoke openly about exploring other faiths, like Buddhism, and got tattoos. And all of it made pearl-clutching parents mad.

"My job is to be a role model, and that's what I want to do, but my job isn't to be a parent," Miley told *Harper's Bazaar* ahead of filming the final season of *Hannah Montana* in 2010. "My job isn't to tell your kids how to act or how not to act, because I'm still figuring that out for myself."

It was an unending satanic panic, and Satan was a teenage girl. Anxious adults were seemingly unable to differentiate between Miley's character on TV and the real-life teenager playing her. And for Disney, the reckless, imitable behavior they'd so feared having in their shows was now happening offscreen—where many of the stars who'd preceded Miley had been able to navigate their ups and downs in private—and the pressure was on Miley to maintain a saintly persona around the clock.

"It *infuriated* me," her *Hannah Montana* co-star Jason Earles said. "The idea that you as a parent think that this fourteen-year-old should be raising your kid for you is absurd. I think we had a responsibility in the show for Miley Stewart to learn lessons and be a slightly better person at the end of an episode than she was at the beginning. But Miley Cyrus had to have the freedom to explore herself, to make mistakes, to figure out her voice and the things that she values."

The fact that Miley didn't crack under that kind of obsessive, dissecting microscope is miraculous, but not entirely an accident. "We needed someone with talent but also the maturity to handle the pressure," Gary Marsh told *Time* of her casting in 2006. "We have brand promises to keep." In addition to Miley's singing talent and "it" factor that lit up the screen, she possessed from childhood what many describe as a disarming, preternatural confidence. "She speaks with the bold, jokey air of someone who is used to being liked—and listened to—by every person in the room," read a 2011 *Marie Claire* profile. "She has a cheerleader's confidence and the laugh of a truck-stop waitress." Miley was self-assured in a way most adults, let alone teenagers, never master.

"Sometimes Miley'd just laugh like, 'They think they can control me.' And sometimes she'd be really upset by it," *Hannah Montana* costume designer Dahlia Foroutan said of the criticisms over the star's behavior. "What I always really admired and respected was who she was surrounded by. Her mother and her manager, Jason [Morey], they always told Miley, it's okay to be yourself. It didn't affect her as much as maybe it would have affected someone else if their management or their parents would have said, 'What are you doing?!' They never did. They were like, 'Miles, you are who you are. You're beautiful. You're wonderful. And everybody loves you.'"

MEANWHILE, MILEY'S SOLO music career continued to skyrocket. Her song "The Climb" reached a peak of number four on the Billboard Hot 100 after its inclusion in the *Hannah Montana: The Movie* soundtrack, and it eventually went six-times platinum. And in 2009, Miley released "Party in the USA," a track co-written by, and originally intended for, Jessie J. With a few lyrical tweaks, it became a distinctly Miley Cyrus track. The vaguely patriotic, immensely listenable bop was soon inescapable. An anthem for college party girls. A rallying cry at sporting events. Gay men made a viral Fire Island parody. *Slate* deemed it "great, goofy—and bipartisan!—fun" that had the power to "heal a fractured nation, at least for three and a half minutes." The song soared to number two and was eventually certified diamond, selling more than ten million units. Even Miley admitting that she'd "never heard a Jay-Z song," despite the lyrical reference, couldn't slow the track's roll. "Honestly, I picked that song because I needed something to go with my clothing line," she said. "It turned out for the best."

When Miley embarked on her Fall 2009 Wonder world tour, sponsored by Walmart to promote said clothing line, she became the first artist to do an arena tour with entirely paperless ticket sales in an attempt to thwart the scalpers that had caused such chaos the last time around. She was sixteen years old. *Hannah Montana* studio teacher Linda Stone accompanied Miley on tour, and, between shows, Miley would complete her requisite geometry homework and English essays while bouncing down the road in her tour bus or tucked into a lounge at whatever hotel they might be staying in for a night.

On stage, Miley still sang a couple of *Hannah Montana* songs, but mostly she performed original songs off her second studio album, *Breakout*. And she did everything entirely as herself. No wig. No split personality. For fifty-six shows across the US, England, and Ireland, the message of the show was: Miley is no longer a young girl playing a rock star. She *is* a rock star. During her set, she launched herself above the crowd in a cascading tutu skirt as she screamed the chorus of "Fly on the Wall." She flew through the air on a prop Harley Davidson motorcycle while belting a cover of "I Love Rock 'n' Roll." She confidently fell backward through a twelve-foot trapdoor, night after night.

"Miley never played it safe. The best thing that you could hope for in an artist is that they know who they are," said Jamal Sims, who served as the Wonder tour's director and choreographer. "She knew the game and what came with it. But she never changed. Miley was always just Miley."

Back in Los Angeles, the *Hannah* team had approached the show's season 3 finale as a potential finale for the entire series. Miley had already shot *Hannah Montana: The Movie*, and it was released in theaters (earning more than $155 million at the global box office) while the third season aired. On the show, Miley Stewart had overcome a finale-worthy existential crisis choosing between Hollywood and Tennessee, and from a production standpoint, the show would be ending with a respectable eighty-five episodes under its belt.

Still, *Hannah* was such a massive success that extending it into a fourth season was an obvious decision from the network's point of view. But to do that, they'd need Miley on board. "Certainly the network was hoping and praying she'd come back," said Rich Correll, who directed that season 3 finale.

By this point, Miley was seventeen, eager to break out of the Disney Channel mold, and had numerous outside opportunities at her disposal. But she was also competitive, and liked the idea of beating *That's So Raven*'s Disney Channel record of one hundred episodes. Plus, there were still unresolved character issues that would be nice to explore in a fourth season, like Miley Stewart finally revealing to the world that she was Hannah Montana. "I think we were all looking for closure, and it was definitely complicated because it was really happening for her [outside of *Hannah*] in a very big way," Rich Ross said. "But she wanted to finish it, otherwise it wouldn't have happened."

Miley agreed to return for a truncated thirteen-episode mini-season. To compensate her without having to massively up the show's production budget and set a precedent for future series, they utilized other Disney divisions, like consumer products, where Miley could be included in a bigger percentage of *Hannah Montana*–related profits.

Since Disney Channel wasn't willing to spend additional money on the series itself, they also considered starting fresh with a lower-paid creative team. But when the network executives discussed ditching Michael Poryes and Steven Peterman with Miley, she refused. The showrunners were told that Miley only agreed to do the final season if they returned, as well. "Ninety-nine-point-nine percent of people would have thrown us under the bus. But she didn't," Poryes said. "It's a testament to Miley and a testament to her character."

Instead, Disney did something similar to what they had done on *Suite Life*. They retitled the show *Hannah Montana Forever* and built new primary sets, meaning the fourth season was technically classified as season 1 of a new show. They moved the Stewarts into a California ranch house. A live horse was added as a recurring character, and Miley and Lilly became roommates who lived in a converted barn on the property. That simple bedroom relocation was actually a huge deal. For the first time, a lead character's bedroom was not under the same roof as their parents', and the network was concerned it would send a bad message, even though Miley was still just a few feet from the main house.

Because *Hannah Montana: The Movie* had been released seven months before production began on season 4—its plot, much to the chagrin of the TV team, had ended with Hannah removing her wig and revealing her real identity to a crowd of townspeople—some of the series writers wanted season 4 to open with Hannah shedding her wig once and for all and coming clean to the world. They could shift the focus of the final season to explore what Miley's life looked like as she attempted to reconcile her two contrasting worlds.

"Creatively, it was very exciting for us. [Original programming head] Adam Bonnett originally said yes. And then after a while, he said no," writer and producer Douglas Lieblein said. "He called us and said, 'I got a call from the merchandising people. There are a million blond wigs in a warehouse in China. She can't take that wig off until after Halloween.' And the way the schedule worked, Halloween was, like, episode eight. The decision on when Hannah took the wig off was based on selling Halloween wigs." (Bonnett said he did "not recall a specific meeting or conversation about delaying the reveal in line with Halloween.")

The series concluded with Miley Stewart choosing friendship over fame, opting to go to college with Lilly instead of making a movie with Steven Spielberg in Europe. They shot and considered an alternate ending: one in which we flash back to "Tennessee, twelve years ago" and see an eight-year-old Miley Cyrus (actually a look-alike young actor named Mary Charles Jones) playing "rockstar" with a doll and telling her parents, played by Billy Ray and Tish, about her dreams of becoming a famous musician one day. The implication was that everything that played out on *Hannah Montana* had been just a figment of young Miley's imagination.

The actual Miley Cyrus watched them film the family scene from the side of the stage and cried.

A WEEK BEFORE the final episode of *Hannah Montana* wrapped on May 14, 2010, Miley released "Can't Be Tamed" as the lead single off her upcoming album of the same name. The music video featured the not-so-subtle imagery of Miley breaking out of a cage, wearing smoky eye makeup and a bondage-accessorized leotard as she writhed against her dancers and spread her literal wings. The internet was, predictably, outraged, forcing another statement from Disney. "Miley, at seventeen, is now making creative choices as a solo recording artist that reflects her own personal style and vision," a Disney spokesperson wrote. "Miley was twelve years old when she began portraying the fictional character of Hannah Montana, who continues to be beloved by millions of Disney Channel fans."

But the irony of the whole thing was that Miley was still signed to Hollywood Records. The music project was entirely Disney sanctioned. "Miley grew quicker than anyone expected, and that *Can't Be Tamed* period of Miley's career was a very controversial one within the company," Hollywood Records' then–general manager Abbey Konowitch said. "We were uncomfortable with how quickly Miley wanted to leave Disney behind and go to a place that wasn't ready to accept her. But at the same time, we respected her. That's where the complications came in."

At this point in her career, Miley wielded enough power to get her way. "That was Miley fighting this system and fighting the norm, and no amount of research or opinion would have changed her mind," Konow-itch added. "We would say, 'We don't want to do that.' And her manager would say, 'Well, that's what she wants to do.' And then, [Disney Music Group head] Bob [Cavallo], coming from an artist background, at the end of the day, the artist wins. Disney Channel and the corporate company weren't thrilled with that, and we did take some heat."

Disney Channel had previously panicked over the imagery of young girls crying in Miley's 2008 music video for "7 Things"—and had only allowed the Brett Ratner–directed clip to air on the network once a focus group of moms assured the channel they weren't bothered by the rawness of the tweens' tears. There was no way the bondage-lite "Can't Be Tamed" video would ever make the on-air cut.

Its lyrics also failed to pass Radio Disney's content review process, so the station couldn't play it. "Did we get requests for it? Absolutely," former Radio Disney DJ Ernie Martinez said. "But because of who we were and what we represented, we just couldn't touch it. Is there a world where Miley could have re-recorded it to be Radio Disney–friendly? Probably, but because of the nature of the song, I don't think it was even worth it."

Then, in December 2010, just before the final season of *Hannah Montana* aired, TMZ posted a video of Miley taking hits on a bong at a house party a few days after her eighteenth birthday. In the clip, Miley has a giggle fit and laughs over a guy she thinks looks like her then-boyfriend, Liam Hemsworth. Public hysteria, once again, ensued. Sources were quick to tell TMZ that Miley was smoking the legal herb salvia, not marijuana. And while Miley has maintained that it really was salvia in that bong, she's also said she was often smoking weed during the *Hannah* years.

"At one point it went from school to *how much weed can I actually smoke and still play a teenage superstar on the Disney Channel?*" she reminisced on Joe Rogan's podcast in 2020. "More than you would fucking think."

The culmination of public backlash led Miley to only tour *Can't Be Tamed* abroad in 2011. The sold-out arena tours from her previous eras were now relegated to South America and Australia. (Konowitch of Hollywood Records said those decisions would have been made by her personal music management, not the label.) "America has gotten to a place where I don't know if they want me to tour or not," Miley said at the time. "Right now I just want to go to the places where I am getting the most love."

Despite—or perhaps because of—whatever outside controversies occurred along the way, 6.2 million people watched the *Hannah Montana* finale in January 2011. Ready to move on from the show and now free from any pressures to conform as a role model at Disney Channel (and the clauses in her contract that stipulated she couldn't partake in controlled substances or make any changes to her hair or physical appearance without Disney's permission), Miley relished her new chapter, chopping off her hair in her *Bangerz* era, twerking on Robin Thicke at the 2013 VMAs, and embracing her stoner persona. "I'm not going to do *Hannah Montana*, but I can give you an update on what she's been up to," Miley said in her 2013 *Saturday Night Live* monologue. "She was murdered."

For many, it was shocking. For Brooke Shields, who played Miley's mom in flashbacks on several episodes of *Hannah Montana* and had also navigated growing up in the public eye, it was totally understandable. "It almost has to be that dramatic because otherwise you're playing in this loop of, 'Oh, they'll figure it out and let me out [of this box] soon,'" Shields said when I spoke to her for a 2021 *Washington Post* piece. "Nobody has any reason to let you out. Miley went out and was like, 'I don't give a shit. I'm going to fucking blow this thing out of the water.' And it shocked and angered people, but she had the balls to do it."

Miley wasn't the first teen star to buck the constraints put on her by her on-screen persona and a puritanical society—just a few years earlier, Jessica Biel posed topless for a men's magazine while on The WB's evangelical soap *7th Heaven*. (That show banished her character to Buffalo.) But Miley *was* the first Disney Channel star to have the level of fame and the spitfire personality to break the confines of what was expected of her at that network.

With Miley, the Disney Channel executives were grappling with how to preserve their hallowed brand while keeping their most powerful star happy. And now, they didn't have just one breakout star and TV series to manage at a time, but a growing roster of mega-famous teens and successful sitcoms, each drawing their own devoted fans and presenting unforeseen challenges.

12

Selena Gomez and
Wizards of Waverly Place

Twelve hundred miles away from Disney Channel's corporate office in Burbank, Cathryn Sullivan spent the early 2000s creating an empire of her own.

Petite and blond, Sullivan had a soft Texas drawl that belied her feisty grit. She'd opened her acting studio in the Dallas suburbs at the turn of the century and built a loyal following of tiny talent who dreamed of striking it big in Hollywood. Since the majority of opportunities for kid actors were on Nickelodeon and Disney Channel, Sullivan trained her young pupils to cater to those networks' needs.

Inside the walls of her studio, she tutored them in auditions, screen tests, chemistry reads, sitcom timing, the art of convincingly working with food props getting dropped on their heads or smashed in their faces, and how to dutifully take direction to mold themselves into whatever vision a producer might have for the part.

"I would mess with them and give them all kinds of direction that didn't even make sense because that's what Disney did," Sullivan said. It was a tactic she'd learned after she'd done a special coaching session with Miley Cyrus for one of her *Hannah Montana* callbacks, only for the network executives to give Miley completely contradictory performance notes in the audition room. "Miley was so mad at me, and then when she got the part and got on set, everything I had told her is what they did for the show," Sullivan said. "They were just screwing with her to see if she could take direction."

And since certain network executives were known to be disarmingly blasé at the auditions, Sullivan would practice doing the same charade with her students, answering pretend phone calls during their readings and sitting stone-faced as the actors cracked jokes. "They wanted to make sure that their stars weren't going to be rattled, that they could handle anything with confidence and not crumble," she said. "That's what my kids could do that everybody else's couldn't."

Back in L.A. in the early 2000s, Disney Channel casting director Joey Paul Jensen had also been working as an acting coach on the side. And when one of her students suggested she do a guest spot teaching at Sullivan's studio, Jensen flew east to see what the fuss was about. She was impressed. Over time, she began looking to Sullivan's studio for talent to cast in Disney Channel projects. She brought Sullivan's son Cody Linley in for a part on *That's So Raven*, which later led to him landing the role of Miley's love interest Jake Ryan on *Hannah Montana*. Soon, Sullivan was a vital pipeline of talent to the network. Selena Gomez, Demi Lovato, Debby Ryan, Madison Pettis, and, more recent, *Bunk'd* star Mallory James Mahoney were all discovered out of her studio.

"Every kid watched Disney. And Selena, Demi, Debby, all of those girls would practice doing that little Mickey Mouse wand thing," Sullivan said. "They all just really wanted to be the person who got to do that one thing."

When I asked Sullivan what it is about Texas that led to it producing so many successful child actors, she didn't have to think long. "There's a distinct way we raise children that's different than in California," Sullivan said. "We're all about loving our kids, but also disciplining them. You don't see a lot of spoiled brats in Texas."

SELENA MARIE GOMEZ's parents had her when they were just sixteen and seventeen years old. Her mom, Mandy Teefey (née Cornett), and dad, Ricardo Gomez, separated when Selena was five, and Mandy raised

Selena in the Dallas–Fort Worth suburb of Grand Prairie while struggling to make ends meet via shifts at Starbucks and Dave & Busters.
"When I was growing up, I was always bullied because I was the outsider, the weird girl with the purple hair and combat boots," Mandy told
The New York Times in 2017. "Then I was a teen mom. You get really
judged."

Mandy dreamed of becoming an actor and often brought Selena,
named after the Mexican American singer Selena Quintanilla, along to
her community theater rehearsals. At times, Mandy and Selena would
have to dig between the car seats to scrounge up enough change for gas
or walk to the dollar store to buy spaghetti for dinner. But when a seven-
year-old Selena told her mom she wanted to be on TV, Mandy found the
funds to enroll Selena in group master classes at Sullivan's studio, as well
as private, one-on-one weekly sessions with Sullivan to help prepare her
for TV auditions.

The sessions weren't cheap—six weeks of group classes cost around
$225, while private sessions were about $40 an hour. But sensing Selena's
promise, Sullivan would hold Mandy's checks until she had the funds in
her account to pay. "Mandy would just put all her money in whatever
Selena wanted to do," Sullivan said. "It really is a rags-to-riches story."

While still in Texas, Selena booked commercials and landed a starring role on the PBS hit *Barney & Friends*, which filmed in Dallas. (In
line at the open casting call, the seven-year-old met another child star
hopeful, Demi Lovato. When both landed parts, the girls—and their
moms—developed a friendship that would stretch into their Disney
days.) "I didn't have to inspire Selena to work harder," Sullivan said.
"She was the hardest working actress I ever had, really, from the very
beginning."

One day, while doing a four-hour private session to prepare for a pilot audition, Sullivan urged Selena to take a recess at the halfway mark.
"I said, 'Why don't we take a break. It's been two hours. You're nine years
old,'" Sullivan recalled. "And she went, 'You know what, you go ahead
and take a break, Miss Cathy. I'm going to look at the notes you gave
me so that the next time we go through this, I know how to fix some
things,'" Sullivan said. "She just wouldn't take a break."

*   *   *

TODD GREENWALD HAD been a writer on the first season of *Hannah Montana* when network development executive Jennilee Cummings asked him to draft a pilot for a Disney Channel family show that involved magic in some way. It was 2006 and the heyday of *Harry Potter*. The Disney theme parks division was rumored to have pulled out of a deal that would have turned J.K. Rowling's franchise into on-site attractions at Walt Disney World (it eventually landed at Universal), but Disney still wanted a stake in the wizarding craze.

"I've never read a *Harry Potter* book, and I've never watched a full *Harry Potter* movie," said Greenwald, who'd previously worked on *Saved By the Bell* and other network teen sitcoms. Despite his ambivalence, he came up with *The Amazing Hannigans*, which then became *The Amazing O'Malleys*, and eventually *Wizards of Waverly Place*, a show about a family of Irish American wizards navigating the human world in New York City. He named the family's boy-girl twins Jordan and Julia after his own two children.

The network loved the pilot script, and Greenwald was offered the choice of two showrunners: one, a Disney Channel veteran with proven experience in the candy-coated genre. The other was an outsider with a rebellious flare: Peter Murrieta. Murrieta was a sharp-tongued improv master who'd performed at Second City in Chicago alongside comedians like Tim Meadows and Chris Farley and understudied for Stephen Colbert before moving to L.A. to focus on writing.

Greenwald chose Murrieta.

"I knew that Peter had a vision that Disney Channel didn't have—and that he would put up a fight. I wanted him to be in their face," Greenwald said. "That single decision was the most important decision of the future of *Wizards of Waverly Place*."

Murrieta's work on the WB sitcom *Greetings from Tucson*—a show he created about an upwardly mobile Irish Mexican American family, based on his own upbringing—had first caught the eye of the Disney Channel executives a few years prior. But when Murrieta consulted his connections, they told him Disney Channel was "tough" to work with, so he didn't pursue anything.

The network reached out again with a tape of the pilot for the failed *Lizzie McGuire* spinoff, *Stevie Sanchez*, asking if Murrieta thought the pilot's star, Selena Gomez, had potential. "She was very charismatic, very sweet," he said. "But also very green." He pushed it aside and took a writing job on the Kelly Ripa sitcom *Hope & Faith* in New York. When that show ended abruptly after just eighteen episodes, Murrieta's agent let him know that Disney Channel was interested in bringing him on to supervise *The Amazing Hannigans* pilot. Murrieta hesitantly agreed to a meeting, and then to a one-year deal.

"I wasn't sure I wanted to do a kid show," Murrieta said. "In my mind, I was like, 'Oh, I'm going to go help run this pilot. Lord knows if it's going to go forward.'"

THE PILOT SCRIPT still needed work, and Murrieta set about revamping it with his own touches. Working with the established title, he kept the Irish American patriarch, but made the mother Mexican American and the kids biracial, similar to the family makeup on *Greetings from Tucson*. "I was looking for things that would make me interested in doing this," he said.

Murrieta remembered Selena from the *Stevie* pilot and wanted to put her in the lead role of Julia. But she had already been cast in a potential *Suite Life* spin-off pilot called *Housebroken*, which co-starred Brian Stepanek as his *Suite Life* character, Arwin, and followed the handyman's adventures rigging up a smart house for his widowed sister and her kids.

Selena, even at thirteen years old, had a knack for sarcasm and deadpan delivery, a skill she'd honed by watching every episode of *Friends* with her mom. "I saw so much of Jennifer Aniston in Selena's delivery, which felt very prime time," original programming head Adam Bonnett said. "Selena had a sweetness mixed with a touch of mischievousness. That's such a winning combination."

After bouncing from a single-episode part on *The Suite Life of Zack*

& Cody to the *Stevie Sanchez* pilot, Selena was poised to finally land a starring role on the network. "It took her a couple of years to really be able to understand comedy," said Catherine Stroud, who, along with Lisa London, had cast Selena in *Stevie* and *Housebroken*. "Disney was supportive of giving her time and project after project to get to the point where she could be the lead because, by then, she had had enough experience that she could start to hear the rhythm of comedy."

But the network had never tested the same lead actor in competing pilots before, and putting Selena in the *Hannigans* pilot would need special approval. Murrieta scheduled a meeting with entertainment president Gary Marsh and pled his case. "Wouldn't casting Selena in both pilots provide an opportunity to see which show was truly better?" Murrieta asked. The pilots could then be judged purely on concept and writing, not the quality of their star, because they'd have her in common. It was a decent argument, and Marsh agreed to let it happen. Selena was now in a win-win situation, guaranteed to lead her own Disney Channel show, no matter which pilot made the cut.

Since Maria Canals-Barrera had played Selena's mom in the *Stevie* pilot, she was perfect to come back as her mother on *The Amazing Hannigans*. They cast *The Hand That Rocks the Cradle* actor Matt McCoy as the patriarch. For the role of Julia's twin brother Jordan, they considered Joe Jonas and Dylan O'Brien, but David Henrie's experience on *That's So Raven* and the CBS hit *How I Met Your Mother* cemented his fate. "I was looking for somebody who was going to have some chops," Murrieta said. "I knew Selena was going to be awesome, but I really wanted to make sure that she had room to grow into it." David would serve as her anchor.

The *Housebroken* pilot tested okay and featured a familiar and beloved *Suite Life* character. But it just couldn't compete against the magical zeitgeist. And the network only had the budget to move forward with one new live-action sitcom each year. "*Housebroken* was a great show," said writer Adam Lapidus, who worked on that pilot. "The problem was, this was all happening right in the middle of Harry Potter— and they were wizards."

Still, the wizards show had problems that needed fixing. When they screened the pilot with focus groups, the Jordan character did not test well. The network pushed to ditch David Henrie and create a new role for a different, younger actor to play Julia's little brother, Max (they eventually cast Jake T. Austin, who had voiced Diego on Nickelodeon's *Dora the Explorer*). But Murrieta was adamant that David needed to stay, too. Not only did David have more experience than the other kid actors on the show, giving them someone to look up to, his character struck a unique chord as a nerd who wasn't ashamed of his smarts and didn't fit a sitcom stereotype. "I'll give you this younger brother," Murrieta relented. "But in exchange, we're going to keep David." The network allowed it, provided that Jordan, now repositioned as Julia's elder brother, didn't drive many stories and was allowed to fade into the background. Murrieta ignored that stipulation.

Because Nickelodeon was also developing a series called *Just Jordan*, the Disney executives requested they change the character's name to avoid conflict. Jordan became Justin, and Julia transformed into Alex, a more "tomboy" name to fit her demeanor. They also recast McCoy and subbed in David DeLuise—the son of comedy legend Dom DeLuise—who Murrieta had worked with on the NBC sitcom *Jesse*. The base salary was one quarter of DeLuise's usual quote, and he felt he'd be debasing himself to move from network to kids' cable. But times were tight, and playing a kooky dad teaching his kids magic seemed like a fun gig. "It's not one hundred percent about the money," DeLuise said. "It's about whether you're going to enjoy it."

DeLuise's Italian heritage led to switching the family name from the O'Malleys to the Russos, and the family's occupation went from running a magic shop to a sandwich shop. Finally, they changed the show title to advertise the wizarding connection right up front: *Wizards of Waverly Place*.

Latino representation on Disney Channel had mainly been limited to Disney Channel Original Movies like *Gotta Kick It Up!* and *The Cheetah Girls*, or supporting characters like the Boulevardez clan on *The Proud Family*. *Wizards* was the first series on the channel to center the Latino family experience through the Mexican Italian Russo clan. The show highlighted cultural touchstones like Alex's quinceañera, and behind the scenes, showrunner Peter Murrieta, executive producer Ben Montanio, and frequent director Victor Gonzalez helped bring authenticity to the storylines playing out on screen. When Shakira guest starred on a 2010 episode directed by Gonzalez, she was in awe of the inclusivity of the set. "There was a moment between setups where she said to us, 'I've never been in America doing anything where there's been this many Latinos,'" Murrieta said. "So, I was very happy to drive that at a time when I don't think that was on anybody's mind."

IT IS A minor miracle that the character of Alex Russo, as audiences know her, exists at all. In kids' programming, and especially in Disney Channel kids' programming, the main character needs to set a good example. They can mess up but, for the most part, they like going to school. They want to participate in extracurriculars. They can be bad at a certain subject. They can have flaws and insecurities. But at their core, they're usually trying their best to be a good kid. (The mold is, of course, skewed by latent sexism: Ren Stevens had to fit it; Louis Stevens did not.)

Selena's *Wizards of Waverly Place* heroine, however, is unabashedly lazy. She hates school. She's grumpy and sarcastic. She does the bare minimum to get by, and she always looks for shortcuts to success. "All the notes were like, 'Why are her arms folded? We don't want to see Janeane Garofalo or Daria,'" Murrieta said. "'That's not our network.'" Echoed writer and producer Matt Goldman, "It was constant resistance to everything we were doing—especially when Alex would not want to go to school or do her homework."

But Murrieta held firm. His own teen years were spent rebelling against authority, listening to punk music, and not wanting to conform. Alex needed to stay true to that lived experience. "Thank God he fought for everything," creator Todd Greenwald said. "We had a responsibility, and kids are impressionable, but everything's not all rosy and hugs." Still, there were compromises. In a season 3 episode where Alex doesn't want to read a book for class, the producers agreed to add a mock PSA on the end of the episode in which Selena, as herself, reminds kids of the importance of reading.

Looking back, Murrieta imagined Alex was possibly bisexual, and that her relationship with the character Stevie (played by Hayley Kiyoko) could have been something more than friends. But that was never discussed or explored at the time. Instead, because giving Miley Stewart a boyfriend had rated so well on *Hannah Montana*, Disney asked that *Wizards* do the same for Alex Russo, and she was given a werewolf love interest in the form of Mason Greyback (Gregg Sulkin)—which also paired well with the growing popularity of *Twilight*.

But while *Hannah* and *Raven* had been star-driven shows with their character's names in the titles, the *Wizards* showrunners were intent on keeping their show an ensemble series. It wasn't *Alex of Waverly Place*, but about the wizards as a family unit. The writers, which included *Friends* veterans Gigi McCreery and Perry M. Rein, incorporated ample "*mija* moments," the mother-daughter heart-to-hearts between Theresa and Alex. And they made sure that Justin and Max continued to have storylines of their own, despite what the network wanted.

"They wanted everything to be about Alex when Selena exploded. And we wanted to keep it balanced," Murrieta said. "So, if you look at the show titles, we started putting Alex's name in the title of every episode, even though it wasn't that much about her. That way they'd think it was an Alex story." In season 3, you can find "Alex Charms a Boy," "Positive Alex," "The Good, the Bad, and the Alex," "Alex's Logo," and "Alex Russo, Matchmaker?" Season 4 brought "Alex Tells the World," "Alex Gives Up," "Alex the Puppetmaster," etc.

But, Murrieta said, "Selena always thought of the show as an ensemble show. When we were trying to get stories over the finish line, she was very supportive so that I could tell substantial stories with Mom and Dad and brothers, not just her."

OFF SET, HOWEVER, Selena was following in the footsteps of her Disney Channel predecessors and becoming a massive star in her own right. Paparazzi began staking out the soundstage parking lot at Hollywood Center Studios and following her on private outings, hoping to capture photos they could then sell to tabloids. "I remember going to the beach with some family members who were visiting, and we saw, far away, grown men with cameras—taking pictures of a fifteen-year-old in her swimsuit," she told *Vogue*. "That is a violating feeling."

The attention she received from fans was more welcome. Young kids adored Selena and gravitated to her innate kindness. Sometimes, Selena's workload meant she would have to miss the usual Friday-night meet and greets with the *Wizards* audience in order to catch a plane or attend an event. But rather than dart out the door with a quick "Love ya! Sorry!" after the cast took their final bows, she often went out to the risers and spoke to the eager fans as a group. "I'm so sorry. I would be here for you, but I have to go do this thing," she told them. "I really wish I could stay. I know I'm only here because of you guys."

Her on-screen dad, David DeLuise, was in awe of her attentiveness. "The kudos that she put to those kids, she was like a Jedi making them think that they were the most important people in the world," he said. "She knew how to talk to the fans. She knew how to say, 'It's not about me. It's about you, God, and *then* me.' She put them above herself."

While shooting the *Wizards of Waverly Place* Disney Channel Original Movie in Puerto Rico, a group outing to see *Watchmen* at a local movie theater quickly turned into a mob scene. But Selena took it in stride, calmly meeting fans and posing for photos. "She was very down to earth with her celebrity in a way that I think was remarkable given her age," the film's producer, Kevin Lafferty, said. To escape the masses, she'd unwind in peace by watching movies on her laptop on set, like Darren Aronofsky's dark addiction drama *Requiem for a Dream*, a film she told Lafferty was her favorite at the time.

When Selena began dating Justin Bieber—America's then–reigning teen heartthrob—in 2010, the media coverage and fan obsession with their relationship became incessant. TMZ hungrily documented their date nights (including the time Justin, inspired by the movie *Mr. Deeds*, rented out the Staples Center for a romantic steak and pasta dinner on the court, followed by *Titanic* playing on the jumbotron), and the *New York Daily News* shared paparazzi photos of what they deemed a "hot and heavy" Hawaiian vacation.

Back on set, some of her *Wizards* co-stars were more skeptical of the romance. "Selena pulled me aside one time and said, 'My parents are not so crazy about this boy I'm dating,'" DeLuise recalled. "I said, 'Well, you have to listen to your parents because they have your best interests at heart.'" And when Justin first came to set to visit Selena, DeLuise walked by as the singer was trying to access the locked soundstage door. "What's the code?" Justin asked. DeLuise narrowed his eyes and feigned obliviousness to the superstar's identity. "And who are you?" he sniped.

Like so many of her predecessors at the Mouse House, Selena felt pressure, both self-imposed and from within the corporation, to always be a good role model for her young fans. "I wasn't a wild child by any means, but I was on Disney, so I had to make sure not to say 'What the hell?' in front of anyone," Selena told *Vanity Fair* in 2023. "It's stuff that I was also putting on myself to be the best role model I could be." And while former PR head Patti McTeague said the biggest misconception about Disney Channel's role in their young talents' lives is that "we actually wanted to control them," and argued instead that the network "just wanted them to be mindful that millions and millions of kids younger than them looked up to them," it was an incredibly heavy burden to put on teenagers.

To THE UNTRAINED eye, *Wizards of Waverly Place* might look the same as the other multi-cam Disney Channel shows of the era, but the *Wizards* team was adamant that they did not want to fit the *I Love Lucy* and *Laverne & Shirley* mold that series executive Adam Bonnett so cherished in the network's other sitcoms. "Disney knew what they had success with, and they just wanted to keep trying to repeat it," *Wizards* writer and producer Matt Goldman said. "Kids are smart. They know when something's the same thing over and over again." ("Every show started with a conversation between me and Gary Marsh, saying, 'What are we going to do differently?'" Bonnett countered. "We always attempted to do something different.")

With Murrieta at the helm, *Wizards* tried to buck the system—and ignited constant friction with the network. "It would be left to me to have the ongoing, passionate conversation with the network who wanted three jokes to a page," Murrieta said. "Many days I would hear, 'Where's the sitcom rhythm?' And I would say back, 'You mean, the rhythm that's killed the sitcom at the network level? The rhythm that people are tired of? Yeah, that's not here. We're not going to do that.'"

Day in and day out, Murrieta went to battle. He and the other *Wizards* creatives felt they were pushing the show to a better place, outside of the network's comfort zone. Goldman had been brought up in the school of Larry David and Jerry Seinfeld at *Seinfeld*. When NBC wasn't pleased with their creative decisions, those men would retort with a version of, "Cancel it, if you don't like it. We're not going out to sea in your ship. We're going out to sea in the ship we built."

"My early mentors had a very strong belief that vision and voice are everything," Goldman said. "And without that, everything falls apart. So, I felt that way, and Peter felt that way. And it created problems with Disney. Disney hated what we were doing, which was very similar to *Seinfeld* when I was there in the beginning: NBC hated *Seinfeld*. They tried to change it every day, and so did Disney with *Wizards*."

Overall, Murrieta said, "Our relationship with the network didn't feel good or healthy. But the show felt great." Before every taping, the cast and producers would form a huddle backstage. One by one, they'd go around the circle, look each other in the eyes, and repeat, "I got your back." It was an us-against-the-world mentality. "We felt like a tight unit," Murrieta said. "It became like we were the punk rock band, and everybody else was Styx and Rush. Whether we took it on ourselves or not, I don't know. But it definitely felt like that's who we became."

Creator Todd Greenwald agreed, "We were very obviously the black sheep of it all."

DESPITE THE CONSTRAINTS and friction behind the scenes, *Wizards* quickly became a ratings success. There was even talk of doing a theatrical *Wizards* movie, but they ultimately only did a DCOM and extended TV special. And while *Wizards* didn't achieve *Hannah Montana*–level ubiquity outside of its audience, its 2012 finale was the highest-rated of any Disney Channel show, drawing 9.8 million viewers. "You'd think when people find out I worked on *Seinfeld* that would impress them the most," Goldman said. "But I can't tell you how many people are as impressed, if not more impressed, by *Wizards*."

And it wasn't just a favorite among fans. In 2007, a shift had begun to occur in the Emmy's Outstanding Children's Program category. In a space previously dominated by news and educational docs, Disney received three of the five nominations that year, for *That's So Raven*, *The Suite Life of Zack & Cody*, and *Hannah Montana*. (The other slots, of course, went to a Linda Ellerbee autism special and a PBS documentary about kids with parents deployed abroad.)

Then, in 2009, the Emmys mercifully split the category in two, pulling the nonfiction programs out for a separate prize and finally giving scripted kids' sitcoms a better shot without Ellerbee in the mix. Disney Channel's only previous Emmy wins in the category had been for the anti-apartheid DCOM *The Color of Friendship* in 2000 and *High School Musical* in 2006. Now, facing its scripted peers alone for the first time at the 2009 ceremony, the second season of *Wizards of Waverly Place* was up against *Hannah Montana* and Nickelodeon's *iCarly*.

Wizards won.

The awards show had stipulated that only the producers should take the stage to accept the trophy, but Murrieta urged the *Wizards* cast to follow him to the podium before anyone could stop them. "I was like, well, whose prize is this?" he said. "It's everybody's." Some may have regretted the inclusion—as DeLuise bounded up the stage stairs, he tripped and broke his collarbone. Still, the actor said, "It felt really, really nice to be able to say: We're an Emmy-winning show. We're making good television. It's not terrible."

WHEN THE *Wizards of Waverly Place* DCOM premiered in 2009, it became the network's second-highest-rated original movie of all time with 11.4 million viewers, only trailing *High School Musical 2*. Network president Rich Ross called Murrieta to congratulate him. And at an industry event, Disney chief Bob Iger made a point to shake hands and thank Murrieta for his work.

Then, everything fell apart.

About six weeks before they wrapped production on season 3 of *Wizards* in the spring of 2010, Murrieta learned secondhand that he was being let go as showrunner for the fourth season, and that series producers Ben Montanio and Vince Cheung would be taking his place. Todd Greenwald would also continue on as an executive producer. That began, as Murrieta put it, "the most dramatic part of my entire career." There were still three episodes of the third season of *Wizards* left to shoot, and no one from the network had directly told Murrieta of his imminent firing. (Disney had a reputation for brutal partings: In 2006, Buena Vista Motion Pictures Group president Nina Jacobson had been unceremoniously ousted over the phone while she was at the hospital with her wife, who was giving birth to their third child.)

Finally, while in postproduction, Murrieta received a call from his agent letting him know his contract on *Wizards* wouldn't be renewed for season 4. Technically, he wasn't fired—he just didn't receive a contract extension like the rest of the cast and crew did. Disney released him from his season 3 contract and paid out a portion of his bonus. And because the cast had already finished for the season, Murrieta made a series of emotional phone calls, saying goodbye to the actors he'd worked with for the past four years.

"They got rid of Peter Murrieta because he was holding true to the integrity of the show, and Disney wanted to change it," DeLuise said. "Peter Murrieta was the reason why the show was funny. He was the reason why the show was good. It was all Peter."

Murrieta felt the decision was largely the result of his constant creative clashes with the network executives. It may have also been, in part, driven by finances. *Hannah* and *Suite Life* both attempted creative changes that decreased costs for their fourth seasons; losing executive producers Steven Peterman and Michael Poryes was initially the answer on *Hannah*, until Miley Cyrus put her foot down and demanded they stay. With *Wizards*, the network didn't replace Murrieta's position and just continued on with Montanio and Cheung steering the ship. ("It just felt time for a change," said original programming executive Adam Bonnett, when asked about the decision.)

But the showrunner's saga wasn't over yet. That summer, *Wizards* received two 2010 Emmys nominations in the Outstanding Children's Program category: one for the third season of the series, and one for the accompanying DCOM. When the network's chief creative officer Gary Marsh called Murrieta to congratulate him on the achievement, it was the first time they'd spoken since everything went down.

"It's really odd," Murrieta remembered Marsh telling him. "I thought because we submitted both the movie and the show that they might cancel each other out."

"Well, Gary, I'm so thrilled to continue to surprise you, even after I'm no longer working for you," Murrieta retorted.

On Emmys night, Murrieta braced for the disappointment of winning nothing, or perhaps worse, winning for the series, in which case he would have to jockey with Greenwald over who gave the speech. If the movie prevailed, however, Murrieta would indisputably claim the glory, since he'd served as its sole executive producer.

The movie won.

"I could feel the gasp. I could feel the bad energy," Murrieta said. He triumphantly took the stage with the *Wizards* cast. "It was a nice cap to it, but it was bittersweet. I made a hit for [Disney]. I won two Emmys. And they still fired me. I don't even know how to be successful enough not to be fired there."

OF COURSE, *Wizards of Waverly Place* soldiered on without Murrieta. And with 106 episodes by the end of its fourth season, it became the longest-running Disney Channel show at the time. But that fourth season just wasn't the same. Without the cantankerous advocate of Murrieta in the creatives' corner, no one pushed back against the network executives and their demands in the same way.

Established supporting characters fell by the wayside as new actors were introduced for possible future franchises. "They brought in all these new kids that they wanted to do other shows with, and it wasn't about our show anymore," DeLuise said. "Suddenly, I'm not even acting with the kids anymore. I'm over here with a guest star or with Maria. It was pretty disheartening."

The finale that Murrieta had envisioned would have seen Justin win the family wizarding competition because he worked hard and wanted it the most. Alex would follow her heart and stay with her werewolf boyfriend, since she didn't care about the prize anyway. And Justin would use his smarts to find a way to bestow powers onto Max. The final scene would pull back to reveal Rachel Dratch reprising her guest role as grown-up Harper and reading the story of *Wizards* to Alex's kids.

In reality, the series was wrapped up in a more predictable bow: Alex is named the family wizard, Justin becomes the headmaster of Wiz-Tech wizarding school, and Max is deemed worthy of one day inheriting the sub shop. "At that point, Disney was like, 'It's a hit show. Peter's gone. We're taking the reins,'" Greenwald said. "The show was on autopilot. People were already halfway out the door. We were all done."

ON THE MUSIC side, Hollywood Records had faced an uphill battle to get Selena on board as an artist. It took two years from when she first joined *Wizards* for her to sign a deal with the label. And when discussions began, she was adamant that she wanted to be a member of a band, not a solo artist. As part of a group, she wouldn't be competing directly with the other, more experienced solo pop stars at the label; in particular, her childhood friend with the powerhouse vocals, Demi Lovato. "Competing head-to-head with both your best friend and an artist in the exact same lane wasn't something that she thought was in her interest," the label's then–general manager, Abbey Konowitch, said.

Plus, Selena was still figuring out her own identity. In her early days, she often wore jeans, Converse, and hipster accessories to red carpet events, and she famously added some subtle cobalt streaks to her hair for a 2007 *Teen Vogue* party, where she excitedly told an interviewer, "I've got some blue going on! I like a little edge."

Selena's team proposed that she front a group, similar to the setup that singer Hayley Williams had with the band Paramore. It would be called

The Scene—a playful nod to the internet trolls who claimed Selena was trying too hard to be "scene," the indie-sleaze subculture that was popular at the time. This was a bad idea, the label felt. Their past musical successes had depended on solo stars using their recognizable names to draw interest. So, the two parties came up with a compromise. Selena would get to have a band, but they would also use her name: Selena Gomez & The Scene. Eventually, after three albums that sold more than five million copies total, the label won the naming battle and Selena dropped The Scene, in both name and actual band members, altogether.

Though she hadn't initially wanted to pursue music, Selena had previously guest starred on two episodes of *Hannah Montana* playing a rival pop singer, and by 2009, Selena was spending her weekends and hiatuses working on her own singing career. But she didn't have a musical background or strong outside music management the way that Miley and Demi did. And because Selena didn't routinely sing in her main Disney Channel projects, other than performing the *Wizards* theme song off camera, she had to fight to be taken as seriously as her contemporaries.

While shooting the music video for the 2009 collaborative charity single "Send It On" that featured Selena, Miley, Demi, and the Jonas Brothers, it became clear that Demi and Miley had been given more solo lines than Selena. Selena's mom, Mandy Teefey, sprang into action.

Mandy pushed for directors Michael Blum and Tracy Pion to record footage of Selena lip-syncing some of the other girls' lines so that she could then record them on the final studio version of the track to equalize their parts, the directors recalled. "Selena's mom was amazing. She was a true manager, like, 'If she's in this, she's going to be in it as much as the other two,'" Pion said. "We wish all moms could be advocates like that."

While Mandy advocated for Selena to get equal treatment, and she and Selena's stepdad, Brian Teefey, co-managed the teenager's career, they didn't come across as typical stage parents. "I would not believe from watching them that her mom had any interest in Selena being in this business," *Wizards of Waverly Place: The Movie* producer Kevin Lafferty said. "It was just that Selena wanted to be in this business, so [Mandy said], 'Fine. Okay, I'll just make sure that she's in a safe and happy place.'" (Lafferty likewise praised *Jump In!* star Keke Palmer's mom for taking a similar stance in her daughter's early career.)

Mandy took on a protective role and used to joke that she was on constant "mole patrol," vetoing tops and dresses that she felt were too revealing for Selena based on whether they covered a mole on her daughter's chest. And Selena praised her mom for allowing her the space to quit working, if she so chose. "If I'm really not enjoying it anymore," Selena told *Elle* in 2011, "she doesn't want me to do it."

But there was only so much a parent could dictate. Years later, when Selena was promoting her solo music, the singer lamented the rote superficiality of an interviewer's questions. "It made me feel like Disney," Selena said in a moment captured in her 2022 documentary *Selena Gomez: My Mind & Me*. "It made me feel like a product."

It was a valid complaint. The entire music ecosystem at Disney was set up in a way that rendered musicians and the music they created as little more than merchandising metrics, no matter how talented the songwriters or the artists may be. While Disney Channel might be encouraging its stars to sign with Hollywood Records, participate in Walt Disney Records' *DisneyMania* albums, or join group sing-alongs like the Disney Channel Circle of Stars, they weren't often endowing them with artistic control.

"The Disney Music Group is just a consumer products division," said Mitchell Leib, who spent years at Hollywood Records before becoming the head of music and soundtracks at the studio. "They don't make or break artists. They inherit artists from the Disney Channel, manage them as best they can during the period that they're creating content for the Disney Channel. Then, once those artists grow up, they don't want to be on Walt Disney Records or Hollywood Records. These aren't competitive record companies. They're consumer products divisions that just happen to operate in records."

STILL, SELENA HAS called her early time at Disney "one of the best experiences of my life." And on the *Wizards* set in particular, "I felt safe, and that's a really hard thing for me to feel," she told co-stars David DeLuise and Jennifer Stone on their *Wizards of Waverly Pod* podcast in 2023. "You guys genuinely loved me, and that's all I could have asked for."

During her time at the network, Selena didn't stir public controversies or face outrage the way Miley did. Like Hilary Duff before her, Selena seemed to toe the line and carry the weight of the Disney brand with ease. "Sometimes I imagined, *girl, you must be tired,*" her *Wizards* mom Maria Canals-Barrera said. "But she was always kind, respectful, humble, prepared. I never saw her ever act out in any way other than being a professional."

Just a month after *Wizards of Waverly Place* wrapped its final episode in May 2011, however, Selena was hospitalized while on a joint promotional tour for her Fox rom-com *Monte Carlo* and her Hollywood Records album *When the Sun Goes Down*. "I was just very malnourished," the then-eighteen-year-old said. "I was low on iron and exhausted." Two days later, she was back performing at an outdoor mall for hundreds of screaming fans. In the following years, she would be diagnosed with the autoimmune disease lupus, undergo a life-saving kidney transplant, and speak openly about her, at times, debilitating mental health struggles.

Even for those who made it look easy while in the throes of the 360-degree circus that came with being a Disney Channel star, it was a years-long exhausting grind, the effects of which followed many into adulthood. Not only did performers endure the physical demands of a packed work schedule, but they bore the mental load of projecting perfection.

As Selena told *Vogue* years later, "That was my job in a way—to be perfect."

13

Jonas Brothers:
Purity Rings and Pre-Made Stars

Steve Greenberg spent his 2004 Christmas break at home with a pile of bad CDs. As the incoming president of Sony's Columbia Records, he had been tasked with sifting through albums by label artists who were on the verge of being cut to see if, by some holiday miracle, there were any worth giving a second chance. He made his way through the stack of ho-hum, forgettable discs, speedily passing each one through his home CD player and tossing them aside—until one Christian pop record gave him pause.

Nicholas Jonas.

Nick was thirteen years old. He'd put out a couple of singles in the Christian market, including a cover of "Higher Love," and recorded an album, but a lack of enthusiasm had shelved the product. Nick's voice reminded Greenberg of a young Taylor Hanson, the lead singer of the trio of brothers whom Greenberg had discovered while at Mercury Records. Greenberg had gone on to produce Hanson's self-written megahit "MMMBop" and its accompanying album, which sold ten million copies worldwide. Perhaps Nick deserved to keep his spot on Columbia's roster.

When Greenberg settled into his office at Columbia's New York headquarters that January, he called Nick and his dad in for a meeting to discuss what his future at the label could look like. During the course of their conversation, Nick casually mentioned he had two older brothers, Joe and Kevin. *Brothers*, Greenberg thought. *I know how to make that work.*

"Do you and your brothers play instruments?" he asked Nick.

"Well, we're learning," Nick replied humbly.

"Great, keep learning," Greenberg said, operating under his belief that if teenagers are self-motivated enough to learn to play rock instruments, they can almost always succeed at being halfway decent. "You're a band."

It had been seven years since "MMMBop." In the interim, a specific type of un-Hanson-like boy band had proliferated. Led by the success of the Backstreet Boys and *NSYNC, groups like O-Town, 98 Degrees, B2K, Westlife, and Dream Street performed with varying degrees of slick dance moves, layered harmonies, and nary an instrument in sight.

Thus, when Greenberg met the Jonas brothers at a dance studio in the city, he found them hard at work rehearsing choreography. Contemporary wisdom had taught the brothers that if they wanted to form a band, they'd need to be dancers, too. But their strengths, like Hanson's, lay more in songwriting and jamming than shimmying in sync. Greenberg offered them an out. "I think they were very relieved that they didn't have to be that," Greenberg said. "They could be a rock band."

The meeting was overseen by the Jonases' dad, Kevin Jonas Sr., who had been shepherding the boys' musical endeavors. Kevin Sr. was a pastor at the Wyckoff Assembly of God church in the family's New Jersey hometown, about forty minutes outside of New York City. He also had songwriting experience and had collaborated on tracks for various Christian artists. "I've worked with a lot of kids who have parents who are very involved," Greenberg said, "and the Jonases' dad was, by far, the most proactive and great of them all."

But even more crucial than the parent-kid dynamic was the one among the three boys. Middle brother Joe and eldest brother Kevin were far better than Greenberg had dared to hope. Joe had done musical theater and loved the spotlight. Kevin had acted in commercials. The three boys had even written and recorded a song called "Please Be Mine" as a group.

Greenberg signed them to the label as a trio and set about picking a band name. They tossed around a variety of monikers: Jonas Jonas Jonas. Jonas Three. Sons of Jonas. J3. In the end, the simple but effective Jonas Brothers won out, and the label began organizing their debut album. Greenberg paired the Jonas Brothers with veteran songwriters for some tracks, but the boys were also talented composers on their own. Columbia decided to push the self-written "Mandy" as their first single with three accompanying music videos, designed to play out like a serialized soap opera when pieced together.

It was 2005. MySpace was thriving. YouTube launched that December. While most major labels were still wary of the internet and utilizing social media platforms, Columbia leaned in, using MySpace's ecosystem of young female creators to spread the word about the band. Greenberg reached out to a variety of third-party creators to design widgets that would play the "Mandy" music videos on users' profiles. As each new video installment was released, the widgets would update on the pages. The creators were thrilled. They were used to being sent lawsuit threats, not music videos to legally use. The executives at Sony, however, were less than enthused.

"People at the Sony Music Group were very upset, like, 'Wait, you're giving our music away for free to be spread by teenage girls?'" Greenberg said. "People hadn't understood that the internet and social media would essentially be the greatest promotional vehicle for music ever created."

As the MySpace campaign took off, MTV's *Total Request Live* took notice. That was another anomaly. "Mandy" wasn't a radio hit like the other tracks dominating *TRL*'s afternoon countdown. It was a mere social media phenomenon. But once *TRL* played the track, radio stations began to follow suit, including Radio Disney. "We thought, 'This is great! We've unlocked the future of the music business!'" Greenberg said.

And then, in the summer of 2006, the internal politics at Sony imploded.

Greenberg and other executives were ousted, leaving acts like Katy Perry, OneRepublic, and the Jonas Brothers—whose debut album, *It's About Time*, was now only getting pushed in a limited release—in an uncertain lurch. Without Greenberg there to champion them, the brothers would likely end up getting dropped. Famed music mogul Johnny Wright, who had signed on as the brothers' personal music manager alongside Phil McIntyre and Kevin Sr., set up a desperate meeting with Bob Cavallo and Abbey Konowitch at Hollywood Records. If Columbia released the Jonases from their contract, would Hollywood sign them?

Based on the influx of requests from listeners, Radio Disney had already been playing the Jonas Brothers' cover of "Year 3000" in constant rotation. The boys had also performed as an opening act for Hollywood Records artists including Aly & AJ and The Cheetah Girls to great success. Hollywood Records' general manager Konowitch was impressed with the way the Jonases had leveraged social media to create a passionate fan base, despite Columbia's apathy. "They had really been blackballed by their label. So, in order to stay alive, they had to do it themselves," Konowitch said. "They had done such a good job that we knew that if we did the right marketing, and if they had a team actually supporting them, they could be huge."

They struck a deal, and in February 2007, Hollywood Records announced that the Jonas Brothers had officially joined the Disney fold.

AS THE JONAS BROTHERS recorded their self-titled Hollywood Records album, the network began to steadily integrate them into Disney Channel content. To ensure maximum exposure for the label's biggest new act, the network scheduled a season 2 episode of *Hannah Montana* in which the Jonas Brothers guest starred to air the same night as the premiere of *High School Musical 2* in August 2007. The *Hannah* episode broke records with 10.7 million viewers, making it basic cable's most-watched episode ever at the time.

And months after the 3D *Hannah Montana* concert film shattered box office records, Walt Disney Pictures set about capturing footage of the Jonas Brothers' 2008 Burning Up tour to create a similar theatrical experience. Bruce Hendricks returned to direct *Jonas Brothers: The 3D Concert Experience* and leaned in to capturing the maniacal devotion of the boys' young female fanbase at their two shows in Anaheim.

"The energy is just indescribable," Hendricks said. "The fans are crying, screaming. I think someone fainted. It was nuts. It was absolutely nuts."

In addition to guest performances from Taylor Swift, Demi Lovato, and the boys' bodyguard "Big Rob," the concert film featured the brothers using foam guns to spray the ecstatic crowd with a white soapy substance. Later, the Jonases soaked themselves while banging on water-doused drums. But Kevin Sr. was wary of the boys being perceived as too sexual. "A lot of times you could see their nipples because they'd be wearing fitted shirts, and they would be soaking wet," tour photographer Elise Abdalla said. "Their team would be like, 'No, you have to crop it. No nipples.' Anything that was too sexy was out."

When the concert movie premiered in February 2009, it didn't shatter any records or perform as well as Miley Cyrus's *Best of Both Worlds* film had, but it still managed to pull in $23.1 million. And people outside the Jonases' target audience were taking notice.

Inspired by the fanfare around the film's release, *South Park* creators Trey Parker and Matt Stone penned a 2009 Jonas Brothers–centric episode titled "The Ring." The "ring" in question was a purity ring, a symbolic piece of jewelry that had risen in popularity during the '90s and early 2000s abstinence-only movement. Christian campaigns like True Love Waits and the Silver Ring Thing urged young people to make a promise to "save themselves" for the right person, usually their future spouse. To really prove their commitment, teens were encouraged to buy a ring, often a simple silver band, that would let potential partners—and the whole world—know they weren't having sex now or for the foreseeable future.

During the time they were on Disney Channel, all three of the Jonas Brothers publicly wore and talked about their purity rings, as did, at various points, Miley Cyrus, Selena Gomez, and Demi Lovato (all of whom dated a Jonas brother). It was too irresistible a trend for *South Park* to ignore.

In "The Ring," Kenny's new girlfriend reveals she recently hooked up with another boy, but that she couldn't help herself: "I was watching the Disney Channel and that show came on with the Jonas Brothers," she tells Kenny. "Every time I see them I get so tingly. I just completely lose control." Hoping to inspire a similarly amorous outcome, Kenny takes her to a Jonas Brothers concert, and over the course of the episode, it's revealed that the Jonases have been forced to keep their purity rings on by the network in order to sell sex to young girls in a non-threatening way. At one point, "the boss," a deceptively upbeat Mickey Mouse, storms in and beats Joe to a bloody pulp as he orders the boys to keep their rings on—or else. "Do we have a problem?" Mickey threatens. "No, Mr. Mouse," Nick stammers in submission.

Papa Jonas was not pleased. "When the *South Park* episode came out, their father was super offended," the tour photographer Abdalla said. "But I was like, don't you think the foam thing *does* look a little weird?"

The brothers were sixteen, nineteen, and twenty-one at the time the episode aired. "When it first came out I didn't think it was funny to be honest," Nick posted in a 2016 Reddit Ask Me Anything (AMA). "But years later and once the purity rings were no longer around, it was very funny to me." In a separate 2016 Reddit AMA, Joe stated that he "loved" the episode and was "so pumped" when it came out. "They were kind of attacking Disney more than me," he wrote, "so I didn't really feel threatened."

But even those directly in the line of fire on the Disney Channel corporate side claim they took the *South Park* episode, and other satirical jabs, in stride. "We were absolutely thrilled because it meant that the rest of entertainment actually noticed us," said former Disney Channel president Anne Sweeney, who was head of the Disney/ABC Television Group at that time. "I thought it was funny."

Similarly, it was a sign that Disney Channel was finally relevant in the cultural zeitgeist when *Saturday Night Live* began parodying the network in skits like "Disney Channel Acting School" (teaching young performers techniques such as "reacting to stinky feet," "spying in a doorway," and wearing clothes that are "as loud and crazy as your acting") in the late 2000s and early 2010s. And Disney Channel happily provided their house graphics for *SNL* to use in the shorts. "No one was thinking we were writing *SNL* or *The Simpsons* or *South Park*. No one was blaming us," former Disney Channel president Rich Ross said. "We had to have a sense of humor about who we were and what we did."

Contrary to popular conspiracy theories, Disney Channel didn't supply purity rings to its talent or indoctrinate them into wearing them. Most
of the stars mentioned above have said they procured their rings from
their parents or hometown churches long before arriving at the channel.
And both Ross and former PR head Patti McTeague balked at the idea
that the network approved of the concept of the rings, which invited endless conversation about the sex lives of teenagers. "Literally, the last thing
we needed or wanted was to have that kind of conversation about what
the actors and actresses were doing in their spare time," Ross said.

For teenagers in the public eye, wearing a purity ring meant adult
interviewers continuously asking them about their virginity and moral
convictions and fellow entertainers taking public jabs. Like when comedian Russell Brand, then thirty-three years old, mocked the Jonas
Brothers and their purity rings during the 2008 MTV Video Music
Awards, prompting eighteen-year-old singer Jordin Sparks (who was
also wearing a purity ring at the time) to use her moment presenting on
stage to tell the crowd, "It's not bad to wear a promise ring because not
everybody, guy or girl, wants to be a slut!"

But even if the network wasn't thrilled about the conversations surrounding their talents' jewelry, it's fair to say that Disney's decision to
employ teens who came with pre-sown puritanical convictions was a
smart business decision for a kids' cable network and music business
hoping to avoid anything beyond a G-rated scandal.

"The Disney brand was embedded in everything that we would do
with their artists. So, how they behaved was an issue; what the lyrics
were to the songs was an issue. We had to always walk the fine line," said
Abbey Konowitch of Hollywood Records. "The Jonas Brothers were
perfect because they were coming from a Christian background, and
so, therefore, they were not coloring out of the lines."

WHEN THE JONAS BROTHERS joined the Disney lineup, it wasn't just in
a musical capacity. The network would find a way for them to be actors,
too. After having the boys audition on the twenty-first floor of Disney

Channel headquarters—a session that involved them reading a scene from *That's So Raven* and Joe Jonas jumping on the conference room table while performing "Mandy"—the executives set about building a show around the siblings.

Producers Michael Curtis and Roger S.H. Schulman, who had led *Phil of the Future*'s second season, were brought in to write a new pilot for the Jonases. They originally envisioned something straightforward with the brothers playing a fictional band, like the 1960s sitcom *The Monkees*, but original programming head Adam Bonnett wanted something higher concept. So they crafted a pilot called *J.O.N.A.S.*, standing for Junior Operatives Networking as Spies, in which the brothers played international spies who go undercover as a rock band. But after filming, the idea proved too expensive, and the dynamic between the brothers was all wrong. Because Kevin was the oldest, they had cast him as the wise leader and Nick as the token goofy little brother. In reality, the roles were flipped.

Bonnett came back to the table and presented a not-so-original idea: "We need to do something more like *The Monkees*," he said. Schulman and Curtis stifled their eye rolls at their earlier pitch being thrown back at them anew. "We looked at each other and went, 'Great idea, Adam,'" Curtis said.

After the failed pilot, the brothers took a break to shoot the Disney Channel Original Movie *Camp Rock*, then returned to work on the retooled single-camera series that would now follow a band of brothers attending regular high school with the restyled title *Jonas*. But unlike previous Disney Channel shows, *Jonas* was a star vehicle starring actual stars from the beginning.

"Disney was used to making stars," Schulman said. "With the Jonas Brothers, they were catching lightning in a bottle, and Disney didn't know what to do with it. They didn't have any tools in that box. So what they substituted was a certain kind of obsequiousness." Because the network executives were wary of upsetting the brothers and their team, they tiptoed around the treatment of their characters in ways they'd never considered on other shows.

"Early in the process, there were a lot of notes from the network saying,

'Oh, no, you can't make fun of Nick like that.' Or, 'Joe looks too egotistical when he makes that joke.' They were sort of on eggshells about the Jonas brothers," Curtis said. "Gradually, over a few episodes, we realized the Jonas brothers were perfectly happy making fun of themselves."

DESPITE THEIR RELATIVE industry pedigree, the brothers received the same standard series contracts as other network stars. Each Jonas would be paid a mere $9,000 an episode for the show's first season with 5 percent bumps for subsequent seasons.

And just as Miley Cyrus and Selena Gomez had done, the Jonas Brothers began working around the clock to fulfill their various obligations. On the weekends, they'd perform concerts before reporting back to the *Jonas* set at 7:00 A.M. on Monday mornings. When shooting wrapped each day, they'd spend their nights writing the original tracks Disney Channel had commissioned for the series. During any breaks, they would often seek to challenge themselves further.

"Nick read somewhere that some guy threw a whiffle ball seventy miles an hour. So he spent two weeks with a whiffle ball and one of those nets and a speed gun," Curtis said. "Any time he was not acting or writing songs, he was throwing that whiffle ball until he threw it seventy miles an hour. They all had their own way of handling the pressure, their own way of coping with it. But it was all very healthy. They had a lot of support, and they were raised right."

The brothers had been brought up to be hard workers and were unnervingly well-mannered. Their parents, Denise and Kevin Jonas Sr., had first met at Bible college in Texas and married at eighteen. "I tended to be strict," their mom, Denise Jonas, told *Today* in 2023. "My husband and I felt like, we're not just raising kids. We're raising adults. And we want to raise them with the integrity and the moral values that we have."

On the *Jonas* set, the brothers personally thanked every crew member for their work at the end of each day. "The first two hundred times they did that, I was a little skeptical," Schulman said. "And then, I realized, yeah, they were taught to do that, but they also mean it." And to onlookers, it appeared Kevin Sr. made sure his obligations as the boys' manager never outweighed his duties as their father. "Their dad used to do check-ins with them all the time to say, 'Hey, where's your head at? Where's your heart? Tell me what you need and what you don't need,'" McTeague recalled.

When *Jonas* premiered in May 2009, it did fine, but not great, given the boys' built-in fandom. As sitcom actors, the brothers were coming across, as one creative put it, exceedingly "dull," and the network decided that if there was going to be a second season, they'd need to overhaul the show from the top.

"We got a call from Adam Bonnett and Gary Marsh, and they said, 'We don't know if we're going to pick up the show yet, but we know it won't be with you guys,'" Curtis recalled.

A few weeks after that ousting, the first season of *Jonas* received a 2010 Emmy nomination for Outstanding Children's Program, pitting it against *Hannah Montana* and *Wizards of Waverly Place*. Years earlier, when *Phil of the Future* hadn't received any Emmy nominations, Bonnett had informed Curtis that Disney Channel didn't submit their lower-rated shows for consideration. "So, with *Jonas*, we made sure that we submitted it ourselves," Curtis said. "We filled out the paperwork and paid the fee. We knew it wasn't a smash hit, but it did okay. And it got nominated."

At the ceremony, the network's outcast creatives commiserated.

"I wonder who's going to win," eventual winner *Wizards*' Peter Murrieta joked to Curtis during the show. "The guys they fired, the other guy they fired, or the guy who's suing them [*Hannah*'s Rich Correll]."

For *Jonas*'s second season, the network reset the show in California, renamed it *Jonas L.A.*, and brought on former *The Office* producer Lester Lewis and frequent DCOM director Paul Hoen as showrunners. They also summoned Marc Warren as a consulting producer to once again come fix a flailing project. (Warren's producing partner Dennis Rinsler had by then retired from the industry completely after the *Cory in the House* debacle.) But the show's kid-centric humor didn't jibe with the type of image that the Grammy-nominated rockers, now in their late teens and early twenties, were hoping to project.

"Biggest regret in regards to the Brothers? Season 2 of *Jonas*," Nick said in their 2019 documentary *Chasing Happiness*. "We shouldn't have done that. It really stunted our growth. I feel like it was just a bad move."

While shooting the series, the boys hid their dissatisfaction on set and fulfilled their obligations without complaint. "We went along with it at the time, because we thought Disney was our only real shot," Joe said in 2013, "and we were terrified that it could all be taken away from us at any moment." But as their albums went platinum alongside a completely forgettable sitcom, it was abundantly clear to the creatives involved: the Jonas Brothers were doing just fine, with or without a scripted series on Disney Channel. "My impression was they didn't really need that show," director Savage Steve Holland said, noting that it had reached a point where "it seemed like the Jonas Brothers maybe didn't need Disney."

BACK IN 2007, when Disney Channel had been casting the lead female role for the original secret-agent-themed *J.O.N.A.S.* pilot, Lily Collins was the frontrunner until her manager pulled her from contention over the salary on offer. ("I think his words were, 'These are slave wages,'" Curtis recalled.) Chelsea Staub, who eventually got the part, became their top pick, but the network was also hoping for more diversity and asked the showrunners to keep looking. Gary Marsh and casting head Judy Taylor joined them to see another batch of girls in person at Disney. None were right for the role, and they wrapped up the session without any new contenders. "There's this one other girl who sent in a tape," Taylor suggested to the showrunners, as Marsh headed out for the evening.

It was Demi Lovato. And she was perfect. "She had a little gap in her teeth, and she was cute as a button," Curtis recalled. He chased Marsh down the hallway and convinced him to return to the room to watch Demi's tape.

"Oh, she's great," Marsh said. "Let's fly her in."

As Demi read scenes and sang with the Jonas Brothers in person, "The hair stood up on the back of all our necks collectively," Schulman said. "You could feel it. It was like, *there's something happening here*."

Marsh was overjoyed. He turned to Schulman.

"This girl belongs on Disney Channel," he said. "But not on your show."

14

Demi Lovato, *Camp Rock*, and a Painful Reality

In the wake of Miley Cyrus's headline-making spree and Vanessa Hudgens's photo leak, Disney Channel finally began to implement a more structured system to help their young performers navigate the increasingly harrowing limelight in 2009.

When Disney Channel president Rich Ross had been a talent coordinator at Nickelodeon early in his career, he'd befriended another talent liaison working at the National Basketball Association named Leah Wilcox. Wilcox had devised a program to help NBA rookies and their families better understand what joining the league entailed, from the sudden surplus of finances to overwhelming fame. Ross noted the two industries' parallels, including how the athletes' families were often from low-income backgrounds, similar to those of many child actors, and unfamiliar with many aspects of the complex industry their child was entering.

"When I knew this thing was blowing up, I called her and said, 'I just don't know how we get people ready,'" Ross recalled. With Wilcox's advice and that NBA system in mind, Ross decided they should be implementing something similar at the network. In 2009, Disney Channel began offering a Talent 101 orientation program for its performers and their families to attend. (Nickelodeon had offered a comparable "Nick 101" class for its talent roster as early as 2002.)

Disney Channel's multipart initiative was overseen by the heads of network casting and talent relations, public relations, and standards and practices. While not mandatory, former PR head Patti McTeague said that talent and their families were "strongly encouraged" to attend.

New performers arriving at the network would be offered a half-day initiation session, usually at the Disney Channel headquarters in Burbank, where the network leaders, as well as external security experts, psychologists, and life coaches, instructed them and their families on navigating the waters and outlined the responsibilities that came with representing the brand (as well as the perks, like an annual allotment of Disneyland tickets). "It was transformative," Ross said. "Part of the education process was self-regulation, to explain to the parents what we expected of them and to make them partners, not adversaries."

One of the biggest lessons they stressed, said *Camp Rock 2* actor Matthew "Mdot" Finley, was "information out is information out," meaning: you can't take back what you say in interviews or post online. To drive home the point, there were PowerPoints and handouts, and a security team who analyzed the kids' devices and accounts to see if they were hackable. It wasn't just compromising personal photos the network was concerned about. It was unreleased music files, future episodic reveals, and anything considered company property. Through the program, the network was "telling them everything we knew about protecting themselves," former president Anne Sweeney said.

The PR team emphasized the importance of making sure each talent's social media profiles reflected their "brand" and the persona they were hoping to build, as well as urged them to share more candid posts every now and then, so that they weren't just plugging projects and could be seen as relatable to fans. And the security experts offered safety tips on how to deal with stalkers and properly outfit home alarm systems, as well as online safety tips, like never posting while you're still in the location of your post. At some sessions, a representative would go around the room, calling out specific details about the actors' lives they'd been able to glean from their digital footprint.

"I know you were at Pinkberry on Sunset Boulevard last Wednesday at 2:00 P.M."

"I know you went to a party three years ago and drank something out of a red plastic cup."

As the 2010s progressed, Disney Channel added additional components to the program: Midway through each production season, McTeague said, they began offering a Talent 102 follow-up course, with guidance for on-set etiquette, communication, and other workplace issues, which was also attended by the series' producers. There were enhanced group media training sessions, which offered workshops and mock on-camera interviews; "Life Skills" sessions, split up by talent age and conducted by pediatricians and experts, discussing developmental topics, stress management, sleep, and nutrition; and for the talent over the age of seventeen, they launched a recurring "Art of . . ." speaker series in 2016 that was held over Sunday dinners. Aaron Paul and his wife, Lauren, led one on the "Art of Kindness"; at another, Nicole Richie spoke to the "Art of Reinvention." "It was an opportunity for young actors to hear from people who they might especially relate to about 'staying grounded' within the entertainment industry," McTeague said. And as each TV series' production came to an end, the actors attended a Talent 103 evening session filled with video reels and speeches that served as a graduation party for the casts and their families, as well as the series creatives and network executives.

The Disney Channel infrastructure was finally beginning to address the colossal fame and pressures on young performers that their time at the network was cultivating. But could it ever be enough?

WHEN DEMETRIA DEVONNE LOVATO was born on August 20, 1992, her mother cradled Demi in her arms and declared, "Someday, they'll all be begging to take your picture!"

Demi's mom, Dianna De La Garza (née Smith), had been a Dallas Cowboys cheerleader in the 1980s and had attempted a short-lived country music career before focusing her attention on making stars out of her three daughters. "You gave up your passions to see that my sisters and I realized ours," Demi wrote in the forward to Dianna's 2017 memoir, *Falling with Wings: A Mother's Story*. "You provided a pathway for us to achieve our goals and dreams, simply because you loved us."

Dianna's life had not been easy. She'd struggled with anorexia, addiction, and depression. Demi's biological father, Patrick Lovato, had allegedly been abusive, and Dianna fled when Demi was still a toddler. She built a new life for herself and her girls with her second husband, Eddie De La Garza, in the suburbs of Dallas. "Over time," Dianna wrote in her memoir, "I convinced myself that if I could just guide my family to stardom, my problems would disappear. The formula in my head looked something like this: stardom = money & recognition = less anxiety & more satisfaction = less depression & more happiness = fairy-tale life."

She put Demi, as well as Demi's older sister, Dallas, and, later, her younger half sister, Madison De La Garza, through an endless parade of piano, voice, acting, and dance classes. Like Mandy Teefey—Selena Gomez's mother—who'd thrown every penny into her daughter's dreams, Dianna and Eddie pawned jewelry and remortgaged their house twice to pay for their girls' pursuits.

It wasn't without cause. Demi (who uses both she/her and they/them pronouns) was a natural talent. Even as a child, she had a dynamic vocal range and could belt songs like a veteran diva. After watching Kelly Clarkson win *American Idol* in 2002, ten-year-old Demi made her email address "littlekelly@yahoo.com" and fantasized about becoming a famous singer just like the "Since U Been Gone" icon. Demi excelled at acting, too, but during classes with Cathryn Sullivan, the Texas-based acting coach said that her pupil "always made it clear to me that she was more interested in singing."

DEMI'S FIRST BIG Disney Channel break came in the form of a very small show. In 2006, network executive Kory Lunsford had recently been put in charge of short-form content. High on the agenda: creating an English version of an Italian interstitial series called *Quelli dell'intervallo*, which had premiered on Disney Channel in Italy the year before as part of an effort to give the international markets a semblance of control over their regional content.

As the Bell Rings marked the first time the network had adapted one of their international shows for the US market. Essentially, it was a low-risk, low-budget political move to demonstrate to the overseas territories that the Burbank office valued their original contributions. It was also a way to test short-form content that might work well when viewed online and on phones, an increasingly popular way that kids were consuming entertainment.

Italy's series had been made by a local production company on a single set. The US version followed suit, casting and shooting out of Austin, Texas. That regional casting announcement was music to Cathryn Sullivan's ears. She submitted all of her suitable acting students and six of them made it through to the chemistry reads, including Demi. But as Sullivan helped her get ready, she realized Demi hadn't prepared for the callback at all.

"'I just don't think I'm Disney material,'" Sullivan recalled Demi wailing. "She was very dramatic about it. And I was like, 'Well, Disney has given you a callback. So, they think you are. Do you want to do this?' She just wasn't sure if she could handle being a Disney star."

A "Disney star" had by then been established as endlessly perky and approachable, and Demi, even in her early teens, had a moody, defiant streak. "She was not a goody-goody girl. She was somebody who said what she wanted to say," Sullivan said. "If you were a Disney star back then, you went the company line."

Demi pulled it together for the audition and won a lead part playing a middle schooler named Charlotte. And while shooting the two- to five-minute episodes, Demi spent her free time on set writing songs and playing guitar. Her talent was undeniable, and Lunsford suggested writing an episode that would allow Demi to showcase her skills. Rather than pay for a new song or cover rights, showrunner Danny Kaplan pushed to use one of Demi's original songs, "Shadow," on the show. When she and her co-star Tony Oller performed it as a duet, it became crystal-clear to those involved that the network needed to find a more substantial platform for Demi's talent on Disney Channel.

BEFORE *AS THE BELL RINGS* aired, Dianna and Demi traveled to Los Angeles for pilot season auditions. To save money on a hotel, they crashed at the downtown loft Selena Gomez and her mom were renting while Selena worked on the first season of *Wizards of Waverly Place*. One day, Demi attended a *Wizards* taping, during which Selena encouraged her friend to do an impromptu performance of Christina Aguilera's "Ain't No Other Man" for the room, which included several network executives. "I was absolutely determined to get [Demi] on the Disney Channel with me," Selena told the *Wall Street Journal* in 2008.

A few weeks later, after Demi and Dianna had returned home to Texas, Disney Channel requested Demi submit a tape to read for the love interest in the *J.O.N.A.S.* pilot. Then, they asked her to travel back to California for a screen test. Dianna and Demi once again crashed with Mandy and Selena. And, after that in-person session, the network's president of entertainment Gary Marsh was convinced that fourteen-year-old Demi had the potential to be huge for the network, much bigger than a supporting character. So, over the next few days, casting director Judy Taylor arranged for Demi to come back and read scenes for the female lead of a new musical Disney Channel Original Movie that became *Camp Rock* and a new sitcom pilot that became *Sonny with a Chance*. Demi landed both. "Everybody knew that she would be the next thing," Kaplan said. "The network basically just took her and said, 'Okay, we're going to recast Demi's role on *As the Bell Rings*.'"

It was a difficult loss for Kaplan. He had begun to worry about Demi's unhappiness on the Texas set and noticed her restrictive eating habits at lunch from the first week of shooting. He said he raised those issues with the network at the time. "Honestly, there were signs," Kaplan said. "But, I don't think anybody really did much about it, and then I lost her. She was gone."

ON THE HEELS of the *High School Musical* phenomenon, the network's excitement was high over *Camp Rock Rules!*, which later became *Camp Rock On* and eventually just *Camp Rock*, a DCOM about kids at a rock-and-roll summer camp. Demi would star as Mitchie Torres, a talented girl with big dreams. And Marsh's original hope was that Jesse McCartney, who had previously turned down *High School Musical*, might agree to star in this film, since the male lead he'd be playing would also be a rock star. Hollywood Records, to which Jesse was signed, loved the prospect. But Jesse was still adamant that he didn't want to be pigeonholed as a "Disney Channel star" and turned them down once again. *Camp Rock* executive producer Alan Sacks pushed for A.J. Trauth, whom he had directed in the 2004 DCOM *You Wish!*, and *Johnny Tsunami*'s Brandon Baker was also discussed as a possibility. Taylor Lautner auditioned, bluffing his way to the final round until, as he's later admitted, it became clear that he could neither sing nor dance.

Finally, Hollywood Records general manager Abbey Konowitch suggested that maybe Joe Jonas could fit the bill as an alternate crossover talent from the label. Marsh wasn't so sure. This was before *Jonas*, and Joe had never had a lead movie or TV role before. Disney Music Group head Bob Cavallo also fretted that it would be bad business to spotlight Joe as a solo singer and break up the Jonas Brothers on screen just as they were taking off as a band. In the end, Marsh agreed to create smaller roles for the other brothers in the film, alongside Joe as the lead.

In September 2007, the Jonases, along with Demi and the ensemble cast, which included Alyson Stoner, Roshon Fegan, Meaghan Jette Martin, and Anna Maria Perez de Tagle, flew to Toronto for rehearsals and shot *Camp Rock* in the surrounding area on a $6.1 million budget, nearly $2 million more than the first *High School Musical*. As a result of the upped production values, they were able to hire cinematographer Dean Cundey, who had worked on everything from *Jurassic Park* to *Halloween*, and stage elaborate musical numbers. But they still worked within TV movie constraints: food fights were messy and complicated to reset for each take, so the kids flung plain spaghetti noodles, sans sauce, to expedite the clean-up process.

In the evenings, the Jonas Brothers headed to a local Toronto studio to record their second album, *A Little Bit Longer*. "They showed up one of the nights with Demi," music producer John Fields recalled, "and she sits down with an acoustic guitar and plays the most Joni Mitchell–ass tune you've ever heard, like the darkest, coolest chords. We were all just blown away."

When *Camp Rock* premiered in June 2008, it drew 8.9 million viewers, just over half of *High School Musical 2*'s record-setting audience, but still a milestone for a non-sequel movie opening. The soundtrack went platinum and made it to number three on the Billboard 200. It was another network hit.

Preparations for a sequel, directed by Paul Hoen, got underway, and just like in the aftermath of *High School Musical*, the fame of its stars exploded. While filming the first *Camp Rock*, the Jonas Brothers had traveled on weekends to play various county fairs. By the time the sequel came out, they were selling out stadiums. But Disney had learned a valuable lesson from *High School Musical*: the *Camp Rock* actors' original contracts included a clause for sequels, diminishing the cast's negotiating power for future films.

The plot of *Camp Rock 2: The Final Jam* pitted the wide-eyed Camp Rock kids against a more polished, well-funded star-making venture across the lake, Camp Star. "We used to joke that Camp Star felt like it was Disney," producer Kevin Lafferty said. "All Camp Star does is take kids who want to be famous and teach them how to sing and dance, and then the Camp Rock kids go, 'They're evil!' We're like, 'Wait. Isn't that us?'"

With an unprecedented $10 million budget, the sequel shoot was lengthened from the standard twenty or twenty-five days to thirty. Despite the crew putting the dummy title *Coin Flip* on all production signage, Canadian Jonas Brothers fans tracked down the production, lining up outside the set gates every day and screaming for the boys. Production manager Victoria Harding came up with the idea of having a lottery for the zealous fans to be extras in the audience for the performance scenes.

But not everyone had an ideal experience on the sequel. Because the *Camp Rock 2* shooting schedule had to work around both the Jonas Brothers' touring schedule and the actual summer camp sessions that took place at their shooting locations, they couldn't begin filming until September and didn't wrap until mid-October. It was a near-freezing fall in Ontario, and the cast had to run around in summer clothes as their lips turned blue from the cold, huddling around space heaters between takes to stay warm. During the first film, the Pajama Jam scene was meant to take place around a campfire but had been moved indoors to keep the cast comfortable on a cold night. On the sequel, such accommodations weren't always granted.

One misty night, Matthew "Mdot" Finley, who played Camp Star antagonist Luke, had to perform his big solo number "Fire" on a slippery vinyl-laid stage. As he did his climactic backflip, he slipped on the landing and his chin crashed into the hard, wet surface. "I remember just seeing blood," choreographer Rosero McCoy said. "I'm like, 'Dude, your chin is hanging off.'" Finley said production bandaged his chin, touched up his makeup, and he continued to perform, periodically changing into fresh white shirts as blood seeped through his bandage. They eventually shut down production, and he went to the hospital to receive stitches. "My safety was definitely disregarded. I don't know whose fault that was or what kind of oversight," Finley said. "But at the time, someone should have been like, 'Yo, what the fuck?'"

Alyson Stoner and Meaghan Martin have also alluded to negative experiences during production. Meaghan caught mono during the *Camp Rock 2* shoot and recalled in a 2022 Instagram post that she was "so sick and being berated, bullied and manipulated by men at least 2x my age" on set. On the production side, Lafferty and Sacks said they did not recall any specific negative incidents that occurred with the cast, other than Meaghan catching mono. "It definitely was a harder movie," Lafferty said. "There was more to shoot and a higher demand—and it was cold."

Demi had known Selena Gomez since they were seven years old and starring together on *Barney & Friends*. At home in Texas, Demi and Selena practiced their BFF red carpet poses and pretended to be Paris Hilton and Nicole Richie texting on their T-Mobile Sidekicks. "What an incredible thing that these two childhood friends both become superstars," *Wizards of Waverly Place* actor Maria Canals-Barrera said. "Often times one of them takes off and one doesn't. Or they both don't make it because it's such a hard business."

By the time Selena and Demi teamed up on screen at Disney for the Disney Channel Original Movie *Princess Protection Program*, fans were already well acquainted with the two stars' off-screen friendship and the shifting dynamics of Disney Channel cliques. Although former network president Rich Ross emphasized that there was "very little friction within our casts—it wasn't like *Grey's Anatomy*," the advent of social media and an increasing number of crossover projects meant Disney Channel stars were beginning to interact with one another at levels previously unknown.

"That's how I met a lot of the other kids from my era and how we networked and bonded," said *Sonny with a Chance* actor Allisyn Ashley Arm, who later married *Kickin' It* actor Dylan Snyder and now goes by Allisyn Snyder. "It was always just at a random thing, like, oh we're all doing international promos today and we're trying to quickly learn a phrase in Japanese together."

The network had also long attempted to foster a somewhat communal spirit among the talent and replicate the quintessential teen socialization milestones they might be missing out on due to their careers. Individual sets often organized their own version of graduation ceremonies or yearbooks for their young cast. And the network facilitated channel-wide holiday parties, dances, and other gatherings for the kids to hang out together—while chaperoned by their parents and under the watchful eye of network executives. "It felt like a junior high dance where no one really knew how to talk to anyone," *Johnny Tsunami* star Brandon Baker said of one social evening. "Everyone just wanted to touch boobs and make out, but all the adults were watching us."

It was Disney High.

"It was beautiful and tragic," Selena has said. "It was everything that every teen goes through, just on a bigger scale. It literally was like high school."

By 2008, the social dynamics of the Disney Channel actors had become complicated. Just like in high schools across America, there was an endless stream of romantic entanglements, teen angst, and friendship alliances. When Demi and Selena began posting lo-fi YouTube vlogs that they filmed together in Selena's bedroom, Miley Cyrus and her friend-slash–backup dancer Mandy Jiroux soon made their own video, appearing to mock Demi and Selena. Miley dated Nick Jonas.

Nick broke up with her. Then Selena dated Nick. Nick broke up with her, and later reunited with Miley. Brenda Song dated Miley's older brother, Trace. Cole Sprouse broke up with Alyson Stoner on Alyson's birthday. Joe Jonas smoked pot for the first time with Miley and Demi. Selena appeared in the Jonas Brothers' "Burnin' Up" music video. And Kevin Jonas stepped out in a "Team Demi and Selena" T-shirt.

"This is their high school campus. So, there is a kind of rivalry that's going to happen no matter what," said Shannon Flynn, the acting coach on *Hannah Montana*, *Jessie*, and other series. "I saw that happen so many times on so many different sets, where there's such a competitive nature. All of those typical high school experiences get amplified by rumors and the press, and even the smallest rivalry can be blown out to be something greater than it actually was."

Whatever complications might have been happening in their stars' interwoven personal lives, Disney was intent on projecting one big happy family on camera, like when Miley, Selena, Demi, and the Jonas Brothers assembled to film the "Send It On" music video in June 2009. Disney hired directors Michael Blum and Tracy Pion—who had previously directed several iconic campaigns at The WB where the actors from *Dawson's Creek*, *Buffy the Vampire Slayer*, and other shows danced and mingled together—to work their magic and convey an image of tight-knit, harmonious Disney Channel stars at the shoot at Pepperdine University in Malibu. "Disney found that what we were really good at was making it feel like there was a giant community," Pion said. "So even though the stars weren't necessarily hanging out and best friends [off camera], it *felt* like that."

While the Disney kids were all consummate professionals on the "Send It On" set and there was no visible tension between then-exes Selena and Nick, or between Miley and Selena in the wake of the You-Tube wars, the teens' handlers carefully orchestrated who could stand by whom during the group shots. And there were times when Miley and Nick, in the midst of their reignited love, would sneak off between takes. "Where's Miley and Nick?" Blum recalled asking an assistant director, who tactfully reported back, "They're in wardrobe. There's some ironing going on, and a little bit of freshening up is needed."

The "Send It On" video was part of Friends for Change, a corporate initiative designed to inspire kids to take care of the earth. But it also inspired fans to continue to obsess over the dynamics between the stars. Earlier generations of Disney Channel fans had been largely ignorant of the network stars' personal lives and what happened off script. Disney Channel's former impact hadn't been large enough to merit teen tabloid coverage of, say, Brandon Baker's fling with his *Johnny Tsunami* co-star Kirsten Storms. And there hadn't been social media to give the famous teens the platform to dole out such information at will. But now, everyone knew about the friendships, relationships, and feuds of the teens they watched on TV.

Still, actors in supporting roles or smaller projects on the network weren't always invited to be part of the on-screen groups and participate in filmed crossovers like the Disney Channel Games or Disney Channel Circle of Stars, leaving them to feel left out and lesser than. Disney Channel wants "to feature the cast that the audience connects to most," Alyson Stoner has said. "But when you're young and you don't yet know how to quantify yourself as an artist versus a product versus whatever, it feels a little personal. And like, 'What's wrong with me?'"

EVEN THE MOST lauded Disney Channel stars struggled to separate their own sense of self from the many roles they played. While filming the Disney Channel Original Movie *Princess Protection Program* in Puerto Rico in the spring of 2008, Selena and Demi experienced the highs and lows that come with being with your best friend 24/7 for several weeks. There were friendship breakups and makeups and occasional screaming matches so loud that their mothers, staying nearby, would have to intervene.

And even though Demi had already filmed *Camp Rock*, she hadn't fully figured out a way to put a protective wall between herself and the characters she played. She felt things deeply and saw her own painful experiences in her character's struggles. "There are so many skills you have to have. To be so young and to have those skills is pretty rare, and Demi definitely did not yet," said *Princess Protection Program* director

Allison Liddi-Brown. "You need time to build that. It's a tough job, what happens to you psychologically."

One *Princess Protection Program* scene involved Demi's character, Princess Rosalinda, getting bullied while working at a frozen yogurt shop. She ends up covered in the sticky treat while everyone laughs and films her. The humiliating scenario, though scripted, dredged up memories of Demi's own experience being severely bullied by her classmates back in Texas. There, they'd tormented Demi over her weight and, she's said, they once passed a suicide petition around school saying they wanted her to kill herself.

"Shooting that really kicked up a lot of stuff from her past," Liddi-Brown said. "After the scene, I went up to her and we were just hugging, both covered in yogurt, and she was crying. I said, 'Well, the good news is: You're an actor because you just did what actors do. You played something that was touching your real life, and it was a very real, very raw, very honest moment, and you're being affected by it right now. The bad news is: You're an actor. It's a tough life, and it's not easy to be a performer and to know how to channel those feelings and what to do with them in a healthy way.'"

It was a lesson Demi was learning in real time.

THE NUMBER OF simultaneous Disney projects that Demi embarked on right away is dizzying. At just fifteen years old, and before anything beyond the *As the Bell Rings* interstitials had even aired, she had two DCOMs, a sitcom, and a Hollywood Records deal all in the bag.

Demi's singing voice was incredible, with a depth and range far beyond her years. For her personal music management, she'd signed with Johnny Wright and Phil McIntyre, who helped co-manage the Jonas Brothers. And the brothers were brought on to co-write tracks for Demi's debut album alongside her. Music producer John Fields, who collaborated with the Jonas Brothers on their three Hollywood Records albums, as well as Demi's first two albums at the label, stressed the level of creative control that the brothers and Demi were able to retain over their music there. "It was completely the opposite of the fabricated Disney bullshit that everyone imagines, like 'It's all written by old people. And it's all by committee,'" Fields said. "No. This was no committee."

Still, even slightly suggestive tracks like "Shut Up and Love Me," which Demi co-wrote with John Mayer for her second album, were shelved. "It's a fantastic song, and they wouldn't let us put it on the album because she was sixteen and they thought it [implied] 'shut up and [something else] me,'" Fields said. Other times, Disney Channel's standards and practices team would veto the lyrics that could be sung on the network, hence "kiss me like you mean it" became "hold me like you mean it" for the "Get Back" music video; and a reference to McDonald's in the track "La La Land" turned into just eating at "Ronald's" on screen. "The channel was way more particular," Fields said. "But on the record side, they kind of just let it happen."

Phil McIntyre was adamant that Demi not be seen as just a "Disney kid," so he pushed Hollywood Records to promote her solo music prior to *Camp Rock*'s release. She embarked on a mini "warm-up" tour, mostly at Six Flags theme parks, in the weeks leading up to *Camp Rock*'s June 2008 premiere, and then joined the Jonas Brothers on their Burning Up tour. This way she wouldn't be perceived as a Disney Channel actor who became a singer, but a singer who became a Disney Channel actor. "It didn't necessarily sit great with Disney Channel or others," Hollywood Records executive Abbey Konowitch said. By diverting the pipeline that the label and the network had by then mastered—Disney Channel lead character to Radio Disney airplay to mainstream coverage—"it put a lot more pressure on us," Konowitch said. "I'm not sure that we thought it was the best idea at the time, but it was."

The new strategy helped skyrocket Demi's pop-punk and rock-infused 2008 debut album, *Don't Forget*, to number two on the Billboard 200 that September, and her 2009 follow-up *Here We Go Again* to number one. "Along with, perhaps, Nick Jonas, the brooding auteur who gives the Jonas Brothers megabrand a dash of thoughtfulness, Ms. Lovato has a kind of alt-Disney aesthetic, simultaneously building the brand and proving its elasticity," *The New York Times*'s Jon Caramanica effused in a 2009 profile.

As Demi garnered legions of her own fans and embarked on the type of concert tours she'd long dreamed of, however, something remained off. "I remember being fifteen years old on a tour bus and watching fans follow my bus with posters and trying to get me to wave outside the window. And all I could do was just sit there and cry," she said while speaking at a mental health summit in 2023. "I remember being in the back of my tour bus watching my fans and crying and being like, 'Why am I so unhappy?'"

WHEN DEMI CAME in for her *Sonny with a Chance* audition—that same week in 2007 when she'd read for *Camp Rock* and *J.O.N.A.S.*—she brought her own props and dunked her head in a bowl of mushy food to get a laugh. She'd wowed the sitcom's producers with her fearless comedy and charmed them with her wide grin and infectious laugh. During the interview portion, they asked her who her favorite singers were.

"Amy Winehouse," she replied right away.

"That should have been a red flag," executive producer Michael Feldman says now.

(Demi had a knack for shocking adults with her morose pop-culture picks: In a 2008 *People en Español* interview, she listed her favorite films as *Donnie Darko* and *Girl, Interrupted*, before being prompted to cite lighter fare like *Elf* and *Mean Girls*.)

Inspired by the popularity of NBC's *30 Rock*, *Sonny with a Chance* was a workplace comedy exploring the behind-the-scenes lives of a group of actors putting on a junior *SNL*-style sketch comedy show called *So Random!* The central character, Sonny Munroe, was a wholesome Midwest girl thrown into the Hollywood machine. To execute the series, Feldman and creator Steve Marmel teamed up with Sharla Sumpter Bridgett and Brian Robbins, a heavyweight producer who'd created *All That* and overseen other comedies at Nickelodeon.

When the cameras were rolling on *Sonny*, Demi was animated and alive, thriving under the spotlight. But when a director yelled "cut," her face immediately dropped. "She was Sonny, and then it was suddenly very cloudy," Feldman said. "She was not a happy kid." For Eric Dean Seaton, who'd become a respected director since his early days as a stage manager on *That's So Raven* and directed thirty-one of *Sonny*'s forty-seven episodes, production was a precarious tightrope every day. "I had rules," Seaton said. "I basically structured the show for Demi, meaning that I would always want to know when she came on set—because then I could see what type of mood she was in."

From Demi's point of view, "I wasn't sleeping, and I was so miserable and angry, too, because I felt like I was being overworked—which I was," she said during a 2020 cast reunion. For the creatives on set, the difference in Demi's demeanor from that of other young Disney actors they worked with was glaring. "Everybody else was so professional, and they so loved what they were doing, and they were so happy to be there," said Dava Savel, who produced *Sonny* after *That's So Raven*. "And Demi, just little by little—she didn't want to do rehearsals. She just wanted her stand-in to do rehearsals for her. I mean, she was really out of line and pissing everybody off. She was just pushing everybody back."

DEMI'S *SONNY* CONTRACT went beyond the standard series terms that many previous Disney Channel stars signed and more closely resembled something out of the old Hollywood studio system. It stipulated that, in addition to Demi's commitment to *Sonny with a Chance* (at the time called *Sketchpad*), she would be required to do two post–*Camp Rock* Disney Channel Original Movies, as well as a theatrical *Sonny* film, if Disney pursued any of those options.

Demi was contracted to receive $38,750 for her performance in the first *Camp Rock*, $75,000 for *Princess Protection Program*, at least $100,000 for the *Camp Rock* sequel, and $10,000 per episode for *Sonny's* first season with a 5 percent bump on the second season (the same series scale Selena was signed to on *Wizards*). If a *Sonny* theatrical movie were to come to fruition, she was locked into a $500,000 base for that picture (half of what Hilary Duff had been able to negotiate for *The Lizzie McGuire Movie* four years earlier).

But Demi had always prioritized music over acting, and now, her music career was heating up faster than *Sonny*. "Acting is just kind of a way to pay for the singing," Demi told *Women's Wear Daily* in 2009, quickly clarifying, "I mean, not anymore. Acting now is like a new challenge, new hobby, a new passion even."

Demi would perform concerts on the weekend and get the rush of hearing thousands of fans scream her name. Then, she'd return to set on Monday to do food gags and pratfalls. "Demi's heart was in the music. The show and the films were not what they wanted to be doing," her *Sonny* co-star Allisyn Snyder said. "They wanted to be in the studio, and they wanted to be going on tour and then they get back here, and it was kind of like going back to school after summer break."

BUT IT WASN'T just about the oppressive schedule and imbalance of passion. The reality was much more painful. Throughout her time on Disney Channel, Demi was struggling with bulimia, self-harm, and substance abuse. "It was really clear right away, even when she was that young, that there were going to be some issues," said Lee Shallat Chemel, who directed an unaired version of the *Sonny* pilot. "Very talented, incredibly ambitious, and obviously, a beautiful singing voice. But there were issues with her mom and her family, and you could see that there was trouble brewing."

Soon after production got underway on *Sonny with a Chance* in September 2008, Demi got sick and had to take a day off of work. Showrunner Michael Feldman said he passed her mom in the studio hallway and asked how Demi was doing.

"Oh, she'll be back to work tomorrow," Dianna assured him.

"That's good, but how is she feeling?" he asked again.

"I told her she needs to buckle up and get back to work, so don't you worry!" Dianna replied.

"I'm not asking you whether she'll be here or not," he said. "I'm asking you from one parent to another, how is your child feeling?"

The combination of a parent whose quality of life is dependent on their child's success and a corporate system that renders sick days for that child a potential financial loss is, fundamentally, working against the health of a child. But why was a teenager who was known to have a variety of personal issues allowed to be put in that high-pressure position in the first place and then allowed to continue with little intervention?

"It was a bad situation," said supervising producer Drew Vaupen, who departed *Sonny* after eleven episodes to create and oversee *Good Luck Charlie.* "We all wanted to help Demi. But she had star power. There was just no way to get to her."

No one wants to say they had the ability to stop the metaphorical bleeding, but concern over Demi's disordered eating and depression was allegedly made known to at least some network executives from as early as 2006. It would take until a public incident at the end of 2010 for meaningful action to be taken.

"People were so concerned, but it's a gentle road to travel. You have to really be respectful of privacy issues. There was never a day that didn't go by that you're not trying to do something to help," *Sonny* line producer Patty Gary Cox said. "I know there was a lot of concern from the network. They were very involved in talking to my executive producers about it and trying to figure out how to help her."

By her own admission, Demi's mother, Dianna, had long avoided confronting the situation. When Demi was in sixth grade, Demi's older sister told Dianna that Demi had been visiting pro-anorexia and bulimia websites. Rather than discuss it with Demi, Dianna ignored the concerns and decided Demi's weight loss was due to a growth spurt. "I even gloated that she might get more jobs because she was thinner," Dianna wrote in her memoir. When Demi had first begun cutting her wrists, the De La Garzas hired a life coach to help. But later, Dianna found bloody tissues in Demi's bed, a sign that she'd resumed cutting. She swept them aside and rushed Demi out the door to make it to the *Sonny* set on time. "So many people—music representatives, television executives, castmates, and management—were depending on Demi to be strong and do her job," Dianna wrote. "Nothing was just a family matter anymore. Walking away wasn't an option."

Demi has also said she was privately coping with losing her virginity as the result of a rape that occurred when she was fifteen, during an initially consensual experience that turned traumatic. She told someone in power about it at the time, but "they [the accused rapist] never got in trouble for it," she said in her 2021 documentary *Dancing with the Devil*.

Demi's bulimia worsened. She was throwing up blood. Gossip blogs shared photos and posts that encouraged commenters to speculate about any changes in her demeanor and appearance. But on the *Camp Rock* sets, Maria Canals-Barrera, who played Demi's character's mom, said she noticed nothing amiss. "It took me a while to believe some of the things I heard later about her struggles," Canals-Barrera said, "because I was completely clueless."

As Demi got older, she—like many teenagers—became more difficult to control. She had begun drinking alcohol at age thirteen. When she passed her high school proficiency exam at age sixteen, she no longer required a guardian on set. That same year, Demi bought her own car with money she had earned and frequently went out with friends until the early hours of the morning. She tried cocaine for the first time at age seventeen.

"What do you say to your child when she is the one paying most of the bills?" Dianna wrote in her memoir. "I couldn't tell her that I'd take her car away when she was the one who owned it. I couldn't take her phone away when she was the one paying to use it. And although I tried to make her follow our rules while she lived under our roof, she was the one paying the rent."

Network and label executives said they were unaware of any serious problems until they later became public. But for a company that loved to micromanage, there were blatant warning signs to even the most ignorant. At Miley Cyrus's sixteenth birthday party at Disneyland in October 2008, Demi posed for photos on the red carpet with what appeared to be visible cutting marks on her wrists. (Her personal publicist at the time attributed the marks to "indentations" left by tight gummy bracelets.) And when Demi was on her first headlining tour in the summer of 2009, opening act and fellow Hollywood Records artist Jordan Pruitt said it was clear that "Demi was going through a really hard time" and that "made it very tumultuous." Jordan added, "Everyone was talking about her drinking and disordered eating."

(In 2019, Jordan filed a since-resolved lawsuit alleging her former music manager sexually abused her, and she also sued Disney and Hollywood Records for allowing her to work with and be unsupervised around him while she was signed to the label in the mid- to late 2000s. When asked about the case, Jordan said, "Unfortunately, all I am legally able to say is 'no comment.'")

On the road, Disney Channel representatives were rarely present. Tours were the domain of the Disney touring entity, its external partners, and the artists' personal management. And as young talent was being pulled in infinite directions across the Disney divisions, the impetus could always be shifted to other parties to take action. Whether it was concern around Demi or any of the other performers, the stance of, "If there's actually a problem, I'm sure someone else is addressing it," became an easy one for those in power to take. And even if Demi's behavior was violating the morals clause that appeared in some of her contracts, what incentive was there for someone working on a project to report her for a breach? They would lose their job if she got fired or sought treatment and the project was canceled.

"You feel a profound sense of responsibility," said Anne Sweeney, then-president of the Disney/ABC Television Group. "But that sense really needs to be shared by everybody: by family, by parents, by agents, by managers. And, sadly, it isn't always the case."

WHILE FILMING THE first *Camp Rock* in 2007, Demi had become instantly smitten with Joe Jonas. The pair finally dated in the spring of 2010, after filming the second movie. But by that same summer, it was over. Joe and Demi announced their breakup, initiated by Joe, in May 2010. Soon, Joe was publicly dating twenty-three-year-old *Twilight* actor Ashley Greene, and when the Jonas Brothers, Demi, and six of their *Camp Rock 2* co-stars went on a fall 2010 concert tour across the US, the Caribbean, and Central and South America, Ashley often tagged along.

Even before they left the US, it was clear Demi was experiencing a downward spiral. Patti McTeague, the former head of Disney Channel PR, said she knew "there was some strife" and that Demi "was hurting" on the *Camp Rock 2* promotional tour. And when interstitial director

Michael Blum shot video footage of Demi and the Jonas Brothers in Florida during their fall tour, he said, "It was clear to me that she was not the Demi I had worked with before."

Then came the grueling international tour schedule. The performers would sometimes leave a concert and head straight to the airport, fly all night, and arrive in a new country by 7:00 A.M. before having to report to the venue that same morning. Everyone was exhausted. The teens were guzzling Red Bull like water to stay awake. Fans swarmed outside the entrances of their hotels and peered through the lobby and restaurant windows, trying to catch a glimpse of the stars.

In an attempt to grant the performers some semblance of normalcy, at every stop, the tour management would book a spare hotel suite, allowing the singers and dancers to congregate in private, rather than deal with the public mayhem that ensued when they ventured out. Inside the suites, they'd split off into small groups of friends to indulge in varying levels of socializing and partying.

Joe and Demi mostly kept their distance from one another, but every night on stage, the exes had to serenade each other with *Camp Rock* duets. "It was painful. She was depressed about the breakup, and she had to literally perform love songs with him," tour photographer Elise Abdalla said. "I felt so bad for her." Three years earlier, Joe and Demi had dressed as Troy and Gabriella from *High School Musical* for Halloween. Now, he was spending the holiday partying with Ashley in coordinating pirate costumes.

Demi, by then eighteen, lashed out at other performers and stuck mainly with her band, dancers, and management team. The combination of overwork, relationship drama, and easy access to drugs and alcohol was a recipe for disaster. Anger issues that had been bubbling since Demi's childhood reached their breaking point over that Halloween weekend in Colombia.

In her 2017 documentary *Simply Complicated*, Demi explained her side of the story:

> "I invited a bunch of people to dinner, my band and my background dancers. I paid for all the alcohol. Somebody ended up getting weed. I

was on Adderall, and we had trashed the hotel. The hotel was threatening us. They went to some of the dancers and asked what had happened. And I think they told on me for using Adderall. Somebody told Kevin Jonas Sr. and [music manager] Phil [McIntyre] and my dad.

"I was very upset. I couldn't believe what had happened. Now, it was out that I was on Adderall. The next day, I was in a lot of trouble. I remember going to Kevin Sr. and saying, 'Listen, I want to thank whoever told on me because I know they were just worried about me, and I just really want to know who told you.' I manipulated him into telling me who it was, and he said it was Shorty. Shorty and I had been really close through *Camp Rock* and *Camp Rock 2*, so when he said Shorty I remember thinking, 'I'm about to beat this bitch up.'"

As the performers and crew sat on the tarmac in their chartered jet waiting to depart Colombia for Peru, Demi boarded the plane, made a beeline for dancer Alex Welch (a.k.a. "Shorty"), and punched her in the face.

"It was on my seat in which the dancer was splatted," *Camp Rock 2* co-star Matthew "Mdot" Finley said. "I was just like, *damn*, Demi."

The plane still had to take off, so the performers were all ordered to get back to their seats amid the bedlam. "It was chaos," Abdalla said. "Everyone was freaking out."

The tour managers were panicking. Nondisclosure agreements were rushed out to those who had been on the plane and witnessed the incident. "You can imagine the kind of things that they were trying to do to keep it on the hush-hush," Finley said. "They will never say the full story. There's Demi's story, there's Shorty's story, and there's the truth. But I'm not here to add any fuel to that." (McTeague said the NDAs would "definitely not" have come from Disney Channel, and that she "had nothing to do with that.")

When the plane landed in Peru, Demi didn't speak to anyone. And she didn't go to the hotel with the rest of the group. "She just disappeared," Abdalla said. Within hours of the incident, Demi had been formally dismissed from the tour. Kevin Jonas Sr. was reportedly the one who made the snap decision to send her back to the US.

Demi and her stepdad, Eddie De La Garza, flew back to Texas, where her mom, Dianna, was at the time. They gathered some of Demi's things from their home in Dallas and then went straight to Timberline Knolls, a treatment center on the outskirts of Chicago. There, Demi was cloistered away from the media coverage and network fallout, as she was diagnosed with bipolar disorder (a diagnosis Demi has said was later amended to ADHD). During her intake process, Demi admitted to regularly drinking alcohol, as well as using cocaine, weed, and Adderall.

The news hit TMZ by Monday. The official word from Demi's team was that she was entering treatment for "emotional and physical issues that she has dealt with for some time."

As the rest of the *Camp Rock* stars continued on the South America tour with a reworked show that omitted Demi, back at Disney Channel, the network executives were once again playing catch-up to an external controversy with one of their stars. "We found out about it after the fact," Sweeney said. "And it was very, very disturbing."

IN THE PAST, when dealing with the fallout from Vanessa Hudgens's photo leak or Miley Cyrus's *Vanity Fair* shoot, the network tacitly or explicitly stood by the talent, kept them employed, and worked through the issues at hand. This time, Disney Channel and Demi effectively cut ties within the week. Because Demi was in a treatment center, there was no direct communication between her and the network leaders in the immediate aftermath of the incident. And Disney made the decision not to delay production on *Sonny with a Chance*, which was scheduled to begin shooting its third season in January 2011. Because the *Sonny* team was already contracted to do the third season of the show and pre-production was underway, canceling the series outright would have meant losing both money and a tangible product to fill the programming void. But it was impossible to continue the same show without Demi there to play Sonny. They needed a new plan.

On November 15—less than three weeks after Demi left the tour and checked into treatment—Disney Channel announced *Sonny* would be reworked to focus on the sketch show within the show, *So Ran-*

dom! "It just seemed like a no-brainer," then–original programming head Adam Bonnett said. Short form clips of *So Random!* sketches had performed well on YouTube, and executive producers Sharla Sumpter Bridgett and Brian Robbins had experience with the pure sketch format on *All That.* They'd pad out the *So Random!* skits with rotating musical guests, including Selena Gomez, Justin Bieber, and Cody Simpson.

"This allows [Demi] the time she needs to get well, without distraction or pressure," a Disney Channel spokesperson told *Variety* of the plan at the time. "Again, we extend our ongoing support to Demi and her family as she works to overcome personal issues."

The outward distance that the network put between themselves and Demi "felt like the right thing to ensure that she was healthy and happy," Bonnett said. "She was still a big part of the Disney family." He added, "She made the wrong choice about how to deal with a situation, and it was unfortunate."

But, to fans, it marked a jarring and sudden disconnect.

The illusion of the perky and relatable teenager portrayed on Disney Channel had been shattered. This wasn't just Miley being provocative. This was a teenager in pain. Young viewers now had easy access to the internet, plus the morning shows, entertainment programs, and tabloid covers in grocery store lines that all spotlighted Demi's breakdown. Tween magazines that were directly targeted at Disney Channel viewers wrote articles detailing the cataclysmic events and speculating, "What led Demi to her breaking point?"

The following April, Demi announced she wouldn't ever be returning to her Disney Channel series, and *So Random!* was canceled when the season concluded. It couldn't weather the combination of expensive production values, constant S&P concern over potentially offensive sketches, and a lack of star power.

Yet, Disney Channel's warm and fuzzy brand meant there was no way they would address Demi's struggles on air or use her experience to speak to wider issues young people might be facing. While Linda Ellerbee had done an entire 2009 "Kids in Rehab" episode on Nick News in response to a wave of young celebrities seeking treatment for substance

abuse, Disney Channel now simply plowed ahead with its standard in-
nocuous programming schedule, which included the *Camp Rock* films
and episodes of *Sonny with a Chance.*

There, Demi was eternally grinning and unbothered, her every ob-
stacle solved by the time the credits rolled.

Epilogue

To have been a Disney Channel star is to be forever recognized, forever scrutinized. *Did you turn out okay? Are you traumatized? Wow, you're so grown up, I feel old! Say the line! Sing the song! Do the bit!* At its worst, it's a parasocial entitlement to a stranger's life and a stubborn refusal to let them grow up and move on. At its best, it's a rarified connection, yoking people from disparate backgrounds together around a partly shared nostalgic experience.

"I didn't realize at the time that being part of a quote-unquote children's show gives you very special access into people's hearts," *Wizards* matriarch Maria Canals-Barrera said. "People come up to me now and they weep, and I just hold them. Because I know what they're crying about. They're crying about remembering who they were at that time in their life—when they were struggling with their identity, whether they fit in, whether they were cool—and a TV show that brought them solace."

And that's the thorny paradox of the Disney Channel story: As the network's heyday programming brought comfort and joy to millions of tender viewers, the coterie of young stars appearing on screen were having to prematurely navigate the pressures of very adult scenarios.

At an age when most teens are still asking their parents for allowance money or earning minimum wage at an after-school job, a child actor might be their family's sole breadwinner and responsible for paying a mortgage. While the average kid can drop out of their school play if they feel overwhelmed or get sick, a professional performer is contractually obligated to see their commitment to a multi-million-dollar production through to the end. Add to that the piercing scrutiny from adults, the media, and fans during a period of immense vulnerability in one's physical and emotional state, and the situation can become a powder keg.

And then the inevitable happens: they grow up.

"One of the built-in issues with the channel is that it is its own world. It's this incredibly intense life when it's happening. It's nonstop," *The Cheetah Girls* and *Lemonade Mouth* executive producer Debra Martin Chase said. "In that world, you are a superstar. You are on kids' walls. They dream about being you and being your best friend. And then all of a sudden you age out. You go from that huge adulation to, *I'm supposed to be a regular person?*"

YET, THE DISNEY Channel of the 2000s couldn't have operated at the level that it did without those larger-than-life teenagers.

"You have the Disney machine and you have the TV network, and that's all great," said Steve Greenberg, who signed the Jonas Brothers at Columbia Records. "But none of it could ever work if you don't have incredibly talented stars to be the artists. You needed a Miley Cyrus. You needed a Selena Gomez. You needed a Jonas Brothers. Maybe their career takes a different trajectory if they don't have that machine behind them, but they were great to start with. The Disney Channel didn't make any of those people great. It just made them big."

By 2010, Disney Channel had grown from a flailing network in search of an identity into a star-making behemoth so broad it couldn't always control its image or look out for its talent. The web of Disney fiefdoms had begun yanking young performers in disparate directions, with each division operating for their own profits. Internal programs like Talent 101 started to add increased structural support at the end of the 2000s, but if those in a young performer's inner circle weren't industry savvy and looking out for them while establishing critical boundaries, the ever-broadening environment and what lie beyond it could be treacherous to navigate.

The performers' paths as adults are varied. Some of the stars reached career highs greater than their Disney Channel days and remain at the top of their field. Some have pursued ventures entirely outside of entertainment: *Wizards of Waverly Place* co-star Jennifer Stone is also an ER nurse. *Good Luck Charlie* star Bridgit Mendler attended MIT and Harvard Law, and became the CEO of a space data startup. *Read It and Weep* star Kay Panabaker is a zoologist. And others have struggled with personal discord and trauma.

"It's an exploitative business," *Even Stevens* and *That's So Raven* showrunner Marc Warren said. "There's that one-thousandth of a percent of incredibly talented kids who are driven and are born to do it. A kid like Shia [LaBeouf], he was doing standup at ten. He was born to do it, and it screwed him up. But would he have been screwed up if he wasn't an actor? Maybe worse. Probably worse."

Some former Disney Channel stars have used their experiences to try to impart positive change for a new generation. Christy Carlson Romano hosted the *Vulnerable* podcast, speaking to many of her former cohorts about their experiences. Demi Lovato directed the Hulu documentary *Child Star*, she's said, to shed light "on important messages about growing up in the public eye, learning to protect our boundaries, and becoming active advocates of our own destinies." Corbin Bleu became the national chair of the Entertainment Community Fund's Looking Ahead program, which offers resources to young performers and their families to help them better handle their finances and transition into a variety of non-entertainment careers in adulthood. "I wish that a program like that existed back then," he said of his *High School Musical* days.

THE DISNEY CHANNEL of the 2010s continued to look much like the Disney Channel of the late 2000s. Gary Marsh took over the network presidency in 2011, and the network kept leaning into loud, brightly lit multi-camera sitcoms, coupled with dramatic original movies and musical crossover projects for its young stars.

Disney Channel developed fresh critical hits, like *Jessie* and *Good Luck Charlie*, and it launched a new wave of actors and singers whose fame long exceeded their time on the network, like Zendaya, Dove Cameron, Sabrina Carpenter, Sofia Carson, Jenna Ortega, and Olivia Rodrigo. Its global reach led to *The Wizards of Warna Walk* in Malaysia, and *The Suite Life of Karan & Kabir* in India, with its international channels generating more than $1 billion in revenue in 2012 alone. "People thought Disney Channel was going to fall off the cliff when *Hannah Montana* went away because it was such a defining show," Marsh said in 2012. "We were so aware of that that we made sure we stacked the deck."

By the time Anne Sweeney resigned as head of the Disney/ABC Television Group in 2014, Disney Channel was available in more than 431 million homes worldwide. "In my daughter's high school yearbook, underneath their pictures, they had favorite class, favorite this, favorite that—and favorite DCOM," Sweeney marveled. "That was unbelievable." In 2015, Disney Channel finally unseated Nickelodeon as the number one kids' network in total daily viewers for the first time.

But the network never again achieved the widespread cultural relevance and ratings heights it managed during the *High School Musical* and *Hannah Montana* era. Rich Ross's time as the head of Walt Disney Studios, the post he'd left his Disney Channel presidency for in 2009, quickly crashed and burned. He was pressured to resign in 2012, after just two and a half years and a string of theatrical bombs. Yet, he said he doesn't regret exiting Disney Channel for the ill-fated role when he did. "I never looked back that it was the wrong decision. I felt I had accomplished what I could accomplish [at the network]," Ross said. "I couldn't really do more. We did everything. Every genre, every country. It never went bigger."

Over the last decade, even with breakout hits like the *Descendants* franchise and the critically acclaimed *Andi Mack*, Disney Channel has lost around 90 percent of its viewers. In 2022, it averaged just 178,000 prime-time viewers, down from nearly two million in 2014. Other kids' cable networks have experienced similar craters. The advent of social media, YouTube, and a multitude of streaming services means the monopolization of children's eyeballs can no longer be contained to a cluster of basic cable channels. Disney Channel's captive audience is now vastly smaller and younger, and the influence of any singular outlet has been drastically diminished in an age of fragmentation and on-demand content.

Some network executives, like Adam Bonnett, hung around until the late 2010s. Marsh remained in the top role, which expanded in 2020 to include Disney Branded Television, until he stepped down in 2021. (Marsh is still involved as an independent producer on various projects—including the 2024 *Wizards of Waverly Place* spinoff.)

By 2020, many of the international Disney Channel networks had shuttered. The focus of Disney's entertainment division is increasingly on the streamer Disney+, where they launched *The Proud Family* reboot and *High School Musical: The Musical: The Series*, starring Olivia Rodrigo. (Notably, rather than signing with Hollywood Records, Olivia launched her chart-topping solo career, complete with expletive-peppered lyrics, on Universal's Geffen Records.)

Disney also planned to reboot *Lizzie McGuire* on Disney+, but after filming two episodes, the project was shelved in 2020. Hilary Duff and Disney met an apparent impasse over how mature the subject matter could be that Lizzie, a character now in her thirties, dealt with on screen. But no matter the content, the streaming industry itself is in a precarious state, and The Walt Disney Company once again finds itself relying almost solely on its theme parks division for company growth.

DISNEY CHANNEL MERITED a single, one-line mention in Bob Iger's 2019 book about leadership and his Disney career. "The Disney Channel, which they launched in the United States, quickly became a success," is all he wrote on the matter. While writing my own one hundred thousand words about the channel, I made a pilgrimage to 3800 West Alameda to soak up the vibes of the place where so much history occurred. The nondescript tower is still the corporate home of Disney Channel, just as it's been since the 1980s.

It was an unusually cold and rainy day in Burbank, the beginning of Southern California's freak "blizzard" of February 2023. Employees flitted in and out to grab a Starbucks in the lobby or get lunch at nearby Olive & Thyme, but Disney's mandatory post-pandemic return-to-office orders were still a few days away from taking effect, giving the building the eerie air of a ghost town. In one corner of the lobby sat the former Radio Disney studio, its floor-to-ceiling glass windows now covered with thick blinds. The space had sat empty since the venture shut down for good in 2021, but the logo from a bygone era of AM radio glory was still etched across the panes.

On the other side of the lobby, I wandered into the small employee gift shop. Racks of Disney-branded notebooks, lanyards, mugs, and shirts lined the walls. Some were emblazoned with The Walt Disney Company logo, others featured images of popular characters, from Moana to Simba to Mickey Mouse. I thought maybe I'd find a tumbler with the network logo or a keychain of Hannah Montana.

"Do you have anything related to Disney Channel?" I asked the twentysomething woman stationed behind the counter.

"No," she said, as a wistful look crossed her face. "I wish."

ACKNOWLEDGMENTS

T, as in Troy? No, T, as in Thank You.

When I first decided in the dark days of 2020 that I wanted to write a book about Disney Channel, I knew it would hinge on finding a team who understood the significance of the subject matter at hand.

I couldn't have asked for a better partner on this journey than Jon Michael Darga at Aevitas Creative Management, who not only still has a pristine collection of *Disneymania* CDs but fielded four years of my outlandish ideas, meltdowns, anxieties, and celebrations while making this book a reality. Thank you, thank you, thank you. I'm so glad we found each other.

To my editor, Sarah Grill at St. Martin's Press, for recognizing the layered story that needed to be told and making sure I wrote the best version of it possible. You championed this project each step of the way with the fervor and dedication I could only expect from a ride-or-die Jonas Brothers fan. And thank you to Hannah Phillips for stepping in and seeing this book through to the finish line with such deftness and enthusiasm.

To Danielle Christopher, for designing the perfect cover art, and to the St. Martin's Press marketing and publicity team, Michelle Cashman, Sara Eslami, Tracey Guest, and Kathryn Hough Boutross, for shouting about *Disney High* from the rooftops.

To the sources who so generously spoke to me over coffee in West

Hollywood, lunch in Orlando, or via Zoom and phone calls from California, Florida, Illinois, New Jersey, New Mexico, New York, North Carolina, Oregon, Tennessee, Texas, Utah, Mexico, Canada, and beyond. Thank you for sharing personal memories that went far beyond superficial platitudes and for being willing to dig deep into the vault to discuss the good, the bad, and the complicated. There are dozens of valued sources whose voices didn't make it into the final manuscript. Even if your quotes weren't used, please know that the anecdotes you shared influenced my reporting and provided crucial context and background. I'm so grateful to you all—we'll just have to do another book.

Of course, the making of this book began long before the publishing process. So, I'd also like to thank my parents for reading to me before I knew how and for making sure the written word was a cornerstone of my life from day one. You let me have every *Baby-Sitters Club* book *and* the official Hanson biography. I love you both so much.

To Rachel Chang, who took a chance on a baby writer applying for a *CosmoGirl* internship and gave me my very first job at *J-14*. You believed in a girl from Florida with zero connections or industry savvy, and I'm forever grateful to have had your guidance and friendship.

To the editors I've been so privileged to work with in recent years, including Stephanie Goodman, Austin Considine, Jeremy Egner, Leslie Horn, Rupa Bhattacharya, and Caitlin Moore. Your edits have sharpened my writing, guided me to be a better reporter, and saved me from myself on numerous occasions.

To Ankita, Bari, Bobbi, Devin, Leslie, Lizzy, Rachel, Sofia, Tanya, and all the friends who cheered me on and helped me see the light at the end of the publishing tunnel. Every bit of encouragement meant the world.

To Caity, who so gamely allowed the *High School Musical* soundtracks to infiltrate our college experience and taught me so much about life. I miss you all the time.

To Bart and Dexter, the two very best cats and writing companions.

To Daniel, every day with you is the best day.

A NOTE ON SOURCES

Quotations found throughout this book are from interviews that I conducted via phone, video, email, and in person between 2020 and 2024, except where otherwise attributed. Contract specifics were obtained from viewing copies of those original documents, unless otherwise cited. Excerpts from dialogue and correspondence that occurred in the 1990s and 2000s were drawn from the memories of sources who said they were either directly involved in or present for those conversations.

NOTES

INTRODUCTION

x   **one of the only industries in the United States:** "Fact Sheet #43: Child Labor Provisions of the Fair Labor Standards Act (FLSA) for Nonagricultural Occupations," U.S. Department of Labor, last modified December 2016, https://www.dol .gov/agencies/whd/fact-sheets/43-child-labor-non-agriculture.

x   **Alyson Stoner coined the phrase "toddler-to-trainwreck pipeline":** Alyson Stoner, "Alyson Stoner Pens Eye-Opening Op-Ed on 'Harrowing' Childhood Stardom: 'Revisit the Script,'" *People*, April 7, 2021, https://people.com/music/alyson -stoner-pens-op-ed-on-childhood-stardom-labor/.

xi   **Disney Channel was the second-most-watched:** Kimberly Nordyke, "USA the top cable channel in 2006," *Reuters,* last modified January 21, 2007, https://www .reuters.com/article/television-cable-dc/usa-the-top-cable-channel-in-2006 -idUSN0335894620070104.

xi   **in 2007, Disney Channel claimed the crown:** Kimberly Nordyke, "OMG! Disney Channel scoops viewers crown," *The Hollywood Reporter*, last modified January 4, 2008, https://www.hollywoodreporter.com/business/business-news/omg -disney-channel-scoops-viewers-101837/.

EPIGRAPH

xv   **My tale is done, there runs:** Jacob Grimm and Wilhelm Grimm, "Hansel and Gretel" in *Grimms' Fairy Tales*, trans. Edgar Taylor and Marian Edwardes (Project Gutenberg, 2001), https://www.gutenberg.org/files/2591/2591-h/2591-h.htm #link2H_4_0020.

PROLOGUE

1   **the 135-acre attraction:** Jeffrey Schmalz, "Nastiness Is Not a Fantasy in Movie Theme Park War," *The New York Times*, August 13, 1989, https://www.nytimes .com/1989/08/13/us/nastiness-is-not-a-fantasy-in-movie-theme-park-war.html.

1   **in order to have an authentic backstage tour:** "Backstage Studio Tour," D23, accessed October 29, 2023, https://d23.com/a-to-z/backstage-studio-tour/.

1. CHANGING OF THE GUARD

7   **Nickelodeon had continued to reign supreme:** Jacques Steinberg, "Rivals Unafraid to Borrow, or Steal, From Each Other," *The New York Times*, February 23, 2009, https://www.nytimes.com/2009/02/24/arts/television/24nick.html.

7   **first proposed the idea of a Disney cable channel in 1977:** "James Jimirro," interview by Marlowe Froke, *Syndeo Institute at the Cable Center*, December 12, 1989, audio, 2:32:04, accessed October 29, 2023, https://syndeoinstitute.org/the-hauser-oral-history-project/i-j-listings/james-jimirro-program-penn-state-collection/.

7   **he dreamed of a place where:** Charles Irvin, "Disney Channel Creator Jim Jimirro on his path to communications, from Penn State to beyond," *Daily Collegian*, November 14, 2022, https://www.psucollegian.com/news/disney-channel-creator-jim-jimirro-on-his-path-to-communications-from-penn-state-to-beyond/article_9c974b34–63bd-11ed-b918–7b130acabdff.html.

7   **70 percent of The Walt Disney Company's revenue:** Aljean Harmetz, "Disney Hopes Eisner Can Wake Sleeping Beauty," *The New York Times*, October 17, 1984, https://www.nytimes.com/1984/10/17/movies/disney-hopes-eisner-can-wake-sleeping-beauty.html.

8   **ranging from $7.95 to $12.95:** Steve Knoll, "Cable TV Notes; The Disney Channel Has an Expensive First Year," *The New York Times*, April 29, 1984, https://www.nytimes.com/1984/04/29/arts/cable-tv-notes-the-disney-channel-has-an-expensive-first-year.html.

8   **then–Disney president Michael Ovitz began poaching:** Sridhar Pappu, "The Queen of Tween," *The Atlantic*, November 2004 issue, https://www.theatlantic.com/magazine/archive/2004/11/the-queen-of-tween/303541/.

8   **After ten years as the president of Nickelodeon:** Sallie Hofmeister, "Key Nickelodeon Executive Quits to Head Venture by Disney, Cap Cities," *The Los Angeles Times*, December 16, 1995, https://www.latimes.com/archives/la-xpm-1995-12-16-fi-14657-story.html.

8   **thirty-eight-year-old:** Sallie Hofmeister, "Chairman of Fox's FX Networks Resigns to Head Disney Channel," *The Los Angeles Times*, February 22, 1996, https://www.latimes.com/archives/la-xpm-1996-02-22-fi-38712-story.html.

11   **During one focus group session in Chicago:** Lacey Rose, "Disney Channel's Gary Marsh on Tabloid Teen Stars, Marvel and the Junk Food Ban," *The Hollywood Reporter*, June 21, 2012, https://www.hollywoodreporter.com/news/general-news/disney-channel-gary-marsh-avengers-miley-cyrus-shia-labeouf-340251/.

12   **as an assistant to prolific TV director John Rich:** Rose, "Disney Channel's Gary Marsh on Tabloid Teen Stars, Marvel and the Junk Food Ban."

12   **including Walter Mondale's failed 1984 presidential bid:** Jon Weisman, "Gary Marsh: Life After Miley," *Variety*, October 20, 2011, https://variety.com/2011/tv/news/gary-marsh-life-after-miley-1118044411/.

14   **featured a whimsical Airstream trailer in the lobby:** Elaine Louie, "An MTV

Look for MTV Central," *The New York Times*, May 15, 1997, https://www.nytimes
.com/1997/05/15/garden/an-mtv-look-for-mtv-central.html.

14   **they'd inhabited since 1986:** "Disney Leases Burbank Space for Two Divisions,"
The Los Angeles Times, June 1, 1986, https://www.latimes.com/archives/la-xpm
-1986–06-01-re-8714-story.html.

16   **more than quintupled Disney Channel's circulation:** John Dempsey, "Disney
Channel tramples rivals," *Variety*, September 4, 2001, https://variety.com/2001/tv
/news/disney-channel-tramples-rivals-1117852202/.

16   **their growth didn't show up:** Dempsey, "Disney Channel tramples rivals."

16   **a deal was brokered with Time Warner:** Christopher Stern, "Time Warner Yields
on Fee," *The Washington Post,* October 10, 2000, https://www.washingtonpost
.com/archive/business/2000/10/10/time-warner-yields-on-fee/05ae992f-262f
-44d2-bf4e-da5037a5ec1b/.

18   **no more than twelve minutes of commercials:** Jeremy Gerard, "House Passes
Bill to Restrict Ads On Children's Television Programs," *The New York Times*, July
24, 1990, https://www.nytimes.com/1990/07/24/us/house-passes-bill-to-restrict
-ads-on-children-s-television-programs.html.

18   **the FCC dictated that advertising for children's products:** "Host Selling" in "The
Public and Broadcasting," Federal Communications Commission, Last modified
September   2021,   https://www.fcc.gov/media/radio/public-and-broadcasting
#HOSTSELLING.

18   **any hint of broader Disney propaganda:** "Host Selling" in "The Public and
Broadcasting."

18   **the rule didn't extend to the interstitial breaks:** "Commercial Limits" in "The
Public and Broadcasting," Federal Communications Commission, Last modified September 2021, https://www.fcc.gov/media/radio/public-and-broadcasting
#COMMERCIALLIMITS.

19   **J.R.R. Tolkien had used the term "tweens":** J.R.R. Tolkien, *The Fellowship of the
Ring: Being the first part of The Lord of the Rings* (New York: William Morrow,
1954), 21.

19   **began to be used in marketing circles:** Daniel Thomas Cook and Susan B.
Kaiser, "Betwixt and Be Tween," *Journal of Consumer Culture* 4, no. 2, 2004,
https://www.sfu.ca/media-lab/cmns320_06/readings/cook_kaiser_betwixt
_between.pdf, 217.

2. THE EXPERIMENTAL ERA

23   **Lee later tragically died by suicide:** Andrew Blankstein, "Disney star committed suicide, was taking drugs for depression, says coroner," *NBC News*, October
8, 2013, https://www.nbcnews.com/news/world/disney-star-committed-suicide
-was-taking-drugs-depression-says-coroner-flna8c11361347.

24   **relegated to a 3:00 A.M. time slot:** Marc Weingarten, "At the Disney Channel,
It's A Diverse World After All," *The New York Times*, May 25, 2003, https://www
.nytimes.com/2003/05/25/arts/television-radio-at-the-disney-channel-it-s-a
-diverse-world-after-all.html.

28   **"Once it started airing, that's when . . .":** Taylor Weatherby, "*NSYNC Reflects on Making U.S. Debut & Competing With Backstreet Boys as Self-Titled Album Turns 20: 'It Was Us Against the World,'" *Billboard*, March 24, 2018, https://www.billboard.com/music/pop/nsync-debut-album-us-20th-anniversary-oral-history-8258181/.

28   **labels agreed to alter lyrics:** Bruce Orwall, "Some Hip Hopes: Disney Channel Spices Up Its Image for Teenagers," *The Wall Street Journal*, October 13, 1999, https://www.wsj.com/articles/SB939767251698416121.

29   **phase out the concert series and external music videos:** Carla Hay, "Disney Channel Scales Back Videos, Concert Programming," *Billboard*, May 13, 2001, https://books.google.com/books?id=jhMEAAAAMBAJ&pg=PA67%23v#v=onepage&q&f=false.

32   **Brown has maintained that she was "available":** Andi Ortiz, "Here's Why Marnie Was Recast in the 'Halloweentown' Franchise: 'There's No Beef,'" *The Wrap*, October 6, 2022, https://www.thewrap.com/why-was-marnie-recast-halloweentown-4.

3. *EVEN STEVENS*: TALENT AND TURMOIL

35   **he used a blusterous opening line:** Christy Carlson Romano, "Even Stevens 20th Anniversary Zoom Reunion!!!," YouTube, June 17, 2020, https://www.youtube.com/watch?v=ClqYALVDCgU.

35   **They felt his character came across:** Kimberly Nordyke, "Disney Channel Becomes a Youth Market Force," *Backstage*, last modified November 4, 2019, https://www.backstage.com/magazine/article/disney-channel-becomes-youth-market-force-21253/.

41   **Cardi B posted an Instagram video:** Tara Martinez, "This Video Of Cardi B Singing An 'Even Stevens' Song Will Make You Feel So Many Things," *Elite Daily*, September 26, 2018, https://www.elitedaily.com/p/the-video-of-cardi-b-singing-we-went-to-the-moon-from-even-stevens-is-everything-12059151.

41   **commuting from her family's home in Milford:** Rosalind Friedman, "14-Year-Old Christy Carlson Romano: The *Parade* Continues," *Playbill*, December 17, 1998, https://www.playbill.com/article/14-year-old-christy-carlson-romano-the-parade-continues-com-101287.

41   **fourteen-year-old Christy:** Christy Carlson Romano, "Christy Carlson Romano: My Private Breakdown," *Teen Vogue*, May 28, 2019, https://www.teenvogue.com/story/christy-carlson-romano-my-private-breakdown.

41   **missed her audition:** Christy Carlson Romano, "How I Lost Princess Diaries To Anne Hathaway," YouTube, September 16, 2021, https://www.youtube.com/watch?v=GQxAZFa_kXg.

42   **contributed to their sexual awakening:** Rachel Shatto, "Hilary Duff Didn't Realize Cadet Kelly Was a Queer Icon," *Out*, January 20, 2022, https://www.out.com/film/2022/1/20/hilary-duff-didnt-realize-cadet-kelly-was-queer-icon.

42   **"the queer girl DCOM Disney never actually gave us":** Anna Menta, "'Cadet Kelly' Is the Queer Girl DCOM That Disney Never Actually Gave Us," *Decider*, November 19, 2019, https://decider.com/2019/11/19/cadet-kelly-on-disney-plus-gay/.

43   **battled an alcohol addiction:** Aaron Gell, "Shia LaBeouf's Dad Has a Lot to Say," *GEN*, November 7, 2019, https://gen.medium.com/shia-labeoufs-dad-would-like -to-say-a-few-things-9818b0204a3c.

43   **spent time in prison for attempted rape:** Gell, "Shia LaBeouf's Dad Has a Lot to Say."

43   **once ran a head shop:** Eric Sullivan, "Shia LaBeouf Is Ready To Talk About It," *Esquire*, March 13, 2018, https://www.esquire.com/entertainment/movies /a19181320/shia-labeouf-interview-2018/.

43   **dress up as clowns and sell hot dogs:** Sullivan, "Shia LaBeouf Is Ready To Talk About It."

43   **he coveted another kid's Fila sneakers:** Mike Hogan, "Landing in Hollywood," *Vanity Fair*, August 2007 issue, https://www.vanityfair.com/news/2007/08/labeouf 200708.

43   **"It wasn't about acting":** Hogan, "Landing in Hollywood."

44   **"Let me tell you about Shia":** Hogan, "Landing in Hollywood."

45   **"I was looking to make money":** Scott Feinberg, "'Awards Chatter' Podcast—Shia LaBeouf ('Honey Boy' & 'The Peanut Butter Falcon')," *The Hollywood Reporter*, October 29, 2019, https://www.hollywoodreporter.com/news/general-news/shia -labeouf-reflects-his-troubled-childhood-transformers-therapy-rising-again -honey-boy-1250660/.

45   **"Our set really was such a solitude":** Romano, "Even Stevens 20th Anniversary Zoom Reunion!!!"

46   **Shia had previously sold a Disney series:** Kevin Conley, "The (Hot-Dog-Vending, Knife-Fighting, Break-Dancing, Spielberg-Wooing) Adventures of Young Shia LaBeouf," *GQ*, April 30, 2008, https://www.gq.com/story/shia-labeouf -transformers; Hogan, "Landing in Hollywood."

46   **Director Alma Har'el has said it was difficult:** Anne Thompson, "Shia LaBeouf Talks About Walking the 'Honey Boy' Tightrope, With Director Alma Har'el as His Net," *IndieWire*, November 4, 2019, https://www.indiewire.com/2019/11 /honey-boy-shia-labeouf-director-alma-harel-oscars-1202187007/.

46   **"Everything in the film happened":** Feinberg, "'Awards Chatter' Podcast—Shia LaBeouf."

47   **"I wrote this narrative, which was":** Jon Bernthal, "Shia LaBeouf," *REAL ONES with Jon Bernthal*, August 31, 2022, https://www.youtube.com/watch?v =nnVKqQiQyTQ.

4. *LIZZIE McGUIRE*: THE TV GIRL NEXT DOOR

52   **She was ready to quit acting:** Richard Harrington, "Keeping Up With Hilary Duff," *The Washington Post*, July 16, 2004, https://www.washingtonpost.com /archive/lifestyle/2004/07/16/keeping-up-with-hilary-duff/eafeae75-2a03-43e4 -af34-b82471246d59/.

52   **raised in Houston and San Antonio:** Sarah Martinez, "Hilary Duff's ties to San Antonio that you probably didn't know about," *My San Antonio*, July 18, 2022,

https://www.mysanantonio.com/entertainment/article/Hilary-Duff-San-Antonio-roots-17308459.php.

52   **"My mom didn't let me get away with shit"**: Lottie Lumsden, "Hilary Duff on growing up in the spotlight and the Lizzie McGuire reboot," *Cosmopolitan UK*, September 29, 2020, https://www.cosmopolitan.com/uk/entertainment/a34142182/hilary-duff-cosmopolitan-uk-november-cover/.

54   **"My mom thought it'd be a great idea"**: Ashley Spencer, "How Lizzie McGuire Reinvented Tween TV and Became a Millennial Obsession," *Vice*, January 12, 2021, https://www.vice.com/en/article/epdmge/lizzie-mcguire-cast-reunites-to-talk-about-disney-series-and-reboot.

56   **averaging around 2.3 million viewers**: Michael Starr, "Starr Report," *The New York Post*, December 11, 2002, https://nypost.com/2002/12/11/starr-report-360/.

56   **"Shortly after the show had begun airing"**: Spencer, "How Lizzie McGuire Reinvented Tween TV."

56   **it was the number one show on cable**: Laura M. Holson, "'Lizzie McGuire' Has Become a Hot Disney Brand," *The New York Times*, December 2, 2002, https://www.nytimes.com/2002/12/02/business/lizzie-mcguire-has-become-a-hot-disney-brand.html.

57   *Lizzie* **books, pencils, sleeping bags, jewelry**: Julia Boorstin, "Disney's 'Tween Machine: How the Disney Channel became must-see TV—and the company's unlikely cash cow," *Fortune*, September 29, 2003, https://money.cnn.com/magazines/fortune/fortune_archive/2003/09/29/349896/index.htm.

60   **legendary wand IDs**: For a deep dive on the Disney Channel theme: *Defunctland*, "Disney Channel's Theme: A History Mystery," November 20, 2022, YouTube, https://www.youtube.com/watch?v=b_rjBWmc1iQ.

61   **all ended the same way**: Disney Channel, "The Best Disney Channel Wand IDs! | Compilation," YouTube, May 24, 2019, https://www.youtube.com/watch?v=s1OIPj_hS-4.

61   **the kids watch themselves**: *Cosmopolitan*, "'Yes Day' Star Jenna Ortega Reacts to Her Iconic Disney Roles!," YouTube, April 5, 2021, https://www.youtube.com/watch?v=YCDkSuVt-Xk.

61   **shaving their legs together**: Bill Bradley, "Here's What Lalaine From 'Lizzie McGuire' Has Been Up To Since The Show Ended," *The Huffington Post*, last modified December 6, 2017, https://www.huffpost.com/entry/what-lalaine-lizzie-mcguire-has-been-up-to_n_7235820.

5. HILARY DUFF: POP STAR AND MOVIE STAR

68   **went gold**: RIAA Gold and Platinum database, accessed October 29, 2023, https://www.riaa.com/gold-platinum/.

69   **"I wanted to make an impression"**: Christy Carlson Romano, "That's So Raven Star Speaks Out on Substance Abuse and Child Acting," *Vulnerable*, April 25, 2023, https://www.youtube.com/watch?v=wazDWkSUhDI.

71   **"We wouldn't get the attention"**: Jill Menze, "The Making of Hilary Duff's

'Metamorphosis,'" MySpace.com, August 23, 2013, retrieved from https://web
.archive.org/web/20131021231432/https://myspace.com/discover/trending/2013
/08/22/oral-history-the-making-of-hilary-duffs-metamorphosis/.

72   **"Hilary had so much personality"**: Menze, "The Making of Hilary Duff's 'Metamorphosis.'"

74   **"What's your favorite food"**: Nickelodeon Kids' Choice Awards carpet, 2002, Retrieved from https://www.youtube.com/watch?v=ai733FPoOFA.

74   **"I'm not here to talk bad about her"**: *Access Hollywood*, 2004, retrieved from
https://www.youtube.com/watch?v=rF1sVECfx1o.

75   **developed an eating disorder over the pressure:** Liza Gebilagin, "How to Get
Strong (and Stay Strong) Like Hilary Duff," *Women's Health Australia*, December 4, 2022, https://womenshealth.com.au/hilary-duff-womens-health-australia
-january-2023/.

75   **"trying to navigate becoming a person"**: Josh Peck, "Hilary Duff is here!,"
Good Guys Podcast, February 27, 2023, https://www.youtube.com/watch?v=C
_A4DSTbEJo&t=131s.

75   **a male *Rolling Stone* reporter made a point:** Mark Binelli, "Hilary Duff: Teenager of the Year," *Rolling Stone*, September 18, 2003, https://www.rollingstone
.com/music/music-features/hilary-duff-teenager-of-the-year-53039/.

75   **David Spade addressed Hilary in the audience:** 2003 Teen Choice Awards, Retrieved from https://www.youtube.com/watch?v=ZF7u5iI2fN8.

75   **"The kids who make it through to here"**: Michael P. Lucas, "Groomed to Be
All That," *Los Angeles Times*, June 23, 2002, https://www.latimes.com/archives/la
-xpm-2002-jun-23-ca-lucas23-story.html.

81   **"a smug, cutesy music video/fashion show"**: Jane Horwitz, "'The Lizzie McGuire
Movie': You Go, Girl—by Yourself," *The Washington Post*, May 2, 2003, https://
www.washingtonpost.com/archive/lifestyle/2003/05/02/the-lizzie-mcguire
-movie-you-go-girl-by-yourself/128db6ac-abc4-4b20-8f83-f1ed69b4ed82/.

81   **Roger Ebert observed that the film:** Roger Ebert, "The Lizzie McGuire Movie,"
Chicago Sun-Times, May 2, 2003, Retrieved from https://www.rogerebert.com
/reviews/the-lizzie-mcguire-movie-2003.

81   **with a $17.3 million haul:** "The Lizzie McGuire Movie," Box Office Mojo, ac-
cessed October 29, 2023, https://www.boxofficemojo.com/release/rl258049537/.

81   **Bob Iger had initiated discussions:** Claudia Eller and Richard Verrier, "Disney, 'Lizzie' Star Parting Ways After Pay Dispute," *Los Angeles Times*, May
24, 2003, https://www.latimes.com/archives/la-xpm-2003-may-24-fi-dizliz24
-story.html.

81   **Dick Cook offered Hilary a multipicture deal:** James B. Stewart, *DisneyWar*
(New York: Simon & Schuster, 2005), 434.

81   **raised to $15,000 by the show's end:** Eller and Verrier, "Disney, 'Lizzie' Star Part-
ing Ways After Pay Dispute."

82   **the $5 million that Susan ultimately wanted:** Eller and Verrier, "Disney, 'Lizzie'
Star Parting Ways After Pay Dispute."

82   **they agreed on:** Allison Hope Weiner, "Hilary's mom on why Duff left 'Lizzie' in

a huff," *Entertainment Weekly*, June 13, 2003, https://ew.com/article/2003/06/13/hilarys-mom-why-duff-left-lizzie-huff/.

82 **Disney refused:** Stewart, *DisneyWar*, 434.

83 **Coogan Account:** "Coogan Law," SAG-AFTRA, https://www.sagaftra.org/membership-benefits/young-performers/coogan-law.

83 **had been $35,000 per episode:** Weiner, "Hilary's mom on why Duff left 'Lizzie' in a huff."

84 **earning a rumored $2 million:** "Duff says goodbye to 'Lizzie'," *NBC News*, August 15, 2003, https://www.nbcnews.com/id/wbna3079874; Addison Aloian, "What Is Hilary Duff's Net Worth In 2023? Everything To Know About The 'How I Met Your Father' Star's $$$," *Women's Health*, January 24, 2023, https://www.womenshealthmag.com/life/a42636843/hilary-duff-net-worth/.

6. THAT'S SO RAVEN-SYMONÉ

85 **drawing up to thirty million viewers:** Mike Barnes, "Regis Philbin, TV Host With the Most Congenial Demeanor, Dies at 88," *The Hollywood Reporter*, July 25, 2020, https://www.hollywoodreporter.com/news/general-news/regis-philbin-dead-host-morning-shows-who-wants-be-a-millionaire-was-88-1126718/.

85 **It took less than three years for *Millionaire*:** Bill Carter, "Who Wants to Bury a Millionaire?," *The New York Times*, May 20, 2002, https://www.nytimes.com/2002/05/20/business/media-who-wants-to-bury-a-millionaire.html.

85 **its meteoric rise showed network executives:** Brian Lowry, "How 'Who Wants to Be a Millionaire' changed the primetime TV rulebook," *CNN*, August 14, 2019, https://www.cnn.com/2019/08/14/entertainment/who-wants-to-be-a-millionaire-column/index.html.

85 **rushed unscripted series into production:** Jim Rutenberg, "'Reality' Shows May Undercut Writers' Strike," *The New York Times*, April 23, 2001, https://www.nytimes.com/2001/04/23/business/reality-shows-may-undercut-writers-strike.html.

86 **shrunk by nearly half:** Scott D. Pierce, "Comedy no longer king," *Deseret News*, June 23, 2004, https://www.deseret.com/2004/6/23/19836137/comedy-no-longer-king.

88 **After doing print modeling:** "Raven-Symoné: 5 Things You Didn't Know About the 'State of Georgia' Star," *The Hollywood Reporter*, June 29, 2011, https://www.hollywoodreporter.com/tv/tv-news/raven-symone-5-things-you-207001/.

89 **"knowing that this is the next step":** TV One TV, "How Raven-Symoné's Dissociative Disorder Impacted Her Memories On 'The Cosby Show' | Uncensored," YouTube, October 13, 2021, https://www.youtube.com/watch?v=tL3lDTOK6CM.

89 **According to Gary Marsh:** Denise Abott, "Milestone: 'That's So Raven,'" *The Hollywood Reporter*, August 1, 2006, Retrieved from https://www.hollywoodreporter.com/business/business-news/milestone-raven-138445/.

90 **the final season of that series:** Jami Ganz, "*The Crown, Friends* among most expensive TV shows ever made," *Entertainment Weekly*, March 8, 2017, https://ew.com/tv/2017/03/08/most-expensive-tv-shows/.

90   **at least three hours of schoolwork a day:** "California Child Labor Laws," *State of California Department of Industrial Relations, Division of Labor Standards Enforcement*, accessed October 30, 2023, https://www.dir.ca.gov/dlse /childlaborlawpamphlet.pdf, 46.

90   **serve as the de facto welfare monitors:** "California Child Labor Laws," 45.

91   **began production in the fall of 2001:** "Raven Symoné To Star in Disney Channel Original Series That's So Raven; Production To Begin in Los Angeles Nov. 9," *Entertainment Wire*, November 8, 2001, retrieved from https://web.archive.org /web/20170406022540/http://www.thefreelibrary.com/Raven+Symone+To+Star +in+Disney+Channel+Original+Series+That's+So...-a079852087.

94   **a "thrilling" move to mirror the reality:** "Making Scents, and a Movie, of Raven's Future," *South Florida Sun-Sentinel*, July 6, 2005, https://www.sun-sentinel.com /2005/07/06/making-scents-and-a-movie-of-ravens-future/.

96   **"When we did that first year":** Veronica Wells, "T'Keyah Crystal Keymáh Talks 'In Living Color,' Caring For A Grandmother Living With Alzheimer's & Raven Symoné," MadameNoire, June 9, 2016, https://madamenoire.com/701421/tkeyah -crystal-keymah/.

96   **quickly began drawing around two million viewers:** Nicholas Fonseca, "Why new Disney icon Raven is not Lizzie McGuire," *Entertainment Weekly*, October 17, 2003, https://ew.com/article/2003/10/17/why-new-disney-icon-raven-not -lizzie-mcguire/.

96   **it was averaging three million:** Allison Samuels, "Why Not Raven?," *Newsweek*, July 31, 2005, https://www.newsweek.com/why-not-raven-121269.

96   **more than four million viewers:** "Broadcast & Cable Nielsens: Week Ending July 31, 2005," Ratings Ryan, August 14, 2021, https://www.ratingsryan.com/2021/08 /broadcast-cable-nielsens-20050731.html.

97   **number one basic cable channel for kids:** "The Walt Disney Company 2004 Annual Report," https://thewaltdisneycompany.com/app/uploads/ar_2004.pdf.

99   **"I do not remember as soon as":** TV One TV, "How Raven-Symoné's Dissociative Disorder Impacted Her Memories On 'The Cosby Show.'"

99   **"I want to bring a new beauty":** Maria Elena Fernandez, "Staying on message is so Raven-Symoné," *Los Angeles Times*, July 12, 2006, https://www.latimes.com /archives/la-xpm-2006-jul-12-et-raven12-story.html.

99   **she was shamed for craving bagels:** Gabrielle Olya, "Raven-Symoné Was Body-Shamed at 7 Years Old on 'The Cosby Show' Set," *People*, July 30, 2015, retrieved from https://web.archive.org/web/20221120193021/https://people.com/health /raven-symone-fat-shamed-on-the-cosby-show-set/.

100   **she was on the Zone diet:** Fonseca, "Why new Disney icon Raven is not Lizzie McGuire."

100   **her dad suggested she get a breast reduction:** Raven-Symoné and Miranda Maday, "Episode 5: Raven & Miranda," *The Best Podcast Ever*, August 7, 2023.

100   **she endured negative feedback:** Julie Mazziotta, "Raven-Symoné Says Body Shaming as a Kid Led to 'So Many Mental Issues,'" *People*, August 7, 2017, https:// people.com/health/raven-simone-body-shaming-mental-issues/.

100 **"My fans know I love my cheese grits"**: Samuels, "Why Not Raven?"

101 **"I was in my own turmoil"**: D'Shonda Brown, "Raven-Symoné Is *Still* Shocked By The Impact Of 'That's So Raven,'" *Girls United*, March 10, 2022, https://girlsunited.essence.com/article/raven-symone-ravens-home-interview/.

101 **"I remember that I wore Abercrombie"**: Elizabeth Wagmeister, "Raven-Symoné Recalls Industry Pushback in Her Teen Years: 'She Looks Too Much Like a Lesbian,'" *Variety*, June 21, 2019, https://variety.com/2019/tv/features/raven-symone-lgbtq-coming-out-1203246873/.

101 **"Disney understood me"**: Alejandra Reyes-Velarde, "After her turbulent days on 'The View,' Raven-Symoné has come 'Home' to Disney," *Los Angeles Times*, June 21, 2018, https://www.latimes.com/entertainment/tv/la-et-raven-symone-ravens-home-disney-channel-20180621-story.html.

102 **"I truly believe that the parents should not"**: Nick Viall, "Going Deeper with Raven-Symoné and Miranda Maday Plus Special Forces and Travis Talks Taylor," *The Viall Files*, September 28, 2023, https://www.youtube.com/watch?v=6XL733MBJGw.

103 **partly of Mexican-Spanish decent**: "One Of The Cheetah Girls is of Hispanic Descent," *People en Español*, September 7, 2007, https://peopleenespanol.com/article/one-cheetah-girls-hispanic-descent/.

104 **"The Cheetah Girls was the first"**: Zeniya Cooley, "*The Cheetah Girls* Gave Black Girls Like Me a Space to Dream," Refinery29, August 15, 2023, https://www.refinery29.com/en-us/2023/08/11494849/cheetah-girls-movie-songs-impact.

106 **merchandise lines targeted at nine to fourteen**: "The Walt Disney Company 2005 Annual Report," https://thewaltdisneycompany.com/app/uploads/ar-2005.pdf.

106 **bring in nearly $400 million**: Faye Brookman, "Critical Mass: Raven Appeals to Anti-Britney Teen," *Women's Wear Daily*, September 23, 2005, https://wwd.com/feature/critical-mass-raven-appeals-to-anti-britney-teen-561287–1973960/.

106 **only a solitary paparazzo showed up**: Samuels, "Why Not Raven?"

106 **"It was so sad"**: Samuels, "Why Not Raven?"

106 **an announced 2007 *That's So Raven* DCOM**: Richard Huff, "'Raven' has Disney raving. Star to also produce '06 shows," *New York Daily News*, June 22, 2005, https://www.nydailynews.com/2005/06/22/raven-has-disney-raving-star-to-also-produce-06-shows/.

107 **an *Adventures in Babysitting* sequel**: Abott, "Milestone: 'That's So Raven.'"

107 **adaptation of Meg Cabot's novel *All-American Girl***: Meg Cabot, "Meg's Diary: Hey, everybody!," July 30, 2003, https://megcabot.com/2003/07/105962129545086759/.

107 **Warner Brothers' remake of *Sparkle***: Michael Fleming, "Raven flocks to pic," *Variety*, August 17, 2003, https://variety.com/2003/film/markets-festivals/raven-flocks-to-pic-1117891004/.

107 **"too young"**: Christina Lee, "Selena Gomez Talks New Album: 'This Is The Next Phase In My Life,'" *Idolator*, June 29, 2015, https://www.idolator.com/7598643/selena-gomez-2015-album-themes.

107 **struck up a friendship at the shoot**: Raven-Symoné and Miranda Maday, "Episode 1: Raven & Miranda," *The Best Podcast Ever*, July 10, 2023.

108   **left to care for her grandmother:** Wells, "T'Keyah Crystal Keymáh Talks 'In Living Color,' Caring For A Grandmother Living With Alzheimer's & Raven Symoné."

108   **7.6 million viewers:** Michael Schneider, "Shows set records for Disney," *Variety*, January 16, 2007, https://variety.com/2007/scene/markets-festivals/shows-set-records-for-disney-1117957517/.

110   **"Once an ugly stepchild":** Boorstin, "Disney's 'Tween Machine."

110   **"People always talk about *Lizzie McGuire*":** Reyes-Velarde, "After her turbulent days on 'The View,' Raven-Symoné has come 'Home' to Disney."

7. *THE SUITE* (AND NOT-SO-SWEET) *LIFE*

111   **skewing about 60 percent female:** Paul Bond, "Q&A: Gary Marsh," *The Hollywood Reporter*, February 10, 2009, Retrieved from https://www.hollywoodreporter.com/business/business-news/qampa-gary-marsh-79123/.

112   **billed as "boy-focused, girl-inclusive":** Brooks Barnes, "Disney Aims for the Boy Audience With a Cable Channel and a Web Site," *The New York Times*, February 12, 2009, https://www.nytimes.com/2009/02/13/business/media/13disney.html.

112   **proved more popular with girls:** Ryan Nakashima, "Cable channel shift reflects Disney's boy trouble," *San Diego Union-Tribune*, Retrieved from https://www.sandiegouniontribune.com/sdut-us-disney-tween-boys-090309-2009sep03-story.html.

115   **idolizing Cindy Crawford:** Ariana Yaptangco, "Brenda Song: 'I'm Really Proud of the Woman I've Become—She's Been Through a Lot,'" *Glamour*, May 20, 2022, https://www.glamour.com/story/brenda-song-interview.

115   **when she was just seventeen:** Yaptangco, "Brenda Song: 'I'm Really Proud of the Woman I've Become—She's Been Through a Lot.'"

115   **emptied her savings account:** Brooke Marine, "Brenda Song, Former Disney Darling, on Returning to TV with *Dollface*," *W Magazine*, November 12, 2019, https://www.wmagazine.com/story/brenda-song-dollface-suite-life-disney-interview.

115   **"I didn't go to my first house party":** Yaptangco, "Brenda Song: 'I'm Really Proud of the Woman I've Become—She's Been Through a Lot.'"

116   **"giving this little Asian American girl":** Marine, "Brenda Song, Former Disney Darling, on Returning to TV with *Dollface*."

116   **Disney didn't allow her to move forward:** Gabe Bergado, "Brenda Song on Her New Series *Dollface*, the Disney Channel Years, and Growing Up," *Teen Vogue*, November 20, 2019, https://www.teenvogue.com/story/brenda-song-dollface.

117   **"A lot had happened in our lives":** Johnni Macke, "Dylan Sprouse Says 'Suite Life of Zack and Cody' 'Saved' Him and His Twin Brother Cole Sprouse," *Us Weekly*, March 19, 2020, https://www.usmagazine.com/celebrity-news/news/dylan-sprouse-says-suite-life-of-zack-and-cody-saved-him/.

117   **their parents, Melanie Wright and Matthew Sprouse, were teaching:** Alex Cooper, "Cole Sprouse: Exploited for Money and Fame," *Call Her Daddy*, March 8, 2023, https://open.spotify.com/episode/2RMnzURpR5OJErVRWrjB70?si=496d236f17ae4918.

117   **"My mother needed an income":** Cooper, "Cole Sprouse: Exploited for Money and Fame."

120   **they'd show a new episode to a room:** Rose, "Disney Channel's Gary Marsh on Tabloid Teen Stars, Marvel and the Junk Food Ban."

121   **Peck pled no contest to charges of lewd acts:** Hugo Daniel, "Pedophile X-Men actor convicted of sexually abusing Nickelodeon child star is STILL working with underage kids," *Daily Mail*, June 8, 2015, https://www.dailymail.co.uk /news/article-3115792/Pedophile-X-Men-actor-convicted-sexually-abusing -Nickelodeon-child-star-working-underage-kids.html.

121   **Drake Bell of Nickelodeon's *Drake and Josh*:** *Quiet on Set: The Dark Side of Kids TV*, directed by Mary Robertson and Emma Schwartz (Business Insider/Investigation Discovery, 2024).

121   **"If we had known the truth":** Emily Longeretta, "Nickelodeon Directors Beth and Rich Correll Apologize for Supporting Brian Peck in Drake Bell Abuse Case: 'We Are Saddened and Appalled,'" *Variety*, https://variety.com/2024/tv/news /nickelodeon-directors-apologize-drake-bell-brian-peck-1235951790/.

122   **since they were eight years old:** Anna Bahney, "Boys Just Want to Be . . . Olsens," *The New York Times*, April 30, 2006, https://www.nytimes.com/2006/04/30 /fashion/sundaystyles/boys-just-want-to-be-olsens.html.

122   **convicted of misdemeanor child molestation:** "Sprouse Manager Convicted of Molestation," *TMZ*, March 3, 2008, https://www.tmz.com/2008/03/03/sprouse -manager-convicted-of-child-molestation/.

124   **due to FCC regulations:** "Host Selling" in "The Public and Broadcasting."

124   **premiered to 5.7 million viewers:** Gary Levin, "Nielsens: Presidential debate fights for numbers," *USA Today*, September 30, 2008, https://usatoday30.usatoday .com/life/television/news/2008-09-30-nielsens-analysis_N.htm.

126   **he got a DUI:** "'Hannah Montana' Star Busted for DUI," *TMZ*, October 17, 2011, https://www.tmz.com/2011/10/17/hannah-montana-mitchel-musso-arrested-dui/.

126   **"I mean, we had a really awesome idea":** Darryn King, "The Post–*Suite Life* Life of Dylan Sprouse," *Vulture*, December 28, 2017, https://www.vulture.com/2017 /12/dylan-sprouse-post-suite-life-life.html.

127   **they graduated with honors:** Crystal Bell, "Dylan And Cole Sprouse Just Graduated From NYU And Our Childhood Is Over," *MTV News*, May 20, 2015, https:// www.mtv.com/news/oq3xjz/dylan-and-cole-sprouse-graduate-college.

8. *HIGH SCHOOL MUSICAL*: THE LITTLE MOVIE THAT COULD

129   **working since she was three:** Danielle James, "Ashley Tisdale Kept Sharpay's Whole Wardrobe From *High School Musical*," *Elle*, December 9, 2022, https:// www.elle.com/culture/a42202055/ashley-tisdale-teen-queens-interview/.

129   **her grandfather was Arnold Morris:** "Arnold Morris Obituary," Legacy.com, accessed October 29, 2023, https://www.legacy.com/us/obituaries/mycentraljersey /name/arnold-morris-obituary?id=19903436.

133   **"I read it and I said":** Mia Galuppo, "Kenny Ortega on 'High School Musical' and His Jump to Netflix: 'There's No Bridge Knocked Down,'" *The Hollywood*

Reporter, September 4, 2019, https://www.hollywoodreporter.com/news/general
-news/kenny-ortega-high-school-musical-his-jump-netflix-q-a-1236547/.

133   **whose mom had been a hairstylist:** Dina Santorelli, "Celebrity Interview: Actor
and Bed & Breakfast Small Business Owner Bart Johnson," *WHY*, accessed October
29, 2023, Retrieved from https://web.archive.org/web/20181012061632/http://www
.workhomeyou.com/resource-detail/686249-celebrity-interview-actor-and-bed.

140   **"In the first movie":** Hal Boedeker, "It's actually Efron singing in 'High School
Musical 2,'" *The Orlando Sentinel*, July 15, 2007, https://www.orlandosentinel.com
/news/os-xpm-2007–07–15-a2story15-story.html.

140   **"To set the record straight":** Kris Greene and Neil Wilkes, "High School Musical," *Digital Spy*, September 21, 2006, https://www.digitalspy.com/tv/a36958/high
-school-musical/.

143   **"Disney is the most progressive":** Ramin Setoodeh, "Director Kenny Ortega on
the Queer Aesthetic of His Movies From 'Hocus Pocus' to 'High School Musical,'" *Variety*, June 30, 2020, https://variety.com/2020/film/news/director-kenny
-ortega-pride-high-school-musical-1234694033/.

143   **pressured to label SpongeBob:** "SpongeBob is asexual, says creator," *Reuters*,
January 29, 2005, retrieved from https://web.archive.org/web/20200425191712
/https://www.theage.com.au/entertainment/spongebob-is-asexual-says-creator
-20050129-gdzgke.html?js-chunk-not-found-refresh=true.

143   **It would take until 2019:** Tony Morrison, "'Andi Mack' makes history with first
Disney Channel character to say 'I'm gay,'" *Good Morning America*, February 11,
2019,   https://www.goodmorningamerica.com/culture/story/andi-mack-makes
-history-disney-channel-character-im-60991622.

144   **ratings-busting 2007 DCOM:** Michael Schneider, "Shows set records for Disney," *Variety*, January 16, 2007, https://variety.com/2007/scene/markets-festivals
/shows-set-records-for-disney-1117957517/.

144   **She had to take it upon herself:** Olivia Singh, "Monique Coleman reveals her
'High School Musical' character wore headbands because the crew didn't know
how to style Black hair," *Insider*, January 26, 2021, https://www.insider.com/high
-school-musical-monique-coleman-taylor-headbands-reason-interview-2021-1.

144   **Monique returned home after the shoot:** "Monique Coleman Tells Fans To
'Dreams Do Come True' As HSM's 10 Year Anniversary Nears," *Just Jared Jr.*, January 19, 2016, https://www.justjaredjr.com/2016/01/19/monique-coleman-tells
-fans-to-dreams-do-come-true-as-hsms-10-year-anniversary-nears/.

144   **"Disney really broke my heart":** Christy Carlson Romano, "High School Musical Actress Monique Coleman on Disney & Becoming #MightyMo," *Vulnerable*,
December 13, 2022, https://www.youtube.com/watch?v=VkYXemNE7os.

145   **Iger officially replaced Michael Eisner:** Frank Ahrens, "Disney Chooses Successor to Chief Executive Eisner," *The Washington Post*, March 14, 2005, https://www
.washingtonpost.com/wp-dyn/articles/A32493-2005Mar13.html.

146   **"Nothing here is better than":** Ken Tucker, "High School Musical," *Entertainment
Weekly*, May 23, 2006, https://ew.com/article/2006/05/23/high-school-musical/.

146   **"hands-down, the most honest":** Stephen Galloway, "Zac Efron on Career Re-

invention, Addiction 'Struggle' and That Fight on Skid Row," *The Hollywood Reporter*, April 30, 2014, https://www.hollywoodreporter.com/movies/movie-news/zac-efron-career-reinvention-addiction-699529/.

146   **on iTunes on January 10:** Gil Kaufman, "What Is 'High School Musical' And How Did It Get To #1?," MTV News, March 1, 2006, https://www.mtv.com/news/9612ww/what-is-high-school-musical-and-how-did-it-get-to-1.

146   **7.7 million viewers in 5 million households:** Ben Sisario, "A Musical for Tweens Captures Its Audience," *The New York Times*, February 8, 2006, https://www.nytimes.com/2006/02/08/arts/television/a-musical-for-tweens-captures-its-audience.html.

146   **had drawn 7.8 million total viewers:** "Premiere of 'Cadet Kelly' Gets Attenshun! Breaks Records, is Highest Rated Disney Channel Original Movie and Most-Watched Telecast Ever on Disney Channel," *Entertainment Wire*, March 11, 2002, retrieved from https://web.archive.org/web/20081204111152/http://findarticles.com/p/articles/mi_m0EIN/is_2002_March_11/ai_83681714.

147   **another 6.1 million viewers:** Paul R. La Monica, "Disney's 'High School' hype," *CNN Money*, July 24, 2007, https://money.cnn.com/2007/07/24/news/companies/disney_highschoolmusical/.

147   **made the biggest jump for a single:** "Beyoncé Still No. 1, 'High School' Breaks Record," Billboard, February 2, 2006, https://www.billboard.com/music/music-news/beyonce-still-no-1-high-school-breaks-record-59830/.

147   **"Surprised? No":** Sisario, "A Musical for Tweens Captures Its Audience."

148   **the first TV soundtrack to reach the top:** Keith Caulfield, "Chart Rewind: In 2006, 'High School Musical' Started Something New," *Billboard*, March 11, 2021, https://www.billboard.com/pro/rewinding-the-charts-in-2006-high-school-musical-started/.

149   **generating revenue for The Walt Disney Company:** "The Walt Disney Company 2006 Annual Report," https://thewaltdisneycompany.com/app/uploads/WDC-AR-2006.pdf, 45.

149   **onto the *New York Times* bestseller list:** John Moore, "'High School Musical': Disney's surprise megahit," *The Denver Post*, July 17, 2008, https://www.denverpost.com/2008/07/17/high-school-musical-disneys-surprise-megahit/.

149   **digital cameras:** Mike Hanlon, "Disney's line of digital cameras for tots and tweens," *New Atlas*, September 8, 2006, https://newatlas.com/disneys-line-of-digital-cameras-for-tots-and-tweens/6126/.

149   **posters, pajamas, board games:** "Addicted to 'HSM,'" *Hartford Courant*, August 27, 2006, https://www.courant.com/2006/08/27/addicted-to-hsm/.

149   **almost ninety million people in more than one hundred countries:** "The Walt Disney Company 2006 Annual Report," 45.

9. EVEN MORE *HIGH SCHOOL MUSICAL*: STARDOM AND SEQUELS

153   **given permission to perform three songs:** Jacques Steinberg, "Back to School," *The New York Times*, March 11, 2007, https://www.nytimes.com/2007/03/11/arts/television/11stei.html.

153   **promoted to a newly created position:** Denise Martin, "Disney Channel taps leading man," *Variety*, September 5, 2005, https://variety.com/2005/scene/markets-festivals/disney-channel-taps-leading-man-1117928539/.

157   **"We were not close":** Ashley Tisdale, "What I've Been Looking For ft. Lucas Grabeel | Music Sessions | Ashley Tisdale," YouTube, May 23, 2017, https://www.youtube.com/watch?v=XDsBDG3y0Pg.

157   **paid him a mere $100,000:** Rachel Abramowitz, "What's after graduation?," *The Los Angeles Times*, August 27, 2007, https://www.latimes.com/archives/la-xpm-2007-aug-27-et-zac27-story.html.

157   **"Personally, I feel no competition":** Steinberg, "Back to School."

158   **Cindy Crawford and her brood:** Brooks Barnes, "The Littlest Big Shots," *The New York Times*, November 4, 2007, https://www.nytimes.com/2007/11/04/fashion/04redcarpet.html.

158   **More than 17.2 million viewers** Nellie Andreeva, "'High School' upstages TV records," *The Hollywood Reporter*, August 19, 2007, retrieved from https://web.archive.org/web/20071018150828/http://www.hollywoodreporter.com/hr/content_display/news/e3i5a787a2fa3a0574d14d791f838e05401.

158   **"Take a bow, Disney Channel":** "'High School Musical 2': OMG! It's a cable ratings record," *Variety*, August 18, 2007, https://variety.com/2007/tv/news/high-school-m-2-22179/.

158   **available in more than ninety-two million homes:** "Premiere of 'High School Musical 2' Breaks Ratings Record," *The New York Times*, August 18, 2007, https://www.nytimes.com/2007/08/18/arts/television/18cnd-disney.html.

160   **"She's damaged":** Gina Keating and Sue Zeidler, "Disney backs star after her apology for nude photo," *Reuters*, September 7, 2007, https://www.reuters.com/article/us-hudgens-nude/disney-backs-star-after-her-apology-for-nude-photo-idINN0746838620070908.

160   **"I want to apologize":** "Vanessa Hudgens 'Embarrassed,' Apologizes for Nude Photo," *People*, September 7, 2007, https://people.com/celebrity/vanessa-hudgens-embarrassed-apologizes-for-nude-photo/.

160   **"Vanessa has apologized":** The Associated Press, "Nude photo emerges of 'High School Musical' star," *The Hollywood Reporter*, September 8, 2007, retrieved from https://www.hollywoodreporter.com/business/business-news/nude-photo-emerges-high-school-149738/.

162   **a $200 million franchise:** Julia Boorstin, "Disney's 'High School Musical' Hits The Big Screen," *CNBC*, October 24, 2008, https://www.cnbc.com/2008/10/24/disneys-high-school-musical-hits-the-big-screen.html.

162   **generated more than $1 billion:** La Monica, "Disney's 'High School' hype."

162   **Ortega floated the idea:** Adam Markovitz, "High School Musical 3: Senior Year," *Entertainment Weekly*, August 15, 2008, https://ew.com/article/2008/08/15/high-school-musical-3-senior-year/.

163   **$30 million:** Borys Kit, "'High School Musical 3' takes L.A. by storm," *The Hollywood Reporter*, October 17, 2009, retrieved from https://www.hollywoodreporter.com/business/business-news/high-school-musical-3-takes-121337/.

163   **a $3 million paycheck:** Markovitz, "High School Musical 3: Senior Year."

164   **pulling in more than $42 million:** "Box Office A+ For 'High School Musical 3,'" *CBS News*, October 27, 2008, retrieved from https://www.cbsnews.com/news /box-office-a-plus-for-high-school-musical-3/.

164   **"What Disneyland's Main Street is":** Richard Corliss, *High School Musical 3: The Critic's Review*," *Time*, October 23, 2008, https://content.time.com/time/arts /article/0,8599,1853513,00.html.

165   **publicly announced** *High School Musical 4:* "Jeffrey Hornaday To Direct High School Musical 4," *Just Jared*, June 1, 2009, https://www.justjared.com/2009/06/01 /jeffrey-hornaday-high-school-musical-4-director/.

165   **"most ambitious series to date":** Nellie Andreeva, "Disney Channel's Music-Driven 'HSM' Offshoot 'Madison High' Gets Pilot Order," *Deadline*, February 17, 2011, https://deadline.com/2011/02/disney-channels-music-driven-hsm-offshoot -madison-high-gets-pilot-order-107324/.

165   **Beanie Feldstein:** Rebecca Brill, "WesCeleb: Beanie Feldstein '15," *The Wesleyan Argus*, April 30, 2015, http://wesleyanargus.com/2015/04/30/wesceleb-beanie -feldstein/.

10. THE RISE OF *HANNAH MONTANA*

167   **"A boom in children's entertainment":** Barnes, "The Littlest Big Shots."

170   **Buddy Sheffield claimed** *he* **originally:** "'Hannah Montana' Lawsuit Settled," *Los Angeles Daily News*, August 4, 2008, https://www.dailynews.com/2008/08/04 /hannah-montana-lawsuit-settled/.

171   **asked to send tapes of all:** Miley Cyrus and Hilary Lifton, *Miles to Go* (New York: Hyperion, 2009), 21–32.

175   **frequent slip-ups calling Miley:** Olivia Harrison, "Miley Cyrus' *Hannah Montana* Character Was Almost Named 'Kylie,'" Refinery29, July 14, 2017, https:// www.refinery29.com/en-us/2017/07/163489/miley-cyrus-hannah-montana -character-named-kylie.

176   **casting directors aren't allowed to ask:** "Are casting directors allowed to ask me about my age, race, ethnicity, nationality, religion, or sexual orientation?," SAG-AFTRA, accessed October 30, 2023, https://servicesagaftra.custhelp.com/app /answers/detail/a_id/1042/~/are-casting-directors-allowed-to-ask-me-about-my -age%2C-race%2C-ethnicity%2C.

179   **brought in 5.4 million viewers:** Jacques Steinberg, "Hannah Montana and Miley Cyrus: A Tale of Two Tweens," *The New York Times*, April 20, 2006, https://www .nytimes.com/2006/04/20/arts/television/hannah-montana-and-miley-cyrus-a -tale-of-two-tweens.html.

179   **"not the finest of its kind":** Robert Lloyd, "'Hannah's' double life as a pop star," *The Los Angeles Times*, March 24, 2006, https://www.latimes.com/archives/la -xpm-2006-mar-24-et-hannah24-story.html.

179   *Suite Life* **was a top-five series:** "The Walt Disney Company 2006 Annual Report," 45.

182   **$400 million to an eye-watering $2.7 billion:** "Disney sees merchandise retail

sales over $30 billion," *Reuters*, June 10, 2008, https://www.reuters.com/article
/industry-disney-license-dc/disney-sees-merchandise-retail-sales-over-30
-billion-idUSN1034177720080610.

185   **Billy Ray had opened for Parton:** Jennifer Hutt, "How Dolly Parton Became the
Godmother of Miley Cyrus," SiriusXM via YouTube, November 21, 2019, https://
www.youtube.com/watch?v=t8LYv3DJC0g.

185   **"She's got to be my fairy goddaughter":** Hutt, "How Dolly Parton Became the
Godmother of Miley Cyrus."

186   **"I have always been known":** Steinberg, "Hannah Montana and Miley Cyrus: A
Tale of Two Tweens."

188   **"breathing life into you":** Sara Delgado, "Miley Cyrus Penned a Letter to Hannah
Montana for the Show's 15th Anniversary," *Teen Vogue*, March 25, 2021, https://www
.teenvogue.com/story/miley-cyrus-letter-to-hannah-montana-15th-anniversary.

11. MILEY CYRUS: ROCK STAR AND ROLE MODEL

189   **losing upward of $20 million a year:** Michael Lev, "Can All Those Upstart Re-
cord Labels Survive?," *The New York Times*, January 5, 1992, https://www.nytimes
.com/1992/01/05/business/can-all-those-upstart-record-labels-survive.html.

190   **"about how totally awesome it is":** Chris Willman, "Music Review: Hannah
Montana (2006)," *Entertainment Weekly*, November 10, 2006, retrieved from
https://web.archive.org/web/20140201212127/http://www.ew.com/ew/article
/0,1557679,00.html.

190   **the first TV soundtrack to debut at number one:** "Billboard 200," *Billboard*, November 11, 2006, https://www.billboard.com/charts/billboard-200/2006-11=11/.

191   **beat new releases from My Chemical Romance:** Chris Harris, "Hannah Montana Rains On My Chemical Romance's 'Parade,'" *MTV News*, November 1, 2006,
https://www.mtv.com/news/o1xq3d/hannah-montana-rains-on-my-chemical
-romances-parade.

192   **"Hell hath no fury like the parent":** Geoff Boucher and Chris Lee, "How much
do you want those 'Hannah' tickets?," *The Los Angeles Times*, October 6, 2007,
https://www.latimes.com/archives/la-xpm-2007-oct-06-et-montana6-story.html.

192   **release a batch of forty-five thousand seats:** Alfred Branch Jr., "Hannah Montana Tour 'Finds' 45,000 Extra Tickets," *Ticket News*, last modified March 17, 2009,
https://www.ticketnews.com/2007/11/hannah-montana-tour-finds-45000-extra
-tickets/.

192   **Taylor Swift's Eras tour Ticketmaster debacle:** Callie Holtermann, "At Ticketmaster Hearing, Taylor Swift Lyrics Were the Headliner," *The New York Times*, January
25, 2023, https://www.nytimes.com/2023/01/25/style/taylor-swift-ticketmaster
-hearing.html.

192   **Fan club members sued:** The Associated Press, "Members sue 'Hannah Montana'
fan club," *Today*, November 13, 2007, Retrieved from https://www.today.com
/popculture/members-sue-hannah-montana-fan-club-wbna21774826.

192   **In St. Louis, the winner:** Belinda Goldsmith, "Parents go to extremes for Hannah Montana tickets," *Reuters*, October 17, 2007, https://www.reuters.com

/article/us-hannah/parents-go-to-extremes-for-hannah-montana-tickets
-idUSN1731159520071018.

192   **In Connecticut, a participant:** Associated Press, "Race in heels trips man on
workers comp," *NBC News*, March 26, 2008, retrieved from https://www.nbcnews
.com/id/wbna23807597.

192   **a Texas mom helped her six-year-old:** "Mother Goes Too Far For Hannah Montana Tix," *Good Morning America*, last modified February 19, 2009, https://
abcnews.go.com/GMA/SummerConcert/story?id=4068368&page=1.

193   **top the box office and gross $31.1 million:** Julia Boorstin, "Disney And Hannah
Montana: A Big Screen Victory In 3-D," *CNBC*, February 5, 2008, https://www
.cnbc.com/2008/02/05/disney-and-hannah-montana-a-big-screen-victory-in-3d
.html.

194   **legally change her name:** "Miley Cyrus One Step Closer to Being Miley Cyrus,"
TMZ, March 24, 2008, https://www.tmz.com/2008/03/24/miley-cyrus-one-step
-closer-to-being-miley-cyrus/.

194   **"cross-category merchandising opportunity":** Mike Duff, "Wal-Mart Launches
Miley Cyrus Apparel Connected to Tour and Youth Strategy," CBS News, June 3,
2009, https://www.cbsnews.com/news/wal-mart-launches-miley-cyrus-apparel
-connected-to-tour-and-youth-strategy/.

194   **Showrunner Michael Poryes sued Disney:** Eriq Gardner, "Hollywood's Deflate-
gate? 'Hannah Montana' Creators Fight 'Perplexing' Arbitration," *The Hollywood
Reporter*, May 5, 2016, https://www.hollywoodreporter.com/business/business
-news/hollywoods-deflategate-hannah-montana-creators-890649/.

195   **"The concept of the show":** Allison Hagendorf, "Episode 15 (feat. Miley Cyrus),"
Rock This with Allison Hagendorf, March 5, 2021, https://open.spotify.com
/episode/157NO7CEE3eE5BifQ9HNfj.

195   **"I began to observe a peculiar phenomenon":** Hayley Mills, *Forever Young: A
Memoir* (New York: Grand Central Publishing, 2021), 131.

195   **The goal was to place:** Joanne Ostrow, "Disney wields its marketing magic," *The
Denver Post*, October 18, 2007, https://www.denverpost.com/2007/10/18/disney
-wields-its-marketing-magic/.

196   **the number one basic cable show:** Carolyn Giardina, "'Hannah Montana' pops
in," *The Hollywood Reporter*, October 18, 2007, retrieved from https://www
.hollywoodreporter.com/business/business-news/hannah-montana-pops-152825/.

196   **nor guardian:** "§11757. Presence of Parents or Guardians of Minors Under Sixteen (16) Years of Age," California Department of Industrial Relations, accessed
October 31, 2023, https://www.dir.ca.gov/t8/11757.html.

198   **"I didn't get recovery days":** Joe Rogan, "Joe Rogan Experience #1531-Miley Cyrus,"
YouTube, September 2, 2020, https://www.youtube.com/watch?v=D7WUMXKV-FE.

198   **Blogger Perez Hilton shared a link:** Tracy Clark-Flory, "Perez pleads panty defense,"
Salon, June 15, 2010, https://www.salon.com/2010/06/15/perez_miley_denial/.

198   **often dubbed her "Slutty Cyrus":** "Slutty Cyrus Caught!," *Perez Hilton*, September 17, 2008, https://perezhilton.com/slutty-cyrus-caught/.

198   **announced her pregnancy at age sixteen:** "Britney's Teen Sister Jamie Lynn

Spears Pregnant," *People*, December 18, 2007, https://people.com/parents/britneys-teen-sister-jamie-lynn-spears-pregnant/.

198 **arrested for drunk driving and cocaine possession:** "Lindsay Lohan Arrested for DUI, Drugs," *ABC News*, July 24, 2007, https://abcnews.go.com/Entertainment/story?id=3408314&page=1.

199 **"The young women on the channel":** Ashley Spencer, "Cole Sprouse on Finding a Healthy Balance in Hollywood," *The New York Times*, April 4, 2022, https://www.nytimes.com/2022/04/04/movies/cole-sprouse-moonshot.html.

199 **"young hot starlets gone wild":** Ann Oldenburg, "Miley Cyrus fulfills her destiny," *USA Today*, last modified January 14, 2007, http://usatoday30.usatoday.com/life/television/news/2007-01-10-miley-cyrus_x.htm.

199 **"There was nothing wrong with it":** "Miley Cyrus 'Really Upset' Over Leaked Photos," *Access Hollywood*, January 5, 2008, https://www.accessonline.com/articles/miley-cyrus-really-upset-over-leaked-photos-61948.

199 **Consumer Reports put out a statement:** "Note to Hannah Montana: Seat belts are necessary not an accessory," *Consumer Reports News*, February 11, 2008, https://www.consumerreports.org/cro/news/2008/02/note-to-hannah-montana-seat-belts-are-necessary-not-an-accessory/index.htm.

199 **"We got caught up in the moment":** Stephen M. Silverman and Michelle Tan, "Billy Ray Apologizes for Not Buckling Up," *People*, February 13, 2008, retrieved from https://web.archive.org/web/20221002074338/https://people.com/celebrity/billy-ray-apologizes-for-not-buckling-up/.

200 **A nineteen-year-old scammer in Tennessee:** Kim Zetter, "Confessed Miley Cyrus Hacker Sentenced to Three Years Probation," *Wired*, October 31, 2011, https://www.wired.com/2011/10/josh-holly-sentenced/.

200 **Bill O'Reilly dedicated a segment:** Wenn, "Newsman Calls for Miley Cyrus Media Conference over Shocking Photos," *Hollywood.com*, last modified June 7, 2014, https://www.hollywood.com/tv/newsman-calls-for-miley-cyrus-media-conference-over-shocking-photos-57206127.

200 **"An editor at a tabloid told me":** Bruce Handy, "Miley Knows Best," *Vanity Fair*, April 28, 2008, https://www.vanityfair.com/culture/2008/06/miley200806.

200 **"The picture disturbs me":** Olivia Vanni, "Photo no-no controversy," *Boston Herald*, April 30, 2008, https://www.bostonherald.com/2008/04/30/photo-no-no-controversy/.

200 **"I feel for her":** Jamie Lee Curtis, "Topless on TV: The Miley Cyrus / *Vanity Fair* Saga," *The Huffington Post*, August 15, 2008, https://www.huffpost.com/entry/topless-on-tv-the-miley-c_b_98990.

200 **Miley quickly put out a statement:** Stephen M. Silverman, "Miley Cyrus: I'm Sorry for Photos," *People*, April 27, 2008, https://people.com/celebrity/miley-cyrus-im-sorry-for-photos/.

200 **"Miley's parents and/or minders were on set":** "Leibovitz Defends Provocative Miley Cyrus Photos," *ABC News*, April 27, 2008, https://abcnews.go.com/Entertainment/SummerConcert/story?id=4736358&page=1.

200 **"IM NOT SORRY":** Miley Cyrus (@MileyCyrus), "IM NOT SORRY Fuck YOU

#10yearsago," Twitter, April 29, 2018, 4:02pm ET, https://twitter.com/MileyCyrus /status/990682726440226817?lang=en.

201 **"A situation was created":** Brooks Barnes, "Revealing Photo Threatens a Major Disney Franchise," *The New York Times*, April 28, 2008, https://www.nytimes.com /2008/04/28/business/media/28hannah.html.

201 SHOULD 'HANNAH MONTANA' BE SEXY?: "Should 'Hannah Montana' Be Sexy?," *ABC News*, April 28, 2008, https://abcnews.go.com/Entertainment/story ?id=4742597&page=1.

202 **retail revenue approached $1 billion:** Barnes, "Revealing Photo Threatens a Major Disney Franchise."

202 **a seven-figure book deal:** Motoko Rich, "A Bookish Miley Cyrus," *The New York Times*, April 22, 2008, https://www.nytimes.com/2008/04/22/arts/22arts -ABOOKISHMILE_BRF.html.

203 **attended by more than five thousand fans at $250:** "Miley Cyrus celebrates Sweet 16 at Disneyland," *Today*, October 6, 2008, retrieved from https://www .today.com/popculture/miley-cyrus-celebrates-sweet-16-disneyland-1c9420468.

203 **"For Miley Cyrus to be a 'good girl'":** Karl Taro Greenfeld, "How Mickey Got His Groove Back," *Portfolio*, May 2008 issue, retrieved from https://web.archive .org/web/20080420044803/http://www.portfolio.com/news-markets/national -news/portfolio/2008/04/14/Disneys-Evolving-Business-Model.

203 **controversy ensued over the "stripper pole":** Monica Herrera, "Miley Cyrus' Pole Dance At Teen Choice Awards Sparks Controversy," *Billboard*, August 12, 2009, https://www.billboard.com/music/music-news/miley-cyrus-pole-dance-at -teen-choice-awards-sparks-controversy-267730/.

203 **"Disney Channel won't be commenting":** Herrera, "Miley Cyrus' Pole Dance At Teen Choice Awards Sparks Controversy."

203 **"I would do that pole dance a thousand times":** Kevin Sessums, "Miley Cyrus: 'I Know Who I Am Now,'" *Parade*, March 21, 2010, https://parade.com/131365 /kevinsessums/miley-cyrus-4/.

203 **The move had been in the works:** Cynthia Littleton, "Rich Ross to head Walt Disney Studios," *Variety*, October 5, 2009, https://variety.com/2009/film/features /rich-ross-to-head-walt-disney-studios-1118009578/.

204 **whose in-house experience had largely been:** "Carolina Lightcap Named President, Disney Channels Worldwide," The Walt Disney Company, November 24, 2009, https://thewaltdisneycompany.com/carolina-lightcap-named-president-disney -channels-worldwide/.

204 **took on expanded duties:** Dawn C. Chmielewski, "Carolina Lightcap named president of Disney Channels Worldwide," *Los Angeles Times*, November 25, 2009, https:// www.latimes.com/archives/la-xpm-2009-nov-25-la-fi-ct-disney25–2009nov25-story .html.

204 **espoused her love of *RuPaul's Drag Race*:** Kevin Sessums, "Miley Cyrus: Country Music 'Feels Contrived On So Many Levels,'" *Parade*, March 17, 2010, https:// parade.com/28010/kevinsessums/0317-miley-cyrus-web-exclusive/.

204 **"My job is to be a role model":** Amy Larocca, "The Real Miley Cyrus," *Harper's*

Bazaar, January 6, 2010, https://www.harpersbazaar.com/celebrity/latest/news /a462/miley-cyrus-cover-interview-0210/.

205   **"We needed someone with talent"**: Jeanne McDowell, "A Disney Star Is Born," *Time*, November 30, 2006, https://content.time.com/time/arts/article /0,8599,1564394,00.html.

205   **"She speaks with bold, jokey air"**: Kimberly Cutter, "The Life of Miley Cyrus," *Marie Claire*, July 21, 2011, https://www.marieclaire.com/celebrity/a11786/miley -cyrus-interview/.

206   **Gay men made a viral Fire Island parody**: David Fudge, "Party in the FIP / Party in the USA / MUSIC VIDEO," YouTube, August 24, 2009, https://www.youtube .com/watch?v=2Ezfk7s1NyY.

206   **"great, goofy—and bipartisan!—fun"**: Jonah Weiner, "Can Miley Cyrus Save Health Care Reform?," *Slate*, September 29, 2009, https://slate.com/culture/2009 /09/miley-cyrus-party-in-the-usa-is-great-goofy-bipartisan-fun.html.

206   **"Honestly, I picked that song because"**: "Miley Cyrus: 'I've Never Heard a Jay-Z Song,'" *Us Weekly*, November 6, 2009, https://www.usmagazine.com /entertainment/news/miley-cyrus-ive-never-heard-a-jay-z-song-2009611/.

206   **the first artist to do an arena tour with**: Ray Waddell, "Miley Cyrus fights scalpers with paperless tickets," *Reuters*, June 21, 2009, https://www.reuters .com/article/us-cyrus-miley-cyrus-fights-scalpers-with-paperless-tickets -idUSTRE55K0CX20090621.

209   **"Miley, at seventeen, is now making creative choices"**: Brooks Barnes, "Sharp Turn for Miley Cyrus," *The New York Times*, May 10, 2010, https://www.nytimes .com/2010/05/10/business/media/10miley.html.

210   **Sources were quick to tell TMZ:** "Miley Cyrus Bong Video Partying With A Bong," *TMZ*, December 12, 2010, https://www.tmz.com/2010/12/10/miley-cyrus-video -bong-hit-smoking-salvia-herb-pyschedelic-birthday-party-hannah-montana/.

210   **Miley has maintained that it really was salvia:** Miley Cyrus (@mileycyrus), "Happy 10 year anniversary to the groundbreaking video of a teenager smoking a bong & saying dumb shit to their friends . . . ," Instagram, December 13, 2020, https://www.instagram.com/p/CIv7IXvptuj.

210   **"At one point it went from school to"**: Rogan, "Joe Rogan Experience #1531-Miley Cyrus."

211   **"America has gotten to a place"**: Marcela Isaza, "Miley Cyrus: Not Enough Love For Me To Tour In The U.S.," *The Huffington Post*, April 15, 2011, retrieved from https://web.archive.org/web/20110419141929/http://www.huffingtonpost.com /2011/04/15/miley-cyrus-not-enough-lo_n_849722.html.

211   **6.2 million people watched:** *The Hollywood Reporter*, "'Hannah Montana' Finale Sets Disney Ratings Record," *Billboard*, January 19, 2011, Retrieved from https:// www.billboard.com/music/music-news/hannah-montana-finale-sets-disney -ratings-record-473581/.

211   **"I'm not going to do *Hannah Montana*"**: Saturday Night Live, "Monologue: Miley Cyrus on the 2013 VMAs-SNL," YouTube, October 7, 2013, https://www .youtube.com/watch?v=Cr_9-Rikttg.

12. SELENA GOMEZ AND *WIZARDS OF WAVERLY PLACE*

215   **shifts at Starbucks and Dave & Busters:** Jia Tolentino, "Selena Gomez on Politics, Faith, and Making the Music of Her Career," *Vogue*, March 9, 2021, https://www.vogue.com/article/selena-gomez-cover-april-2021.

215   **"When I was growing up":** Margy Rochlin, "Selena Gomez (and Others) on Adapting 'Thirteen Reasons Why' for Netflix," *The New York Times*, March 22, 2017, https://www.nytimes.com/2017/03/22/arts/television/selena-gomez-thirteen-reasons-why-netflix.html.

215   **dreamed of becoming an actor:** Alex Morris, "Selena Gomez Wasn't Sure She Was Ready To Tell This Story," *Rolling Stone*, November 3, 2022, https://www.rollingstone.com/music/music-features/selena-gomez-my-mind-and-me-documentary-new-music-only-murders-in-the-building-1234620268/.

215   **walk to the dollar store:** *E! Special: Selena Gomez*, 2011, As cited in https://www.irishmirror.ie/showbiz/celebrity-news/selena-gomez-i-momma-4718895.

216   **rumored to have pulled out of a deal:** Brian Delpozo, "How 'Harry Potter' Almost Ended Up at Disney World—And Why the Deal Fell Apart," *AllEars.net*, June 7, 2020, https://allears.net/2020/06/07/how-harry-potter-almost-ended-up-at-disney-world-and-why-the-deal-fell-apart/.

221   **"I remember going to the beach":** Tolentino, "Selena Gomez on Politics, Faith, and Making the Music of Her Career."

222   **rented out the Staples Center:** "Justin Bieber: My Big Surprise Date With Selena Gomez," *TMZ*, September 26, 2011, https://www.tmz.com/2011/09/26/justin-beiber-selena-gomez-dinner-daate-staples-center-demi-lovao-titanic-surprise-los-angeles-movie-mr-deeds/.

222   **a "hot and heavy" Hawaiian vacation:** "Selena Gomez and Justin Bieber get hot and heavy with beach romp in Hawaii," *The New York Daily News*, May 27, 2011, https://www.nydailynews.com/entertainment/gossip/selena-gomez-justin-bieber-hot-heavy-beach-romp-hawaii-article-1.144476.

223   **"I wasn't a wild child":** Julie Miller, "Selena Gomez Survived Social Media and, With Her New Music, Is Ready to Leave Darkness Behind," *Vanity Fair*, February 15, 2023, https://www.vanityfair.com/hollywood/2023/02/selena-gomez-hollywood-issue-2023.

225   **drawing 9.8 million viewers:** Michael Starr, "The Starr Report," *The New York Post*, January 10, 2012, https://nypost.com/2012/01/10/starr-report-2172/.

225   **Disney received three of the five nominations:** "Outstanding Children's Program-2007," Emmys, accessed on October 30, 2023, https://www.emmys.com/awards/nominees-winners/2007/outstanding-childrens-program.

225   **the second season of *Wizards of Waverly Place*:** "Outstanding Children's Program-2009," Emmys, accessed on October 30, 2023, https://www.emmys.com/awards/nominees-winners/2009/outstanding-childrens-program.

225   **with 11.4 million viewers:** Rick Kissell, "Disney's 'Wizards' casts spell over ratings," *Variety*, August 30, 2009, https://variety.com/2009/scene/markets-festivals/disney-s-wizards-casts-spell-over-ratings-1118007918/.

226   **unceremoniously ousted over the phone:** Laura M. Holson, "Nina Jacobson

Has Her Revenge on Hollywood's Old-Boy Network," *The New York Times*, December 9, 2016, https://www.nytimes.com/2016/12/09/fashion/nina-jacobson-hollywood-diversity-hunger-games-american-crime-story.html.

228 **It took two years:** "Selena Gomez Joins Hollywood Records?," *Just Jared*, May 9, 2008, https://www.justjared.com/2008/05/09/selena-gomez-hollywood-records/.

228 **"I've got some blue going on!":** Hannah Dailey, "Watch Selena Gomez Poke Fun at Her Younger Self in New TikTok: 'Got Some Blue Going On!,'" *Billboard*, July 16, 2021, https://www.billboard.com/music/music-news/selena-gomez-tiktok-teen-vogue-video-blue-hair-9602357/.

230 **she was on constant "mole patrol":** Jeanne Wolf, "The Very Sweet Life of Selena Gomez," *Parade*, June 21, 2009, https://parade.com/130844/jeannewolf/sweet-life-of-selena-gomez/.

230 **"If I'm really not enjoying it":** "Selena Gomez: The Advice My Mom Gave Me That I Live By," *Hollywood Life*, June 7, 2012, retrieved from https://www.yahoo.com/entertainment/selena-gomez-advice-mom-gave-live-224231803.html.

230 **"It made me feel like Disney":** *Selena Gomez: My Mind and Me,* directed by Alek Keshishian (2022, Apple TV+), streaming.

230 **"one of the best experiences":** Raquelle Stevens, "The value of friendship," *Giving Back Generation*, Spotify, May 31, 2022, https://podcasters.spotify.com/pod/show/givingbackgeneration/episodes/The-value-of-friendship-e1j70kt.

230 **"I felt safe":** David DeLuise and Jennifer Stone, "Ep 4: Selena Gomez Reveals Her Biggest Mistake," *Wizards of Waverly Pod*, YouTube, February 27, 2023, https://www.youtube.com/watch?v=97TBj7Svgy4.

231 **"I was just very malnourished":** Patrick Gomez and Melody Chiu, "Selena Gomez: I Was 'Malnourished' and 'Exhausted,'" *People*, June 13, 2011, https://people.com/celebrity/selena-gomez-explains-cause-of-hospitalization/.

231 **"That was my job in a way":** Tolentino, "Selena Gomez on Politics, Faith, and Making the Music of Her Career."

13. JONAS BROTHERS: PURITY RINGS AND PRE-MADE STARS

235 **in February 2007, Hollywood Records announced:** "The Jonas Brothers Sign Record Deal With Disney's Hollywood Records," PRNewswire, February 8, 2007, Retrieved from https://web.archive.org/web/20070213073434/http://sev.prnewswire.com/entertainment/20070208/LATH11608022007-1.html.

235 **with 10.7 million viewers:** Andreeva, "'High School' upstages TV records."

237 **"When it first came out":** Francesca Bacardi, "Nick Jonas' Reddit AMA Addresses Relationship With Miley Cyrus, the Famous Purity Rings and More," *E! News*, March 31, 2016, https://www.eonline.com/news/753054/nick-jonas-reddit-ama-addresses-relationship-with-miley-cyrus-the-famous-purity-rings-and-more.

237 **Joe stated that he "loved" the episode:** Joe Jonas, "I'm Joe Jonas, former flat iron hair model, ask me anything!," Reddit, October 11, 2016, https://www.reddit.com/r/IAmA/comments/56zxcj/im_joe_jonas_former_flat_iron_hair_model_ask_me/.

237 **skits like "Disney Channel Acting School":** Saturday Night Live, "Disney Chan-

nel Acting School-SNL," YouTube, September 18, 2013, https://www.youtube.com/watch?v=MeSd7Q7oThc.

238 **"It's not bad to wear a promise ring"**: "Jordin Sparks & Russell Brand Spar Over Purity Rings At VMAs," *NBC New York*, September 8, 2008, https://www.nbcnewyork.com/local/jordin_sparks___russell_brand_spar_over_purity_rings_at_vmas/1855232/.

240 **"I tended to be strict"**: Scott Stump, "Does the Jonas Brothers' mom have a favorite Jonas Brother? They think so," *Today*, August 21, 2023, https://www.today.com/popculture/jonas-brothers-mom-denise-interview-rcna100956.

241 **brought on former *The Office* producer**: Richard Huff, "Disney keeps up with the Jonases: 'JONAS' picked up for second season," *The New York Daily News*, November 8, 2009, retrieved from https://web.archive.org/web/20230511144829/https://www.nydailynews.com/entertainment/tv-movies/disney-jonases-jonas-picked-season-article-1.414812.

242 **"Biggest regret in regards to the Brothers?"**: *Chasing Happiness*, directed by John Lloyd Taylor (2019, Prime Video), streaming.

242 **"We went along with it at the time"**: Jennifer Vineyard, "Joe Jonas: My Life As a Jonas Brother," *New York Magazine*, December 9, 2013, https://web.archive.org/web/20131202232806/https://www.vulture.com/2013/11/joe-jonas-talks-jonas-brothers.html.

14. DEMI LOVATO, *CAMP ROCK*, AND A PAINFUL REALITY

244 **as early as 2002**: Lucas, "Groomed to Be All That."

246 **"Someday, they'll all be begging"**: Dianna De La Garza and Vickie McIntyre, *Falling with Wings: A Mother's Story* (New York: Feiwel and Friends, 2018), 79.

247 **pawned jewelry and remortgaged**: De La Garza and McIntyre, *Falling with Wings: A Mother's Story*, 158.

247 **After watching Kelly Clarkson win**: *The Tonight Show Starring Jimmy Fallon*, "Demi Lovato Celebrates Their 30th Birthday on The Tonight Show (Extended) | The Tonight Show," YouTube, August 16, 2022, https://www.youtube.com/watch?v=-xIPBJsisYE.

248 **a way to test short-form content**: Emily Nelson and Stacy Meichtry, "Low-Budget Disney Show, a Hit in Italy, Heads to Other Countries, Web, Phones," *The Wall Street Journal*, October 9, 2006, https://www.wsj.com/articles/SB116035917893286429.

249 **"I was absolutely determined"**: Peter Sanders, "Disney Revs Up Tween Star Machine," *The Wall Street Journal*, June 17, 2008, https://www.wsj.com/articles/SB121366103826779219.

250 **as he's later admitted**: *Marie Claire*, "Taylor Lautner and Tay Lautner Talk Camp Rock Auditions, Hidden Talents, & Their New Podcast," YouTube, March 17, 2023, https://www.youtube.com/watch?v=Va9Rj__fzLg.

250 **it drew 8.9 million viewers**: Kimberly Nordyke, "Disney's 'Camp Rock' scores big ratings," *The Hollywood Reporter*, June 21, 2008, Retrieved from https://www.hollywoodreporter.com/business/business-news/disneys-camp-rock-scores-big-114313/.

251   **as their lips turned blue:** Alyson Stoner, "A Child's Body: Open Access | Dear Hollywood Episode 2," YouTube, August 18, 2023, https://www.youtube.com/watch?v=SZN8luP8Kvs.

251   **huddling around space heaters:** "Demi Lovato and Jonas Brothers rock out one last time in 'Camp Rock 2: The Final Jam,'" *The New York Daily News*, August 29, 2010, retrieved from https://web.archive.org/web/20170612095300/https://www.nydailynews.com/entertainment/tv-movies/demi-lovato-jonas-brothers-rock-time-camp-rock-2-final-jam-article-1.200713.

252   **"so sick and being berated":** Meaghan Jette Martin (@meaghanjette), "As I shared yesterday in my story-I had a really difficult time filming Camp Rock 2, not only was Tess butchered after giving her such a lovely character arc . . . ," Instagram, August 27, 2022, https://www.instagram.com/p/ChxHn61MWO6/.

253   **"It was beautiful and tragic":** "Selena Gomez Talks 'Wizards' Reunion, Growing Up On The Disney Channel & Taylor Swift," *The Huffington Post*, March 15, 2013, https://www.huffpost.com/entry/selena-gomez-talks-about_n_2814049.

254   **Cole Sprouse broke up with Alyson Stoner:** Stacey Grant, "'Suite Life''s Alyson Stoner Says Cole Sprouse Dumped Her On Her Birthday," *MTV News*, December 9, 2016, https://www.mtv.com/news/dn9nu0/cole-sprouse-alyson-stoner-dated-podcast.

254   **smoked pot for the first time:** Vineyard, "Joe Jonas: My Life As a Jonas Brother."

255   **"to feature the cast that the audience":** Allison McClain Merrill, "The Disney Channel Games: Extras," *Past Foot Forward*, August 29, 2023, https://pastfootforward.com/2023/08/29/the-disney-channel-games-extras/.

256   **they'd tormented Demi over her weight and:** "Demi Lovato talks childhood bullying, Raya dating, mental health awareness: 'I have an awesome life today,'" *Yahoo Music*, September 17, 2017, https://www.yahoo.com/entertainment/demi-lovato-talks-childhood-bullying-raya-dating-mental-health-awareness-awesome-life-today-201814869.html.

257   **"Along with, perhaps, Nick Jonas":** Jon Caramanica, "Tween Princess, Tweaked," *The New York Times*, July 15, 2009, https://www.nytimes.com/2009/07/19/arts/music/19cara.html.

258   **"I remember being fifteen years old":** Hannah Dailey, "Demi Lovato Opens Up About Bipolar Diagnosis, Gender Fluidity & Ignoring Instagram Comments," *Billboard*, May 12, 2023, https://www.billboard.com/music/music-news/demi-lovato-bipolar-diagnosis-gender-fluidity-ignoring-instagram-comments-1235328548/.

258   **she listed her favorite films as:** Laura Kusnyer, "Philosophizing with 15-Year-Old Demi Lovato," *People en Español*, June 19, 2008, https://peopleenespanol.com/article/philosophizing-15-year-old-demi-lovato/.

259   **"I wasn't sleeping, and I was so miserable":** Matthew Scott Montgomery, "Sonny With a Chance/So RaNDoM Reunion!," YouTube, April 25, 2020, https://www.youtube.com/watch?v=9jPlB88FKLY.

259   **"Acting is just kind of a way":** Nick Axelrod, "Tween Queen: The Rise of Demi Lovato," *Women's Wear Daily*, July 1, 2009, https://wwd.com/fashion-news/fashion-features/tween-queen-the-rise-of-demi-lovato-2199121/.

261   **She told someone in power about it:** *Demi Lovato: Dancing with the Devil*, directed by Michael D. Ratner (2021, OBB Pictures and SB Films), YouTube, https://www.youtube.com/watch?v=6FW-glAaTKU.

262   **She tried cocaine for the first time:** Alex Cooper, "Demi Lovato," *Call Her Daddy*, Spotify, August 23, 2022, https://open.spotify.com/episode/0z8lON88xft N1xP161drGS.

262   **"What do you say to your child":** De La Garza and McIntyre, *Falling with Wings: A Mother's Story*, 248.

262   **"indentations" left by tight gummy bracelets:** Natalie Finn, "Demi Lovato Wears Bracelets, Doesn't Cut Herself," *E! News*, December 11, 2008, https://www.eonline.com/news/72945/demi_lovato_wears_bracelets_doesnt_cut_herself.

263   **initiated by Joe:** Cristina Everett, "Joe Jonas: 'It was my choice to break up' with Demi Lovato," *The New York Daily News*, May 25, 2010, https://www.nydailynews.com/2010/05/25/joe-jonas-it-was-my-choice-to-break-up-with-demi-lovato/.

264   **"I invited a bunch of people to dinner":** *Demi Lovato: Simply Complicated*, directed by Hannah Lux Davis (2017, Phillymack Productions), YouTube, https://www.youtube.com/watch?v=ZWTlL_w8cRA.

266   **was later amended to ADHD:** Caryn Ganz, "How Honest Can Demi Lovato Be?" *The New York Times*, March 16, 2021, https://www.nytimes.com/2021/03/16/arts/music/demi-lovato-interview.html.

266   **Demi admitted to regularly drinking alcohol, as well as:** De La Garza and McIntyre, *Falling with Wings: A Mother's Story*, 277.

266   **The official word from Demi's team:** "Demi Lovato Leaves Jonas Bros. Tour to Get Treatment for 'Emotional and Physical Issues,'" *ABC News*, November 2, 2010, https://abcnews.go.com/Entertainment/actress-singer-demi-lovato-treatment-emotional-physical-issues/story?id=12038895.

266   **Disney Channel announced *Sonny* would be:** Michael Schneider, "New gameplan for 'Sonny With a Chance,'" *Variety*, November 15, 2010, https://variety.com/2010/tv/news/new-gameplan-for-sonny-with-a-chance-1118027468/.

267   **"The allows [Demi] the time she needs":** Schneider, "New gameplan for 'Sonny With a Chance.'"

267   **an entire 2009 "Kids in Rehab" episode:** Laurel Pantin, "Nick News 'Kids in Rehab' Episode," *Teen Vogue*, October 16, 2009, https://www.teenvogue.com/story/nick-news-kids-in-rehab-episode.

EPILOGUE

271   **became the CEO of a space data startup:** Michael Sheetz, "Disney star turned space CEO: Bridgit Mendler launches satellite data startup backed by major VCs," CNBC, updated February 20, 2024, https://www.cnbc.com/2024/02/19/disney-star-bridgit-mendler-launches-satellite-startup-northwood-space.html.

271   **"on important messages about growing up":** Larisha Paul, "Demi Lovato Will Lend Personal Expertise to 'Child Star' Documentary in Directorial Debut," *Rolling Stone*, March 16, 2023, https://www.rollingstone.com/tv-movies/tv-movie-news/demi-lovato-directorial-debut-with-child-star-documentary-1234698192/.

272   **generating more than $1 billion in revenue:** Ron Grover and Lisa Richwine, "The Disney Channel: more than just a pretty face," *Reuters*, February 10, 2012, https://www.reuters.com/article/disney-international/the-disney-channel-more -than-just-a-pretty-face-idINL2E8D9AE520120210.

272   **"People thought Disney Channel":** Rose, "Disney Channel's Gary Marsh on Tabloid Teen Stars, Marvel and the Junk Food Ban."

272   **available in more than 431 million homes:** Janice Min, "Disney Shocker: Top Exec Anne Sweeney to Exit to Become TV Director (Exclusive)," *The Hollywood Reporter*, March 11, 2014, https://www.hollywoodreporter.com/news/general -news/anne-sweeney-top-disney-exec-687567/.

272   **In 2015, it finally unseated Nickelodeon:** Mikey O'Connell, "TV Ratings: Disney Channel Finally Snaps Nickelodeon's Viewership Streak," December 30, 2015, https://www.hollywoodreporter.com/news/general-news/tv-ratings-disney -channel-finally-851598/.

272   **He was pressured to resign:** Brooks Barnes, "Rich Ross, Disney Studio Chairman, Is Forced Out," *The New York Times*, April 20, 2012, https://archive.nytimes .com/mediadecoder.blogs.nytimes.com/2012/04/20/rich-ross-disney-studio -chairman-quits/.

272   **lost around 90 percent of its viewers:** Alex Dudok De Wit, "Disney, Nick, And Cartoon Network Saw Double-Digit Ratings Plummet (Again) This Year," *Cartoon Brew*, December 31, 2021, https://www.cartoonbrew.com/business/disney -nick-and-cartoon-network-saw-double-digit-ratings-plummet-again-this-year -211989.html.

272   **it averaged just 178,000 prime-time viewers:** Gavin Bridge, "Was 2022 the Death Knell for Kids TV?," *Variety*, January 5, 2023, https://variety.com/vip/was -2022-the-death-knell-for-kids-tv-1235478975/.

273   **Marsh remained in the top role:** Cynthia Littleton, "Longtime Disney Channels Chief Gary Marsh Segues to Production Pact," *Variety*, September 21, 2021, https://variety.com/2021/tv/news/gary-marsh-disney-channel-descendents -producer-1235070026/.

273   **The focus of Disney's entertainment division:** Andrew Ross Sorkin, Ravi Mattu, Sarah Kessler, Michael J. de la Merced and Ephrat Livni, "Bob Iger Tweaks Disney's Strategy on Streaming," *The New York Times*, August 10, 2023, https://www .nytimes.com/2023/08/10/business/dealbook/bob-iger-tweaks-disneys-strategy -on-streaming.html.

273   **relying almost solely on its theme parks:** Brooks Barnes, "Disney, Challenged Elsewhere, Plans to Spend $60 Billion on Parks and Cruises," *The New York Times*, September 19, 2023, https://www.nytimes.com/2023/09/19/business/media /disney-parks-expansion.html.

273   **"The Disney Channel, which they launched":** Robert "Bob" Iger, *The Ride of a Lifetime: Lessons Learned from 15 Years as CEO of the Walt Disney Company* (New York: Random House, 2019), 58.

274   **the venture shut down for good:** Tyler Aquilina, "Radio Disney to shut down in 2021," *Entertainment Weekly*, December 5, 2020, https://ew.com/music/radio -disney-to-shut-down-in-2021/.

INDEX

ABOUT THE AUTHOR

Hughes Fioretti Photography

Ashley Spencer is a culture writer and reporter whose work has appeared in *The New York Times, The Washington Post, Los Angeles Times, Vanity Fair, The Guardian, The Hollywood Reporter, Vice, Vulture,* and elsewhere. *Disney High* is her first book.